武汉实验外国语学校校本课程

丛书主编／李　茵　丛书副主编／王永汉

Learn It

二级

外语学校初中英语综合运用能力等级教程

外语类总主编　徐　涛　蔡文静

本 册 主 编　钱晶晶　徐　佳

本 册 编 者　钱晶晶　徐　佳　蔡文静　孙宇敏　樊　娲

向　丹　赵　军　李　欢　夏涓涓　张金霞

WUHAN UNIVERSITY PRESS

武汉大学出版社

武汉实验外国语学校校本课程

（外语类）

总 主 编

徐　涛　蔡文静

丛书编委会成员

序

如果说，一所一流的大学关注学术研究、创造精神，那么，一所一流的中学应该关注什么？

或许，98 年前的教育家蔡元培先生签署的第一部《中学校令》就能给我们以启迪："中学以完足普通教育、造成健全国民为宗旨。"看似普通的一句话，其中却蕴含着这样的真知灼见：教育的落脚点，最后，必须落脚在学生的能力素养及健康成长上。（"完足普通教育"、"健全国民"本身就包含有个体学习能力素养、终身学习意识等多种涵义。）这与 1996 年国际 21 世纪教育委员会向联合国教科文组织提交的报告《教育——财富蕴藏其中》中所包含的最核心的观点"教育要使学习者学会掌握'学习的四大支柱'"（"学会认知"、"学会做事"、"学会共同生活"和"学会生存"）有内在的关联。也与当下盛行的 PISA（Programme for Internaltional Student Assessment，国际学生评估项目，它是经济合作与发展组织的成员共同开发的项目，其目的是测试十五岁学生是否掌握了参与未来知识社会所必需的基础知识和基本技能，从而建立一套学生评价方面的教育指标）所要求的三大基本方面——阅读能力、数学能力、科学能力，以及其他诸如学习态度、学生如何管理他们的学习等方面的要求，有异曲同工之妙。他们的共同点都在于：教育的核心在于"育人"、"立人"，她必须关注"人"的能力的增强、素质的提升、道德的健全等。

如此说来，在教育的价值取向多元化的今天，一些成年人难逃教育的浮躁和功利化，重温蔡先生的这句话，对于今天的我们而言，是否会有着更多的意味？

对于一所好的学校而言，除了应有较好的物质条件，但更重要的是，应该具有自己的博大胸襟和精神气质。

需要说明的是，这种精神气质和博大胸襟突出表现为：培养走向未来、具有国际视野的人才和有责任感、敢于担当的人，其教育的视野要涵盖现实，更要超越现实。关切的目光绝非只停留在作为"表层"的分数及当下，更要穿越前者，抵达"深层"的价值取向、文化积淀和更为纵深、辽阔的未来！而最能折射这种气质及视野的，我以为，体现在这所学校的方方面面，包括教学安排、课堂氛围、师生关系、社团活动、社会实践、校园环境、学校管理模式、作业布置方式及特色等。其中，学校校本课程的设置及落实，也是众多校园文化、气质承载及体现方式之一。

校本课程的设置与否，也是判断一所学校是否真的将学生的成长放在首位的参考条件之一。丰富多彩的校本课程，植根于对"新课程标准"理念的真切理解，更植根于学生群体的个体差异性和强烈求知欲的现实语境，植根于当下乃至未来的知识社会对学生能力的长远要求，更植根于学生个体的终身学习的需要。它直观地展现出一所学校的精神气质和文化内涵！

作为一所具有基础性、实验性和开放性的现代化学校，我校已在多年的摸索和发展中，培养出众多活跃在外交、文化及社会各个领域的优秀人才，并逐渐形成自己特有的校园文化："一个载体"——以外语教学为载体，"三个特色"——外语特色、开放特色、素质教育特色，五个“学生培养目标内涵”——自主精神、公民意识、科学态度、人文情怀、领袖气质。正是在这样的校园文化的指引下，武汉实验外国语学校形成了“重视学生个性发展，一切为了孩子，为了孩子的一切”的办学特色，在社会上享有较高的声誉。

作为我校特色学科的外语，自然是走在校本课程的最前列。本套“武汉实验外国语学校外语校本课程”丛书，共分为四类课程：一是阅读类，二是听力类，三是社团活动类，四是教学研讨类。

具体来说，阅读类课程选择的是我校在长期外语教学实践中，已经证实为“经典”的阅读文本，与教材呼应，同时又适度提高，是我们武汉实外的学生必须要读的好读物；听力类课程是作为“武汉实外初中听力等级教程”的一部分，其中的内容既包括英语歌曲、英文演讲，也包括精彩英语对话等，内容生动，时代性突出，也贴近学生们的心灵及生活；社团活动类课程主要展现了我校的社团活动及 duty show（作者注：“值日报告比赛”——一种在课前5分钟，由单人或多人以小组方式展示的包含有表演、电影配音、专题探研诸如“好莱坞电影中的美国生活方式”等成果的教学活动）的精华，学生们的开阔视野和风采都让教师们感受到他们这代人的希望和茁壮成长，其中的“活动现场”、“学生感悟”、“教师点评”的栏目文字能最大限度再现活动的魅力，并带给人思考的愉悦；最后一类是“教学研讨”类课程，它是我校外语老师一直坚持进行的“共同成长”教研活动过程及成果的展现，我校所有外语教师都积极参与其中，并以包括听力课、口语课、概念课、活动课等在内的多种课型，展现出了她们不同风格但却同样精彩的教学活动。

综上所述，这套校本课程是武汉实验外国语师生们精神面貌的生动再现与历史的见证。她记录并见证了一位位外语教师的辛勤善思，记录并见证一个个实外学生的可喜成长，也记录和见证了一个个外语课堂的诗意瞬间，同时，她更体现出这所学校所蕴藏的一种精神气质，一种奔跑的姿态，预示着学校更美好的发展前景。

希望这套“武汉实验外国语学校校本课程”丛书，能给予每一位读者一些触动和思考，也祝福武汉实验外国语学校的发展前景更加辉煌灿烂！

是为序。

全国人大代表
武汉市政府参事　李菁
武汉实验外国语学校校长

2012-8-17

前　言

近年来,“减负增效”的呼声愈来愈高。减负背景下是学生书本多、课程多、作业多的现实局面。针对减负,新课程标准提出了从教师、教材、课堂等多方面进行减负的要求。力求“减负不减责任,减负不减质量”。

一直以来,一线教师都在不断探索,如何有效、保质地编写课本教程。既能切实反映学生的学习情况,又能切实减轻学生的负担。因为减负,不是所谓的不布置作业,而是要制止繁琐重复地对学生进行机械练习的题海战术。一本好的课后辅导教材,应该既能实现检测学生学习效果的目的,同时也能让学生通过有限、有效的题目设计获得相应的知识。

《Learn It》作为武汉实验外国语学校的校本课程,编者均为教学经验丰富的一线教师。在本书的编写过程中,编者精简而精炼地对课程内容进行了汇编,以帮助学生更有效、更轻松地使用本书。

首先,《Learn It》精简练习数量。编者根据每堂课学生掌握知识的情况,精心挑选和设计有针对性的题目,使学生的英语综合运用能力在每堂课后的练习中得到巩固和提升。《Learn It》综合了每堂课的重要知识点,既能帮助学生更好地掌握知识技能,减轻学生的作业负担,同时也能帮助教师及时高效地检验学生的课堂学习情况,减轻教师批阅作业的负担,以便有更多的时间辅导学生。

其次,《Learn It》内容紧扣课本,题目设计不乏趣味性。在保证学生落实每堂课知识的前提下,激发学生的求知欲望,维持其思维的活跃性。外语学校学生对文化的兴趣浓厚,《Learn It》的内容涵盖了多个领域的各种文化,让学生在完成作业的同时接受“润物细无声”的文化滋养。此外,《Learn It》采用的一课一练的编排设计更方便学生练习,也方便教师批阅。

最后,由于我们能力有限,加之时间仓促,本书难免存在不少问题,恳请同行专家赐教指正。

编　者

2012 年于武汉实验外国语学校

目录 CONTENTS

Exercises

目录 CONTENTS

Tapescripts

Keys

Exercises

Unit 1

Section One

一、单项选择。

( ) 1. Please give me ________. I want to write a letter.

A. a paper B. some papers

C. some pieces of papers D. a piece of paper

( ) 2. —What's the matter with you?

— ____________________

A. Not at all. B. I'm sorry.

C. I don't feel very well. D. That's right.

( ) 3. —________ the empty cup away and ________ me a cup of tea, please.

—OK. Wait a minute.

A. Take; bring B. Take; carry

C. Bring; take D. Bring; carry

( ) 4. It's dark here; turn ________ the light, please.

A. off B. on C. down D. up

( ) 5. Do you want ________ with me?

A. go shopping B. to go shop C. to go shopping D. shopping

( ) 6. —Can I ________ your dictionary?

—Sorry, I ________ it at home.

A. lend; left B. borrow; left

C. lend; forget D. borrow; forget

( ) 7. There ________ more gardens in our school next year.

A. is B. are C. will be D. shall be

( ) 8. —________ do students exercise a week?

—Three or four.

A. How much B. How long

C. How many times D. How often

( ) 9. Drinking milk ________ good ________ our health.

A. are; to B. is; to C. is; for D. are; for

( ) 10. Susan ________ us very well, she's an excellent cook.

A. looked like B. looked at
C. looked for D. looked after

二、首字母填词。

1. January the f ________ is New Year's Day.
2. —Where is my watch?
   —I can't f ________ it.
3. Zhao Ming n ________ goes to school late.
4. My mother often goes to the s ________ to buy different things.
5. We play ping-pong in the g ________ .

三、回答问题。

1. What is your name?（李丽欣）
____
2. Nice to meet you.
____
3. See you tomorrow.
____
4. What day is today?（9 月 5 日）
____
5. When is your birthday?（1 月 19 日）
____

四、句型练习。

换一种说法。

1. Bring me those spoons.
____
2. Give him that parcel.
____
3. Read her the poem.
____
4. Show them the film.
____
5. I am going to tell this news to you.
____

用代词取代画线部分名词。

6. Can you turn off <u>the radio</u>?
____
7. Show us <u>those photos</u>.
____

8. Can you try on this coat?

____

9. Pass Sam the knife.

____

10. I am going to give this fork to you.

____

五、改写句子。

1. He often does his homework after supper.（改成一般疑问句）
   ________ he often ________ his homework after super?
2. The plane takes off at 9：15 in the evening.（改成否定句）
   The plane ________ take off at 9：15 in the evening.
3. They were excited at seeing the film.（改成感叹句）
   ________ ________ they were at seeing the filming!
4. He learned to play the piano when he was five years old.（对画线部分提问）
   ________ did he learn to play the piano?
5. Peter joined in the singing group 2 months ago.（对画线部分提问）
   ________ joined in the singing group 2 months ago?

Section Two

一、单项选择。

(　　) 1. —Hi, Jane! You look very beautiful today.
—________
A. I don't think so.　　B. No, not at all.
C. Don't say so, please.　　D. Thanks a lot.

(　　) 2. Do you need shoes ________ sports? We have lots of shoes ________ very good prices.
A. for; at　　B. for; with　　C. at; with　　D. in; at

(　　) 3. My mother looked ________ when she heard the news.
A. worry　　B. worries　　C. worried　　D. worrying

(　　) 4. The problem is very difficult. Can you ________?
A. work out it　　B. work it out
C. work them out　　D. work out them

(　　) 5. —Could you please give me ________?
—Sure.
A. some advice　　B. an advice　　C. any advice　　D. any suggestion

(　　) 6. ________ Jennifer was reading a magazine, his sister was listening to the pop music.

A. What time　　B. When　　C. While　　D. Since

(　　) 7. Now children, turn to page ________ and look at the ________ picture in Lesson Two.

A. twentieth; one　　B. twenty; one

C. twentieth; first　　D. twenty; first

(　　) 8. —There are fifty students in our class. 80% students love junk food. What does 80% mean?

—It means ________.

A. most of the students　　B. some of the students

C. all of the students　　D. none of the students

(　　) 9. If you want to lose weight, you have to eat ________ food for dinner.

A. fewer　　B. more　　C. few　　D. less

(　　) 10. —You'd better drink some hot tea.

—That ________ a good idea.

A. sounds　　B. sound like　　C. sounds like　　D. either A or C

二、翻译句子。

1. 李老师正在给她的班级上课。

____

2. 不要看窗外。

____

3. 你可以在池塘里看到什么？

____

4. 有两个孩子正在操场上玩耍。

____

5. 我可以看到一架飞机正在天上飞。

____

三、按照时间先后顺序排序。

①April Fool's Day ②Valentine's Day ③Christmas ④New Year's Day ⑤Mother's Day

________　________　________　________　________

四、句型练习。

1. There are some boys.

They are sitting beside a tree.（合并）

____

2. I can see a girl.

She is swimming across the river.（合并）

____

3. There is a cat lying under the chair. (一般疑问句)

____

4. I can see a boy listening to the radio in the dorm. (否定句)

____

5. The UFO is flying over the city. (对画线部分提问)

____

五、改写句子。

1. David is having fun. (改为同义句)
   David is ________ ________.
2. Now the students are visiting the zoo. (用 usually 代替 now 改写句子)
   The students ________ ________ the zoo on holidays.
3. Peter seldom meets his friends. (对画线部分提问)
   ________ ________ ________ Peter ________ his friends?
4. her, see, Lisa, grandmother, always, to, on Sundays, goes (连词成句)
   ____
5. Sun Qian usually walks to school. (改为同义句)
   Sun Qian usually ________ to school ________ ________.

六、完成对话。

A: (1) ____?

B: I have a headache.

A: (2) ____?

B: I'm busy preparing for the exam so I don't have the time. But I've taken some aspirin.

A: Then, (3) ______________________________ now?

B: I'm feeling much better now, thanks.

Section Three

一、单项选择。

( ) 1. —This is Lily, my sister.
—________________
—Very glad to see you.
A. Thank you very much. B. How are you? I'm fine.
C. Morning. I'm Dora. D. Hi. My name is Dora.

( ) 2. Maria likes documentaries ________ cartoon, ________ she doesn't like thrillers.
A. and; and B. or; and C. but; but D. and; but

(　　) 3. It's foolish ________ you to do that.

A. for　　B. of　　C. to　　D. with

(　　) 4. ________ is from America.

A. One of the boys　　B. All of the boys

C. Some of the boys　　D. One of the boy

(　　) 5. It's important to be ________ and ________.

A. politely; help　　B. politely; helpful

C. polite; helpful　　D. polite; help

(　　) 6. They asked for a ________.

A. news　　B. bread　　C. drink　　D. information

(　　) 7. —________ do you go back to your hometown?

—Twice a month.

A. How soon　　B. How often

C. How long　　D. How many times

(　　) 8. —What ________ you ________?

—I am ________ my sister.

A. do; do; babysit　　B. are; doing; babysiting

C. did; do; babysitting　　D. are; doing; babysitting

(　　) 9. —________ are you going to stay?

—________ a week.

A. When; About　　B. How; For

C. How long; For　　D. What; About

(　　) 10. ________ Chinese are looking for ways to learn English well before Beijing 2008 Olympics.

A. Thousand　　B. Thousands　　C. Thousand of　　D. Thousands of

二、介词和副词填空。

1. Is the accessories department ________ this floor?
2. Can you imagine anyone ________ that sweater?
3. Sorry, madam. These scarves are not ________ sale.
4. What are you going to buy Jeff ________ his new flat? He moved last week.
5. Do you often shop ________ catalog or ________ the Internet?
6. What problems do you have ________ answering questions in class?
7. Look at your pants! They have holes ________ them!
8. What is the woman ____________ glasses looking ____________?

三、完形填空。(2006年长沙市初中毕业学业考试)

Did you watch NBA 55th All-Star Game? If you watched it, you wouldn't __1__ Shaquille O'Neal's wonderful play.

Shaquille O'Neal is in Miami Heat now. He was born on March 6th, 1972. He is 2.16

meters tall. When he was young, he was very ___2___. His strong hands gave him a good start of life. Shaquille liked playing ___3___. But when he was a high school student in Grade Two, he wasn't good at basketball yet. Just at that time, he ___4___ his good coach, Dale Brown. Then he began his hard practice. In 1992, he joined NBA, ___5___ for Magic Team, then Lakers, and later Miami Heat in 2004. He had a great ___6___. He has joined All-Star Game ten times, won NBA Finals MVP (most valuable player) three times, ___7___ got the gold medals for the USA in the Olympic Games. He was named one of the fifty ___8___ players in NBA history.

Shaquille O'Neal is strong and tall. People call him "Large Shark". But he is good at ___9___, too. He has already had six CDs. It's really one of the happiest things in the world to listen to his CDs while ___10___ him play basketball.

( ) 1. A. remember B. forget C. see
( ) 2. A. thin B. sick C. strong
( ) 3. A. basketball B. soccer C. volleyball
( ) 4. A. missed B. met C. left
( ) 5. A. playing B. singing C. dancing
( ) 6. A. idea B. success C. party
( ) 7. A. and B. but C. although
( ) 8. A. worst B. slowest C. greatest
( ) 9. A. music B. history C. math
( ) 10. A. making B. helping C. watching

四、句型练习。

变否定句。

1. Sam and Bob want to make a toy car.

____

2. They usually get up early every day.

____

3. I always stay at home at the weekends.

____

变一般疑问句。

4. Jim lives in Paris.

____

5. Diana and Maria begin work at 8 o' clock every morning.

____

6. I like eating fresh fruit.

____

对画线部分提问。

7. She usually reads English <u>in the morning</u>.

____

Section Four

一、单项选择。

(　　) 1. I'm ________ him, but I can ________ nothing, because there is something wrong with my ________.

A. listen; hear; eyes　　B. listening to; hear; ears

C. listening; hearing; ears　　D. listen to; hear; eyes

(　　) 2. The weather is not ________ it was yesterday.

A. so cold as　　B. as colder than

C. so colder as　　D. very colder than

(　　) 3. Study harder, ________ you'll not pass the coming exam.

A. or　　B. and　　C. but　　D. if

(　　) 4. Li Ming did his homework ________, so he left school last.

A. easily　　B. quickly　　C. happily　　D. slowly

(　　) 5. —Hello, Could I speak to Jane, please?

—________

A. I'd like to.　　B. Goodbye.　　C. I think so.　　D. Hold on, please.

(　　) 6. ________ of his parents has been to the Great Wall.

A. Both　　B. All　　C. None　　D. Neither

(　　) 7. I've never seen ________ like that.

A. such a boring play　　B. a such boring play

C. so a boring play　　D. a so boring play

(　　) 8. I want to do ________.

A. different something　　B. different anything

C. something different　　D. anything different

(　　) 9. —What about ________?

—OK, let's go!

A. play bowling　　B. playing bowling

C. to play bowling　　D. to playing bowling

(　　)10. —How do you get there?

—________________

A. I by bike to get there.　　B. I take the bike there.

C. I get there by bus.　　D. both A and B.

二、翻译句子。

1. 她是个可怕的长舌妇。

____

2. 我将在这个磅秤上称自己的体重。

____

3. 我的爷爷奶奶就住在我们家隔壁。

____

4. 李老师通常7点钟离开家。

____

5. 你能告诉我去火车站的路吗？

____

三、阅读理解。（2006年长沙中考）

Are you the only child in the family? If so, you are the most important in your family. Parents are the closest people to you in the world. But a lot of middle school students have a problem. They feel they're not as close to their parents as before. They even don't think their parents are fair to them.

Some students complain that their parents often say a lot to them, but never listen to them. Some say their parents don't allow them to play computer games when other classmates are doing that. Others say when they're making phone calls to friends, their parents like to ask if they're speaking to a boy or a girl. These make them very unhappy. Some students even decide to leave home because they're afraid to tell their parents when they have done something wrong, especially when they do badly in exams. Then they usually think running away is the only choice. But they don't know running away may bring them some more problems.

Problems are parts of life. Here are some suggestions for you to solve your problems.

1) Find a good chance to talk with your parents. Don't be afraid to tell them your feelings.

2) Get help from others like good friends or teachers.

3) Keep a diary to help you understand more about yourself and your feelings.

4) Show your parents you're growing up. Then they'll feel you're no longer a child.

If you follow the advice, you'll have a happy life and never think of running away.

(　　) 1. According to the article, ________ are the closest people to an only child.

A. teachers　　B. classmates　　C. parents

(　　) 2. Which of the following is **TRUE**?

A. Parents don't love their children now.

B. Middle school students don't have any problems.

C. Some students don't think their parents are fair to them.

(　　) 3. We'd better ________ if we have problems with them.

A. talk with our parents

B. quarrel with our parents

C. leave our parents

(　　) 4. Why does the author advice us to keep a diary?

A. Because it's our homework.

B. Because it can help us practice writing.

C. Because it can help us understand ourselves better.

(　　) 5. This article is about some middle school students' ________.

A. friends　　B. hobbies　　C. problems

四、句型练习。

1. Mrs. Green does the housework every day.（一般疑问句）

____

2. Sandy is riding his bicycle.（变否定句）

____

3. He ①<u>usually</u> goes to school ②<u>by bus</u>.（对画线部分提问）

Q①: ____

Q②: ____

4. We often go to the library on Sundays.（用"tomorrow"把句子改成将来时）

____

Section Five

一、听写单词。

1. ________　2. ________　3. ________

4. ________　5. ________　6. ________

7. ________　8. ________　9. ________

10. ________

二、选出相对应的答语。

1. (　　) A. I have a stomachache.

2. (　　) B. We should keep away from sick poultry（家禽）.

3. (　　) C. Of course, go ahead.

4. (　　) D. Less than eight hours.

5. (　　) E. Much better.

三、听短对话，选出最佳答案。

(　　) 1. A. For three years.　B. They are interested in it.

C. Chinese history.

(　　) 2. A. They're in Russian style.　B. They're in European style.

C. I'm not sure.

( ) 3. A. He likes Chinese culture. B. Chinese.
C. Too hot.

( ) 4. A. In the living room. B. In his bedroom.
C. In his mother's bedroom.

( ) 5. A. Twenty-one. B. Twenty. C. William.

四、单项选择。

( ) 1. —Have a nice weekend!
—________________
A. The same to you. B. Be careful.
C. I think I can. D. Glad to see you.

( ) 2. —Will there be more people in 100 years, do you think?
— ________, I hope.
A. No, there isn't B. No, there aren't
C. No, there won't D. No, they won't

( ) 3. He feels ________ and works ________.
A. good; bad B. well; well C. good; well D. bad; good

( ) 4. He ________ a souvenir at the zoo yesterday.
A. buys B. bought C. was buying D. buy

( ) 5. Give me ________.
A. two kilos of fruits B. two kilos of fruit
C. two kilo of fruit D. two kilo of fruits

( ) 6. If it ________ fine tomorrow, we'll go swimming.
A. is B. will be C. is going to be D. was

( ) 7. Ten years ago, there were no railways ________ the two cities.
A. above B. among C. between D. over

( ) 8. Mary is ________ busy, because she has ________ homework to do today.
A. too many; much too B. too much; much too
C. much too; too much D. many too; too much

( ) 9. Dave is ________ than ________ boy in our class.
A. smarter; any other B. smartest; any other
C. smart; any one D. smartest; any

( ) 10. My backpack is ________ beautiful than ________.
A. much; her B. more; she
C. much more; hers D. much; hers

( ) 11. The library ________ from Monday to Sunday. So I can go there to read books every day.
A. opens B. is opening C. is closed D. closes

(　　) 12. When you want to say goodbye to your friend after the party, you can say: ________

A. Take care.　　B. Good evening.

C. Never mind.　　D. That's all right.

(　　) 13. The restaurant is ________ the corner. You can't miss it.

A. in　　B. on　　C. of　　D. under

(　　) 14. —Which girl is Susan?

—The girl ________ short hair is Susan.

A. in　　B. of　　C. on　　D. with

(　　) 15. —When is Christmas Day?

—It's ________.

A. in 2011　　B. on November 25

C. in December　　D. On Friday

五、首字母填词。(2005年无锡中考)

In the old days, London was (1) k ________ as a city of fog. The fog was as thick as pea soup. London's fog was (2) c ________ by factory smoke, so it was called "smog". The smog was so thick that car and bus drivers could (3) h ________ see the road in front of them even during the daytime. People had to (4) w ________ "smog-masks" over their faces when they went out.

In December 1952, a very thick dark (5) c ________ came down over the city. It was the (6) w ________ smog Londoners had ever had. Nearly fifty people died in road accidents. Many more people (7) b ________ very unhealthy. After three weeks, the smog began to (8) l ________ slowly. Life in London came back to normal. But not long after that, over 4,000 people died as a (9) r ________ of the smog.

In 1956, the British (10) s ________ burning coal in houses and factories in the city. London's air got cleaner.

六、完形填空。

One day Mark Twain was invited to __1__ a lecture in a small town. He met a young man he knew. The young man told Mark Twain that he had an uncle __2__ never laughed or smiled. The young man said that nobody and nothing could possibly make his uncle smile or laugh.

"Please __3__ your uncle to my lecture tonight," said Mark Twain. "I'm sure I can make him laugh."

That evening the young man and his uncle sat __4__ the front row. Mark Twain spoke directly to the old man. He told some rather funny stories, __5__ made everyone in the hall laugh. But the old man never __6__ smiled. Mark Twain told __7__ stories he knew. But the old man's face was still a blank. At last, Mark Twain stopped. He felt very tired and disappointed.

__8__ later, Mark Twain told a friend of his about __9__ had happened. "Oh," said his friend, "I know that old man. He has been __10__ for years."

( ) 1. A. send	B. give	C. work	D. make
( ) 2. A. which	B. whom	C. whose	D. who
( ) 3. A. take	B. carry	C. fetch	D. bring
( ) 4. A. in	B. on	C. with	D. at
( ) 5. A. with which	B. those	C. which	D. these
( ) 6. A. even	B. ever	C. still	D. yet
( ) 7. A. the funniest	B. funniest	C. the most funny	D. most funny
( ) 8. A. These days	B. Some days	C. Other days	D. Those days
( ) 9. A. how	B. which	C. what	D. that
( ) 10. A. foolish	B. deaf	C. blind	D. dead

七、阅读理解。(2005年云南省中考)

Many years ago, when I was working as a volunteer at a hospital, I got to know a little girl named Lisa. The poor little girl had a very serious disease and was dying. The doctor had done his best but no medicine really worked. The only chance to save her seemed to be a blood transfusion(输血) from her five-year-old brother. The little boy had the same disease before and had developed the antibodies(抗体) to fight the illness.

The doctor talked to the little boy about what they planned to do, and asked him if he would be willing to give his blood to his sister. I saw him hesitate (迟疑) for a moment. He took a deep breath and said, "Yes, I'll do it if it can save Lisa."

As the transfusion was going on, the little boy lay quietly in bed next to his sister. He looked at her and smiled all the time. When everything was done and the colour returned to his sister's face, his smile disappeared and he looked a little afraid. He looked up at the doctor and asked, "Will I start to die now?"

He was too young to understand the doctor. He thought he would have to give all his blood to his sister. But he agreed.

( ) 1. What happened to the little girl named Lisa?

A. She died of a very serious disease.

B. She got better with the antibodies from her brother.

C. She lost her little brother.

D. The transfusion failed and her illness got worse.

( ) 2. The doctor waited the little boy to ________.

A. give all his blood to his sister

B. give some of his blood to his sister

C. give his life to his sister

D. get the same disease as his sister

( ) 3. How did the five-year-old boy understand the doctor's plan?

A. He thought he was going to lose all his blood.

B. He thought he was going to be killed.

C. He thought he was going to die together with his sister.

D. He thought he was going to die when he grew up.

(　　)4. What did the boy feel when the doctor talked to him about the transfusion?

A. He was unhappy to help his sister.

B. He was so afraid that he refused to do anything.

C. He was worried about his sister.

D. He was willing to give his blood.

(　　)5. The writer still remember the story many years later ________.

A. because the little girl had a very strange disease

B. because the sister and brother had the same disease

C. because the doctor saved the little girl's life

D. because of what the boy did for his sister

八、句型练习。

1. Pass Jim the salt.（把句中的名词都改成代词）

____

2. There is a dog. The dog playing in the garden.（合并）

____

3. Tim comes from Australia.（改为否定句）

____

4. I sometimes help my mother in the afternoon.（对画线部分提问）

____

5. She usually gets up at 6 : 00.（对画线部分提问）

____

6. He never goes to work on foot.（用"next week"把句子改成将来时）

____

九、用适当的句子填空。

A：So Jimmy，(1)________________ vacation?

B：I'll probably fly to Hangzhou to stay with my uncle.

A：What will you do then?

B：Maybe (2)________________.

A：Go hiking，that's great! And don't you ever think of (3)________________ on the West Lake?

B：We'll definitely go boating，too. (4)________________?

A：Well，some relatives are coming over from Singapore. So I'll spend some time with them and show them around the city of Xiamen.

B：Oh，a family get-together. That's nice. (5)________________!

A：Thank you. You，too.

Unit 2

Section One

一、单项选择。

(　　) 1. Sam is a poor man with ________ money but ________ friends. He's happy.

A. little; many　B. a little; much　C. few; many　D. a few; much

(　　) 2. Let me ________. I'll telephone you tomorrow.

A. look　B. see　C. know　D. to see

(　　) 3. My brother Li Lei often ________ a bus to school.

A. take　B. takes　C. by　D. carries

(　　) 4. He is ________ old to work in the factory.

A. very　B. quite　C. much　D. too

(　　) 5. He is good at playing ________ soccer instead of ________ piano.

A. the; the　B. /; the　C. /; /　D. /; the

(　　) 6. Your shoes are new, but ________ are old.

A. I　B. my　C. mine　D. mines

(　　) 7. The shirt is too ________, I can't afford it.

A. cheap　B. expensive　C. much　D. high

(　　) 8. —What is Kathy like?

—________________

A. She likes swimming.　B. She is like a student.

C. She is easygoing.　D. She is of medium build.

(　　) 9. —What's your ________?

—It is 504, North Lake Road.

A. address　B. e-mail address

C. telephone number　D. area code

(　　) 10. —What nationality are you?

—________________

A. I am from China.　B. I am Chinese.

C. I live in China.　D. I was born in China.

二、首字母填词。

1. I don't think it's h________ for her to spend so much time alone.

2. How many hours do you s ________ every night?
3. Does it make a big d ________ if you eat fruit every day?
4. What's your f ________ program?
5. Most students e ________ three or four times a week.
6. What's the hospital's t ________ number?
7. What c ________ are they in?
8. Ann and I are good f ________.
9. She passed her driving t ________ when she was 17.
10. Is y ________ brother a Chinese student?

三、句型练习。

变否定句。

1. She has a lot of books.

____

2. They have a lot of glue.

____

3. There is a lot of jam in the can.

____

4. I can see some rice in the bowl.

____

变一般疑问句。

5. I want an orange.

____

6. There are a lot of shoes in the locker.

____

7. His daughter eats an apple every day.

____

对画线部分提问。

8. She has a little ink.

____

9. There are many sandwiches in the basket.

____

10. I need some cake.

____

四、补全对话，每空一词。

Mary: Hello, this is Mary.
Mr. White: Hello, this is Mr. White, Peter's father.
Mary: Hello, may I speak to Peter?
Mr. White: Sorry, he is not(1) ________.
Mary: Could you tell me when he'll come back?
Mr. White: I'm afraid I can't. Can I take a(2) ________ for him?

Mary: Please tell him that I(3) ________ he will come to my birthday party next Sunday.

Mr. White: Thank you for (4)______ Peter to your party. By the way, (5)______ will it begin?

Mary: It will start at half past five.

Mr. White: OK.

Mary: Thank you. Goodbye.

Mr. White: Goodbye.

Section Two

一、单项选择。

(　　) 1. His brother, Bruce, caught a lot of ________ on Sunday.
A. bird　　B. fish　　C. duck　　D. dog and cat

(　　) 2. Look at these ________. Victor has ________ aunt and two uncles.
A. photos; a　　B. photos; an
C. photoes; the　　D. photograph; an

(　　) 3. —Do you mind my taking this place?
—________. It's for Mr. Smith.
A. Not at all　　B. Yes, please
C. Yes, of course not　　D. Better not

(　　) 4. —________________________
—I'm a worker.
A. What are you doing?　　B. Who are you?
C. What do you do?　　D. What do you like?

(　　) 5. My mother does some ________ on Sundays.
A. wash　　B. to wash　　C. washes　　D. washing

(　　) 6. ________ twenty-fifth of ________ December is ________ Christmas Day.
A. The; the; a　　B. The;the;the
C. The;/; /　　D. /; /; the

(　　) 7. —Hi. Lin Tao. I'm looking for you.
—____________________
A. Excuse me .　　B. What's the matter?
C. What's up?　　D. What's trouble?

(　　) 8. I'm very nervous when the ________ ask me questions.
A. interviewees　　B. interviews
C. interviewers　　D. interviewer

(　　) 9. Welcome to our school. ________, our school is the biggest one in the city.
A. By the way　　B. In the way
C. On the way　　D. Show the way

(　　)10. ________ you ________ English every day?

A. Are; reading　　B. Does; read
C. Do; read　　D. Is; reading

二、根据前后关联填词。

1. January ________ March　　2. May ________ July
3. September ________ November　　4. two ________ four
5. ________ six seven　　6. eleven ________ thirteen
7. eighteen nineteen ________　　8. first ________ third
9. Tuesday ________ Thursday　　10. Sunday ________ Tuesday

三、完形填空。

Today Neil is __1__ near a river. Suddenly his knife falls into the __2__. He is very __3__ because the knife is the birthday present his father gave him, but it is __4__ now. Then at once a kind old woman comes up and asks Neil what is wrong. "I lose my __5__," he says. "It falls into the water when I am playing here." The woman gives him a gold(金的)knife and asks, "Is this your knife?" "No," says the boy. The old woman gives him a silver one and asks __6__, "And this one?" "No," again says the boy. Then she gives him 7__ iron knife. "Yes, that's __8__!" calls out the happy boy. "I know it __9__," the old woman says. "Now I will give you the gold knife and the silver knife because you are a/an __10__ boy."

(　　) 1. A. reading　B. sleeping　C. listening　D. playing
(　　) 2. A. sea　B. water　C. lake　D. mud
(　　) 3. A. sad　B. happy　C. angry　D. exciting
(　　) 4. A. broken　B. well　C. lost　D. heavy
(　　) 5. A. bag　B. knife　C. money　D. clothes
(　　) 6. A. again　B. too　C. either　D. also
(　　) 7. A. a　B. an　C. the　D. /
(　　) 8. A. me　B. I　C. my　D. mine
(　　) 9. A. enough well　B. well enough　C. good enough　D. enough good
(　　) 10. A. interesting　B. clever　C. lazy　D. honest

四、句型练习。

1. Mr. Grant has a bag of tea.（对画线部分提问）

____

2. I have①only one bicycle.
I have ② only one bicycle.（对画线部分提问）
①: ____
②: ____
3. How much paper do you need?（2）
回答: ____
4. How many bones does your dog want?（3）
回答: ____

五、完成句子。

1. What's wrong?（变同义句）

   ________ is ________ ________?

2. Why don't you give her some flowers for her birthday?（变同义句）

   ________ ________ ________ her some flowers for her birthday?

3. Linda found her cute dog somewhere.（变否定句）

   Linda ________ ________ her cute dog ________.

4. I was shopping at this time last Saturday.（对画线部分提问）

   ________ ________ ________ ________ at this time last Saturday?

5. Eli was at the cinema while her brother was studying in the library.（对画线部分提问）

   ________ ________ Eli while her brother was studying in the library?

Section Three

一、单项选择。

( ) 1. It's 8 : 40 p. m. Yes, it's ________ in the evening.

A. twenty to nine B. twenty past nine
C. forty eighty D. nine past forty

( ) 2. This dictionary is ________.

A. my brother's one B. my brothers ones
C. my brother one D. my brother's

( ) 3. Why don't you get ________ to read?

A. something B. everything
C. anything D. nothing

( ) 4. —Susan, go and join your sister cleaning the yard.

—Why ________? John is sitting there doing nothing.

A. him B. he C. I D. me

( ) 5. The music sounds ________.

A. very beautiful B. very beautifully
C. enough beautiful D. fine

( ) 6. The doctor asks her not to eat ________ meat every day.

A. too much B. much too C. too many D. lot of

( ) 7. Did you sleep ________?

A. good B. fine C. well D. OK

( ) 8. How many lessons ________ you ________ on Friday?

A. are; having B. is; having C. do; have D. does; have

( ) 9. Jeff is studying ________ an English exam.

A. for B. at C. of D. with

( ) 10. I'm going to work ________ interesting when I grow up. Maybe Paris. I like art.

A. nowhere　　B. somewhere　　C. anywhere　　D. elsewhere

二、翻译句子。

1. 你可以用面粉和水做点糨糊。

____

2. 他有多少钱？

____

3. 她的书包里装满了书。

____

4. 我将把这幅画挂在这里。

____

5. 外面天气怎样？

____

6. 我的伞漏雨。

____

7. 你认为这个音乐怎样？

____

8. 这个杯子是用什么做的？

____

三、用所给词的适当形式填空。

1. Who usually ________ (cook) the meal at home?
2. Sally ________ (teach) English in a middle school.
3. Look! Don ________ (introduce) his friends to Frank.
4. Alex always ________ (go) to school on foot.
5. Please be quiet. The baby ________. (sleep)
6. Be quick! I ________ (wait) for you at the gate now.
7. There ________ (be) many mice and a cat in the house.
8. Don't ________ (touch) the buttons.
9. — Where is Tom?
   —He ________ (repair) his bicycle.
10. Ron ________ (study) English at the moment.

四、句型练习。

1. What's the date today?（回答问题）

2 月 21 日________________　　4 月 18 日________________

8 月 17 日________________　　3 月 2 日________________

10 月 3 日________________　　7 月 31 日________________

2. 用下列单词造句(可以改变词形和增加必要的词汇)

bag/plastic/make/expensive

①______________________________

cloudy/today

②____

look/how/outside?

③____

3. Your hairstyle looks smart.（对画线部分提问）

____

五、完形填空。（2005 年无锡中考）

Some friends hired a bus to go to the beach for their holiday. When they __1__ the bus late at night to go home, someone was __2__ on the ground beside it. They looked at him and __3__ that he was a man from their town who hadn't come in their bus. He was very __4__. "I suppose he came in another bus," one of the men said, "and __5__ it when it left for home __6__ he was drunk. Now he's come to our bus to go back." Then two men put him into the bus. He didn't __7__ up during the drive back, and when the bus arrived they took him to his __8__. They knocked at the door for several minutes, and then a __9__ opened a window and said, "It's no use __10__ there. They've gone to the beach. And they'll be back in a few days."

(　　) 1. A. stopped　B. changed　C. passed by　D. returned to

(　　) 2. A. lying　B. singing　C. reading　D. playing

(　　) 3. A. wondered　B. reported　C. found　D. explained

(　　) 4. A. sad　B. ill　C. tired　D. drunk

(　　) 5. A. caught　B. missed　C. met　D. lost

(　　) 6. A. because　B. if　C. though　D. so

(　　) 7. A. get　B. wake　C. stand　D. look

(　　) 8. A. town　B. office　C. home　D. hotel

(　　) 9. A. driver　B. conductor　C. guide　D. neighbour

(　　) 10. A. crying　B. knocking　C. searching　D. complaining

Section Four

一、单项选择。

(　　) 1. Don't you have any bananas?

A. Yes, we don't.　B. No, we do.

C. No, we don't.　D. Yes, we have.

(　　) 2. — ________ is he?

— He is thirteen years old.

A. How　B. How many　C. How much　D. How old

(　　) 3. ________ skirt is yours?

A. Whose　B. Where　C. How　D. Which

(　　) 4. ________ too many sweets is bad for your teeth.

A. Eat　B. Eats　C. Eating　D. /

(　　) 5. — My mother is ill in bed. She has a bad cold.

— ______________

A. Really? You'd better see a doctor B. I hope you feel better soon.

C. I'm sorry to hear that. D. Oh, really.

(　　) 6. Father wants me ______ a teacher.

A. to be B. to do C. am D. are

(　　) 7. Give him ______ to eat, please.

A. something delicious B. delicious something

C. anything delicious D. delicious anything

(　　) 8. — Is this ______ ball, Joe?

— No, it's not ______.

A. your; my B. your; mine C. yours; my D. yours; mine

(　　) 9. — Does Daniel often play ______ you?

— No. He often looks ______ things on the Internet.

A. for; on B. with; out C. with; for D. for; out

(　　) 10. When the light is red, you ______ cross the road. You ______ wait for the green light.

A. can; must B. can; must not

C. can't; must D. can't; must not

二、句型练习。

1. The chocolate tastes sweet.（对画线部分提问）

____

2. the policeman /strong/ big feet（连词成句）

____

3. It feels like silk.

（一般疑问句）______________________________

（对画线部分提问）______________________________

4. Jake likes playing football very much.

（否定句）______________________________

（一般疑问句）______________________________

5. Jessie is rollerblading in the park.（对画线部分提问）

____

6. There are 34 tourists on the tour bus.（对画线部分提问）

____

7. The bank is across from the hospital.（对画线部分提问）

____

三、阅读理解。（2005年无锡中考）

The Internet can show you lots of jobs all over the world. If you want to find a job on the Internet, use the words "job search" or "employment" to find the websites you need. Type in what you want and where you want to work. In a few seconds, a list of jobs will appear on the screen. You can also type in the name of a company to learn about jobs there. Many websites list full-time and summer jobs.

Job search websites can help you in other ways, too. They show you how to write a good resume（履历）and how to get ready for an interview. They also tell you what to say to an interviewer on the telephone. Some websites give you interview conversations to practise. One website even has a dictionary of interview words. A good employment website can be a big help in your job search.

Good luck with your job-hunting.

(　　) 1. What should you do first if you want to find a job on the Internet?

A. To type in "job search" or "employment" to find the websites.

B. To write a good resume.

C. To get ready for an interview.

D. To get an English dictionary.

(　　) 2. Some employment websites tell you how to have a job interview ________.

A. face to face　　B. in an e-mail

C. in a letter　　D. on the telephone

(　　) 3. From the passage, we know that ________.

A. you can't look for a summer job on the Internet

B. some websites show you how to write a resume

C. if you type in the name of a company, you will get a job there easily

D. the Internet can only show you a list of jobs of your own country

(　　) 4. The underlined word "job-hunting" means ________.

A. searching a job　　B. giving a job

C. doing a job　　D. changing a job

(　　) 5. What's the main idea of the passage?

A. The Internet lists a large number of companies.

B. You can find many websites on the Internet.

C. It's about how you can use the Internet to find a job.

D. There are different ways for you to look for jobs.

Section Five

一、听写单词。

1. ________　2. ________　3. ________
4. ________　5. ________　6. ________
7. ________　8. ________　9. ________
10. ________

二、选出相对应的答语。

1. （　　）　A. I'm twelve.
2. （　　）　B. I'm in Class 3, Grade 1.
3. （　　）　C. That's Tony.
4. （　　）　D. A-double-P-L-E.
5. （　　）　E. I'm from Canada.
6. （　　）　F. It's 8836415.
7. （　　）　G. It's a pencil.

三、听对话，选出正确答案。

（　　）1. What color is the bag?
A. Red.　B. Yellow.　C. White.

（　　）2. Who is Nick's good friend?
A. Mary.　B. Kate.　C. Simon.

（　　）3. How many students are there in Jim's class?
A. Twenty-two.　B. Forty.　C. Forty-two.

（　　）4. Where's the reading room?
A. In front of the teaching building.
B. Behind the teaching building.
C. On the left of the teaching building.

（　　）5. Whose sweater is it?
A. It's Nick's.　B. It's Jim's.　C. It's Jill's.

四、单项选择。

（　　）1. —Look at ________ animal. It's funny and interesting.
—Which one do you mean? ________ black one with a long tail?
A. an; The　B. an; An　C. the; The　D. the; An

（　　）2. —What happened to Tom?
—He was crossing the street ________ a motorbike hit him from behind.
A. while　B. when　C. until　D. because

（　　）3. —Are you learning art now during your spare time?
— No. I'm not. I've stopped ________ Chinese medicine instead.
A. to learn　B. learning　C. to drop　D. to give up

（　　）4. — Mom, I've got a fever.
— So ________. How did you catch it?
A. have you　B. you have　C. have I　D. did I

（　　）5. — Does the child need any help?
— No. He is old enough to ________ himself.
A. put on　B. wear　C. dress　D. take care

（　　）6. — Why not borrow some money from your friends?

— But I know ________ of the people here except you.

A. nobody B. none C. all D. no one

( ) 7. — What are you going to do tomorrow?

— I'm not sure. I ________ make a trip to Hangzhou with my girlfriend.

A. may B. am going to C. will D. shall

( )8. ________ people come to Jilin to visit Mount Changbai every year.

A. Thousands of B. Thousand of C. Thousand D. Thousands

( ) 9. They felt so ________ that they ________ go home earlier.

A. excited; could B. excitedly; could

C. excited; couldn't D. excitedly; couldn't

( )10. — Could you tell me how to get to Center Street?

— ____________________

A. Don't ask me. B. You're welcome.

C. Thank you all the same. D. Sure. You can take the No. 1 bus.

( )11. By the time I got home, the show ________ already ________.

A. had; finished B. have; finish

C. is; finish D. is; gone

( )12. When ________ the car invented?

A. is B. were C. been D. was

( )13. I love writers ________ tell their own stories.

A. who B. whose C. which D. where

( )14. Weeks went ________ without any news of them.

A. by B. on C. past D. in

( ) 15. He is used to ________ in the study.

A. reads B. reading C. sing D. sang

五、阅读理解。(2005年无锡中考)

One Sunday, Mark decided to go sailing in his boat with his friend Dan, but Dan happened to be away. Dan's brother John offered to go instead though he did not know anything about sailing. Mark agreed and they set out to sea.

Soon they found themselves in a thick fog. Mark was afraid they would be hit by a big ship. Just at that time he saw a large buoy (浮标) through the fog, so he decided to tie the boat to it for safety. As he was getting onto the buoy, however, he dropped the wet rope. The boat moved away in the fog, carrying John who didn't know how to use the radio. He drifted (漂泊) about and was not seen until twelve hours later.

Mark spent the night on the buoy. In the early morning he fell asleep. He was having a bad dream when a shout woke him up. A ship, Californian, came up and he climbed onto it and thanked the captain. The captain told him that john had been picked up by another ship and the ship's captain had sent out a message. "Without the message, I wouldn't have found you on the buoy," he said.

(　　) 1. Which of the following explains why Mark and Dan didn't go sailing together?

A. Dan asked his brother to go instead.

B. Dan was in some other place.

C. Mark didn't think Dan knew anything about sailing.

D. Mark would like to go with john.

(　　) 2. Mark tried to tie the boat to the buoy so that ________.

A. he could spend the night on it

B. he and John could go on sailing when the fog cleared

C. it wouldn't be hit by other ships

D. he might be picked up by a passing ship

(　　) 3. John and Mark got away from each other because ________.

A. there wasn't enough room for them on the buoy

B. Mark failed to tie the boat after getting onto the buoy

C. Mark thought it safe to stay on the buoy but John didn't

D. John had been asked to stay in the boat to radio for help

(　　) 4. How was Mark found on the buoy?

A. With the help of John, the captain of Californian knew where to find him.

B. John sent a message to Californian by radio.

C. He shouted as soon as he saw Californian.

D. The captain of Californian saw him as the fog cleared.

(　　) 5. At the end of the passage, the underlined word "he" was ________.

A. mark

B. John

C. The captain who sent the message

D. the captain who got the message

六、选用下列所给的词的适当形式填空。

these, an, cake, same, number, how, three, that, not, where

1. She's in Class ________.
2. Answer question ________ 4.
3. — ________ old are you? — I'm 22.
4. — What's that in English? — It's ________ orange.
5. "Write" and "right" are pronounced the ________.
6. I hope to see you tomorrow, but if ________, leave me a message.
7. Would you like a slice of chocolate ________?
8. ________ is he from?
9. Is ________ your toy?
10. Are ________ your students?

七、句型练习。

变否定句。

1. There are a lot of tomatoes in the fridge.

____

2. That man is going to sing a song.

____

变一般疑问句。

3. It sounds nice.

____

4. She needs a lot of bread.

____

对画线部分提问。

5. My father wants <u>two tubes of</u> toothpaste.

____

八、看图造句。

(My mother, be, math)

1. ______________________________

(Jill, be, birthday)

2. ______________________________

(not, smoke, classroom)

3. ______________________________

(I, come, from)

4. ______________________________

Unit 3

Section One

一、单项选择。

(　　)1. — What is ________?

— It's two o'clock.

A. the date　　B. date　　C. time　　D. the time

(　　)2. What time ________ your father usually go to work?

A. do　　B. don't　　C. does　　D. doesn't

(　　)3. Sam gets up ________ six o'clock every morning.

A. in　　B. on　　C. at　　D. about

(　　)4. Most of the students in this school go to school ________ foot.

A. by　　B. on　　C. in　　D. with

(　　)5. — Where does Lucy study?

— She ________ Wuhan Foreign Languages School.

A. studys at　　B. studying in　　C. studied on　　D. studies at

(　　)6. After a week's hard work, we'd better ________.

A. have a try　　B. have a shower

C. have a cold　　D. have a rest

二、请根据所给的时间写出对应的英语表达法（在需要的时候用 **past** 和 **to**）。

eg: 2 : 00 →It's two o'clock.

1. 7 : 00 → ________________　　2. 1 : 28 → ________________
3. 2 : 02 → ________________　　4. 12 : 45 → ________________
5. 11 : 35 → ________________　　6. 4 : 57 → ________________
7. 5 : 30 → ________________　　8. 9 : 15 → ________________

三、请用另一种表达方式表述下列的时间。

1. It's two forty. → ____________　　2. It's six ten. → ________
3. It's half past three. → ____________　　4. It's a quarter to five. → ________
5. It's twenty-five to nine. → ________________
6. It's a quarter past twelve. → ________________

四、请用方框中适当的冠词填空。

a an the ×(零冠词,即不用冠词)

1. I go to school by ________ bike every day.
2. Open ________ door, please.
3. There is ________ “m” in the word “match”.
4. ________ sun is bigger than ________ moon.
5. It’s ________ August now.
6. They’re having ________ breakfast now.
7. There is ________ cat in the room. ________ cat is hers.
8. Does she have to stay at ________ home every night?
9. His parents want him to go to ________ college.
10. Wang Mei plays ________ piano very well.
11. Tom often gets online in ________ cafeteria.

五、改错题。下列句子每句都有一个错误,请写出正确的句子。

1. My work start at seven thirty.

____

2. When do you usually arrive the cinema on Sundays?

____

3. The TV programme is going to be over at half to eleven.

____

4. Mike goes to work by foot.

____

5. I usually after school do my homework.

____

六、根据图片和提示仿照例句写句子。

Sandy; 7 : 30
What time does Sandy usually have breakfast?
Sandy usually has breakfast at 7 : 30.

1. Mr. Lee; 8 : 15

____

____

2. I; 2 p. m.

____

____

3. Kate; 9 : 50

____

____

4. the students; in the morning

____

____

5. Alan; at noon

____

____

6. Lily; in the afternoon

____

____

Section Two

一、单项选择。

(　　)1. Some students seldom have a good sleep ________ because they have too much homework to do.

A. in night　　B. on noon　　C. at evening　　D. at night

(　　)2. The cinema ________ at 9 : 00 a. m. and ________ at 12 : 00 p. m.

A. starts; finishes　B. leaves; shuts　C. opens; closes　D. starts; ends

(　　)3. He was born ________ a rainy day ________ 1997.

A. at; on　　B. on; in　　C. at; on　　D. by; in

(　　)4. — My watch is five minutes slow.

— You'd better ________ the clock ________ by five minutes.

A. take; back　　B. catch up; with

C. put; back　　D. put; forward

(　　)5. Thursdays and Fridays are ________ in Britain.

A. weekdays　　B. national holidays

C. weekends　　D. red-letter days

(　　)6. Beijing and Paris are in different ________.

A. time zones　　B. cities　　C. nationalities　　D. countrysides

二、请用适当的介词填空。

1. Joe's father stops work ________ about ten.
2. I usually wear casual clothes ________ T-shirts.
3. We arrived ________ the airport ________ noon.
4. Sammy is a waitress ________ a restaurant.
5. Can I go to the shopping center ________ subway?
6. My mother is very busy ________ work.
7. The children come home from school ________ the evening.
8. How do you like travelling ________ air?
9. Mary goes to the cinema ________ foot.
10. Skating is good ________ winter.

三、请根据下面的日历回答问题。

July 2011

Su	Mo	Tu	We	Th	Fr	Sa
					1	2
3	4	5	6	7	8	9
10	11	12	13	14	15	16
17	18	19	20	21	22	23
24	25	26	27	28	29	30
31		↑				

1. What day is it today?
____
2. What's the date today?
____
3. What's the date tomorrow?
____
4. What day is July 18th?
____

四、仿照例句写出下列时间的英文表达式。

6 : 00 a. m. → 6 o'clock in the morning

1. 07 : 00 p. m. →____________　　2. 03 : 00 a. m. →____________
3. 08 : 30 a. m. →____________　　4. 04 : 45 p. m. →____________
5. 02 : 54 p. m. →____________　　6. 11 : 55 a. m. →____________
7. 01 : 18 a. m. →____________　　8. 09 : 15 p. m. →____________

五、根据图表填入正确的频率副词。

seldom, sometimes, usually, never, often, always, hardly

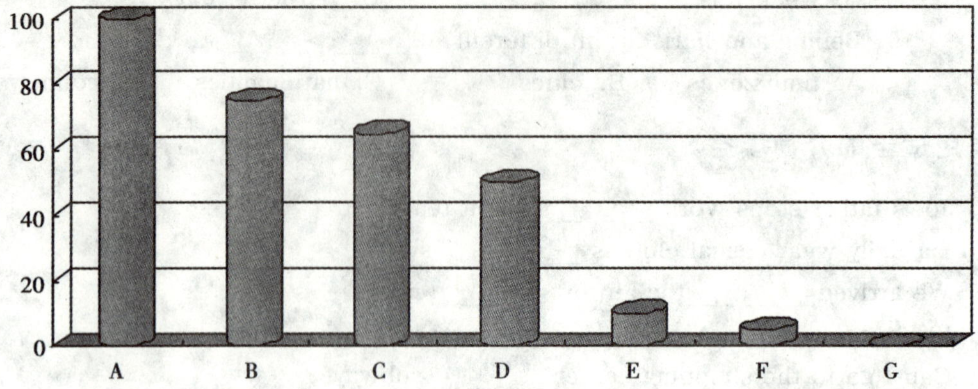

A. ______ B. ______ C. ______ D. ______ E. ______ F. ______ G. ______

六、句型练习。

1. Mike often gets up at 6：30.（变一般疑问句）

____

2. My family always go to Brighton in summer.（变一般疑问句）

____

3. The plane leaves at 15：00.（变否定句）

____

4. We have some Brazilian coffee.（变否定句）

____

5. Mike often goes to bed at 21：30.（对画线部分提问）

____

6. Steffen works in the book store.（对画线部分提问）

____

7. My uncle usually travels by train.（对画线部分提问）

____

8. What's the time?（换一种说法）

____

9. What date is it today?（换一种说法）

____

七、请用五句话描述一下你的日常生活。

1. ______________________________
2. ______________________________
3. ______________________________
4. ______________________________
5. ______________________________

Section Three

一、单项选择。

( )1. —________ do you arrive ________ the cinema?
— At eleven thirty.
A. How; at B. When; in C. What; by D. What time; at

( )2. What a lazy boy! He ________ does his homework on time.
A. always B. usually C. never D. often

( )3. We can see some old men swimming in the river even ________ a cold morning.
A. on B. in C. at D. for

( )4. You should think ________ before spending all that money on clothes.
A. one time B. once C. two times D. twice

( )5. — What about going out for a walk?
— Sorry, I'm ________ a great book.
A. in front of B. at the back of
C. in the middle of D. in the front of

二、用括号内动词的适当形式填空。

1. Tommy ________ (like) swimming.
2. After dinner she often ________ (watch) TV with her parents.
3. Nick and Nancy ________ (not like) PE.
4. What day ________ (be) it today?
5. The show ________ (finish) at 11 p.m. every weekend.
6. Children ________ (go) to school in daylight.
7. When spring ________ (come), everything ________ (begin) to grow.

三、将下列汉语翻译成英语。

1. 休闲服________ 2. 国际团体________ 3. 意味着________
4. 社会活动________ 5. 在傍晚________ 6. 在图书馆________
7. 体育比赛________ 8. 起床________ 9. (日、月)升起________

四、选出适当的动词完成下面的词组。

make do play have go

1. ________ the violin 2. ________ a cold 3. ________ friends
4. ________ sports 5. ________ a choice 6. ________ skating
7. ________ housework 8. ________ some washing 9. ________ a talk

10. ________ for a walk 11. ________ exercises 12. ________ basketball

五、用一周内的某一天完成下列句子。

1. ________ is named after the Moon in many languages.
2. In some cultures, ________ is considered unlucky.
3. ________ is in the middle of the common 5-day workweek.
4. The church service is usually on ________.
5. ________ is the usual day for elections in the United States.
6. In the United States, Thanksgiving Day is a festival celebrated on the fourth ________ in November.
7. ________ is the sixth day of the week according to international standard.

六、将下列词语组成正确的句子。

1. often, cat, chase, the, does, mouse, the
____
2. town, lives, a, small, Paris, she, in, near
____
3. tea, people, at, have, four, British, about, o'clock
____
4. that, by, morning, goes, train, work, to, every, businesswoman
____
5. does, at, do, school, homework, his, Jack, not
____
6. the, have, a, I, cafeteria, ten, in, break, at
____

七、完形填空。(2006年浙江省绍兴市中考)

My name is Wang Kun and my sister is Wang Wei. Since middle school, we have dreamed about taking a great trip by __1__. When we graduated from college, we finally got the __2__ to do it.

We started our long bike ride __3__ the Mekong River(湄公河) in October. __4__ it was autumn, the snow had already started to fall in Tibet. Our legs felt so heavy and __5__ that we thought they were ice. Have you ever seen __6__ ride bicycles? Wang Wei was in front of me as usual. I knew I didn't need to encourage __7__. To climb up the mountain road was hard work but to go __8__ the hills was great fun. When we reached a valley, it became much warmer. We had to __9__ our clothes. In the early evening, we stopped to __10__ our tents and then we ate. After supper, Wang Wei went to __11__ but I stayed awake. At midnight, the sky became clear and the stars were __12__. There was almost no __13__, only the sound of the fire. What a __14__ night! We have already traveled so far. We are reaching Dali in Yunnan Province. There our cousins Dao Wei and Yu Hang will __15__ us in the ride trip. I'm sure we'll have a greater time together.

( )1. A. bus B. bike C. train D. plane
( )2. A. chance B. experience C. information D. instruction
( )3. A. in B. on C. along D. above
( )4. A. Although B. Because C. When D. If
( )5. A. warm B. hot C. comfortable D. cold
( )6. A. snow men B. businessmen C. engineers D. foreigners
( )7. A. him B. her C. me D. them
( )8. A. back B. over C. up D. down
( )9. A. wash B. carry C. change D. dry
( )10. A. put up B. put on C. put away D. put down
( )11. A. work B. sleep C. travel D. run
( )12. A. colourful B. dim C. light D. bright
( )13. A. wind B. fog C. cloud D. rain
( )14. A. busy B. boring C. noisy D. quiet
( )15. A. greet B. join C. visit D. interview

Section Four

一、单项选择。

( )1. The Langland Hotel ________ Central London and is close to the British Museum and the world famous London Zoo.
A. situate in B. is situated in
C. is situating in D. situates

( )2. The newly-built airport has the most advanced ________, and provides perfect service.
A. communities B. programmes C. activities D. facilities

( )3. — What do you usually do on the computer?
— I usually get a lot of ________ by getting online.
A. information B. letters C. message D. ideas

( )4. In China, students can have a ten-minute ________ between classes in most schools.
A. off B. pause C. break D. leave

( )5. — Would you like to go shopping?
— ________________.
A. No, I'd like to B. No, I don't
C. Yes, I'd love to D. Yes, I do

( )6. It ________ dark late in the evening in summer.
A. gets B. is getting C. got D. get

(　　)7. — Why doesn't the little boy introduce ________ to ________.

— Maybe he is too shy.

A. him; me　　B. himself; me

C. me; him　　D. me; himself

二、根据句意填写单词，单词首字母已经给出。

1. Most families make dumplings to get prepared for the Spring Festival on the last day of the year in lunar c ________.
2. He saves a q ________ of his salary each month to buy an ipad.
3. He is dressed in a s ________ suit today, and looks energetic.
4. When spring begins, the British people put the clocks f ________ by one hour.
5. Doing a ________ in the gym is a good way to improve one's health.
6. Please try to finish the job as soon as p ________.
7. The boss fired his s ________ today.

三、用所给词的适当形式填空。

1. Frank asks his new friend Jack to write the ________ (introduce) to his book of photographs.
2. Hugh Grant is a famous ________ (Britain) actor.
3. There are several ________ (company) in this area.
4. The shop is ________ (close) every Monday.
5. Ted ________ (fly) to America twice a month.
6. Mary ________ (teach) history in that school.

四、阅读理解。阅读下面短文，并根据短文内容选择正确答案。(2006年重庆中考)

Mr. and Mrs. Brown lived in a house near London. They had only one child and he was very young. Mr. Brown often came back home from work very late when his wife and child were asleep. He usually opened the front door with his key and came into the room quietly.

One night he forgot to bring his key. He had to ring the doorbell, but his wife didn't wake up. He rang it again. Again nothing happened. Then Mr. Brown knocked at the bedroom window and even shouted loudly. Still his wife didn't wake up. He thought for a moment. At last he had an idea. Then he began to speak like a small child. "Mom!" he said, "I want to drink some water." His wife woke up right now and opened the door for him.

(　　)1. How many children did Mr. and Mrs. Brown have?

A. One.　　B. Two.　　C. Three.　　D. None.

(　　)2. Mr. Brown couldn't open the door one night because ________.

A. he came back late　　B. his wife and child were not at home

C. he spoke like a small child　　D. he forgot to bring his key with him

(　　)3. Mr. Brown didn't ________ to wake up his wife.

A. sing a song　　B. knock at the window

C. ring the doorbell　　D. shout

(　　)4. ________ opened the door at last.

A. Mr. Brown　B. Nobody　C. Mrs. Brown　D. The child

(　　)5. Which of the following is TRUE?

A. Mr. and Mrs. Brown lived far from London.

B. Mr. Brown opened the back door with his key.

C. Mrs. Brown often opened the door for Mr. Brown.

D. Mr. Brown rang the doorbell twice that night.

五、句型题。

1. It's often hot in summer.（变否定句）

____

2. There are two thousand students in this college.（对画线部分提问）

____

3. Her mother sometimes works at home.（对画线部分提问）

____

六、选出下列词语的正确意思。

(　　)1. hall　　A. a place or event where people dance to popular music

(　　)2. disco　　B. a small amount of food that you eat between meals

(　　)3. snack　　C. in a loyal and honest way

(　　)4. faithfully　　D. a large room used for meetings, concerts, or other public events

七、写作题。

Andy 今年 13 岁，在 St. Mary 中学读书。请以他的身份给 King's College 写一封信询问他们的寒假课程。要求 40 ~60 字。信的格式已经给出。

要点：1. 写信的目的。

2. 自我介绍。

3. 希望获取学校的有关信息。

Dear Sir/Madam,

____

____

____

____

____

____

Yours faithfully,

Andy

Section Five

一、听写单词。

1. ________ 2. ________ 3. ________ 4 ________ 5. ________
6. ________ 7. ________ 8. ________ 9. ________ 10. ________

二、听问题选答案。

( )1. A. At home. B. It's Monday. C. I don't know.
( )2. A. It's January 1st. B. It's Sunday. C. It is rainy.
( )3. A. It is Christmas. B. It is March 3rd. C. It is wet.
( )4. A. On September 10th. B. At 8 o'clock. C. By bike.
( )5. A. On Monday. B. Twice a week. C. At 7 a. m.
( )6. A. The library. B. Chinese. C. Athens.

三、听对话并回答问题。

( )1. A. It's seven o'clock. B. At eight o'clock. C. It's late.
( )2. A. A professor. B. A writer. C. We don't know.
( )3. A. Table tennis. B. Tennis. C. Football.
( )4. A. Three past six. B. Six o'clock. C. Three to six.
( )5. A. It's May 31st. B. It's May 30th. C. It's June 1st.
( )6. A. At School. B. In a factory. C. In a shop.
( )7. A. Study. B. Go to school. C. Go swimming.

四、听下面几段对话并完成每段对话后的几个小题。

听对话，回答第 1 ~3 题。

( )1. Why does Mike telephone Cathy?
A. They haven't seen each other for a long time.
B. He wants to invite her to his birthday party.
C. He wants to invite her to the party in his new house.

( )2. When will the party begin?
A. At eight o'clock on Sunday.
B. After eight o'clock on Saturday.
C. Before eight o'clock on Sunday.

( )3. Which of the following is TRUE?
A. Cathy won't go to the party because she is busy.
B. Cathy will go to the party because she is looking forward to the party.
C. Cathy won't go to the party because she doesn't know Mike's new address.

听对话，回答第 4 ~ 7 题。

(　　)4. Where is Jim going for his holiday?

A. He hasn't decided yet.　　B. He is going to the country.

C. He is going to the seaside.

(　　)5. What is Mary going to do for her holiday?

A. She is going to the country.　　B. She is going to stay at home.

C. She is going to the seaside.

(　　)6. Who is going to have a holiday abroad?

A. Jim.　　B. Jim's wife.　　C. Nobody.

(　　)7. Why isn't Mary going abroad?

A. She needs peace and quietness when she is on holiday.

B. She wants to buy a car by the sea.

C. She wants to save money for her car.

五、听短文并填空。

Spring Festival is usually in late January or early February. It is the first day of the Chinese year. This is a very (1)________ festival for all Chinese people. Before the festival, people are busy. They clean their houses and go shopping for food, (2)________ and new clothes.

In Guangzhou people go to the flower (3)________ to look at all the beautiful flowers. Many people buy flowers, too. On the (4)________ before Spring Festival, people usually have a big supper with their family. After supper, they watch TV or go out. At Spring Festival people go and visit their friends and family. They eat nice food. The children love this time. They can get "(5)________ money".

六、单项选择。

(　　)1. We'd better go home before it ________ dark.

A. changes to　　B. becomes　　C. gets　　D. turning

(　　)2. The football match is ________ Saturday afternoon.

A. in　　B. by　　C. on　　D. with

(　　)3. We sometimes play badminton ________ lunchtime.

A. in　　B. at　　C. on　　D. with

(　　)4. ________ is the second day of a week according to international standard.

A. Wednesday　　B. Tuesday　　C. Monday　　D. Sunday

(　　)5. He visits the theatre sometimes, ________ he?

A. is　　B. isn't　　C. comes　　D. doesn't

(　　)6. He ________ goes to sleep late.

A. doesn't　　B. not　　C. never　　D. no

(　　)7. They won't visit the museum if it ________ tomorrow.

A. will rain　　B. rains　　C. to rain　　D. is raining

(　　)8. Many people telephone the travel agency to ask for further ________ about a tour to Hong Kong.

A. information　B. news　C. messages　D. ideas

(　　)9. The car company ________ just outside the city.

A. is situated　B. located　C. situated　D. lies in

(　　)10. His interests ________ cooking and photography.

A. hold　B. including　C. contain　D. include

七、完形填空。(2004 年江西省南昌市中考)

I stood in the doorway, watching my older brother carefully putting clothes into his bag . I coughed uneasily. Finally __1__ that I was there, Rocky turned toward me with a sad smile.

"I'm __2__ tomorrow," he said.

"I know." My __3__ was almost a whisper(低声). I was __4__ at myself for being so weak, but I wasn't about to cry.

"My __5__ is early, so there is still __6__ time to come to the airport," he said. Seeing the __7__ look on my face, he quickly added, "I promise(答应) I won't leave without saying goodbye."

I tried to say __8__ , but didn't. It's always __9__ to keep quiet if you're about to cry. "You promised you wouldn't cry," he said to me, thinking that I was close to __10__ .

I remember the day he taught me how to ride a bike. __11__ I thought he was always right behind me, holding the seat to keep me from __12__ . I was happy with this, but he knew he couldn't hold me up all my life. He told me that one day he would have to let go.

His coughing stopped my thinking . What was left to say? How could I say __13__ to the person who taught me everything?

The next morning I __14__ , looked at my alarm clock, and realized he had left __15__ ago. We never even said goodbye.

Goodbye, Rocky! Although he may have been many miles away, I knew he heard me, even if it was only an answer in his heart.

(　　)1. A. forgetting　B. realizing　C. watching　D. learning

(　　)2. A. arriving　B. living　C. coming　D. leaving

(　　)3. A. voice　B. sound　C. noise　D. word

(　　)4. A. glad　B. moved　C. angry　D. pleased

(　　)5. A. ship　B. flight　C. train　D. bus

(　　)6. A. enough　B. little　C. no　D. busy

(　　)7. A. surprised　B. excited　C. sad　D. happy

(　　)8. A. anything　B. everything　C. something　D. nothing

(　　)9. A. stranger　B. better　C. worse　D. easier

(　　)10. A. tears　B. smiles　C. words　D. sadness

( )11. A. At last B. From now on C. At first D. So far
( )12. A. riding B. running C. walking D. falling
( )13. A. goodbye B. hello C. yes D. sorry
( )14. A. gave up B. stood up C. looked up D. woke up
( )15. A. minutes B. hours C. days D. weeks

八、阅读理解。阅读下面短文,并根据短文内容选择正确答案。(2004年襄樊市中考)

Young people can have problems with their minds. Some students become worried because they have to study very hard. Others have trouble getting on well with people like their parents and classmates.

Liu Wei, a Junior 2 student from Hefei, could not understand his teacher and was doing badly in his lessons. He became so worried about it that he started to cut his finger with a knife.

Another student, 14-year-old Yan Fang from Guangzhou, was afraid of exams. She got very worried in the test, and when she looked at the exam paper. She couldn't think of anything to write.

A recent report from *Jiefang Daily* says about 18% of Shanghai teenagers have mental(心理的,精神的) problems. Their troubles include being worried and very unhappy, and having problems in learning and getting on with people. Many students who have problems won't go for advice(劝告) or help. Some think they will look stupid (愚蠢) if they go to see a doctor. Others don't want to talk about their secret.

Liang Yuezhu, an expert on teenagers from Beijing Anding Hospital has the following advice for teenagers:

* Talk to your parents or teachers often.
* Take part in group activities and play sports.
* Go to see a doctor if you feel unhappy or unwell.

( )1. The students who often become worried or have trouble getting on with others may have ________.
A. mental problems B. a headache
C. knives with them D. no parents

( )2. Liu Wei cut his finger with a knife because ________.
A. he was afraid of his teacher
B. he wanted to frighten his parents
C. he was so worried about his studies
D. his finger was badly hurt

( )3. Yan Fang 's problems happened whenever ________.
A. she studied very hard B. she had exams
C. she talked with her parents C. she thought of something

( )4. Students who have problems won't ask others for help because ________.
A. they won't let others think they are stupid

B. they don't think doctors can help them

C. they don't want to tell their secret to others

D. both A and C

(　　)5. Liang Yuezhu's advice tells us that ________.

A. it's better for the students who have mental problems to join others

B. it's unnecessary for them to be with others

C. only group activities and sports can help them

D. teachers and parents can't do anything about mental problems

九、句型题。

1. I would like some vegetables.（变否定句）

____

2. The film starts at a quarter to three.（对画线部分提问）

____

3. My birthday is in August.（对画线部分提问）

____

4. Jason walks to school every day.（换一种说法）

____

5. Tim usually goes to work by taxi.（换一种说法）

____

十、填入正确的词语使文章完整。

I have the same routine (1)________ Monday (2)________ Friday. I get up at six every day. I dress myself quickly and have breakfast (3)________ half past six. After breakfast I go to school. I don't ride a bike. I go to school (4)________ foot.

I have four lessons (5)________ the morning. I do morning exercises (6)________ my classmates after the second lesson. At eleven thirty, I have lunch (7)________ school. In the afternoon, I have three lessons. After class, we often have sports (8)________ the playground. I study hard and always help my classmate (9)________ their lessons. School is over at five.

After supper I read newspapers or watch TV for half an hour. I prepare my lessons (10)________ half past seven and nine. I go to bed at nine.

Unit 4

Section One

一、词汇练习。

1. These five days are weekdays. They are ______, ______, ______, ______ and ______.
2. We call them weekends. They are ______ and ______.
3. weak ______（反义词）　　4. sick ______（近义词）
5. terrible ______（近义词）　　6. well ______（近义词）

二、请用两种表达方式写出以下时间。

1. 9：05 ______ ______
2. 10：15 ______ ______
3. 12：30 ______ ______
4. 1：15 ______ ______
5. 4：45 ______ ______
6. 6：55 ______ ______
7. 11：35 ______ ______

三、参照例句写出句子。

1. mother / pretty / new sunglasses
   What's mother like?
   She looks pretty. She has new sunglasses.
2. Sue / neat and tidy / a pretty skirt
   ______
   ______
3. Billy / naughty / dirty hands
   ______
   ______
4. Peter / strong / great muscles
   ______
   ______

5. Lily / tired / headache
How does Lily feel?
She feels tired. She has a headache.
6. Lucy / hot / a temperature
____
____
7. Sandy / terrible / a toothache
____
____
8. Frank / sick / a stomachache
____
____
9. Tony / awful / measles
____
____
10. Ms. Li / tired / headache / take an aspirin
What's the matter with Ms. Li?
She feels tired.
She has a headache, so she must take an aspirin.
11. Mother / bad / earache / call the doctor
____
____
____
12. Mike / sick / stomachache / drink some medicine
____
____
____
13. Simon / ill / mumps / remain in bed
____
____
____

四、单项选择。

(　　) 1. How do you read "August 9, 2007"?
A. Two thousand and seven, August, nine
B. Two thousand and seven, August ninth
C. August the ninth, two thousand seven
D. August the ninth, two thousand and seven

(　　) 2. How about ________ with us?
A. come　　B. coming　　C. to come　　D. comes

( ) 3. Why ________ send an e-mail to Billy?
A. don't B. not you C. do you D. don't you

( ) 4. — ________ is he going to stay in the city?
— For three weeks.
A. When B. How long C. How long ago D. How often

( ) 5. I plan ________ the books to the library this afternoon.
A. return B. to return C. returning D. returned

( ) 6. Let ________ the blackboard.
A. him cleaning B. him to clean C. he clean D. him clean

( ) 7. — ________ is a box of chalk, please?
— One yuan. ________ boxes do you need?
A. How many; How many B. How much; How much
C. How many; How much D. How much; How many

Section Two

一、单项选择。

( ) 1. Look at this cake. It ________ a star.
A. look like B. is likes C. likes D. is like

( ) 2. You should use ________ ruler because I need to use mine.
A. yourself B. your own C. own D. your self

( ) 3. Is there ________ in today's news?
A. anything interesting B. something interested
C. nothing interesting D. interesting anything

( ) 4. Your dad's nephew is your ________.
A. niece B. cousin C. sister D. brother

( ) 5. That's not ________ pen. It's ________.
A. my; her B. your; mine C. his; his D. her; your

( ) 6. You ________ hand it in at once. You may hand it in tomorrow.
A. needn't B. may not C. can't D. must not

二、根据图片写出英文标志。

1. ____________

2. ____________

3. ____________

4.  ________

5.  ________

6.  ________

三、句型练习。

把下列句子改为否定句。

1. Put a penny in the slot.
____
2. The machine works.
____
3. Drink this medicine.
____
4. It tastes awful.
____

把下列句子改为一般疑问句。

5. Mother must finish the work at once.
____
6. We can't talk in the library.
____
7. He will go to the concert this Friday.
____
8. I need a piece of paper.
____

四、翻译下列句子。

1. 他运气真好！
____
2. Sandy 怎么啦？
____
3. 爸爸患了流行性感冒。
____
4. 几点了？
____
5. 他患了重感冒。
____
6. 为什么他喝这个药？
____

7. 它尝起来像毒药。

____

8. 他们感觉很虚弱，所以他们必须待在床上。

____

9. Billy 正坐在后座上。

____

10. 他在沙发上睡着了。

____

11. 你不能在这里停车。

____

12. 不要玩火柴！

____

Section Three

一、首字母填词。

1. You look sick, so you should drink some m ________.
2. Sandy and Sue have flu, so they must s ________ in bed.
3. My mother t ________ is English.
4. I feel hot. I have a t ________.
5. He has a toothache, so he must go to the d ________.
6. He has mumps, so he must r ________ in bed.
7. I'd like to put some s ________ jam on the toast.
8. These mushrooms contain a deadly p ________.
9. She has a headache, so she must take an a ________.
10. What's the m ________ with you, Sue?

二、单项选择。

(　　) 1. We're going to have a flower-show ________.
A. next week　B. yesterday　C. last month　D. now

(　　) 2. I'm happy ________ your letter and I'm happy ________ your success.
A. to receive; for　B. to receive; about
C. receive; for　D. receive; about

(　　) 3. — May I ________ a message?
— Of course. Hold on for a moment. I'll ________ the message for you.
A. take; leave　B. leave; take
C. taking; leaving　D. leaving; taking

(　　) 4. Please ask him ________. It's bad for your health.
A. not to eat too much　B. to not eat too much

C. not eat too much　　　D. eat not too much

三、对画线部分提问。

1. He looks tired.

____

2. Simon feels ill.

____

3. She is going to see me on Monday at 9：00.

____

4. Billy must take an aspirin.

____

5. They must stay in bed.

____

6. Peter should see the doctor.

____

7. Bill is well-behaved.

____

8. You mustn't park here because it's a no parking area.

____

9. You look pretty today.

____

10. Mr. Black can fix the machine.

____

四、将下列句子换一种说法。

1. How do you like the music?
   What do you ________ ________ ________ music?
2. It has a funny taste.
   It ________ ________.
3. You mustn't smoke or spit here.
   No ________ ________ ________ here!
4. What is the weather going to be like tomorrow?
   ________ is the weather ________ ________ ________ tomorrow?
5. Sandy has measles, so he can't go to school.
   ________ Sandy has measles, he can't go to school.
6. How many books has she?
   How many books ________ ________ ________?
7. How can I help you?
   What ________ I ________ ________ you?
8. Where are you from?
   Where ________ ________ ________ ________?

9. It looks like metal.

It ________ ________ metal.

10. The children are having a swim.

The children ________ ________.

五、完形填空。(2005 年上海市中考)

Jose is a student at a medical college. He is on the way to becoming a __1__. Jose lives at home with his parents, a disabled elder sister and two younger brothers. Both his parents have full-time jobs and Jose works __2__ time in a restaurant to help the family.

Several weeks ago Jose's father began feeling bad chest pains. When he went to a doctor, he was told that there was something wrong with his __3__ and he needed to be operated on and would have to give up his __4__ for at least one year.

Faced with large medical __5__ and loss of almost two thirds of the family's income for the next year, Jose's mother wanted him to drop out of __6__ and do more work to help the family. Jose loves his family very much and knows the sacrifices they have made for his __7__, but, if he drops out now, he will lose the whole term's credit. That will be too much for __8__. He doesn't know what to do. He spoke to his girlfriend, Maria, and she told him to __9__ in school. He also spoke to his uncle, Carlos, but he thought that his first __10__ was to help his family get through the difficult times ahead. What should Jose do?

(　　)1. A. professor	B. pilot	C. waiter	D. doctor
(　　)2. A. one	B. part	C. all	D. different
(　　)3. A. heart	B. car	C. watch	D. glasses
(　　)4. A. holiday	B. job	C. family	D. studies
(　　)5. A. money	B. pay	C. expense	D. care
(　　)6. A. restaurant	B. home	C. office	D. school
(　　)7. A. education	B. life	C. work	D. health
(　　)8. A. the family	B. his parents	C. his sister	D. him
(　　)9. A. remain	B. live	C. do	D. talk
(　　)10. A. work	B. job	C. duty	D. service

Section Four

一、填空。

写出下列人称代词的反身代词。

1. he ________　2. she ________　3. I ________　4. we ________

5. it ________　6. you ________　7. they ________

写出下列词的复数形式。

8. strawberry ________　9. library ________　10. potato ________

11. sandwich ________　　12. hero ________　　13. photo ________

二、原文填空。

1. Show me your ________. Say "Ah".
2. He still has a bad cold, so ________.
3. Mrs. Boffin stops. "________, dear," Professor Boffin says.
4. ________________, and they take Professor Boffin, too!
5. And have some potatoes. ________.
6. Of course. ________.
7. ________, Sandy. Your hair's very long.
8. A haircut! Of course, not! ________!
9. —What are those boys doing?
   —____.
10. Billy! Look in the mirror! Why, Sandy? ________________!
11. What's it like, Sandy? Is it ________?
12. Ugh! It tastes like ________!

三、单项选择。

(　　) 1. I like ________ photos ________ parties.
　A. take; at　B. to take; in　C. taking; at　D. to taking; at

(　　) 2. Thanks ________. I'll finish my homework on time.
　A. for your help　B. at your help　C. for help me　D. your help

(　　) 3. — Must I arrive here at 3 o' clock?
　— No, you ________. You can come here later.
　A. needn't　B. mustn't　C. needn't to　D. don't

(　　) 4. Oh, I'm hungry. And I'd like ________.
　A. have something to eat　B. to have something to eat
　C. have something for eat　D. to have something for eat

(　　) 5. There are two ________ on the table and some ________ under the table.
　A. radioes; potatoes　B. radios; potatoes
　C. radioes; potatos　D. radios; potatos

(　　) 6. ________ students are waiting outside.
　A. Two hundred　B. Two hundreds of
　C. Hundred of　D. Two hundreds

(　　) 7. Here is a present ________ you ________ my best wishes.
　A. to; for　B. to; with　C. to; as　D. for; with

(　　) 8. How can you ________ your friends?
　A. keep touch with　B. keep in touch
　C. keep in with　D. keep in touch with

四、阅读理解。(2004年上海市中考)

Geoffrey Payne talks for the first time about the night his wife was killed. The judge thought it was he who killed his wife. Now he wrote to a magazine from the prison(监狱) about what happened on the night of 13 October, 1999.

I had to stay late at the hospital that night to do an operation. I finally left at about 11 p. m. I drove home slowly because the weather was terrible—the wind was blowing and it was raining heavily, I was turning into our road when a man suddenly ran in front of my car. I almost hit him but I stopped just in time. I was frightened and the man looked frightened, too. I got out of the car but he ran away before I could ask if he was all right. It was very strange.

When I got home, the lights were on but it was very quiet. I called to my wife but there was no answer. Then I remembered that she was out at a concert.

I was still very upset about what happened on the road, so I made myself a drink. Then I went upstairs to have a bath. I saw that the window in the bedroom was open. This was strange because my wife always locked the doors and windows before she went out. She was afraid of burglars(夜盗者). When I went to close it, I found Ellen. She was lying on the floor. There was blood everywhere. I rushed over and felt for her pulse but she was dead. I sat on the floor beside her body and was too frightened to do anything.

The next thing I knew, the sky was getting light. I can't remember a thing about that night. In the morning I phoned the police. They arrived about half an hour after I phoned them. But it seemed like hours. During that time I tried hard to remember anything I could about the night before. I couldn't stop thinking about the man in the road. *What was he doing at that time of night in our quiet neighbourhood? Why did he look so frightened! Why did he run away?*

(　　) 1. Geoffrey Payne was a ________.

A. doctor　　B. policeman　　C. judge　　D. taxi driver

(　　) 2. ________ while Payne was turning into his road that night.

A. A man suddenly ran in front of his car

B. His wife called him from the concert hall

C. A man stopped him and asked him the way

D. A man hit Payne 's car with a big stone and ran away

(　　) 3. When Payne got home, he found ________.

A. Ellen waiting for him

B. the bedroom window closed

C. Ellen lying on the floor, blood all over

D. a burglar in his house

(　　) 4. After he found Ellen dead, Payne ________.

A. called the police at once

B. called out for help

C. tried to find out who killed his wife

D. sat beside his wife's body without knowing what to do

(   ) 5. In this passage Payne tried to ________.

A. say something about his family

B. show he was very sorry for his wife's death

C. tell why his wife was killed that night

D. make people believe the man in the road probably killed his wife

Section Five

一、把你所听到的句子写在下面的横线上。

1. ________________________________
2. ________________________________
3. ________________________________
4. ________________________________
5. ________________________________
6. ________________________________
7. ________________________________
8. ________________________________

二、听下面一段短文，根据短文内容，判断下列句子的正误，将 T 或 F 填入题前的括号内。

(   ) 1. There are two hills far from his home.

(   ) 2. The school is next to the valley.

(   ) 3. He walks to school every day.

(   ) 4. There is a small river next to school, over which there is a stone bridge.

(   ) 5. The playground in front of the teaching building is small.

(   ) 6. Children often climb the trees after school.

(   ) 7. When autumn comes, all the teachers and students will help farmers with their harvest.

三、听下面五段小对话，根据对话内容选择最佳答案。

(   ) 1. How does David often go to school?

A. On foot. B. By bus. C. By bike.

(   ) 2. What is the relationship between them?

A. Strangers. B. Good friends. C. Father and daughter.

(   ) 3. What does the woman want to have?

A. A cup of coffee. B. A cup to tea. C. A cup of juice.

(　　) 4. When does the concert begin?

A. 9 : 00.　　B. 9 : 15.　　C. 8 : 45.

(　　) 5. What will the girl do tomorrow?

A. She will go boating. B. She will go skating. C. She will go fishing.

四、选择下列词语的正确解释。

(　　) 1. poison　　A. something used for treating illness

(　　) 2. remain　　B. to stay in the same place without moving or leaving

(　　) 3. silence　　C. a substance that can kill you or make you sick

(　　) 4. dangerous　D. a period of complete quiet

(　　) 5. medicine　　E. able to or likely to cause danger

五、用下列词的适当形式填空。

1. He looks ________ (fun) in a red colored dress.
2. I don't feel ________ (good). I have a stomach-ache.
3. You mustn't ________ (waste) our time.
4. I ________ (finish) all my work before I ________ (leave).
5. I ________ (leave) in a minute.
6. Let's ________ (begin) the game now!
7. Everybody ________ (call) him Mr. Liu.
8. The sun ________ (rise) in the east and ________ (set) in the west.
9. —Where is Mac? —He ________ (run) on the grass.
10. It is very cold these days. It ________ (snow) soon.

六、对画线部分提问。

1. I must see Tim on Monday at one o'clock.

____

2. You must have a haircut.

____

3. You can't park here because it's a no parking area.

____

4. Simon is well-behaved.

____

5. My mother has a headache.

____

七、完形填空。

Three __1__ ago, my family got our first computer. __2__ the beginning of this summer, I found it was too old and I wanted to get a __3__ one. After my father and I talked for a long time, he __4__ . We went to many shops and read many ads. __5__ we bought an HP computer.

During the first week, I noticed __6__ our computer had some problems. I spent many hours __7__ to fix it, but it __8__ work. So I __9__ to phone the HP company and ask them __10__ to work out my problem. They told me to wait until the next morning because all their workers were __11__ that day.

The next morning two workers came. It took them many hours to mend it, but the computer __12__ did not work. My dad had no other way but to return the whole thing.

A few days later, we decided that I should go on the Internet and order some parts to build a new computer by __13__. It was not an easy job for me to build a new computer. I tried many times, and in the end I was successful. From these setbacks(挫折), I have learned a lot. Now I believe that if the HP computer hadn't had any problems, __14__ I would not have learned how to build the new one. Even though I spent lots of time on it, I know it wasn't __15__.

(　　) 1. A. days　B. weeks　C. months　D. years
(　　) 2. A. At　B. On　C. To　D. For
(　　) 3. A. big　B. new　C. cheap　D. small
(　　) 4. A. won　B. paid　C. agreed　D. received
(　　) 5. A. At first　B. At last　C. At once　D. At times
(　　) 6. A. if　B. that　C. what　D. how
(　　) 7. A. try　B. tried　C. to try　D. trying
(　　) 8. A. do　B. did　C. don't　D. didn't
(　　) 9. A. hoped　B. have　C. had　D. liked
(　　) 10. A. how　B. what　C. why　D. where
(　　) 11. A. free　B. sad　C. busy　D. exciting
(　　) 12. A. already　B. always　C. still　D. usually
(　　) 13. A. themselves　B. himself　C. itself　D. myself
(　　) 14. A. or　B. then　C. so　D. and
(　　) 15. A. a waste of time　B. a successful job
C. a good computer　D. a bad company

八、阅读理解。

Chicago on a Budget（预算）

How to have fun in Chicago without spending a lot of money?

Sightseeing

The Art Institute（学院）of Chicago has a fine collection of photos and paintings. The ticket is $10.00, but go on Tuesdays and you'll get in free.

The Sears Tower is the world's third tallest building. By going to the 103rd floor, you can get a great view of the whole city! All for only $8.50.

Free show

There are free concerts in Grant Park in summer. They are held from Wednesday to Saturday nights at 7 : 30 pm.

The Oprah Winfrey Show and *The Jenny Jones Show* both offer(提供) tourists free tickets. For *The Oprah Winfrey Show* you'll have to book tickets at least a month before.

Places to stay

You can stay in a hotel for $100 to $300 a day. However, you can get a room in the dormitory(宿舍) at Roosevelt University for $215 for a whole week! But you have to stay for 30 days to get this great rate(价格).

(　　) 1. The writer wrote this passage for telling us ______.

A. Chicago is a big and beautiful city

B. where we can see fine photos and paintings

C. how to make a cheap trip in Chicago

D. there are many free concerts in Chicago

(　　) 2. It will cost you ______ if you visit the Art Institute instead of the Sears Tower on Sundays.

A. more　　B. less　　C. the same　　D. nothing

(　　) 3. You may go to ______ if you like to get a great view of the whole city.

A. the Art Institute　　B. the Sears Tower

C. Roosevelt University　　D. Grant Park

(　　) 4. You have to spend at least ______ in all for a month to stay in a dormitory room at Roosevelt University at a good rate.

A. $100　　B. $300　　C. $250　　D. $860

(　　) 5. According to this passage, which of the following statements is NOT true?

A. You are free to go to the Art Institute on Tuesday.

B. There are free concerts in Grant Park in summer.

C. The Sears Tower is one of the world's tallest buildings.

D. You can get tickets to *The Oprah Winfrey Show* as soon as you arrive.

九、选出适当的选项填在下列横线上。

A. The newspaper said it was the worst play of the year.

B. I was afraid you'd say that.

C. The film *Walking in the Rain* is on.

D. To see a film or to watch a play?

E. I don't think so.

F. We just missed it.

G. That should be enjoyable.

A：Sam，we haven't gone out for over a month. Let's go somewhere this evening.

B：Fine. Where would you like to go? (1)________

A：A new play is on this week. Let's go and watch it, shall we?

B：It got very bad reviews. (2)________

A：How about the film *Dancer in the Dark*! (3)________

B：We've already seen it. Don't you remember?

A：Then let's go to the neighbourhood cinema. (4)________

B：Good. What time does it start?

A：15 minutes ago. (5)________

B：Well, I guess all we can do is to stay home and watch television.

A：(6)________Now it will take me another month to get you interested in going out.

十、按照实验顺序将下列步骤排序。

It's too dangerous to stand near a rocket when it blasts off. But you can use a balloon and string to make a model of how a rocket works. Try this activity to build your own model. Put them into right order.

A. Blow up the balloon and clip the clothespin to the end so air cannot escape.

B. Tape the balloon to the middle of the straw.

C. Move the straw with the balloon close to a chair. Make sure the end with the clothespin is closest to the chair.

D. Move the chair apart until the string is tight and level.

E. Tie one end of the string to a chair. Tie the other end to another chair that is about 4 meters (13 feet) away.

F. Remove the clothespin.

G. Thread one end of the string through a straw(吸管).

H. Cut a piece of string about 5 meters (16 feet) long.

I. Measure how far the balloon moves. Record the distance.

____

Unit 5

Section One

一、写出下列动词的过去式。

1. is ________ 2. are ________ 3. am ________ 4. come ________
5. go ________ 6. sit ________ 7. find ________ 8. tell ________
9. write ________ 10. say ________ 11. buy ________ 12. make ________

二、首字母填词。

1. Last Saturday we went to the f ________. We had a good time.
2. Today is January the first. Y ________ was December the thirty-first.
3. This afternoon we found a very interesting storybook in the l ________.
4. — What are you doing, Jerry? — I am looking for my k ________ to the door.
5. — Where is the thief? — He is in p ________ now.
6. Sue is brushing her teeth in the b ________.
7. Oh, look at your long hair! Go to the b ________ at once to get it cut!
8. Did Sandy write in his d ________ the day before yesterday?
9. My brother has got a toothache, so he has to see the d ________.
10. As the new term begins, I'm going to the s ________ to get some stationery.
11. Sandy went to the g ________ to buy some fruits and vegetables.
12. Mother went to the b ________ to buy some beef.

三、参照例句写出句子。

1. Father / church / yesterday
Was father at church yesterday?
When was father at church?
Where was father yesterday?
2. Sandy / bed / last night
____
____
____

3. Sue / the funfair / this morning

____

____

____

4. The baby / the pram / the night before last

____

____

____

5. Mother / the grocer's / two hours ago

____

____

____

四、句型转换。

1. Father was in the country yesterday evening.（变否定句）

____

2. There were some pictures in the parcel last night.（变否定句）

____

3. Sue folded her clothes last night.（变否定句）

____

4. The children were at the barber's the night before last.（变一般疑问句）

____

5. Sandy had breakfast yesterday morning.（变一般疑问句）

____

6. There was some snow on the mountains last winter.（变一般疑问句）

____

7. Tony had a new schoolbag last term.（对画线部分提问）

____

8. The horse was in the field the day before yesterday.（对画线部分提问）

____

9. Sandy and Sue were at home a short time ago.（对画线部分提问）

____

10. Mother was in the village a month ago.（对画线部分提问）

____

11. Professor Boffin went to the cinema just now.（对画线部分提问）

____

五、单项选择。

（　　）1. —What does your sister like doing in her spare time?

—She ________ watching TV.

A. likes B. liked C. has liked D. had liked

( ) 2. —When ________ Jessy ________ to New York?

—Yesterday.

A. does; get B. did; get C. has; got D. had; got

( ) 3. —How clean the bedroom is!

—Yes, I am sure that someone ________ it.

A. cleans B. cleaned C. has cleaned D. had cleaned

( ) 4. —Would you please lend me your bike?

— ____________

A. Sure. B. No, thanks.

C. Never mind. D. It was a pleasure.

( ) 5. — How are you doing, Daisy?

—________, thank you.

A. I'm OK B. I'm a teacher C. I'd love to D. I'm coming

( ) 6. —Don't try to ________ anything from me, Mary.

—I know nothing about it, mum! I was sleeping at that time!

A. hear B. cheat C. lie D. hide

( ) 7. —Why do you get up so early in the morning, Tarcy?

—I generally make it a ________ to be up by 7 to read English.

A. plan B. wish C. secret D. rule

Section Two

一、写出下列国家对应的首都。

1. America ________ 2. Germany ________ 3. England ________

4. France ________ 5. Italy ________ 6. Japan ________

7. Ireland ________ 8. Greece ________ 9. Spain ________

二、单项选择。

( ) 1. The story happened ________ the morning of May 1,1990.

A. in B. for C. at D. on

( ) 2. — Where ________ you ________ lunch just now?

— At school.

A. did; have B. did; had C. have; had D. shall; have

( ) 3. There ________ a sports meeting in our school next month.

A. is going to have B. are going to be

C. will have D. is going to be

( )4. —Where did you go on holiday this summer? England?

—You are ________ . We went on a 10-day tour to Paris.

A. funny　　B. right　　C. cool　　D. close

(　　)5. —Do the dishes, Mike, or I will tell mum!

—Mind your own ______, Sue!

A. action　　B. duty　　C. business　　D. way

三、翻译下列句子。

1. 你总是那么粗心。

______

2. 前天你在学校吗?

______

3. 你怎么啦?

______

4. 我正在写日记。

______

5. 也许小猫在床下。

______

6. 几分钟以前她还在这儿。

______

四、根据图片及例句完成下列句子。

1. 
(I / a long time ago)
I was in Italy a long time ago.

2. 
(we / six months ago)
______

3. 
(they / in 2005)
______

4. 
(he / the year before last)
______

5. 
(Peter / last week)
______

五、读下面的短文，给短文中的每段话选择适当的小标题。

Welcome back to the start of a new school year. I hope you all had an enjoyable summer break. A special welcome goes to all the new families who have joined us at Sunshine.

(1)________ Please call up the school office if anyone has changed the address or phone number.

(2)________ The cost for a school meal has increased to $1.85 per day. This is $9.25 per week.

(3)________ Our club is open from 8 : 25 am until school starts and costs $1 per day. There is no need to book a place—just turn up! The menu includes bread, cereal, fruit and a drink. Milk is still offered at the morning break.

(4)________ Please note that from 9 : 00 am—3 : 00 pm all visitors must use the main entrance in Cambridge Square and not cut through the playground. This is especially important when children are out at break times and having PE classes.

(5)________ If you have any unwanted Barbie dolls, Action Men or toy cars, we would love to have them for our lunchtime play areas.

A. Playground toys　　B. Breakfast club

C. School meals　　D. Children's information

E. Access to school

Section Three

一、单项选择。

(　　)1. —We need to ________ a time to have a talk, now!

—What about tomorrow? I am too busy today.

A. put up　　B. fix up　　C. use up　　D. look up

(　　)2. —May I watch TV for a while?

—No, you ________ . You have to finish your homework first.

A. shouldn't　　B. needn't　　C. mustn't　　D. won't

(　　)3. —What should I do here?

—Just put all the things ________ they were.

A. where　　B. when　　C. whose　　D. which

(　　)4. —Hi, Sunny. Your new flat is so nice!

—Thanks, ________________.

A. don't mention it　　B. my pleasure

C. help yourself　　D. make yourself at home

(　　) 5. —I really hope to keep in touch with Lily.

—Sorry. I don't know ________.

A. what her name is　　B. what her job is
C. what her number is　　D. when she left

二、用适当的数量词填空。

1. I like the little ________ of chocolate that you get at the party.
2. Have you got any ________ of jam?
3. Jerry bought four ________ of beer yesterday.
4. We're going to need three ________ of flour to make this cake.
5. Can I use your ________ of toothpaste, please?
6. I'd like a ________ of cigarettes, please?
7. How many ________ of matches do you have?
8. This ________ of beans cost \$2.
9. I need a ________ of soap to clean my hands.
10. I'd like a ________ of soup, please!

三、根据图片回答问题。

1.  How did he feel?
____

2.  How many kinds of animals were there in the field?
____

3.  How was the weather that day? Where was the bird?
____
____

4.  Where were they? What were they?
____
____

四、完形填空。

I still remember very clearly my first visit to the dentist's with my mother. When I walked into the office, I saw many people waiting, and they all looked __1__. I began to worry. I sat beside my mother, and she __2__ a story to me from a children's magazine. __3__ later, a nurse called us, and led us into __4__ room. I was told to climb into a big

__5__. I saw a drill and other strange things __6__ me and I was frightened. The dentist looked into my mouth and examined each tooth carefully. Finally he said my teeth were all __7__. I was glad the examination was __8__ and was anxious to leave, so I paid __9__ when he showed me the right way of tooth brushing. Later on in my life whenever I had a toothache, I wished I had __10__ him carefully.

( )1. A. happy B. nervous C. excited D. ill
( )2. A. spoke B. said C. told D. read
( )3. A. Sometimes B. Sometime C. Some time D. Some times
( )4. A. operation B. operating C. other D. another
( )5. A. chair B. door C. desk D. bench
( )6. A. around B. behind C. under D. over
( )7. A. well B. fine C. sick D. bad
( )8. A. end B. finish C. over D. gone
( )9. A. no attention B. no attention to C. attention D. attention to
( )10. A. noticed B. listened to C. heard D. understood

Section Four

一、原文填空。

1. I'm writing in my ________.
2. ________ are very clever men, Professor Boffin.
3. —You were at the ________.
   — I'm not going to write that in my diary!
4. Last week, mother, father and the children had lunch at a ________.
5. There ________ some cakes in this tin a minute ago.
6. It was ________ 24th.
7. How ________ ago were you in America?
8. Where's the key ________ my car, dear?
9. ________ it's in your car.
10. It's not very ________! It says "School, School, School!"

二、用所给词的适当形式填空。

1. Tom and Mary ________ (arrive) in Wuhan last month.
2. Mike ________(not go) to bed until 12 o'clock last night.
3. Mary ________ (post) the parcel yesterday morning.
4. There ________ (be) no one here a moment ago.
5. Did Sandy ________ (clean) his teeth this morning?
6. Mother didn't ________ (visit) Mrs. Gasbag yesterday evening.
7. Sue ________(have) some bananas but she didn't have strawberries yesterday.

8. Last week Sandy and Billy ________ (be not) in the village.
9. My mother ________ (not do) housework yesterday.
10. She watches TV every evening. But she ________ (not watch) TV last night.
11. ________ your father ________ (go) to work every day last year?
12. What time ________ you ________ (get) to Beijing the day before yesterday?
13. How long ago ________ (be) he in America?
14. ________ (be) the children at church last Sunday?
15. ________ (be) the thief in prison the night before last?

三、单项选择。

( ) 1. "No parking" means you ________ park here.
A. can't B. shouldn't C. needn't D. mustn't

( ) 2. Don't ________ it over!
A. pours B. pouring C. pour D. poured

( ) 3. — Your hair is too long. You must have a haircut.
— All right. I will go to the ________ this afternoon.
A. haircutter's B. bakers' C. barber D. barber's

( ) 4. — Where are the children?
— They are ________ a fight in the playground.
A. having B. doing C. playing D. going

( ) 5. There is going to ________ a meeting next week.
A. have B. has C. is D. be

四、翻译。

1. 去年在这些山上有许多雪。

____

2. 昨天在碗柜里有许多蛋糕，但是今天没有了。

____

3. 多久以前孩子们在游乐场？

____

4. 妈妈刚刚去了果蔬店。

____

Section Five

一、听写句子。

1. ____
2. ____
3. ____

4. ____________________

5. ____________________

6. ____________________

二、听下面五段小对话,选择正确的答语。

( ) 1. When will the man see the dentist?

A. On Friday. B. On Saturday. C. On Monday.

( ) 2. Why is the man in a hurry?

A. He is going to catch the plane.

B. He is going to drive the car.

C. He is going to catch the train.

( ) 3. Which box does the man like?

A. The bigger one. B. The smaller one. C. Both of them.

( ) 4. What does the girl's sister do?

A. A teacher. B. A reporter. C. A doctor.

( ) 5. What is the weather like in Tianjin?

A. Windy. B. Cloudy. C. Sunny.

三、听下面一段对话,选择最佳答案。

( ) 1. People in the dialogue are ________.

A. classmates B. a couple

C. mother and son D. father and daughter

( ) 2. They are talking about ________.

A. whether to go to the theatre B. whether to grow vegetables

C. whether to live in the city D. whether to have a barbecue

( ) 3. Who is for living in the suburbs?

A. Mr. Lee. B. Mrs. Lee.

C. Mr. Lee's father. D. Mrs. Lee's father.

( ) 4. Who is for moving to the city?

A. Mr. Lee. B. Mrs. Lee.

C. Mr. Lee's father. D. Mrs. Lee's father.

( ) 5. They decide to leave the matter to ________.

A. Mr. Lee's father B. Mrs. Lee's mother

C. Mr. Lee's mother D. Mrs. Lee's father

四、听下面一段短文,选出正确的选项。

( ) 1. The sponge is an animal that has ________.

A. a tail B. many holes C. a head

( ) 2. Which of the following does this story lead you to believe?

A. The sponge lives where there are ancient people.

B. The sponge eats whatever the water may bring.

C. Sponges bite the divers.

(　　) 3. Where does the sponge live?

A. It lives where men dive.

B. It lives in the air.

C. It lives under water.

(　　) 4. The main idea of the whole story is that ______.

A. the sponge is very different from most animals

B. people in ancient times were clean

C. we do not use sponges from the sea any more

五、用适当的词语填空。

1. If you want to pray, you will go to the ______.
2. If you want to buy some cakes, you will go to the ______.
3. If you want to cook a piece of steak, you will go to the ______ to buy some beef.
4. If you want to buy some crayons, you will go to the ______.
5. If you want to buy some fruits, you will go to the ______.
6. If you have got a pain on your teeth, you will go to the ______.

六、对画线部分提问。

1. Tom bought twelve strawberries last week.

____

2. She drove the car very carefully.

____

3. They lit a fire a few minutes ago.

____

4. He is going to have a birthday party this Sunday at home.

____

5. The girl under the tree is my sister.

____

七、完形填空。

Mother's day is a holiday for mothers. It is celebrated in the United States, England, Sweden, India, Mexico and many other __1__. Little by little, it __2__ widely celebrated. Mother's day falls on the second Sunday in May. __3__, many people send __4__ of love to their mothers. Those whose mothers are still living __5__ a pink or red rose, while those whose mothers are __6__ wear a white one.

The __7__ of a day for mothers was first given by Miss Ana Jarvis of Philadelphia. As a result of her hard work, the celebration for the first American Mother's Day __8__ in Philadelphia on May 10, 1908. Soon the __9__ became popular all over the __10__ and around the world.

( )1. A. homes B. schools C. countries D. cities

( )2. A. gives B. becomes C. stays D. begins

( )3. A. For a long time B. In the morning C. At a time D. On that day

( )4. A. presents B. things C. hello D. calls

( )5. A. put B. take C. wear D. dress

( )6. A. ill B. healthy C. dead D. busy

( )7. A. idea B. plan C. need D. meeting

( )8. A. held B. was holding C. was held D. is held

( )9. A. day B. year C. month D. time

( )10. A. country B. America C. place D. England

八、阅读理解。

On Nov. 18th, 1908, three men went up in a balloon. They started early in London. The headman was Augusta Gaudron, and the other two men were Tannar and Maitland. They had a big balloon and they were ready for a long way.

Soon they heard the sea. They were carrying the usual rope, and it was hanging down from the basket of the balloon. At the end of the rope they had tied a metal box. This could hold water, or it could be empty. So they were able to change its weight. It was for use over the sea. They were also carrying some bags of sand.

After the sun rose, the balloon went higher. It went up to 3,000 metres, and the air was very cold. The water in the balloon became ice. Snow fell past the men's basket, and they could see more snow on the ground. The men tried to throw out some more sand; but it was hard. They tried to break the icy sand with their knives, but it was not easy. The work was slow and they were still falling, so they had to drop some whole bags of sand. One of them fell on an icy lake and made a black hole in the ice.

At last they pulled the box into the basket. It was still snowing; so they climbed to get away from the snow. They rose to 5,100 metres! Everything became icy. They were so cold that they decided to land. They came down in Poland heavily but safely. They had travelled 1,797 kilometers from London!

( )1. Three men flew in balloon ________.

A. for nearly 1,800 kilometers B. to another city

C. to visit Poland D. less than a century ago

( )2. The metal box was used for ________.

A. carrying the bags of sand B. keeping drinking-water

C. carrying ropes of the basket D. changing weight

( )3. When the balloon went up higher, ________.

A. the temperature of the balloon began to fall

B. they saw the sun went down

C. they made a hole in the basket with their knives

D. they could see a black hole on the ground

(　　)4. The balloon landed ________.

A. in London　　B. on the sea

C. on a lake　　D. in a foreign country

(　　)5. Which of the following is NOT true?

A. The three men started their journey before the sun rose.

B. The balloon began to go up when they threw bags of sand out of the basket.

C. When they pulled the box into the basket, the balloon began to climb up.

D. The three men had to land because they felt cold.

九、按照文章结构及段落内容准确排序。

A. In the end, sadly people buried him in 6′×4′land—that is what everybody needs.

B. Once there was a farmer. He was happy with whatever he had. But his elder brother was richer than him. One day, he thought that his brother was getting richer and richer day by day. As his mind wandered, he thought he should also be richer.

C. So he bought some gifts and went to Chief. He presented the gifts to him and told him the purpose of his coming. Chief welcomed him and accepted the gifts. He told him that he could have the land without giving him anything. He could take as much land as he could cover by walking the land before sunset. He should start in the morning and whatever distance he could cover during the day, he could have that land.

D. Then he started saving some money to buy more land and after a long time, as he had enough money to buy more land, he thought of Chief. Chief had very large land.

E. The farmer got very happy to hear this offer. Now he could have lots of land without paying anything. He came in the morning and started running, not walking, so that he could cover the largest area. In order to cover the largest area, he neither took his food, nor drank water, nor took any rest. He just continued running. Without eating, or drinking, or rest, he got very tired when he came back in the evening, and as he came back to Chief, he got very tired and died.

____

Unit 6

Section One

一、单项选择。

(　　) 1. — What's your hobby?
— I like ________.
A. go fish　　B. going fish　　C. go fishing　　D. going fishing

(　　) 2. It is difficult for me ________ stories in English.
A. write　　B. writes　　C. writing　　D. to write

(　　) 3. I think reading books is ________.
A. relaxing　　B. relax　　C. relaxed　　D. relaxes

(　　) 4. Do you think it is good ________ children to go shopping?
A. for　　B. as　　C. at　　D. of

(　　) 5. — ________?
— I like dolphins best.
A. What would you like　　B. What animals do you like best
C. How do you like the animals　　D. Is there any animal do you like

(　　) 6. — Can you tell me how to ________ videos with this camera?
— That's easy! Let me show you.
A. rent　　B. play　　C. make　　D. do

(　　) 7. — ________ you attend the evening classes?
— I don't like the courses there.
A. Why not　　B. Why don't　　C. How about　　D. What about

二、看图片并写出其对应的兴趣爱好。

1. 　2. 　3. 　4. 

5.  6.  7.  8. 

9.  10. 

11.  12. 

Picture 1 ________ Picture 2 ________ Picture 3 ________

Picture 4 ________ Picture 5 ________ Picture 6 ________

Picture 7 ________ Picture 8 ________ Picture 9 ________

Picture10 ________ Picture 11 ________ Picture 12 ________

三、写出下列动词的现在分词形式。

1. carry ________ 2. go ________ 3. lay ________ 4. make ________

5. spend ________ 6. have ________ 7. pass ________ 8. hit ________

9. come ________ 10. watch ________ 11. swim ________ 12. fly ________

13. lie ________ 14. ride ________ 15. write ________ 16. teach ________

17. begin ________ 18. shop ________ 19. see ________ 20. ski ________

四、仿照例子完成下列习题。

eg:I / dance / sing

I don't like dancing but I like singing.

1. Sandy / take photos / collect stamps.

____

2. The Clarks / play chess / play cards

____

3. Lucy and Lily / swim / play hopscotch

____

4. My brother / study / play computer games

____

5. Those boys / play basketball / play football

____

6. The cat / eat mice / eat fish

____

五、用动词的适当形式填空。

1. Ben ________ (like) singing very much.
2. Sue ________ (draw) a picture now.
3. I am used to ________ (swim) in the river in winter.
4. Do you hate ________ (smoke)?
5. Tom often ________ (have) dinner at home.
6. Billy ________ (do) not like PE because he is fat.
7. The Smiths often ________ (watch) TV in the evening.
8. She ________ (go) to work from Monday to Friday.
9. She enjoys ________ (listen) to music.
10. I haven't finished ________ (read) the novel.
11. My aunt ________ (look) after her baby carefully.

六、找出下列每组中与其他词不同类的词。

eg:	A. apple	B. pear	C. panda (circled)	D. banana
( )1.	A. badminton	B. riding	C. hang-gliding	D. guitar
( )2.	A. photography	B. painting	C. poster	D. dancing
( )3.	A. forget	B. carry	C. watch	D. fight
( )4.	A. interesting	B. good exercise	C. expensive	D. creative
( )5.	A. camera	B. actually	C. television	D. pottery
( )6.	A. discos	B. cartoons	C. comedies	D. soaps

Section Two

一、单项选择。

( ) 1. — Did you watch the movie *The Twilight Saga: Eclipse* yesterday?
— Yes, but it was really ________. I was ________.
A. excited; exciting B. interested; interesting
C. boring; bored D. relaxing; relaxed

( ) 2. Gregory is a ________ designer and his work always amazes us.
A. expensive B. creative C. imagination D. difficult

( ) 3. —What's on the ________ tonight?
— There is a television series called *Gossip Girls*.
A. cinema B. box C. show D. display

( ) 4. — Which ________ do you like best?
— I like *The Big Bang Theory*. I was really good fun.
A. sport B. film C. cartoon D. soaps

( ) 5. — What do you usually do in your spare time?

— I usually sit in front of the television. I'm really a TV ________.

A. fans　　B. slob　　C. potato　　D. player

(　　) 6. — Don't make a ________. You baby brother is asleep.

— All right.

A. sound　　B. voice　　C. noise　　D. bed

二、根据图片判断下列电视节目和电影的类别。

1. 

____

2. 

____

3. 
____

4. 

____

5. 

____

6. 
____

7. 

____

8. 

____

三、仿照例子完成下列习题。

eg: I / eat

What are you doing?

I'm eating.

1. I / go sightseeing

____

____

2. We / play tennis

____

____

3. the baby / drink milk

____

____

4. the girls / skip

____

____

5. Kate / do aerobics

____

____

6. My parents / bake a cake

____

____

四、用现在进行时写句子。

1. Lily / learn to / speak French

____

2. it / snow / now

____

3. they / watch a basketball match / on TV

____

4. he / close the window

____

5. look / the dog / bark

____

6. listen / the baby / cry

____

7. they / have a meeting / at eleven o'clock

____

8. she / smile to herself / in the mirror now

____

五、句型练习。

1. Frank is climbing the hill.（变一般疑问句）

____

2. We are having a Chinese lesson now.（变一般疑问句）

____

3. He is drinking a cup of coffee.（变否定句）

____

4. We are picking apples on a farm these days.（变否定句）

____

5. I'm eating some vegetables.（对画线部分提问）

____

Section Three

一、单项选择。

(　　) 1. Look! Tim is ________ a new bike today.

A. jumping　　B. running　　C. riding　　D. taking

(　　) 2. I can't catch up with the fashion, because the clothes style ________ all the time.

A. has changed　B. is changed　C. changed　D. is changing

(　　) 3. It was too late to ________ after the party; therefore I called a taxi.

A. on foot　B. pick up　C. catch a bus　D. sit a train

(　　) 4. Thanks to your help, ________ in the room is in good order now.

A. everything　B. anything　C. something　D. nothing

(　　) 5. The doctor asked her to stay ________ for two or three days.

A. at the bed　B. in the bed　C. in bed　D. on bed

(　　) 6. Mike enjoys ________.

A. to play the badminton　B. playing the badminton

C. to play badminton　D. playing badminton

(　　) 7. I like ________. Would you like ________ with me this afternoon?

A. swimming; swimming　B. to swim; to swim

C. swimming; to swim　D. to swim; swimming

二、改错题。下列句子每句都有一个错误，请写出正确的句子。

1. Everything are fine.

____

2. Watching videos is really a good fun.

____

3. I'm liking playing golf now.

____

4. I was surprising to learn that he was taking drugs.

____

5. Do you think the graph is correct for people in your age?

____

三、完形填空。(2006 年广州中考)

I have always been interested in clowns. The earliest thing I can remember, as a child of three, is seeing a pair of clowns — one very fat, and the other very __1__. A traveling circus came to our town and my parents took me to see it. When we arrived at the circus, everyone was laughing at the clowns. I didn't understand why they were laughing, __2__ I laughed too.

While I was __3__, the fat clown came and sat down next to me. "Shall we dance?" he asked, then __4__ me up and began dancing. I felt frightened and began to cry. __5__ then I have been interested in clowns. They make me laugh a lot, although they still make me a bit __6__, too.

In life, we sometimes laugh at things that __7__ us. We often laugh most at people who make us nervous. When we laugh, we relax and __8__ ourselves. People who never laugh can become worried and ill. Laughter is like medicine and a clown is like a __9__.

There have always been, and there will always be clowns, because people need to laugh. Laughter is the best kind of __10__ in life.

(　　)1. A. happy　B. thin　C. kind　D. lucky

( )2. A. and B. so C. or D. but
( )3. A. dancing B. eating C. laughing D. crying
( )4. A. picked B. threw C. hung D. pushed
( )5. A. Before B. Since C. By D. From
( )6. A. tired B. silly C. afraid D. sick
( )7. A. trouble B. surprise C. interest D. frighten
( )8. A. play B. love C. enjoy D. understand
( )9. A. doctor B. nurse C. friend D. teacher
( )10. A. dream B. medicine C. care D. color

四、介词填空。

1. Sam is doing aerobics ________ the gym.
2. Tom and Henry are playing tennis ________ a tennis court.
3. Gina is running ________ the running track.
4. We often swim ________ the swimming pool in summer.
5. I want to buy some envelopes ________ the shop.
6. Would you like to have a cup of coffee ________ the café?
7. I sometimes take photos ________ my friend's camera.
8. Two men are waiting ________ the train ________ a station.

五、用动词的适当形式填空。

1. We usually ________ (play) hide-and-seek after school.
2. She ________ (not eat) at the moment.
3. Do you like ________ (write) letters?
4. Would you like ________ (fly) a kite?
5. Do you mind me ________ (sit) next to you?
6. It is said that the books about the earthquake now ________ (sell) well.
7. There is a little girl ________ (water) flowers in the garden.
8. Please don't forget ________ (clean) the room while I am away in Beijing.
9. John likes soccer very much and he ________ (spend) about one hour ________ (play) it every day.
10. It ________ (rain) hard outside. You have to stay at home.

六、句型题。

1. Elsa likes watching sports and films.（变一般疑问句）
____
2. Look at these horses.（变否定句）
____
3. The girl is living with her grandparents at present.（变否定句）
____
4. Grace is reading <u>in the yard</u>.（对画线部分提问）
____

5. My teacher doesn't like games shows.（对画线部分提问）

____

6. Andy likes fishing because it is interesting.（对画线部分提问）

____

7. Norman is from Scotland.（换一种说法）

____

Section Four

一、单项选择。

(　　) 1. Listen! Some of the girls ________ *We Wish You Merry Christmas*.
A. are singing　B. sing　C. will sing　D. sang

(　　) 2. The show is really ________ and everyone is ________ in it.
A. interesting; interesting　B. interesting; interested
C. interested; interesting　D. interested; interested

(　　) 3. — Dad, why should I stop ________ computer games?
— For your health, my boy. I'm afraid you ________.
A. to play; must　B. playing; have to
C. to play; can　D. playing; may

(　　) 4. — You forgot ________ the lights again.
— Really? I won't next time.
A. turn off　B. turns off
C. turning off　D. to turn off

(　　) 5. Although Bill isn't rich enough, he often ________ money to the poor.
A. will give　B. was giving
C. gives　D. gave

二、连词成句。

1. still, the, the, growing, of, is, world, now, population

____

2. service, I, day, listen, world, every, the, to, BBC

____

3. playing, they, on, are, court, a, squash

____

4. monkey, Jack, and, playing, his, garden, are, disk, look, together, in, the, flying

____

5. all, write, world, me, from, people, to, over, the

____

6. jacket, my, I, a, for, for, son, am, looking

____

三、用正确的时态填空。

1. — ________ the students ________ (read) English.
   — Yes, they are.
2. We ________ (play) football now.
3. Sally ________ (work) six days a week.
4. Look! The birds ________ (sing) in the tree.
5. Julia ________ (like) ________ (draw) now.
6. My mother ________ (cook) in the kitchen right now.
7. It's six in the afternoon. The Smiths ________ (have) lunch together.
8. Tom ________ (brush) his teeth at the moment.
9. Cathy ________ (live) in a flat in London.

四、阅读理解。(2004 年上海市中考)

Here are four messages on Alan Marshall's answer phone.

Monday 9 : 21

Alan? Alan, if you're at home, please answer the phone. Are you really not there? Well, I'd just like to say that I'm very angry with you—and your father is too. You know how much he loves our monthly family lunches. This is the fifth one you've missed. I hope you've got a really good reason this time. Oh, umm, this is your mother speaking.

Monday 10 : 02

Mr. Marshall, this is Steffi Rosen, Mr. Prince's assistant. I'm calling to confirm(确认) tomorrow's lunch with Mr. Yamada of Rising Sun Computer Games. Mr. Prince wants you to know that this meeting is very important. Please remember to bring the interactivity designs(互动设计) with you. He says that Mr. Yamada is ready to pay for the world rights (版权) on your new game! The restaurant is The Four Stars in Gower Street and I've booked a table for a quarter past One. Be there on time—please!

Monday 11 : 23

My name is Karen Miller. I'm a producer at Interactive Computer Games, Australia. I saw your game "Kill the Enemy!" at the International Computer Game Fair. I think your work is great and I'd like to discuss buying the rights for my part of the world. Someone at the fair said that you're working on a new game which is even more interactive. How interactive can you get? Perhaps we can interact over lunch? I'm in London until Wednesday. My mobile number is 027747 6130800.

Monday 12 : 31

Hello, Alan. It's Daisy. Did you have a good weekend? How's the new game going? I miss you. Bye.

判断下列句子是否符合电话留言内容,符合的用 T 表示,不符合的用 F 表示。

(　　) 1. Alan's parents don't want him to miss their monthly family lunches.

(　　) 2. Mr. Prince invites Mr. Yamada to lunch in order to buy the world rights on his new game.

(　　) 3. Karen Miller, an organizer of the International Computer Game Fair, came to London to order Alan's new game.

(　　) 4. It is said that Alan is working on a more interactive new game.

(　　) 5. Daisy calls to ask Alan out for the weekend.

(　　) 6. Alan does a very good job of designing computer games and is always very busy.

五、句型题。

1. You are sending an e-mail.（变一般疑问句）

____

2. The students are planting some trees now.（变否定句）

____

3. The old man is sleeping right now.（对画线部分提问）

____

4. The boy is playing squash under the big tree.（对画线部分提问）

____

5. It is really good fun.（换一种说法）

____

六、将下列汉语翻译成英语。

1. 肥皂剧________ 2. 创造性的________ 3. 细节________
4. 对……有好处________ 5. 最喜爱的节目________ 6. 跑道________
7. 健身训练________ 8. 自然风光片________ 9. 调查表________
10. 您忠实的________ 11. 壁球场________ 12. 体育运动中心________
13. 老幼皆宜________ 14. 照看孩子________ 15. 访谈节目________

Section Five

一、听写单词。

1. ________ 2. ________ 3. ________ 4. ________ 5. ________
6. ________ 7. ________ 8. ________ 9. ________ 10. ________

二、听问题选答案。

(　　)1. A. I like table tennis. B. I'm sorry I'm busy. C. I go to the park.
(　　)2. A. Comedies. B. I like English. C. My TV is broken.
(　　)3. A. At home. B. In the supermarket. C. In America.
(　　)4. A. Next month. B. As soon as possible. C. At 8 o'clock.
(　　)5. A. Just for fun. B. It's tiring. C. I don't like films.
(　　)6. A. Seven hours. B. Twice a week. C. It's difficult for me.

三、听对话并回答问题。

(　　)1. A. 85791038. B. 85761066. C. 85781088.

(　　)2. A. 5.　　B. 7.　　C. 8.

(　　)3. A. Every day.　　B. Sometimes.　　C. Never.

(　　)4. A. They will go to the classroom.
B. They will meet at 9：00.
C. They won't meet.

(　　)5. A. It's very beautiful.
B. It's too expensive.
C. It's not his favourite.

(　　)6. A. Swim with Bob.
B. Plant trees with Linda.
C. Have a picnic with Linda.

(　　)7. A. In a library.　　B. At the bookstore.　　C. At the zoo.

四、听下面几段对话并完成每段对话后的几个小题。

听第一段对话，回答第1~3题。

(　　)1. Who is answering the phone?
A. Sally.　　B. Jim.　　C. Dave.

(　　)2. When did Jim go out?
A. Half an hour ago.　　B. An hour ago.　　C . We don't know.

(　　)3. Which statement is NOT true?
A. Jim is going to get some paint.
B. Jim may stop at the pub on the way back.
C. Dave won't call again.

听第二段对话，回答第4~7题。

(　　)4. Where is the man going?
A. The man is going to a bank.
B. The man is going to a hospital.
C. The man is going to a flower shop.

(　　)5. How can the man get there?
A. Go ahead until he sees a tall building on the left.
B. Go along the road and turn left at the second crossing.
C. Go along the road and turn right at the second crossing.

(　　)6. Where is the bank?
A. Near the hospital.　　B. Inside the park.　　C. Behind the flower shop.

(　　)7. What is the dialogue about?
A. It's about getting some money from the bank.
B. It's about how the man can buy some flowers.
C. It's about asking the way to a hospital.

五、听短文并填空。

There are many kinds of TV programs on TV. I like to watch (1) ________, game shows and comedies. But cartoons are my favorite. I usually watch TV for thirty

(2)________ a day and the program I watch is a cartoon called *Doraemon*. It is on TV from six thirty to seven o'clock, Monday to (3)________. A lot of people watch it at that time. It's an interesting cartoon. *Doraemon* is drawn by a Japanese cartoonist. Doraemon is a (4)________ robot and the star of the cartoon. He can do many incredible things. For example, he can go traveling (5)________ or make people smaller or bigger. *Doraemon* is a good TV program. It is my favorite TV show.

六、单项选择。

( )1. Some children ________ in the river. Can't you see?
A. are swimming　B. swim　C. swims　D. will swim

( )2. They ________ online in the evening. They do their homework.
A. are chatting　B. can't chatting
C. don't chat　D. don't chatting

( )3. Now many students ________ reading *Harry Potter*.
A. likes　B. liking　C. are liking　D. like

( )4. Because the shop ________ down, all the dresses are sold at half price.
A. shuts　B. is closing　C. will break　D. putting

( )5. Besides good ________, the restaurant offers different kinds of traditional Fujian dishes.
A. service　B. food
C. education　D. fitness

( )6. Vincent grows ________ in English. He shows great ________ in English.
A. interested; interest　B. interest; interested
C. interested; interesting　D. interests; interesting

( )7. My little son enjoys ________ TV after supper.
A. watches　B. watching
C. watch　D. to watch

七、根据所给的信息填出所缺单词，首字母已经给出。

1. He sticks the stamp on the e________.
2. A dog's mother begins t________ puppies from birth. She makes them wait for food; she controls when they play and how far they travel.
3. I learn to use my digital camera in the free p________ courses.
4. Austria is f________ for its music.
5. This job is so boring. I wish I could do something more c________.
6. They had an enjoyable and r________ holiday.
7. Some students were playing basketball, while others were running on the t________.
8. I am working on the p________. This pretty jug is my work.
9. He plays a Russian spy in the comedy d________ *Sleepers*.
10. I put on my g________ gloves and dig in the soil.

八、阅读理解。(2006 年广东省汕头市中考)

ADVERTISEMENTS	
HONGNAN RESTAURANT 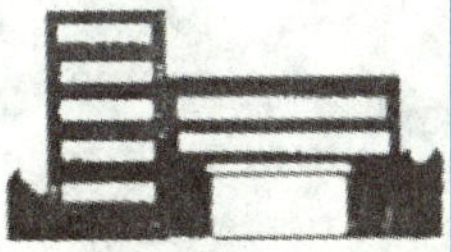 **Tel**: 83386223 **Add**: 635 Grand Road **Open**: Mon. to Fri. 7 : 00 a. m. —2 : 30 p. m. 5 : 00 p. m. —9 : 00 p. m. Sat. & Sun. 7 : 30 a. m. —2 : 00 p. m. 5 : 00 p. m. —10 : 00 p. m.	**HISTORY MUSEUM**  **Tel**: 87796960 **Add**: 69 Hong Kong Road One of Guangdong's largest museums specia-lized (专门) in Guangdong history of the native (本地) people. **Open**: Mon. to Fri. 9 : 00 a. m.—5 : 00 p. m. Sat. & Sun. 9 : 00 a. m.—3 : 00 p. m.
BAIHE SHOPPING CENTER **Tel**:87872738 **Add**:5300 Shanghai Road **Open**:Mon. to Fri. 10 : 00 a. m.—11 : 00 p. m. Sun. to Sat. 9 : 00 a. m.—10 : 30 p. m. 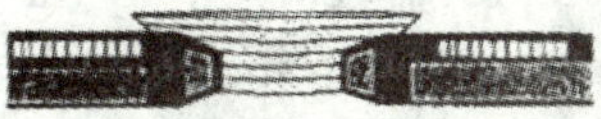	**FULL HOTEL** **Tel**:83338989  **Add**:368 East Huanshi Road **Breakfast**: 6 : 30 a. m. —9 : 00 p. m. **Lunch**:11 : 30 a. m. —2 : 00 p. m. **Dinner**:5 : 30 a. m. —10 : 00 p. m. **Coffee Shop**: Mon. to Fri. 7 : 00 a. m. —10 : 00 p. m. Sun. to Sat. 8 : 00 a. m. —10 : 00 p. m.

(　　)1. If you want to go out for lunch on Sunday, you can call at ________.

A. 83386223 or 83338989　　B. 87679690 or 83386223

C. 83338989 or 87872738　　D. 87872738 or 876796960

(　　)2. If you want to buy a new dress, you can go to ________.

A. 69 Hong Kong Road　　B. 368 East Huanshi Road

C. 5300 Shanghai Road　　D. 635 Grand Road

(　　)3. ________ isn't open for two and a half hours in the afternoon on weekdays.

A. Full Hotel　　B. Hongnan Restaurant

C. History Museum　　D. Baihe Shopping Center

(　　)4. On Sunday morning, the coffee shop in Full Hotel doesn't open until ______.

A. 6 : 30 a. m.　　B. 7 : 00 a. m.　　C. 7 : 30 a. m.　　D. 8 : 00 a. m.

(　　)5. You can know ________ when you visit History Museum.

A. the history of South China

B. the history of Guangdong's native people

C. the history of Shanghai

D. the history of Hong Kong

九、完形填空。(2005年陕西省中考英语试卷——课程改革实验区)

Dear Dad,

Happy birthday to you!

On this special day I'd like to talk to you __1__ a special way.

I don't think I'm good at __2__ you my thought face to face with you, so I'm writing to show my deep love for you.

You're not a rich man or a famous person. But in my heart, you are one of the greatest __3__ in the world. I'm __4__ you.

You're __5__ interested in fame and wealth(名利). You do __6__ things like paying phone bills on time, and working as a worker in your factory. The smile on your face shows you're pleased with the family. You take good care of my grandparents. You help me with my schoolwork and do some shopping with Mom on Sundays.

In the past, I didn't care __7__ you were with me or not. Now I am sorry to say I __8__ you the respect(尊重)before. But I am thankful for what you have done for me.

I am quite lucky that I have __9__ a great father. And I feel happy that now I can let you __10__ how much I love you. You are successful as a son, a husband, a father, and a friend.

Wish you happy forever!

Yours,

David

( )1. A. in B. at C. by D. on

( )2. A. talking B. saying C. speaking D. telling

( )3. A. businessmen B. man C. men D. worker

( )4. A. worried about B. proud of C. afraid of D. sorry for

( )5. A. always B. ever C. already D. never

( )6. A. ordinary B. interesting C. wonderful D. popular

( )7. A. whether B. that C. what D. where

( )8. A. will show B. don't show C. didn't show D. have shown

( )9. A. too B. so C. very D. such

( )10. A. to know B. know C. knew D. knowing

Unit 7

Section One

一、单项选择。

( ) 1. When is the swimming pool ________ to the public?
A. opening B. open C. opened D. opens

( ) 2. — ________ you swim?
— Yes, but I am not a swimmer.
A. Can B. May C. Need D. Must

( ) 3. — What a day! It's raining again. I'm afraid we can't go hiking tomorrow.
— Don't worry. It won't ________ long.
A. last B. drop C. rain D. fall

( ) 4. I told you the truth only yesterday. ________ I say it again?
A. Must B. Can C. May D. Will

( ) 5. — What's wrong with your brother?
— Oh, he fell to the ground and hurt himself while he ________ his bike.
A. is riding B. was riding C. rides D. will ride

( ) 6. — Would you please tell me ________ to do online shopping?
— Sure. Let me show you.
A. how B. what C. which D. when

( ) 7. ________ I work seven days a week.
A. Some time B. Sometime C. Sometimes D. Some times

二、根据图表写句子。

	very well	a little	not at all
John			
Lily and Lucy			

eg：John can play football very well.

1. John ______
2. John ______
3. Lily and Lucy ______
4. Lily and Lucy ______
5. Lily and Lucy ______

三、用下列方框中的词填写句子。

me you him her them us it

1. Mary, please show ______ your picture. I can't wait.
2. Tom, please pass ______ the glasses. Mother wants to read the newspapers.
3. Jenny, who taught ______ English last term? Was ______ Mr. Smith?
4. Sam is my brother. Do you like to play football with ______?

四、用所给单词的适当形式填空。

1. The bus was very crowded, so she wanted (take) ______ a taxi.
2. She enjoys (read) ______ novels before going to bed.
3. It took him two hours (finish) ______ his homework.
4. He has made up his mind (work) ______ hard.
5. Would you like (watch) ______ the football match this afternoon?
6. The child stopped (walk) ______ and listened to the music.

五、用以下提示写句子。

eg：(telephone)
I can make phone calls because there's a telephone.

1. (typewriter)
______
2. (camera)
______
3. (fax machine)
______

六、句型转换。

1. It's time for breakfast.（改为同义句）
It's time ______ ______ breakfast.
2. Sandy has supper at 6：00 p. m. every day.（改为否定句）
Sandy ______ ______ supper at 6：00 every day.
3. Simon can play football very well.（改为同义句）
Simon is ______ ______ playing football.
4. He goes running every morning.（对画线部分提问）
______ ______ ______ he ______ running?

5. You can't walk on the grass.（改为祈使句）

________ walk on the grass, please.

七、选择正确的动词，用其适当的形式填空。

fly visit do dance go

1. You can't watch TV. You must finish ________ your homework.
2. Would you like ________ to see the film with us now?
3. Let's practise ________ every Friday after school.
4. We are all looking forward to ________ Beijing Zoo.
5. Sally, with his cousin, often ________ kites at weekends.

Section Two

一、单项选择。

(　　)1. Today she looks ________. Look! She is looking ________ at his son.
A. happy; happy　B. happily; happily
C. happy; happily　D. happily; happy

(　　)2. Bob doesn't know the answer to the question. I don't know ________.
A. too　B. either　C. also　D. as well

(　　)3. Excuse me, is there ________ in the office?
A. somebody else　B. else somebody
C. anybody else　D. else anybody

(　　)4. ________ people know ________ about it.
A. Only a little; more　B. Very few; /
C. Very little; /　D. Very a few; more

(　　)5. His teacher often tells us ________ much time ________ TV.
A. not to spent; watch　B. to not spend; watching
C. don't spend; watch　D. not to spend; watching

(　　)6. I hope you can give me ________.
A. some advices　B. many advices
C. two pieces of advice　D. two advice

二、根据下列图表，完成句子。

Sunny English Club
For students
4:30—6:00 p.m.　Every Saturday
200 yuan a month
9 Zhouyu Street
Tel: 3786290
Foreign teachers, English songs and films and more!

续表

Ocean Museum 9：00—5：30　From Thursday to Sunday ticket：50 yuan 132 Xueyuan Street Tel：5439871 Show you a full picture of sea lives！	Health Centre 9：00—6：30 16 Yongle Street Tel：3801451 Free examinations for those over 70. Give you good advice to keep healthy！

eg：Sunny English Club is open ***between*** half past four ***and*** six in the afternoon，every Saturday.

Sunny English Club is open ***from*** half past four ***to*** six in the afternoon，every Saturday.

1. Ocean Museum ____________________
2. Ocean Museum ____________________
3. Health Centre ____________________
4. Health Centre ____________________

三、根据例句选择方框中的词或词组写句子。

walk，talk in sentences，crawl，read，cry，kick a ball，hold something，use a knife and fork，drink from a cup

eg：At birth，babies can cry，but they can't crawl.

1. At six months，they can __________，but they can't __________.
2. At one year，they can __________，but they can't __________.
3. At two years，they can __________，but they can't __________.
4. At three years，they can __________，but they can't __________.
5. At five years，they can __________，but they can't __________.

四、阅读下面的文章，完成句子。

Stephen Hawking was born in 1942. He's a world famous scientist and expert（专家）on space and time. Stephen is trying to find the answer to some very big questions such as：How did the universe begin？How will it end？

Stephen was a student at university. He studied math and science. Then，at the age of twenty，he became very ill. He was so young，but the doctors said to his family，"He has only two more years to live." The doctors were wrong—he didn't die. He can't walk now，but he uses a wheelchair. He talks with the help of a computer. After Oxford，Stephen went to Cambridge University. Three years later，in 1965，he became a doctor of Philosophy（哲学）.

Because of his health problem，it was difficult for him to draw diagrams or to write. So he started to think in pictures. With this new way of thinking，he became one of the most famous scientist in the world. In 1981，he met the Pope（教皇）in Rome. They talked about his ideas. Then in 1988，he wrote his first important book，*A Brief History of Time*. It sold more than 5.5 million copies in 333 different languages.

1. Stephen Hawking is famous for his research on ________________.
2. He ________________ instead of walking.
3. When he was 20, his disease was so serious that the doctors said that ________________.
4. Stephen's new way of thinking is ________________.
5. The title of Stephen's first important book is ________________.

五、选出下列句子中错误的一项并将其改正在后面的横线上。

1. When(A) I reach(B) the studio, I look(C) the timetable(D). (　　)________
2. I(A) want Rita(B) type(C) a letter(D). (　　)________
3. I get up(A) and(B) go run(C) before(D) breakfast. (　　)________
4. I switch on them(A) and make sure(B) there are(C) no problems(D). (　　)________
5. I do(A) different something(B) to help(C) me relax(D). (　　)________

Section Three

一、单项选择。

(　　) 1. Look, the teddy bear ________ a cat.
A. is like　B. is likes　C. look like　D. look likes

(　　) 2. Mother often sees ________ at the weekend.
A. her all friends　B. all her friends
C. her friends all　D. all of the her friends

(　　) 3. We often have bread and milk ________ breakfast. They are good for our health.
A. for　B. on　C. at　D. in

(　　) 4. —________ do you come here for? —To ask you for help.
A. What　B. Why　C. How　D. Who

(　　) 5. I will buy a pen ________ a present ________ my cousin.
A. as; to　B. like; for　C. as; for　D. like; to

(　　) 6. Can you tell me how ________ a ghost?
A. dress up　B. to dress up as a
C. to dress up as　D. can dress up as

(　　) 7. — How often does he go to school? — ________.
A. 3 times　B. 5 times　C. A few times　D. 3 times a week

二、完形填空。

Mr. Brown lived by the sea. He had a big __1__ and had to work hard, or his wife and children would be hungry. So he had to __2__ early in the morning. After breakfast he left for the sea in a small boat. He always hoped to __3__ more fish. One morning the man got to a good place for __4__. He threw a long rope with many hooks（钩子）into the water. He found it __5__ and pulled the hooks out of the water. He saw there were some gold chains（金链）on the hooks. He was, of course, very __6__. "I'll sell the gold chains for a lot of __7__." He thought to himself. "I'll build a new house, buy lots of expensive things. I'll be __8__ man in the world." Mr. Brown went on drawing his net（收网）and didn't notice（注意）what was __9__ to his boat. It began to sink（下沉）. As he was pulling the gold chain, the boat sank into the sea. He __10__ not only the gold chains, but also his boat and life!

(　　) 1. A. house	B. family	C. farm	D. factory
(　　) 2. A. get up	B. go to bed	C. go home	D. go to work
(　　) 3. A. buy	B. find	C. catch	D. eat
(　　) 4. A. resting	B. sleeping	C. swimming	D. fishing
(　　) 5. A. dangerous	B. light	C. heavy	D. safe
(　　) 6. A. glad	B. helpful	C. worried	D. strange
(　　) 7. A. food	B. fruit	C. clothes	D. money
(　　) 8. A. richer	B. the richest	C. poorer	D. the poorest
(　　) 9. A. listening	B. happening	C. thinking	D. saying
(　　) 10. A. found	B. had	C. lost	D. got

三、原文填空。

1. Sally Oliver meets two people with very different ________.
2. I play the saxophone in a ________ after work.
3. I'm an ________. My job is to ________ new things.
4. I do all my ________ work here.
5. I drink tea all day—I can't work ________ it.
6. I often ________ juggling.

四、用所给动词的正确形式填空。

1. ________ (not speak) with food in your mouth. It is not polite.
2. When something ________ (worry) me, I can always go to her for help.
3. Why not ________ (ring) the doorbell more loudly? Then someone will hear us.
4. Look! The women's pet dog ________ (chase) leaves in the garden over there.
5. Those hunters ________ (not hunt) any animals after they came into the forest.
6. I'm pleased with him because he is always willing ________ (share) his things with his friends.
7. Sandy enjoys singing for people better than ________ (tell) funny jokes.
8. It is careless of the boy ________ (knock) my dictionary and pens off the desk.
9. The headmaster ________ (think) of her life in the USA when she saw the picture on the wall.

五、用以下方框内的词填写句子。

me you him her us them

1. I think Tony is at home now. Can you phone ________?
2. It's Mr. Smith's birthday on Sunday. Can you send ________ a card?
3. Hello, Mum. Jenny and I are at Roy's house. Can you come and meet ________?
4. My grandparents live in another city. I always visit ________ in December.
5. Don't worry. I can help ________ with your English.

六、句型转换。

1. I like looking for new ideas.（对画线部分提问）
   ________ ________ you like ________ for?
2. I like English best.（改为同义句）
   English is my ________.
3. My father is an engineer. He works or big company.（合为一句）
   My father ________ ________ an engineer in a big company.
4. That girl eats eggs in the morning.（改为否定句）
   That girl ________ ________ eggs in the morning.
5. They enjoy playing tennis after school.（改为一般疑问句）
   ________ they ________ playing tennis after school?
6. The home address is in the top-right corner of the envelope.（对画线部分提问）
   ________ ________ the home address?
7. His brother has eaten a lot of vegetables.（对画线部分提问）
   ________ ________ his brother eaten?
8. I'd like to buy a new bike.（改为一般疑问句）
   ________ you ________ to buy a new bike?

七、首字母填空。

Charlie Chaplin broke into (1) s ________ business at the (2) a ________ of five because his mother, a music-hall performer, lost her voice (3) d ________ the performance and had to (4) l ________ the stage, and Charlie went on and (5) s ________ a well-known song. Halfway through the song a shower of money threw onto the stage. Charlie (6) s ________ singing and told the audience he (7) w ________ pick up the (8) m ________ first and then finish the (9) s ________. The audience (10) l ________. This was the first of millions of laughs in Charlie Chaplin's fabulous career.

Section Four

一、单项选择。

(　　)1. This shirt is very cheap. I'll ________ it.

A. bring　　B. love　　C. want　　D. take

(　　)2. —Is Sally from America?

—No. Sally is an ________ girl, but she's in ________ now.

A. America; England　　B. English; America

C. American; English　　D. England; America

(　　)3. Please ________ the picture. What can you ________?

A. look at; see　　B. see; look at

C. look at; look at　　D. see; see

(　　)4. The yellow coat ________ my new T-shirt and it ________ me very well.

A. matches; matches　　B. fits; matches

C. matches; fits　　D. fits; fits

(　　)5. It's time ________ an English lesson.

A. having　　B. to have　　C. have　　D. to having

(　　)6. Tom needs some help ________ his homework. Can you help ________?

A. to; he　　B. with; him　　C. to; him　　D. with; his

(　　)7. Amy thinks mooncakes are too sweet. She ________ eats them.

A. often　　B. always　　C. usually　　D. seldom

(　　)8. People use QQ to ________ with each other on the Internet.

A. speak　　B. say　　C. talk　　D. tell

(　　)9. — You look very cool today, Simon.

— ________________

A. Really? Thank you.　　B. Oh, I don't think so.

C. No. I am not cool at all.　　D. The same to you.

(　　)10. Sometimes I ________ some music on and ________ the drum.

A. get; run　　B. put; play　　C. play; play　　D. get; play

二、用所给词的适当形式填空。

1. It's interesting for us ________ (chat) with each other after lunch.
2. The students in our school practise ________ (run) once a day.
3. Your name is Lily. What about ________ (she)?
4. — Look! What's on those ________ (shelf)? — They are new CDs.
5. Mum says we should ________ (not eat) too many sweet snacks.
6. ________ (with) your help, I will never finish cooking the meal.
7. ________ (cross) the road when the light is green.
8. We are looking forward to ________ (visit) the World Park.
9. Thanks for ________ (give) us so much good advice in our study.
10. How did they celebrate ________ (child) Day last year?
11. My uncle ________ (fly) to Shanghai once a week.
12. —Who is the ________ (one) to come to school? —Oh, it's Mary.
13. At the moment the Greens ________ (cook) for dinner together.

三、根据本单元内容判断下列表述的正误。

(　　) 1. Jenny, the sound engineer working in a recording studio, goes to work on foot every day.

(　　) 2. Jenny's job is quite difficult, so she doesn't like it.

(　　) 3. Jenny can have a rest at home on weekends.

(　　) 4. Ian is an inventor who always gets up very late.

(　　) 5. First Ian turns on the answerphone because he can't speak to people when he has an idea.

四、阅读理解。

One day, a poor farmer took a bag of wheat(小麦) to town. He didn't know what to do when the bag fell off his horse. The bag was too heavy for him to lift. He hoped that someone would come and help him.

A minute later, a man came over. But the farmer's heart sank(下沉) when he saw the man because he was the great man in town. The farmer was afraid to ask him for help.

As soon as he came up to the farmer, the great man got off his horse and said, "You need my help, don't you? Let me help you." Then he took the bag and put it onto the horse.

"Sir," asked the farmer, "how can I pay you?"

"Well," the great man answered, "if you see anybody in need of help, do the same for him."

(　　)1. What happened when the farmer took his wheat to town?

A. The farmer couldn't find the way to town.

B. The bag of wheat fell off the horse.

C. The bag of wheat was lost.

D. The farmer fell off the horse.

(　　)2. Who came up after a while?

A. An old man.　B. A boy.　C. A man.　D. A rich farmer.

(　　)3. What did the great man do when he saw the farmer?

A. He helped the farmer to put the bag back onto the horse.

B. He walked past the farmer without saying anything.

C. He just said "Hello!" to the farmer.

D. He asked another man to help the farmer.

五、根据中文提示完成句子。

1. — Where is the ________(政府) office?

— It's on the second floor.

2. It is not polite to ask for a stranger's telephone number because it is too ________（私人的）.
3. I read an interesting ________（广告）in the newspaper.
4. Gun powder is one of the greatest ________（发明）in ancient China.
5. Pay attention to the ________ ________（营业时间）of this shop.
6. She was appearing in ________（公众）for the first time since her illness.
7. I always listen to music for ________（放松）.

Section Five

一、听下面五段对话，选出与对话意思相符的图片。

(　　)1. What's Jim going to do next Sunday?

A. 　B. 　C. 

(　　)2. Which sign can they see?

A. 　B. 

C. 

(　　)3. What does the man want to buy first?

A. 　B. 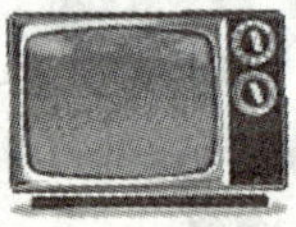　C. 

(　　)4. What does the man's father do?

A. 　B. 　C. 

(　　)5. What does the woman want to learn?

A. 　B. 　C. 

二、听下面五段对话，选择正确答案。

( )1. When is the woman's birthday?
A. On December 24. B. On December 25. C. On December 26.

( )2. Where were the woman and her father four years ago?
A. In China. B. In England. C. In America.

( )3. Where are the two speakers?
A. In the bus. B. At the bus stop.
C. In the Children's House.

( )4. Who runs the fastest?
A. Lucy. B. Lily. C. Kate.

( )5. When did the early bus leave?
A. At 6 : 25. B. At 6 : 30. C. At 6 : 35.

三、听下面几段对话，选择正确答案。

听下面一段对话，回答第 1 ~2 题。

( )1. What are they talking about?
A. A photo. B. A newspaper. C. A magazine.

( )2. What do you know about Tom?
A. He is shorter than Maria. B. He is younger than Maria.
C. He is thinner than Maria.

听下面一段对话，回答第 3 ~4 题。

( )3. Where does the woman want to go?
A. The bus station. B. The supermarket. C. The post office.

( )4. Which bus can take the woman there?
A. The No. 7 bus. B. The No. 1 bus. C. The No. 6 bus.

听下面一段对话，，回答第 5 ~7 题。

( )5. How is the man going to the zoo tomorrow?
A. By bus. B. By car. C. On foot.

( )6. When are they going to meet?
A. At 9 am. B. At 8 am. C. At 10 am.

( )7. Where are they going to have lunch?
A. In the zoo. B. At Mr. Wu's home. C. At school.

四、听短文，完成信息表。

• 9 : 00 a. m.	• Meet at __1__
• __2__	• Bus leaves
• 10 : 00 a. m.	• Arrive at South Hill School
• 10 : 30 a. m.	• __3__
• 11 : 45 a. m.	• Presentation of cup and medals
• 1 : 15 p. m.	• Get on the bus in front of the restaurant

( )1. A . the school gate B. the cinema gate C. Wildlife Restaurant

(　　)2. A. 9：15 a. m.　　B. 9：20 a. m.　　C. 9：25 a. m.

(　　)3. A. Bus leaves from the cinema
B. Get off the bus
C. The match starts

五、单项选择。

(　　)1. The shop ________ at 8：00 a. m. and it ________ for ten hours every day.
A. opens; is open　　B. is opened; opens
C. is open; has opened　　D. opened; opens

(　　)2. —Is this your sweater, Joy?
—No, It's not ________ sweater. ________ is yellow.
A. my; My　　B. my; Mine　　C. mine; Mine　　D. mine; My

(　　)3. I am thirsty. Could you let me have ________ coke?
A. little　　B. any　　C. some　　D. other

(　　)4. I don't want to read this book. There is ________ in it.
A. something interesting　　B. nothing interesting
C. interesting something　　D. interesting nothing

(　　)5. —Is the woman a teacher?
—Yes. She teaches ________ English.
A. you　　B. us　　C. our　　D. your

(　　)6. Look at the photo of my family. The boy ________ my father and my mother is me.
A. in　　B. on　　C. between　　D. of

(　　)7. This suit ________ him ________ very young.
A. makes; look　　B. make; looks　　C. makes; looks　　D. make; look

(　　)8. At the sports meeting, Amy ran ________.
A. as fast as she can　　B. as soon as she could
C. as fast as she could　　D. as sooner as she can

(　　)9. If you live near the shopping mall, you ________ go far to buy things.
A. have to　　B. haven't to　　C. don't have to　　D. needn't to

(　　)10. Those ________ people all have new ideas to ________ new things.
A. creating; invite　　B. creative; invent
C. creative; invented　　D. creating; inviting

(　　)11. — You look unhappy. What's wrong with you?　— I scored ________ points in my class.
A. the fewest　　B. the least　　C. the most　　D. fewer

(　　)12. I think ________ with friends is better than ________.
A. chat; watching TV　　B. chatting; watching TV
C. chatting; watch TV　　D. chat; watch TV

(　　)13. The workers wore glasses over their eyes to keep them ________.
A. save　　B. safe　　C. safely　　D. clearly

( )14. In the past, there was ________ library ________ hospital in my hometown.

A. no; and B. no; or C. not; and D. not; or

( )15. Don't eat ________ sweet food, or you'll be ________ fat.

A. too much; much too B. much too; much too

C. too much; too much D. much too; too much

六、完形填空。

Once there was a king who told some of his people to dig a pond(池子). The king then told his people that one person __1__ each family had to bring a glass of milk during the night and put it into the pond. So, by the morning, the pond should be __2__ of milk.

After __3__ the order, everyone went home. As one man prepared his milk, he thought that since everyone was bringing milk, he would just __4__ a glass of water and put that into the pond instead. __5__ it was dark at night, no one would notice it, so he quickly went and put the water into the pond and __6__ home.

In the morning, the king went to visit the pond. To his __7__, the pond was only filled with water! What happened? Yes! Everyone had the same idea __8__ that man. They all thought, "I don't have to waste my milk. Someone else will do it."

Dear friends, when you plan to help poor people or people in trouble, do not think that __9__ will take care of it. Instead, it starts with you. If you don't do it, no one else will, so change yourself and make a __10__.

( )1. A. at B. from C. on D. with

( )2. A. filled B. empty C. crowded D. full

( )3. A. giving B. refusing C. receiving D. offering

( )4. A. hide B. steal C. waste D. drink

( )5. A. If B. Since C. While D. After

( )6. A. left B. came C. returned D. arrived

( )7. A. surprise B. satisfaction C. joy D. taste

( )8. A. with B. to C. as D. of

( )9. A. others B. the others C. none D. neither

( )10. A. face B. mistake C. living D. difference

七、阅读理解。

"Dreams may be more important than sleep. We all need dreams," some scientists say.

Dreams take up about one quarter of our sleeping time. People have several dreams each night. Dreams are like short films. They are usually in colour. Some dreams are like old films. They come to us over and over again. That may be because the dreamer is worrying about something. Dreaming may be a way of trying to find an answer.

Some people get new ideas about their work from dreams. They may think about their work all day. These ideas can carry over into dreams.

Sometimes we wake up with a good feeling from a dream. But often we can't remember the dream. Dreams can go away quickly.

Too much dreaming can be harmful. The more we sleep, the longer we dream. The mind is hard at work when we dream. That is why we may have a long sleep and still wake up tired.

(　　)1. It may be less important to sleep than to ________.

A. think　　B. dream　　C. work　　D. study

(　　)2. Dreams and films are usually ________

A. very long　　B. in colour　　C. about work　　D. very sad

(　　)3. Why do some people often dream about their work?

A. Because they are tired in the daytime.

B. Because they are not interested in their work.

C. Because they may think about their work all day.

D. Because they have too much work to do.

(　　)4. Which of the following is NOT true?

A. Dreams may be helpful to people sometimes.

B. Too much dreaming may be bad for people.

C. People always remember their dreams quickly.

D. People sometimes wake up tired if they have a lot of dreams while sleeping.

(　　)5. The story mainly tells us ________.

A. what dreams are　　B. people like sleep

C. dreams are like films　　D. we always remember dreams

八、首字母填空。

Only Mother Love is (1)t ______ love. It gives everybody everything all his life. When you are still a baby, mother takes good care of you as much as (2)p ______. In your waking hours she always holds you in her (3)a ______. When you are ill, she stops her work right now to look after you day and night and forgets about (4)h ______. When you are growing up day by day, she feels very happy. When you are old enough to go to school, mother still looks after you all the time. On cold winter days, she always tells you to put on (5)m ______ clothes. She always stands in the wind waiting for you (6)b ______ from school. When you hurry(匆忙) to leave home with little breakfast, she always feels worried about you at home. She usually knows about your study and (7)s ______ much money on your school things. When you do well at school, you will see the brightest (8)s ______ on her face.

Mother is always ready to give everything she has to her children, not to (9)r ______. What true love it is in the world! We will (10)r ______ Mother Love forever!

Unit 8

Section One

一、根据你所学过的课文填空。

1. Mrs. Boffin: Go to the ______ and get ______ and some ______ please, dear.
   Professor: Good morning. ______________, please?
2. Mrs. Boffin: Don't ________! Oh! Look at those eggs!
3. Mother, father and Sue ________. Sandy ________.
4. They all had ________, ________ and ________. "Yum! Yum!" Sandy said.
5. "________________?" father asked.
   "Yes, thank you, Dad," Sue answered. "It was a lovely treat," Sandy said.

二、仿造例句写句子。

eg: Were there any bananas in the basket yesterday? / on the table
There weren't any bananas in the basket yesterday.
There were some bananas on the table yesterday.

1. Was there any snow on the mountain last month? /in the tree
   ____
   ____
2. Were there any students on the playground 5 minutes ago? / in the classroom
   ____
   ____

eg: greengrocer / watermelons
The greengrocer didn't have any watermelons yesterday, but he has some today.

3. baker / hamburger
   ____
4. stationer/ colour pencil
   ____

eg: Sandy/ a hamburger/ a cake
Did Sandy have a hamburger?
He didn't have a hamburger, but he had a cake.

5. Miss Green/ lunch/supper
   ____

____

三、用所给词的适当形式填空。

1. That boy was angry and he ______________ (hit) the naughty dog.
2. I went to the supermarket and ______________ (get) some oranges.
3. She ______________ (ask) her teacher some questions yesterday.
4. We ______________ (have) some noodles this morning.
5. Wendy ______________ (see) a toy rabbit in her bed. She was very happy.
6. What about ______________ (go) to the movies?
7. The family ______________ (have) a holiday last month.
8. ______________ (not play) in the street!
9. — May I ______________ (use) your dictionary?
   — Of course. Please ______________ (go) and get it.
10. Can you ______________ (drive) a car, Bob?

四、单项选择。

(　　) 1. — Why did he ________ to Beijing?
— Because he ________ to work there.
A. come; wanted　B. came; want　C. go; want　D. go; wanted

(　　) 2. — ________ she do her housework yesterday afternoon?
— No, she ________.
A. Did; doesn't　B. Does; didn't
C. Did; didn't　D. Was; wasn't

(　　) 3. — Did they ________ an Maths class this morning?
— Yes, they ________.
A. have; had　B. had; did
C. had; had　D. have; did

(　　) 4. ________ he enjoy ________ the orange juice in that bar?
A. Does; drink　B. Did; drinking
C. Is; drinking　D. Had; drank

(　　) 5. — ________ Sandy and Sue have toast for breakfast?
— Yes, they did.
A. Did　B. Does　C. Do　D. Have

(　　) 6. He ________ anything in the book store last week.
A. didn't bought　B. Don't buy　C. bought　D. didn't buy

(　　) 7. Mother was out yesterday afternoon, so I ________ the supper.
A. cook　B. cooked　C. cooks　D. is cooking

五、句型转换。

1. Tony kept in bed the day before yesterday.（改为否定句）

____

2. Give him a carrot!（改为否定句）

____

3. You'd better stay at home all day.（改为否定句）

____

4. Draw those animals on the wall.（改为一般疑问句）

____

5. We went to the station with grandpa today.（改为一般疑问句）

____

6. Mom put some sticking-plaster around Sandy's finger.（改为一般疑问句）

____

7. Father and Sandy had <u>some steak</u>.（对画线部分提问）

____

8. I went to the dentist's <u>this afternoon</u>.（对画线部分提问）

____

9. Get some eggs for me, please.（换一种说法）

____

10. Show me the newspaper, please.（换一种说法）

____

Section Two

一、根据你所学过的课文填空。

1. Grandmother and grandfather ________ this morning.
   They ________________________.
2. We ________ for them at the ________.
   They ________ train. The train ________ at ________.
3. "What lovely flowers!" Mrs. Boffin said.
   "________, dear," Professor Boffin said.
4. "It's the 27th __________. I __________ this year."
5. Mrs. Boffin smiled.
   "My birthday ______________," she answered.
   "But thank you __________. __________."

二、仿造例句写句子。

eg: Tom/ a banana /an apple
    Tom wanted a banana. He didn't want an apple.

1. Grace/a flute/a water-pistol

____

2. Sam/ a shave/a haircut

____

eg：watched television/ yesterday/the day before yesterday
Did you watched television yesterday?
No, I didn't watch television yesterday.
I watched television the day before yesterday.

3. tasted the cake/ last night/ this evening

____

____

____

4. paid the bill/ this afternoon/ this morning

____

____

____

eg：father answered the telephone/ this morning/ this afternoon
Father didn't answer the telephone this morning.
He answered the telephone this afternoon.

5. Sue poured gravy over her food/ this morning/this evening

____

____

6. The children copied their exercises/last night/ the night before last

____

____

三、单项选择。

(　　)1. We ________ a good time last weekend.
A. have　B. had　C. had not　D. there was

(　　) 2. — Where ________ you last Sunday?
— I ________ at home.
A. were; was　B. are; am　C. were; am　D. are; was

(　　) 3. She doesn't ________ her homework in the afternoon.
A. doing　B. to do　C. does　D. do

(　　) 4. He ________ his key. He needs some help.
A. lose　B. is losing　C. lost　D. losed

(　　) 5. — Did they ________ an English class this morning?
— Yes, they ________.
A. have; had　B. had; did　C. had; had　D. have; did

(　　) 6. Is the boy ________ something?
A. eats　B. eat　C. eating　D. ate

(　　) 7. What ________ you ________ last night?
A. did; do　B. was; doing　C. were; did　D. did; did

四、句型转换。

1. There was some cream in the bowl.（改为否定句）

____

2. He played basketball after class.（改为否定句）

____

3. There were many vegetables in the refrigerator yesterday.（改为否定句）

____

4. We had a nice dinner last night.（改为一般疑问句）

____

5. She has to finish her homework before dinner.（改为一般疑问句）

____

6. We lived in Wuhan.（改为一般疑问句）

____

7. I would like to have a cup of tea.（改为一般疑问句）

____

8. The new term began at <u>February 3rd</u>.（对画线部分提问）

____

9. The dictionary was <u>Susan's</u>.（对画线部分提问）

____

10. They were <u>in the garden</u> the night before last.（对画线部分提问）

____

五、将下列短语或句子翻译成相应的英文表达。

1. 祝你长寿

____

2. 迟到总比不到好

____

3. 西蒙昨天没有上学，他得了感冒。

____

4. 爸爸前天付好了账单。

____

Section Three

一、看图写句子。

eg: 

the day before yesterday

I played badminton with my parents and my sister the day before yesterday.

this afternoon

Alice didn't read a book under the tree this afternoon.

1. 

last month

2. 

yesterday afternoon

3. 

last night

4. 

this evening

二、单项选择。

(　　) 1. We'll ________ our class in an hour.
A. began　B. beginning　C. to begin　D. begin

(　　) 2. — Where is your mother, Sue?
— She ________ the flowers in the garden.
A. waters　B. has watered　C. is watering　D. watered

(　　) 3. The glasses he ________ a moment ago are broken. He needs a new pair.
A. wore　B. wear　C. wearing　D. worn

(　　) 4. You'd better ________ Jim about plans just yet.
A. don't tell　B. not tell　C. not telling　D. not to tell

(　　) 5. — Hurry up! We're all waiting for you.
— I ________ for an important phone call. Go without me.
A. wait　B. was waiting　C. am waiting　D. waited

(　　) 6. Let's get some water and ________ the classroom.
A. clean　B. cleaning　C. to clean　D. cleaned

(　　) 7. He usually goes to school by bus, but yesterday he ________ a taxi.
A. takes　B. took　C. is taking　D. will take

三、阅读理解。

I heard the bees long before I saw them.

It was a very hot afternoon, and we decided to cool off in the river near my home. As we climbed down a small rocky hill towards the water, my boyfriend John suddenly started to shout then jumped into the water below. Peter and Mary quickly followed but

I was too far away to jump. I was trapped.

I heard a low hum(嗡嗡声), which was growing louder. From a distance, the group of bees looked almost like a cloud of smoke. As it got closer, I realized it was actually thousands of bees flying towards me.

All I could do was cover my face with my hands. Crazily, I thought that if I sat very still(不动的), the bees would think I was just another rock.

After a few seconds, I knew my plan hadn't worked. The bees were attacking me. I could hear my friends shouting at me to get down to the pool fast.

But it wasn't so easy. I was in great pain and the only way I could get away was to use my hands to climb down the rocks. However, I was afraid to do that at first because my face would be unprotected. The noise the bees made was so loud and frightening, but I had no choice.

I rushed down the rocks and jumped into the pool, but I don't remember doing it. I was just so happy to be free from the pain. I was safe, and the water felt wonderful.

But we still weren't out of danger. Every time we tried to climb out of the pool, the bees flew back over our heads. We spent the next three hours in the water, putting our heads under the water from time to time to avoid the bees until they finally lost interest.

( ) 1. How many people went swimming that day?

A. Two. B. Three. C. Four. D. Five.

( ) 2. The underlined word "it" (in paragraph 3) refers to "________".

A. a rock B. the group of bees

C. a hill D. the river

( ) 3. At first why didn't the writer want to climb down the rocks?

A. She was afraid she would fall.

B. She was too far away from the pool.

C. She thought the bees would follow her.

D. She didn't want her face to be unprotected.

( ) 4. How did the writer escape the bees?

A. She covered her face with her hands.

B. She hid behind the rocks.

C. She jumped into a water pool.

D. She pretended to be a rock.

( ) 5. In what order are the following mentioned in the story?

a. The writer rushed down the rocks.

b. John jumped into the water.

c. The low hum grew louder.

d. The bees flew back over their heads.

e. The bees were attacking the writer.

A. b, c, e, a, d. B. b, a, e, c, d.

C. c, d, e, a, b. D. c, b, d, e, a.

Section Four

一、根据你所学过的课文填空。

1. They went home today and ______________________.
   On the way ______________________.
   "______________," grandpa said.
2. Yesterday ______________. It was Sandy's unlucky day.
   In the morning ______________.
3. In the evening ______________, but Sandy didn't mind at all.
   "______________" he said, and ______________!

二、写出下列动词的过去式形式。

1. is/am ________	2. cut ________	3. ask ________
4. put ________	5. arrive ________	6. meet ________
7. shut ________	8. sleep ________	9. light ________
10. read ________	11. say ________	12. spend ________

三、为每个单词选出正确的词义。

(　　) 1. course　　A. a person who takes other people's things and keep for himself or sell those for money
(　　) 2. stationery　　B. part of a meal served at one time
(　　) 3. share　　C. give trouble or pain to
(　　) 4. thief　　D. materials for writing; paper, pens, etc.
(　　) 5. hurt　　E. to have, use, pay or take part in something with others

四、单项选择。

(　　)1. I saw ________ enjoy ________ in the park.
　　A. them; themselves　　B. they; them
　　C. she; herself　　D. her; hers

(　　)2. We often ________ our teacher ________ help.
　　A. ask; to　　B. asks; for
　　C. ask; for　　D. want; to

(　　) 3. I wasn't ________ about the exam. He ________.
　　A. worry; wasn't, either　　B. worried; wasn't, either
　　C. worry; wasn't, too　　D. worried; wasn't, too

(　　) 4. The used car ________ 500 dollars.
　　A. cost　　B. pay　　C. worth　　D. spend

( ) 5. The number of the boy babies ________ much larger than that of the girl babies these years.

A. are B. was C. is D. were

( ) 6. We usually have classes ________ the afternoon. But we don't have any classes ________ Friday afternoon.

A. on; on B. in; in C. on; in D. in; on

五、句型转换。

1. My cotton shirt feels as smooth as the silk one.（变为否定句）

____

2. He bought some flowers for his wife yesterday.（变为一般疑问句）

____

3. I didn't finish my homework.（对画线部分提问）

____

4. He liked playing games when he was young.（对画线部分提问）

____

5. I didn't go out because of the rain.（对画线部分提问）

____

六、完形填空。(2011年武汉市中考)

I didn't cry when I learned I was the parent of a disabled child. I just sat still and didn't say anything.

When Jenny was old enough, I sent her to a kindergarten(幼儿园). On the first morning, Jenny spent hours playing by herself. It seemed that she felt very __1__. However, to my joy, Jenny's classmates always __2__ her, "You got all your spelling words right today!" In fact, her spelling list was the __3__. Later, she faced a very painful __4__ — at the end of the term, there was a game which had __5__ to do with physical education. But Jenny was __6__ in it.

My husband and I were anxious about the day. I wanted to let my child stay home! But my heart wouldn't let me off that easily. So I __7__ a pale, unwilling Jenny onto the school bus.

At the kindergarten, I was quite worried because of her __8__ action, Jenny would probably hold up her team. The game went well until it was time for the sack (麻袋) race. Surely Jenny would find it __9__. Now each child had to climb into a sack, jump to the finishing line, return and climb out of the sack. I noticed Jenny standing near the end of her line of players.

But as it's her turn to join, a change took place in her __10__. The tallest boy behind Jenny placed his hands on her waist (腰). Two other boys __11__ in front of her. The moment the player before Jenny stepped out from the sack, the two boys

__12__ the sack suddenly and kept it open while the tall boy lifted Jenny and __13__ her into it. A girl nearby took her hand and supported her __14__ Jenny got her balance. Then she jumped forward, smiling and proud. In the cheers of the teachers, schoolmates and parents, I silently thanked the warm, understanding people in life who made it __15__ for my disabled daughter to be like her fellow human beings. Then I finally cried.

( ) 1. A. excited	B. lonely	C. happy	D. weak
( ) 2. A. greeted	B. expected	C. encouraged	D. followed
( ) 3. A. easiest	B. longest	C. smallest	D. tidiest
( ) 4. A. choice	B. problem	C. result	D. exam
( ) 5. A. nothing	B. anything	C. everything	D. something
( ) 6. A. forward	B. fast	C. behind	D. up
( ) 7. A. threw	B. pushed	C. knocked	D. fixed
( ) 8. A. slow	B. quiet	C. quick	D. secret
( ) 9. A. stupid	B. simple	C. relaxing	D. difficult
( ) 10. A. school	B. family	C. team	D. heart
( ) 11. A. ran	B. lay	C. walked	D. stood
( ) 12. A. picked up	B. gave up	C. cut up	D. made up
( ) 13. A. drove	B. hid	C. put	D. hit
( ) 14. A. when	B. until	C. after	D. unless
( ) 15. A. popular	B. special	C. necessary	D. possible

Section Five

一、将你听到的单词或短语写在下面的横线上。

1. ______	2. ______	3. ______	4. ______
5. ______	6. ______	7. ______	8. ______
9. ______	10. ______	11. ______	12. ______
13. ______	14. ______	15. ______	16. ______
17. ______	18. ______	19. ______	20. ______

二、选出你所听到的句子。

( ) 1. A. Can we meet at the theatre?
B. Shall we meet at the theatre?
C. Let's meet at the theatre.

( ) 2. A. They are going to the art gallery on Tuesday.
B. They are going to go to the garden on Tuesday.
C. They are going to go to the art gallery on Tuesday.

( ) 3. A. Let me show you the park.

B. Let me show you around the park.

C. Let me tell you about the park.

( ) 4. A. Mrs. Black often meets her friends for tea.

B. Mrs. Black often gives her friends tea.

C. Mrs. Black often meets her friends at tea time.

( ) 5. A. My little brother always goes to school by car.

B. My mother always cuts her fingers.

C. My little brother always counts on his fingers.

三、听句子，并选择正确的答语。

( ) 1. A. He wants to see the doctor. B. He looks ill.
C. He looks like a doctor.

( ) 2. A. Quite far away. B. I take the bus.
C. More than 30 minutes.

( ) 3. A. Yes, it's next to the park. B. No, I don't know.
C. Yes, I can.

( ) 4. A. It likes fish. B. It's white and black.
C. It's one year old.

( ) 5. A. OK, be quick please. B. It's very kind of you.
C. Thank you all the same.

( ) 6. A. He lost his schoolbag. B. He was very sad.
C. He is crying.

( ) 7. A. About 5 minutes' walk. B. It's more than 5 minutes.
C. It's 5 minutes' long.

( ) 8. A. Every 2 days. B. For 2 days.
C. In 2 days.

( ) 9. A. I don't like it. B. Yes, there's something wrong with it.
C. It doesn't work.

( ) 10. A. They will go home by car. B. They will be very tired.
C. They will be football stars.

四、听句子，选出一个与你所听到的句子意思相近的选项。

( ) 1. A. Football is the American people's favourite sport.

B. Not all Chinese people like football.

C. Many Chinese like football, but Americans don't.

( ) 2. A. Mary doesn't like the cake at all.

B. Mary likes the cake a lot.

C. The cakes are not delicious at all.

( ) 3. A. The teacher knows no one in the class.

B. The teacher knows someone in the class.

C. The teacher knows all the students in the class.

(　　) 4. A. Dick and Jones like football.
B. Dick and Jones don't like basketball.
C. Dick likes basketball, Jones likes too.

(　　) 5. A. Peter works for ten hours and forty-five minutes.
B. Peter works for nine and a half hours.
C. Peter works for eleven hours and fifty minutes.

五、单项选择。

(　　) 1. We ________ a good time last weekend.
A. have　B. had not　C. had　D. there was

(　　) 2. ________ she at school yesterday afternoon?
A. Is　B. Were　C. Did　D. Was

(　　) 3. Anybody, ________ me a hand.
A. to give　B. gives　C. give　D. giving

(　　) 4. I'll stay here for ________ two days.
A. the other　B. others　C. another　D. the others

(　　) 5. ________ down the radio, because the baby is sleeping.
A. Turning　B. Turn　C. Turned　D. To turn

(　　) 6. He ________ home last week and he likes ________ home every week.
A. go; going　B. went; going　C. goes; go　D. went; go

六、根据你所学过的课文填空。

1. I'm ________ that I haven't any matches.
2. Don't hit your ________ like that!
3. Last week, mother, father and the children had lunch at a ________.
4. Grandma and grandpa had some lovely ________ for us.
5. Professor Boffin carried the ________ of flowers home.
6. It ________ in the middle of the road and it stopped all the ________.
7. We laughed but the car drivers were very ________.
8. The donkey noticed the ________ and jumped up.
9. We arrived at the ________ at half past eleven and said goodbye.
10. Mother put some ________ on Sandy's finger and it hurt a lot!

七、根据要求变换句型。

1. I can go to school by bike.（改为否定句）

____

2. I had a maths lesson an hour ago.（改为一般疑问句）

____

3. Mom cut her finger last night.（对画线部分提问）

____

4. Sandy had lunch at school.（对画线部分提问）

____

5. Give him a carrot, please.（换一种说法）

____

八、完形填空。

A new term has begun. Teachers are __1__ about the fact that new students are not easy to handle. They like to bring cellphones and MP3 players to school. What is __2__, some students even use cellphones to do with out-of-class matters in class, or sometimes just for fun. Some other students listen to MP3 players when they are having a lesson that they are not interested in. Are these new students really that __3__? "Yes," says Delaney Kirk, a professor at Drake University. __4__ she adds it's not their fault. Instead, the things that they bring into school—cellphones, MP3 players and so on—and the teachers are to blame. Kirk first began thinking about students' manners six years ago. "I had my first class in which students were sleeping or talking to each other. It seemed that learning well __5__ nothing to do with them," she says. "At first, I got worried about this, but then I said to myself, 'You're teaching __6__, and you need to manage this ... ' These students need to know more about manners. It's time to help them develop some good __7__. They shouldn't waste time doing nothing when they are young. Sooner or later, they might regret the time they have wasted." Kirk also __8__ a list of suggestions to help teachers better manage their classes. The following are among her suggestions: Tell students how they will benefit by taking the class. On the first day of class, emphasize its importance __9__ giving some homework that students must turn in next time. Do not allow them to bring cellphones and MP3 players to the class at all. Decide __10__ formal and informal the class will be.

(　　) 1. A. excited　B. worried　C. surprised　D. interested

(　　) 2. A. bad　B. worse　C. good　D. better

(　　) 3. A. rude　B. polite　C. friendly　D. curious

(　　) 4. A. But　B. However　C. And　D. Therefore

(　　) 5. A. learned　B. did　C. had　D. shared

(　　) 6. A. management　B. English　C. Chinese　D. lessons

(　　) 7. A. ideas　B. speeches　C. habits　D. classes

(　　) 8. A. makes　B. brings　C. gets　D. takes

(　　) 9. A. of　B. on　C. at　D. by

(　　) 10. A. what　B. how　C. which　D. why

九、阅读理解。

We know that many animals do not stay in one place. Birds, fish and other animals move from one place to another at a certain time. They move for different reasons: most of them move to find food more easily, but others move to get away from places that are too crowded.

When cold weather comes, many birds move to warmer places to find food. Some fish give birth in warm water and move to cold water to feed. The most famous migration (迁移) is probably the migration of the fish, which is called "salmon". This fish is born in fresh water but it travels many miles to salt water. There it spends its life. When it is old, it returns to its birthplace in fresh water. Then it gives birth and dies there. In northern Europe, there is a kind of mouse. They leave their mountain homes when they become too crowded. They move down to the low land. Sometimes they move all the way to the seaside, and many of them are killed when they fall into the sea.

Recently, scientists have studied the migration of a kind of lobster (龙虾). Every year, when the season of bad weather arrives, the lobsters get into a long time and start to walk across the floor of the ocean. Nobody knows why they do this, and nobody knows where they go.

So, sometimes we know why humans and animals move from one place to another, bur at other times we don't. Maybe living things just like to travel.

( ) 1. Most animals move from one place to another at a certain time to ________.

A. give birth　　B. enjoy warmer weather

C. find food more easily　　D. find beautiful places

( ) 2. The fish called "salmon" spends a long life in ________.

A. salt water　　B. its birthplace　　C. fresh water　　D. rivers

( ) 3. The mice in northern Europe move when ________.

A. they give birth　　B. the weather is bad

C. the place gets too crowded　　D. they haven't enough food

( ) 4. The lobsters move ________.

A. to the fresh water　　B. to the sea floor

C. at a certain time　　D. to find more food

( ) 5. What is the main idea of the passage?

A. Animals move in order to find food more easily.

B. The migration of the fish called "salmon" is the most famous migration.

C. Living things move from one place to another because they like to travel.

D. Sometimes we know why and how living things move from one place to another, but sometimes we don't.

Unit 9

Section One

一、根据你所学过的课文填空。

1. During the night ______________________________.
   He sat up in bed and ____________.
2. We both ________. The light ________. We were both afraid.
3. Then we ________. "I was hungry," father said. "____________.
   Do you want one?"
4. This morning mother got up early ______________.
   The kitchen ______________!
5. Then father, Sandy and I went downstairs as well.
   "______________?" mother asked.
   "______________," father answered.

二、根据例句写句子。

eg: Mother brought them some bread / during the morning / the meal
Did mother bring them some bread during the morning?
She didn't bring them some bread during the morning.
She brought them some bread during the meal.

1. Father sat at his desk/during the lesson/the day
   ____
   ____
   ____
2. Sue made a snowman/ during the game/this morning
   ____
   ____
   ____
3. The sun shone everyday/ during March/August
   ____
   ____
   ____

4. The children came home/this evening/this afternoon

____

____

____

5. The children wore their uniform/ on Friday/ on Monday

____

____

____

三、写出下列动词的过去式形式。

1. bring ________	2. buy ________	3. fight ________
4. think ________	5. hold ________	6. make ________
7. stand ________	8. tell ________	9. shine ________
10. drink ________	11. drive ________	12. eat ________
13. give ________	14. go ________	15. come ________
16. wear ________	17. take ________	18. forget ________

四、用所给词的适当形式填空。

1. — Where ________ they ________ (spend) the summer holiday?
   — They plan ________ (go) to Europe.
2. Can you ________ (drive) a car, Bob?
3. He is good at ________ (swim).
4. The bird ________ (be) in the tree ten minutes ago, but now it ________ (fly) over the trees.
5. Tim doesn't ________ (like) tea. He ________ (like) coffee.
6. ________ (be) there any bicycles in the street last night?
7. — Where ________ (be) the children now?
   — They ________ (be) here a minute ago. Perhaps they ________ (have) a P. E. lesson in the playground.
8. The baby can ________ (dress) himself. Look! He ________ (put) on his socks now.
9. Mother usually ________ (have) tea with her friends on Fridays, but next Friday she ________ (go) to the concert.
10. We'll be free this afternoon. How about ________ (visit) the art gallery?

五、单项选择。

( ) 1. The boy ________ fifteen years old next year.
A. is going to be B. will C. is growing to be D. is

( ) 2. You'd better ________ the window, it's too cold outside.
A. not to open B. not open C. not opening D. don't open

( ) 3. — Where ________ you last Sunday?

— I ________ at home.

A. were; was　B. are; am　C. were; am　D. are; was

(　　) 4. I hope I ________ visit the museum some day.

A. am　B. can　C. was　D. do

(　　) 5. — What happened ________ him?

— He had a car accident last week.

A. in　B. on　C. for　D. to

(　　) 6. We ________ a good time last weekend.

A. have　B. had　C. were　D. had not

(　　) 7. Be careful. The train ________.

A. is going to come　B. comes　C. is coming　D. will come

六、将下列句子翻译成相应的英文表达。

1. 昨天早上我们两人都迟到了。

____

2. 昨晚他看见爸爸在厨房喝茶。

____

3. 我今天早上看见妈妈穿过了公园。

____

4. 晚饭时妈妈给他们拿了些牛排。

____

5. 我们两个都很害怕独自在家。

____

Section Two

一、根据你所学过的课文填空。

1. ________________________________ and passed it to Lillie.
2. Lillie read it and ________________.
3. I didn't read it because ________________.
   He ________________.
4. During play time ________________.
   It said: ________! "________________" I said.

二、根据例句写句子。

eg: Jim and Tom usually drink some coffee. / at tea time

They drank some coffee at tea time as well.

When did they drink coffee?

1. The children usually have some bananas. / during lunch

____

____

2. Mother usually goes shopping. / in the afternoon

____

____

3. Lucy usually go to school by bus. / on Friday

____

____

eg：Father wrote a letter. / in the morning / in the evening

Did father write a letter in the morning?

He didn't write a letter in the morning.

He wrote a letter in the evening.

4. Sandy and Sue ran to school. / this morning/yesterday morning

____

____

____

5. A thief broke the window. / this evening/ at midnight

____

____

____

6. Sandy showed his water-pistol to his friends. /during the lesson /during playtime

____

____

____

三、写出下列动词的过去式形式。

1. write ________	2. run ________	3. ring ________
4. sing ________	5. ride ________	6. wake ________
7. speak ________	8. break ________	9. show ________

四、单项选择。

(　　) 1. — One of my friends had a car accident last month.

— ________

A. That's too bad!　　B. I see.

C. I'm sorry to hear that.　　D. It's OK.

(　　) 2. My mother tells me ________ online for long time.

A. not stay　　B. to not stay

C. not to stay　　D. not stayed

(　　) 3. —I'm going to Beijing for a holiday.

— ____________________

A. Good bye.　　B. You are right.

C. It's good.　　D. Have a good time.

(　　) 4. I'm going to the library ________ some books on geography.

A. borrow　　B. to borrow

C. borrowing　　D. to lend

(　　) 5. You'd better ________ silent about this.

A. not keep　　B. keeping

C. to not keep　　D. not kept

(　　) 6. —________

— Nothing but a little sick.

— Take care of yourself, dear.

A. What's that?　　B. What's your name?

C. Is it wrong?　　D. What's the matter?

五、阅读下面的短文，根据其内容从所给的 12 个单词中选出最恰当的 8 个填入空中。

in; serious; spent; working; but; on; keeps; weak; ahead; edge; grows; side

After two weeks of worry, a farmer in the north of England was very happy yesterday. James Tuke, a farmer who (1) ________ sheep, lost his dog, Sally, when they were out working together a fortnight ago.

"Sally was running (2) ________ of me," he said, "and disappeared over the top of the hill. I whistled and called (3) ________ she didn't come. She's young, so I thought perhaps she'd gone back to the farmhouse (4) ________ her own. But she wasn't there. Over the next few days I (5) ________ as much time as I could looking for her. I was afraid that I would never see her again. Then a neighbour said she'd heard an animal crying while she was out walking near the (6) ________ of a cliff. I rushed out and found Sally on a shelf of rock halfway down. She was thin and (7) ________ but she had no (8) ________ injuries. She was really lucky!"

六、将下列句子翻译成相应的英文表达。

1. 早上教室里非常乱，而且灯都开着。

____

2. 下午时 Professor Boffin 又忘记了带雨伞。

____

3. 妈妈像往常一样下午和朋友们一起喝咖啡。

____

Section Three

一、根据例句写句子。

eg: The wind blew very hard. / today/yesterday

Did the wind blow very hard today?

The wind didn't blow very hard today.

The wind blew very hard yesterday.

1. The sun set very early. / in October/ in December

______

______

______

2. Father began work very late. / on Tuesday morning/on Monday morning

______

______

______

3. Sue hurt her head very much. / an hour ago/a few minutes ago

______

______

______

eg：Sandy and Sue are going to go to school on foot. /this morning

They went to school on foot this morning as well.

When did Sandy and Sue go to school on foot?

4. Miss Smith's going to draw a picture. / this evening

______

______

5. The children are going to go to the funfair. / after school

______

______

6. Sue's going to give a speech. / on Friday

______

______

二、单项选择。

(　　) 1. He ______ magazines in the morning and ______ TV in the evening.

A. watched; saw　　B. read; watched

C. looked; watched　　D. saw; watched

(　　) 2. I don't know if she ______ to the beach. If it ______, she will go.

A. goes; won't rain　　B. goes; doesn't

C. will go; doesn't rain　　D. will go; won't go

(　　) 3. Can you ask him ______ a message ______ your father?

A. have; to　　B. to take; to

C. to give; for　　D. bringing; for

(　　) 4. You may go and ask him. He knows ______ about that.

A. few　　B. a few　　C. little　　D. a little

(　　) 5. When I saw an old friend of ______, I stopped ______ to him.

A. me; talking　　B. mine; to talk

C. mine; talking　　　D. me; to talk

(　　) 6. — ________ is it from here?

— It's about ten minutes' walk.

A. How long　B. How far　C. How often　D. How soon

三、阅读理解。(2010年武汉市中考英语A卷)

One midnight, a little girl woke up to pass water. She by herself got up and down her bed, walked to the bedroom door and opened it. She looked outside and walked back, for it was so dark in the hall that she feared.

Her mother said, "Don't be afraid, honey. Take courage!"

"What's courage?" she asked, running to her mother's bed.

"Courage is the brave breath," her mother answered.

"Mum, do you have courage?"

"Certainly."

The girl held out her little hands, saying, "Mum, blow some of your breath of courage to me."

After her mother blew out two mouthfuls of breath into her little cold hands, the little girl clenched her fists(握拳) nervously, afraid that the "breath of courage" would run away. Then with her fists clenched, she walked out of the bedroom towards the bathroom with nothing to fear.

Her mother said to herself, "It will be nice if someone can blow some kind of 'breath' to me. Then I can hold it in my hands too when I feel terrified or lost."

In fact, mostly, what we are terrified of is nothing but the fear in our mind. Who we should defeat(战胜) is nobody but ourselves.

(　　) 1. The girl walked back because ________.

A. the bathroom was too far away

B. her mother wouldn't go with her

C. she was too afraid of the dark

D. the bedroom door was locked

(　　) 2. We learn from the reading that ________.

A. the girl went to the bathroom by herself

B. the girl pretended to be terrified of nothing

C. the girl's mother was able to blow brave breath

D. the girl's mother was very proud of herself

(　　) 3. To stop "mother's breath" from running away, the girl ________.

A. held out her little hands　　B. clenched her fists

C. talk to her mother　　D. held her own breath

(　　) 4. The writer mainly wants to tell us that ________.

A. adults are always brave enough

B. children learn to be brave quickly

C. the fear in one's mind is the real problem

D. the mother can deal with anything with breath

(　　) 5. Which is the best title of the passage?

A. The Fearless Mother.　　B. One Lonely Girl.

C. One Midnight.　　D. The Breath of Courage.

Section Four

一、根据你所学的课文填空。(每空填一词)

1. The other day it rained ________, so we ________.
2. We ________ a ________.
3. We ________ a ________ of ________, some ________ ________ and some string.
4. We worked ________ for two hours.
5. At last the ________ was ________.
6. We ________ his ________.
7. Then Sandy ________ the ________ and our ________ ________.
8. He ________ ________ ________.

二、单项选择。

(　　) 1. When I was ________ high school, I had a part-time job ________ McDonald's.

A. in; inside　　B. from; in　　C. on; at　　D. in; at

(　　) 2. I don't enjoy computer games now, but I ________ like them when I was younger.

A. was used to　　B. used to　　C. would　　D. shall

(　　) 3. — Hi! You look tired.

— Yes, I'm busy ________ for my English exam tomorrow.

A. written　　B. do　　C. preparing　　D. to work

(　　) 4. If you don't know the meaning of a word, ____ it ____ in a dictionary.

A. look; out　　B. find; out　　C. look; up　　D. watch; out

(　　) 5. "Sir, can you please drive faster? I have to get to the station as soon as possible.

My train ________ in 20 minutes."

A. started　　B. goes　　C. will leave　　D. come

(　　) 6. He told me that he preferred ________ at home rather than ________ out for a walk.

A. to stay; go　　B. to sleep; walking

C. live; to come　　D. sat; to be

三、阅读短文，用所给词的适当形式填空。

Dear Anne,

I'm sorry I (1)________ (not write) to you these days, but I've been working hard. When I (2)________ (receive) your letter I (3)________ (sing) in a play at school. When I finished that, I went on holiday with some friends. I meant to send you a postcard, but I (4)________ (forget) to take your address with me. How are you getting on at college? You (5)________ (not say) much about this in your letter. I hope you still (6)________ (like) it. I have done many things recently. I've (7)________ (learn) (8)________ (drive) and my parents sometimes (9)________ (lend) me their car. Maybe I (10)________ (go) to London and see you one day.

Best wishes,

Andy

四、句型转换。

1. Cathy was writing a letter at 9 pm yesterday.（变为否定句）

____

2. I was having a shower when the postman knocked at the door.（变为一般疑问句）

____

3. John had breakfast at 7∶30 this morning.（变为一般疑问句）

____

4. Henry goes to the library <u>once a month</u>.（对画线部分提问）

____

5. The children worked <u>busily</u> this morning.（对画线部分提问）

____

五、完形填空。（2010年黄石市中考）

I believe listening is a powerful medicine. It was Sunday. I had the last __1__ to see and I got into her room. she was an old woman, sitting on the bed, trying to __2__ her socks. Usually I said something like this: "How are you feeling? The nurse says your son is visiting you today. I believe you are __3__ seeing him."

She __4__ me with a serious voice, "Sit down, doctor. This is my story, not yours."

I was surprised and __5__. I sat down and helped her with the socks. she began to tell me that her only son lived not far from her, __6__ she had not seen him for five years. She believed her health problems were worse because of __7__ her son. After hearing her story and helping her put on her socks, I asked if there was __8__ I could do for her. She __9__ her head and smiled. All she wanted me to do was to __10__.

Each story is __11__. Some are clear; others are not. Some are true; others are not, yet all those things do not really __12__. What matters to the storyteller is that the story is heard.

Listening to someone's story costs nothing but it is the key to healing. I often __13__ what the woman taught me, and I __14__ myself of the importance of stopping, sitting down and truly listening. I __15__ the power of listening.

( ) 1. A. doctor B. nurse C. patient D. student
( ) 2. A. take off B. get off C. clean out D. put on
( ) 3. A. looking forward to B. asking for C. worrying about D. going on
( ) 4. A. impressed B. stopped C. asked D. greeted
( ) 5. A. excited B. mad C. embarrassed D. angry
( ) 6. A. or B. so C. but D. if
( ) 7. A. missing B. loving C. understanding D. meeting
( ) 8. A. nothing else B. anything else C. nothing D. everything
( ) 9. A. shook B. dropped C. waved D. moved
( ) 10. A. see B. smell C. listen D. feel
( ) 11. A. terrible B. different C. similar D. true
( ) 12. A. happen B. appear C. matter D. change
( ) 13. A. think of B. dream of C. get over D. laugh at
( ) 14. A. teach B. ask C. remind D. cheer
( ) 15. A. talk about B. show off C. believe in D. run out of

Section Five

一、将你所听到的单词写在下面的横线上。

1. ________ 2. ________ 3. ________ 4. ________
5. ________ 6. ________ 7. ________ 8. ________
9. ________ 10. ________ 11. ________ 12. ________
13. ________ 14. ________ 15. ________ 16. ________
17. ________ 18. ________ 19. ________ 20. ________

二、根据你所听到的问题选出正确的答语。

( ) 1. A. You are right. B. No, there isn't. C. Sorry, I don't know.
( ) 2. A. He is leaving. B. I'll watch TV. C. He walks to school.
( ) 3. A. I'm fine. B. Of course. C. That's all right.
( ) 4. A. Twice a month. B. Next week. C. By boat.
( ) 5. A. I have seen it. B. It's interesting. C. The cinema is new.
( ) 6. A. It's me. B. It's Lilly's. C. It's over there.
( ) 7. A. She is fine. B. She is reading. C. She is a doctor.
( ) 8. A. Every morning. B. At home. C. On foot.
( ) 9. A. It's good. B. Yes, please. C. Sorry, we won't do it again.
( ) 10. A. When he was a boy. B. It's in China. C. Because he liked it.

三、根据你所听到的对话选择正确答案。

( ) 1. A. She lives in London.
B. She doesn't like London.
C. She likes London.

( ) 2. A. Because she needs a quiet place.
B. Because she likes to listen to the songs.
C. Because she finds a new job.

( ) 3. A. It's rainy. B. It's fine. C. It's cold.

( ) 4. A. She likes Italian food very much.
B. The dinner was too expensive.
C. The food was as good as she expected.

( ) 5. A. She likes the story very much.
B. She thinks the music is very beautiful.
C. She thinks the dialogue is funny.

四、根据你所听到的短文选择正确答案。

( ) 1. How much do Peter and Linda receive from their parents?
A. Three dollars. B. Four dollars. C. Five dollars.

( ) 2. How do they get the money?
A. Their parents give them the money for free.
B. They do the housework and earn the money.
C. They sell food and CDs.

( ) 3. What does the money use for?
A. They use it to buy their food. B. They use it to buy some gifts.
C. They use it for their hobbies.

( ) 4. What should NOT Peter do every day?
A. Wash the dishes after dinner. B. Take out the garbage.
C. Clean the garden.

( ) 5. What are NOT their hobbies?
A. Reading novels. B. Going to the movies.
C. Listening to the music.

五、写出下列动词的过去式形式。

1. blow ________ 2. know ________ 3. throw ________
4. fly ________ 5. draw ________ 6. swim ________
7. rise ________ 8. set ________ 9. begin ________
10. hurt ________

六、用所给词的适当形式填空。

1. — They escaped from the prison.

— Oh, really? But how?

— They ________ (dig) an underground tunnel.

2. The cards sold in the shops ________ (be) so expensive. Why not make some cards ourselves?
3. — I don't feel like ________ (eat) anything.

   — You'd better ________ (go) to see a doctor.
4. I ________ (break) my leg last night, and it really ________ (hurt).
5. Bruce is used to ________ (lie) in bed after doing sports.
6. Try to get used to ________ (do) so much homework every day.
7. I locked the door in order to ______ (keep) the children from ______ (enter).
8. I like writing letters to my best friends instead of ________ (use) a computer.
9. My sister ________ (fall) and ________ (hurt) herself when she was riding.
10. We waited for Tom for quite a long time last Sunday. He often kept us ________ (wait).

七、句型转换。

1. She had to look after her younger brother.（改为否定句）

____

2. This cake tastes delicious.（改为否定句）

____

3. You'd better have some drink.（改为否定句）

____

4. I can go skating tomorrow.（改为一般疑问句）

____

5. He took his children to the seaside yesterday.（改为一般疑问句）

____

6. He must stay at home because of the heavy snow.（改为一般疑问句）

____

7. I didn't finish my homework because I had a cold.（对画线部分提问）

____

8. This dress cost her 1,000yuan.（对画线部分提问）

____

八、完形填空。

I have a good mother. She has always made sure we eat very __1__. We live __2__ the sea and have fish about four times a __3__. We eat fresh fruit and vegetables every day. We don't eat __4__ sugar or fat(脂肪). A lot of my school friends eat many sweets every day but I only eat a few. And I'm not too heavy, so I __5__ have to be thinner. I'm quite healthy. I don't often get cold, __6__ I had a bad cold and a high temperature last week because I played football in the __7__. I don't often get things __8__ flu(流感) either. Last winter almost all my classmates got flu—but I didn't. I don't get these things

__9__ I take a lot of exercise and I am very __10__. Two years ago I broke my __11__ while I was playing football and I couldn't __12__ my arm for a month. So as you can __13__ from what I've said, I'm an __14__ person. But there's one thing I really love—playing football. I'm the captain of the class team at school. Because of this, I must have a good diet(饮食), and as I've said, this isn't a problem because my mother __15__ us so well.

( ) 1. A. slowly B. safely C. healthily D. quickly
( ) 2. A. in B. under C. above D. near
( ) 3. A. day B. week C. month D. year
( ) 4. A. much B. any C. delicious D. good
( ) 5. A. sometimes B. often C. always D. never
( ) 6. A. so B. but C. and D. for
( ) 7. A. rain B. sun C. field D. forest
( ) 8. A. for B. like C. of D. with
( ) 9. A. because B. while C. if D. when
( ) 10. A. busy B. tall C. helpful D. strong
( ) 11. A. foot B. arm C. hand D. head
( ) 12. A. open B. pull C. move D. find
( ) 13. A. hear B. see C. write D. describe
( ) 14. A. ordinary B. important C. interesting D. exciting
( ) 15. A. feeds B. trains C. invites D. interviews

九、阅读理解。

Perhaps the only test score that I remember is the 55 when I was in high school.

The test was the final for a course. I remember waiting anxiously as my teacher Mr. Right passed out our papers one by one. It was a rather difficult test. I heard my classmates ***groaning***, and I could tell by the groans that the scores weren't looking good.

Mr. Right put my paper on my desk. There in big red numbers, circled to draw attention, was my score, 55!

I lowered my head, and covered the score up quickly. A 55 is not something that you wanted your classmates to see.

"The scores were not very good, none of you passed," Mr. Right said. "The highest score in the class was a 55."

A 55. That's me!

Suddenly my sad look didn't look so bad. I had the highest score. I felt a lot better.

I walked home alone that day with the low but high score. My father knew that I had a big test that day and asked me as soon as I got home, "How did you do in your test?"

"I made a 55," I said.

A frown (皱眉) now stood on my father's face. I knew I had to explain immediately. "But Dad, I had the highest score in the class," I proudly stated. I thought that explanation would make a difference.

"You failed!" my father replied.

"But it's the highest!" I insisted.

"I don't care what others had, but you failed. What matters is what you do!" my father firmly said.

For years, my father was always that way. It didn't matter what others did, it only mattered what I did and that I did it excellently.

We often don't understand the wisdom（智慧）of good parents until we ourselves stand in the parenting shoes. My father's words have carried me throughout life.

(　　) 1. The word ***groaning*** is the closest in meaning to ________.

A. singing　B. laughing　C. complaining　D. quarreling

(　　) 2. In class, to hide my score from my classmates, I ________.

A. lowered my head　B. covered my score up

C. walked home alone　D. explained immediately

(　　) 3. A frown stood on my father's face because he thought ________.

A. I did a bad job in the test　B. I became the worst student

C. I gave a good excuse　D. I stood in his shoes

(　　) 4. We can infer from the passage that ________.

A. the father was strict with his child

B. the writer was always poor in tests

C. Mr. Right was worried about the writer

D. the writer was always happy with his scores

(　　) 5. Which is the best title of the passage?

A. The Final Test.　B. That's Me!

C. My Strict Teacher.　D. Scores, Important?

期中考试(一)

卷面分值:100 分　考试时间:100 分钟

第一部分

(80 分)

一、听力理解部分 (25 分)

第一节 (共 6 小题, 每小题 1 分,满分 6 分)

听下面 6 个问题。每个问题后有三个答语,从题中所给的 A、B、C 三个选项中选出最佳选项。听完每个问题后,你都有 5 秒钟的时间来作答和阅读下一小题。每个问题仅读一遍。

(　　)1. A. I want a sandwich.　B. Yes, I'd like to.　C. Here's your book.

(　　)2. A. It's Saturday.　B. It's fine.　C. It's Spring Festival.

(　　)3. A. It's from my mother.　B. It's very nice.　C. It's in your backpack.

(　　)4. A. I have an old watch.　B. I have a cold.　C. I'm going to school.

(　　)5. A. For five days.　B. By air.　C. I visited some museums.

(　　)6. A. I'm relaxed.　B. On weekends.　C. I like to play chess.

第二节 (共 5 小题, 每小题 1 分,满分 5 分)

听下面 5 段对话。每段对话后有一个小题,从题中所给的 A、B、C 三个选项中选出最佳选项。听完每段对话后,你都有 10 秒钟的时间来回答有关小题和阅读下一小题。每段对话仅读一遍。

(　　) 7. A. 9:15.　B. 9 o'clock.　C. 8:45.

(　　) 8. A. A magazine.　B. Taking pictures.　C. A new machine.

(　　) 9. A. In a shop.　B. In a hospital.　C. In a school.

(　　) 10. A. Bus stop.　B. Train station.　C. Airport.

(　　) 11. A. He wants some oranges.
B. He wants some eggs.
C. He wants some cakes.

第三节 (共 14 小题,每小题 1 分,满分 14 分)

听下面 4 段对话或独白。每段对话或独白后有几个小题,从题中所给的 A、B、C 三个选项中选出最佳选项。听每段对话和独白前,你将有时间阅读各个小题;听完后,各小题将给出 5 秒钟的作答时间。每段对话或独白读两遍。

听第 12 段材料，回答第 12 ~ 14 题。

(　　)12. Where are the speakers talking now?

A. On the telephone.　　B. At the station.　　C. On the plane.

(　　)13. What is the woman doing?

A. She is booking(预定) her flight ticket.

B. She is talking about her traveling.

C. She is making sure she has booked her flight ticket.

(　　)14. When will the woman fly to New York?

A. This Monday, March 8.

B. Next Monday, March 18.

C. Next Monday, March 8.

听第 13 段材料，回答第 15 ~ 17 题。

(　　)15. What month does the boy think is the best time to visit Hong Kong?

A. July.　　B. August.　　C. May.

(　　)16. How many things does the boy mention that travellers can do in Hong Kong?

A. Three.　　B. Four.　　C. Five.

(　　)17. What does the girl want to do now?

A. To visit Hong Kong.

B. To visit her friends.

C. To go swimming in the sea.

听第 14 段材料，回答第 18 ~ 20 题。

(　　)18. How many kinds of salads are talked about?

A. Only one.　　B. Three.　　C. Two.

(　　)19. What did the man order?

A. Onion soup and a tomato salad.

B. Spicy tofu and a vegetarian burger.

C. Spicy tofu and a house salad.

(　　)20. What kind of drink did the man order?

A. Orange juice.　　B. Apple juice.　　C. Peach juice.

听第 15 段材料，回答第 21 ~ 25 题。

(　　)21. How many days did the speaker spend in Miami?

A. Fourteen days.　　B. Ten days.　　C. Two days.

(　　)22. Where did they enjoy a wonderful sight of the world?

A. In the Science Museum.　B. On the plane.　　C. Along the beach.

(　　)23. What did they do in the morning when the weather was not too hot?

A. They used to go dancing in a disco.

B. They used to have breakfast outdoors.

C. They used to go sightseeing.

(　　)24. What can we learn about the speaker and John?

A. They didn't like the beach at all.

B. They had a good time on the beach.

C. They enjoyed traveling in hot weather.

( )25. Which of the following is NOT mentioned in the passage?

A. How they felt when they had to leave.

B. What the weather was like every day.

C. What they bought in Miami.

请同学们将试卷翻到第二部分,完成听写部分的试题。

二、单项选择(15 分)

( )26. ________ the empty cup away and ________ me a cup of coffee.

A. Take; bring B. Take; carry C. Bring; take D. Bring; carry

( )27. — What do you always eat ________ lunch?

— An egg and some noodles.

A. from B. on C. for D. in

( )28. The accident happened ________ the morning of July 21st, 2011.

A. on B. in C. at D. to

( )29. — May I have a rest now?

— No, you ________.

A. can't B. must C. needn't D. should

( )30. ________ fine the weather is!

A. What a B. How a C. What D. How

( )31. I ________ this pair of shoes, but they are not big enough for me to wear.

A. tried B. tried on C. puts on D. wore

( )32. — Jennifer's home is not far from our school.

—Let's go ________.

A. on foot B. by feet C. with foot D. on feet

( )33. — ________ do you get together?

— We're so busy. That's why we can only meet twice a year.

A. How long B. How often C. How much D. When

( )34. — What's the time ________ your watch?

— It's 5 : 30.

A. by B. on C. for D. over

( )35. I was born in a small town ________ just south of Cleveland.

A. situates B. situated C. is situates D. situating

( )36. John ________ America next month.

A. is leaving for B. is leaving to

C. is leaving at D. is leaving in

( )37. —________ does the concert last?

— Three hours.

A. How soon B. How often

C. How long D. How many

(　　)38. You can have a trip to the countryside ________ your spare time.
A. at　　B. of　　C. in　　D. with

(　　)39. Tom suggested we ________ separately, but Jim suggested ________ together in one car.
A. to go; going　B. go; going　C. going; go　D. go; to go

(　　)40. She had better ________ a doctor if it gets any worse.
A. to see　　B. see　　C. saw　　D. seeing

三、完形填空（10分）

Long long ago a thief stole a bag of money from a farmer's house. The __41__ went to the judge and asked __42__ help. The judge ordered __43__ the people of the farm to come before him. He took out a number of sticks of the same size and gave one stick to __44__ man. Then he said, "Come before me again tomorrow. I'll know which __45__ you is the thief, because the thief's stick will be one inch __46__ than the others." The thief was afraid to be found out and so he cut an inch __47__ the stick.

The next day the thief's stick was found to be one inch __48__ than any __49__ stick. __50__ this way the thief was found out and put into prison.

(　　)41. A. thief　　B. farmer　　C. stick　　D. man
(　　)42. A. to　　B. of　　C. for　　D. from
(　　)43. A. all　　B. every　　C. each　　D. whole
(　　)44. A. one　　B. other　　C. each　　D. any
(　　)45. A. from　　B. for　　C. to　　D. of
(　　)46. A. long　　B. longest　　C. longer　　D. short
(　　)47. A. out　　B. off　　C. to　　D. of
(　　)48. A. shorter　　B. longer　　C. thinner　　D. wider
(　　)49. A. another　　B. other　　C. others　　D. the other
(　　)50. A. On　　B. At　　C. In　　D. To

四、阅读理解（30分）

A

TV PROGRAMMES(节目)

Channel(频道)1	Channel 2
18:00 Around China	17:45 Computers today
18:30 Cartoon network	18:10 Chinese arts
19:00 News	18:30 English classroom
19:30 Weather report	18:50 Animal world
19:40 Around the world	19:25 China's 2004
20:10 TV play: *Sisters*	20:20 Sports
21:00 English for today	21:00 TV play: *Big Family*
21:15 Popular music	21:45 English news
21:55 Talk show	22:00 Music

( ) 51. You want to know something about Japan, you can watch ________.

A. Weather report B. China's 2004

C. Around the world D. Animal world

( ) 52. You are a football fan. You may watch TV at ________.

A. 19:00 on Channel 1 B. 19:40 on Channel 1

C. 20:20 on Channel 2 D. 21:15 on Channel 1

( ) 53. How long does the TV play *Sisters* last(持续)?

A. 30 minutes. B. 50 minutes.

C. 90 minutes. D. 120 minutes.

( ) 54. You can watch ________ if you want to learn English.

A. English news B. English classroom

C. English for today D. A, B and C

( ) 55. Children often like to watch ________.

A. Cartoon network B. News

C. Weather report D. Sports

B

Hainan	Island
Capital:	Haikou
Population:	more than 7 million
What to see:	Wanquan River
	Dongshan Ridge
	Hot Springs
	Hairui Tomb

Hainan Island is the second largest island of China. Haikou, the capital of Hainan Province, is in the northeast of the island. It is the largest city on the island. It is a pretty city with an interesting flower market. In the south of the island, there is scuba diving, fishing and boating. If relaxing is in your plan, then there are long white beaches to walk along. Everybody knows Sanya because of "Tianya Haijiao" — "the edge of the sky and the rim of the sea".

Hainan Island is the place to be, whether it's summer or winter!

( )56. What's the capital city of Hainan Province?

A. Sanya. B. Haikou. C. Wenchang. D. Qionghai.

( )57. What can't people do in the south of Hainan Island?

A. Scuba diving. B. Fishing.

C. Skating. D. Boating.

( )58. Which season is good for people to go and visit Hainan Island?

A. In spring and autumn. B. In summer.

C. In winter. D. Any season is OK.

( )59. Which city is famous for "Tianya Haijiao"—"the edge of the sky and the rim of the sea"?

A. Haikou.　B. Sanya.　C. Tianjin.　D. Dalian.

(　　)60. Which of the following is NOT clear in the reading?

A. The population of Hainan Island.

B. What people can see on the island.

C. Where to relax.

D. The time people can go to the market to buy beautiful flowers.

C

There is a saying that the British like a nice cup of tea in the morning and a nice cup of tea at night. And at half past seven, ***their idea of heaven*** is a nice cup of tea. They like a nice cup of tea with their dinner and a nice cup of tea before they go to bed. ***There is a lot to be said about a nice cup of tea!***

Sometimes it seems that no one likes tea as much as the British do. But in fact, tea is liked in many countries around the world. In China and Japan, tea was first used as a medicine. Many years later, people there drank tea as a beverage(饮料).

People in the world like to drink different kinds of tea, green, black or red as some people call it, served in different ways. But they all know that drinking tea is good for one's health.

(　　)61. The main idea of the first paragraph(自然段)is ________.

A. how many cups of tea the British drink each day

B. the British like talking about tea

C. the British can't live without drinking tea

D. tea is very important in the life of the British

(　　)62. The phrase "***their idea of heaven***" means ________.

A. the happiest thing for them

B. their thoughts

C. their God

D. the worst thing for them

(　　)63. The sentence "***there is a lot to be said about a nice cup of tea***" means ________.

A. they enjoy eating with a nice cup of tea

B. there is a lot of tea

C. they talk much about a nice cup of tea

D. there is a talk while drinking tea

(　　)64. From the passage we know tea was used as a medicine in ________ many years ago.

A. the world　B. British

C. many countries　D. China and Japan

(　　)65. This passage mainly tells us ________.

A. people in different countries like drinking different tea

B. tea is liked by people in many countries

C. how many kinds of tea there are in the world

D. tea is medicine

第二部分

(20 分)

一、听写,听一篇文章并根据所听内容补全所缺单词 (5 分)

With the development of the Internet, a large number of people do shopping on the Internet. Shopping online becomes more and more __1__.

People have different opinions on shopping on the Internet. Some think it's __2__. You don't need to spend a lot of time choosing something from shop to shop. You can just sit in front of the computer, and search on the Internet for the things you like.

However, some people don't like shopping online. They think it's not safe, and once cheated, people will have nowhere to complain about. What's more, people can't see the goods. If clothes are __3__ online, they can't be tried on personally.

I am convinced that shopping online would be a __4__ way than the traditional one. All you need to do is to sit in front of your computer and click the mouse. The goods come in all __5__, sizes and colors on the Internet. If you feel unsure about those, you can have a chat with the sellers online till you are certain on the things you will buy.

1. ________ 2. ________ 3. ________ 4. ________ 5. ________

二、将单词与符合的意思匹配(5 分)

( ) 1. comedy — A. a set of pages that show the days, weeks, and months of a year

( ) 2. questionnaire — B. a play, film, or television programme that is intended to make people laugh

( ) 3. calendar — C. light of day

( ) 4. casual — D. informal

( ) 5. daylight — E. a written set of questions which you give to a large number of people in order to collect information

三、句型转换(5 分)

1. Lucy had to clean her bedroom this afternoon. (变否定句)

____

2. Sandy got a fever. (变一般疑问句)

____

3. The music sounds <u>terrible</u>. (对画线部分提问)

____

4. What's the weather like today? (换一种说法)

____

5. The thief was in prison the night before last.（对画线部分提问）

____

四、用所给词的适当形式填空(5 分)

1. Our school is ________ (situation) in Longyang Avenue, where there isn't so much traffic problems.
2. They always enjoy ________ (read) some magazines and ________ (play) football after class.
3. The teachers advised us ________ (do) some exercise outdoors during the break in winter.
4. Why not ________ (have) a cup of tea with me after school?
5. Mary ________ (cut) his finger a short time ago.

期中考试(二)

卷面分值:100 分　考试时间:120 分钟

第一部分

(80 分)

一、听力理解部分(25 分)

第一节(共 6 小题,每小题 1 分,满分 6 分)

听下面 6 个问题。每个问题后有三个答语,从题中所给的 A、B、C 三个选项中选出最佳选项。听完每个问题后,你都有 5 秒钟的时间来作答和阅读下一小题。每个问题仅读一遍。

(　　)1. A. Pretty good.　B. Very nice.　C. Fine, thanks.

(　　)2. A. It's here.　B. At 9 : 00 p. m.　C. In the room.

(　　)3. A. Canada.　B. They are new.　C. They are friends.

(　　)4. A. That's right.　B. It's a cat.　C. It's Jim.

(　　)5. A. It's OK.　B. It's black.　C. It's Mike's.

第二节(共 5 小题,每小题 1 分,满分 5 分)

听下面 5 段对话。每段对话后有一个小题,从题中所给的 A、B、C 三个选项中选出最佳选项。听完每段对话后,你都有 10 秒钟的时间来回答有关小题和阅读下一小题。每段对话仅读一遍。

(　　)6. Where does the man mean?
A. He likes English better.
B. He likes math better.
C. He likes neither of them.

(　　)7. What can we know about Jack?
A. Jack isn't in the office.
B. Jack is busy in the office.
C. Jack is asking the way to the office.

(　　)8. What are they talking about?
A. The new room.
B. Their school.
C. The air in the office.

(　　)9. What is the price of ten bags?

A. $14.95.　　B. $10.99.　　C. $2.99.

(　　)10. When is Bob probably going home this afternoon?

A. At 1：00.　　B. At 2：00.　　C. At 4：00.

第三节(共 14 小题,每小题 1 分,满分 14 分)

听下面 4 段对话或独白。每段对话或独白后有几个小题,从题中所给的 A、B、C 三个选项中选出最佳选项。听每段对话和独白前,你将有时间阅读各个小题;听完后,各小题将给出 5 秒钟的作答时间。每段对话或独白读两遍。

听第 11 段材料,回答第 11 ~13 题。

(　　)11. Where are the man and woman?

A. In a shop.　　B. At home.　　C. At the doctor's.

(　　)12. What's wrong with the man?

A. He has got a headache and a bad cough.

B. He has got a stomachache.

C. He makes a mistake.

(　　)13. What will the man have to do next?

A. To go home at once and have a good meal.

B. To take some medicine and have a good rest.

C. To stay in hospital for some time.

听第 12 段材料,回答第 14 ~16 题。

(　　)14. Where are they talking?

A. In a bookstore.

B. In a clothes store.

C. In a food store.

(　　)15. What's the man's favourite color?

A. Yellow.　　B. Green.　　C. White.

(　　)16. When did the conversation happen?

A. In summer.　　B. In spring.　　C. In autumn.

听第 13 段材料,回答第 17 ~20 题。

(　　)17. What happened to Jane?

A. She was almost hit by a car.

B. Her license was taken away.

C. She was badly ill.

(　　)18. What was Jane doing while she was crossing the street?

A. She was talking with their friends.

B. She was listening to news.

C. She was reading a newspaper.

(　　)19. Which is TRUE about Jane?

A. She felt afraid and sorry.

B. She was very careful while crossing the road.

C. She would go to the hospital.

(　　)20. What is NOT Bill's suggestion?

A. Jane should take the driver's license away.

B. Jane should remember the number of the car.

C. Jane should take more care while crossing the road next time.

听第 14 段材料,回答第 21 ~25 题。

(　　)21. What did the writer go to town to do?

A. Go to the park.　　B. Visit her uncle.

C. Do some shopping.

(　　)22. Why did the writer go to the phone box and stay there?

A. It rained suddenly and she had no umbrella with her.

B. She wanted to phone her mother.

C. She waited for her friend there.

(　　)23. What did the writer think the young man wanted to do?

A. Clean the phone box.　　B. Repair the phone.

C. Use the phone.

(　　)24. How long did the man wait?

A. About 5 minutes.　　B. About 10 minutes.

C. About 15 minutes.

(　　)25. Why was the writer embarrassed?

A. She couldn't get out of the phone box.

B. She made the man wait so long.

C. She did something foolish.

请同学们将试卷翻到第二部分,完成听写部分的试题。

二、单项选择 (15 分)

(　　)26. The light is ________. You don't need to turn on your torch.

A. on　　B. off　　C. up　　D. down

(　　)27. There is ________ fat and sugar in junk food.

A. too many　　B. too much　　C. many too　　D. much too

(　　)28. I don't like to buy this sweater. It's ________ expensive.

A. too much　　B. much more　　C. far more　　D. much too

(　　)29. I plan to go to France this summer. I ________ to Paris.

A. never have been　　B. have been never

C. have never been　　D. never been

(　　)30. My parents ________ far away from here when they were young.

A. lives　　B. lived　　C. live　　D. living

(　　)31. Would you like ________ to my birthday party next week?

A. going　　B. go　　C. to go　　D. went

(　　)32. — What can I do for you?

— ________

A. I'd like a watch.　　B. That's OK.

C. It doesn't matter.　　D. Of course not.

(　　)33. — Why not ________ your clothes? The weather is so nice.

— I'd love to, but I have to finish my homework first.

A. washing　B. wash　C. to wash　D. to washing

(　　)34. This hotel is a five star hotel which ________ in Maple Street.

A. is situated　B. situates　C. situating　D. situate

(　　)35. — ________ juice would you like?

— ________ is OK.

A. How much; A few　B. How many; Few

C. How many; A little　D. How much; A little

(　　)36. — I'm sorry I'm late for the party.

— ________

A. No, you aren't.　B. Yes, you are.

C. That's all right.　D. You are welcome.

(　　)37. — Must I clean the room now?

— No, you ________. You can do it tomorrow.

A. mustn't　B. must　C. needn't　D. need

(　　)38. It's the library! So you ________ know shouting is not allowed here.

A. can　B. must　C. needn't　D. need

(　　)39. There is going to ________ a meeting next week.

A. have　B. has　C. is　D. be

(　　)40. James and I ________ each other since we were very young.

A. knew　B. have known　C. had known　D. were knowing

三、完形填空（10分）

One night a man came to my house. He told me, "There is a family with eight __41__. They have not eaten for days." After I asked him where the family was, I took some __42__ with me and left.

When I got to that family, I __43__ those little children were too hungry to say __44__. There was no sadness(悲伤) in their eyes, just the deep pain of hunger. I gave the food to the mother. She took half of it, and then __45__. When she returned, I asked her, "__46__ did you go?" She gave me this simple __47__, "To my neighbors—they are also __48__!"

I was not surprised that she gave, because poor people are always very kind. But I was surprised that she knew her __49__ were hungry. Usually, when we are in trouble, we always __50__ ourselves first, and we have no time for others.

(　　)41. A. children　B. workers　C. farmers　D. teachers

(　　)42. A. flowers　B. wine　C. food　D. water

(　　)43. A. showed　B. watched　C. looked　D. found

(　　)44. A. a sentence　B. a word　C. it　D. nothing

(　　)45. A. came in　B. came back　C. got in　D. hurried away

(　　)46. A. When　B. Where　C. How　D. Why

(　　)47. A. question　B. key　C. answer　D. lie

(　　)48. A. ill　　B. unhappy　　C. tired　　D. hungry

(　　)49. A. people　　B. neighbors　　C. family　　D. children

(　　)50. A. think of　　B. talk about　　C. laugh at　　D. look for

四、阅读理解(30分)

A

An American went to a small town in South America for his holidays. Few people went there because it was far away from cities. One day he fell ill and wanted very much to see a doctor.

The American went to find out how he could find a fine doctor there. A man told him, "That's very easy. If there's a patient that a doctor can't cure, the doctor has to put a balloon over his clinic(诊所)."

The American thought, "If there are fewer balloons, the doctor will be better." He began to look for the best doctor along the street. First he found a clinic with 20 balloons. After a few minutes he found another one with 30 balloons. He thought they weren't the best.

At last he found the third clinic. Only 5 balloons were there. He was very happy and went in. "Wait a minute," said the doctor. "I'm too busy, you know. This clinic opened yesterday." The American was very surprised and said to himself, "Where can I find the best doctor?"

(　　)51. Few people went to the small town for their holidays because ________.

A. it was too small　　B. it was dangerous

C. it was very dirty　　D. it was far from cities

(　　)52. The American wanted to find a clinic ________.

A. because he didn't feel well

B. to see if there were balloons over it

C. to find out how a doctor worked there

D. because his son had a headache

(　　)53. There were ________ balloons over the second clinic than the first one.

A. less　　B. more　　C. better　　D. worse

(　　)54. How long was the third clinic open?

A. For a week.　　B. For a month.　　C. For two days.　D. For a year.

(　　)55. The doctor in the third clinic was ________.

A. the best in the town　　B. better than the first one

C. very friendly to everyone　　D. not the one the American wanted

B

Instruction

Indication(指示): Cough cause by cold

Take three times a day after meals

Dosage(剂量): Adults: 2 spoons each time

Children: 8—14 years, one spoon

4—7 years, 1/2 spoon

Not fit for children below the age of 4 years

Notes: 1. Store in a cold place

2. Using before Oct. 2008

Pharmacy company:

Tel & Fax: 021-56317708

E-mail: cmxc@ 126. com

Add: No. 10 Nanjing Road, Shanghai, China

(　　)56. A sick child at the age of ________ can't take this medicine.

A. three　B. five　C. six　D. four

(　　)57. If Mrs. Green wants her seven-year-old son to take this medicine, she should give him ________ each time.

A. two spoons　B. one spoon

C. half a spoon　D. a quarter spoon

(　　)58. How much should Mrs. Green give her seven-year-old son this medicine a day?

A. Three spoons.　B. One and a half spoons.

C. Six spoons.　D. Two- thirds spoon.

(　　)59. In which month of 2008 can Mrs. Green give her son the rest medicine?

A. September.　B. October.

C. November.　D. December.

(　　)60. If you want to contact the pharmacy company, which of the following ways can't you use?

A. Using QQ.　B. Faxing.

C. Writing.　D. Sending e-mail.

C

Scientists have always wanted to know more about the other worlds in space.

Years ago they knew many things about the moon. They knew how big it was and how far away. But they wanted to know more about it. The only way to find out more was to send men to the moon.

The moon is about 384,000 kilometres away from the earth. A plane cannot fly to the moon because the air reaches only 240 kilometres. Then there is no air. But something can fly even there is no air. That is a rocket.

How does a rocket fly? There is gas in the rocket. The gas is made very hot. When the gas rushes out of the end of rocket, it makes the rocket fly up into the sky.

Rockets can fly far out into space. Rockets with man in them have already reached the moon. Several rockets without men in them have flown to another planet much farther away than the moon. One day rockets may be able to fly to any place in space.

(　　) 61. Scientists ________ about the moon before they sent rockets to it.

A. knew everything　B. knew something

C. didn't know anything　D. didn't know anything

(　　) 62. Which of the following is right according to this passage?

A. The moon is about 240 kilometres away from the earth.

B. A plane can fly 384,000 kilometres away from the earth.

C. A plane can't reach the moon without air.

D. Several rockets with men in them have flown to other worlds farther away than the moon.

(　　) 63. Men can fly to the moon ________.

A. with a plane　　B. in rockets

C. without rockets　　D. in planes

(　　) 64. Rockets can ________ now.

A. knew something about the moon　　B. go anywhere in space

C. reach the moon　　D. fly without men

(　　) 65. A rocket can fly because ________.

A. the gas is made very not　　B. it flies very fast

C. there is no man in it　　D. the gas in it is working

第二部分

(20 分)

一、听写,听句子并根据所听内容补全所缺单词(5 分)

1. I w ________ a letter to my friend Jane and looked forward to her letter then.
2. It's very difficult to get rid of bad h ________.
3. He is always late. It isn't w ________ waiting for him.
4. The wedding was m ________. So many people crowded to see it.
5. It is said that the storm caused s ________ damage. A lot of people died and hundreds of people became homeless.

二、将单词与符合的意思匹配(5 分)

(　　) 1. fingers　　A. customer

(　　) 2. simple　　B. a short film that is made by photographing a series of drawings

(　　) 3. client　　C. to move slowly on the floor with hands and knees

(　　) 4. lifestyle　　D. easy or not difficult to understand

(　　) 5. crawl　　E. five parts extending from each hand

(　　) 6. treat　　F. something unusual which gives pleasure

(　　) 7. course　　G. involving the use of imagination to produce new ideas or things

(　　) 8. creative　　H. ways of living

(　　) 9. cartoon　　I. the things you do every day

(　　)10. routine　　J. one part of a meal put on the table at one time

三、用所给词的适当形式填空（5 分）

1. We usually ________ (swim) in that river when we were children.
2. They ________ (sleep) very well last night.
3. She ________ (rise) with the first rays（光线）of the sun this morning.
4. The man ________ (lose) a lot of money yesterday.
5. They ________ (fly) the kite the day after tomorrow at the river bank.
6. —________ you ________ (get) a pain in your stomach?
   — Yes, it really ________ (hurt).
7. There were many students in the playground, ________ (be) there?
8. There ________ some steak on the table a few minutes ago, but there ________ (not be) any now.
9. John is a student ________ (invent), and he likes ________ (invent). He ________ already ________ (invent) many things in these three years.
10. The boy has got a bad cold. You'd better ________ (take) him to hospital.

四、句型转换（5 分）

1. He hurt his leg the other day.（改成一般疑问句）

   ____

2. We ate some moon cakes and drank some tea on Mid-Autumn Festival.（改成一般疑问句）

   ____

3. She has got a wonderful idea.（改成一般疑问句）

   ____

4. Wash your hands quickly.（改成否定句）

   ____

5. The children sang songs to celebrate the New Year's Day.（改成否定句）

   ____

6. Tom bought twelve strawberries last week.（对画线部分提问）

   ____

7. She drove the car very carefully.（对画线部分提问）

   ____

8. They lit a fire a few minutes ago.（对画线部分提问）

   ____

9. He is going to have a birthday party this Sunday at home.（对画线部分提问）

   ____

10. Andy spent 5 pounds on the apples yesterday.
    Andy ________ 5 pounds ________ the apples yesterday.

Unit 10

Section One

一、单项选择。

(　　)1. I don't like Bali now because it's too ________. Many people go there for vacation.

A. cold　　B. crowded　　C. hot　　D. lonely

(　　)2. I'd like to go to the ________ because I like climbing. It's ________.

A. seaside; noisy　　B. forest; quiet

C. mountains; exciting　　D. desert; empty

(　　)3. — ____________________

— It was delicious.

A. How was the food like?　　B. What was the food?

C. What the food was about?　　D. How was the food?

(　　)4. There are six people in the room, ________ Peter and Tom.

A. including　　B. includes　　C. included　　D. include

(　　)5. The big house has ________ beautiful furniture in it.

A. many　　B. much　　C. a number of　　D. many of

(　　)6. Yesterday I talked to Amy on the phone and she ________ happy.

A. looked　　B. sounded　　C. smelled　　D. tasted

(　　)7. What about ________ meat for lunch?

A. to buy some　　B. buying some

C. to buy any　　D. buying any

二、用括号中所给的词把下列句子变成一般过去时。

eg: I often go to school by bike. (yesterday)

I went to school yesterday.

1. I buy a magazine every morning. (yesterday morning)

____

2. Mr. Black misses the train and is late for work. (the day before yesterday)

____

3. Jessica spends much money on her clothes. (last year)

____

4. Steven gives up learning Chinese because he thinks it is too difficult. (last month)

____

5. My PE teacher is a professional tennis player. (5 years ago)

____

三、用方框中所给词的适当形式填空，使短文正确、通顺、连贯（每词限用一次）。

wonder, big, old, somebody, pleased, money, richer, take, many, receive

Many years ago there was a poor man. He had an (1)________ tree in his garden. On the tree there were many fine oranges. One day, he found one of his oranges much (2)________ than the others. It was as big as a football. (3)________ had ever seen such a big orange. The poor man took the orange to the king. The king was so (4)________ that he gave the poor man a lot of (5)________ for it.

When a (6)________ man heard of it, he said to himself, "It's only an orange. Why has the king given him so much money for it? I will (7)________ my gold cup to the king. He will give (8)________ money to me."

The next day when the king (9)________ the gold cup, he said to the rich man, "What a nice cup! I will show you something (10)________. Please take this great orange."

四、根据句意，用括号中所给单词的适当形式填空。

1. I hoped you ________(bring) it here earlier just now.
2. After the earthquake, many ________ (home) people live in the tents.
3. It is silly of you ________ (not forgive) others for their faults.
4. —Look at the sign, please. Don't talk loudly!
   —Sorry. I ________(not notice) it.
5. —The bus is leaving right now, but Jack hasn't arrived yet.
   —Well, he said he ________(come) here on time.
6. You ________ (hear) the news last night?
7. They ________ (write) letters the whole morning. They didn't have a rest.
8. You'd better ________(read) this book now.
9. He wants ________(clean) his room next week.
10. Jim often helps his mother ________(cook) supper.
11. Yesterday I ________(write) a letter to my uncle.
12. Tomorrow he ________(leave) for Beijing.
13. In 1987 his mother ________(die).
14. Do you enjoy ________(play) at home?
15. His mother went out without ________(look) at him.

五、写出下列动词的过去式。

1. run ______ 2. have ______ 3. listen ______ 4. read ______ 5. send ______

6. see ________ 7. leave ________ 8. find ________ 9. stand ________ 10. sit ________
11. come ________ 12. buy ________ 13. think ________ 14. thank ________ 15. study ________

Section Two

一、单项选择。

( ) 1. I am sure that I will see many places of ________ during my stay in Australia.
A. interest B. interesting C. interested D. more interesting

( ) 2. Last Sunday, I went shopping with my mother, ________ we bought many things.
A. and B. because C. or D. but

( ) 3. — Would you please not take photos here? Look at the sign. — ________
A. No, I don't. B. Yes, I do. C. Sorry, I will. D. Sorry, I won't.

( ) 4. Lucy became a famous ________ when she was just 11 years old.
A. piano B. violin C. violinist D. golf

( ) 5. When my father was fourteen, he started ________ a football team.
A. to play with B. to play for C. playing with D. playing as

( ) 6. Deng Yaping went to Tsinghua University and ________ English and management.
A. majored in B. major in C. majored for D. major for

( ) 7. — ________ didn't she come to school last night?
—Because she was ill.
A. When B. Why C. Where D. How

二、用括号内所给单词的适当形式填空。

1. When Mike was three years old, he started ________ (play) soccer.
2. Please ________ (not put) these clothes here.
3. Who ________ (buy) a new bike yesterday?
4. It was 8:00. The boys ________ (play) football on the playground.
5. He ________ (watch) TV and then read a storybook last night.

三、句型转换。

1. I was born in Jinan in 1990. (对画线部分提问)
________ and ________ ________ you ________?
2. They did their homework after supper. (改为否定句)
They ________ ________ their homework after super
3. She begins to work at 8 : 00 every morning. (改为同义句)
She ________ ________ at 8 : 00 every morning.
4. They lived in Beijing for two years. (对画线部分提问)

______ ______ ______ they live in Beijing?

5. He went to bed at ten last night.（对画线部分提问）

______ ______ ______ he ______ to bed?

四、根据所给图片信息和英语提示，完成句子。

1. enjoy, skate, two years ago

____

2. have dinner, yesterday

____

3. ill, take some medicine, yesterday evening

____

4. visit Great Wall, happily, last year

____

五、下面两封是 Celia 写给她的老师 Mr. Scott 的信以及 Mr. Scott 给她的回信。

Dear Mr. Scott,

I'm writing to complain about my deskmate, Lana.

She likes junk food(垃圾食品) and she always brings some to school. After she eats it, she drops the litter into my desk. She also has a bad habit. After she borrows my pencil, she doesn't return it. I get angry when she copies(抄袭) my homework. And she sometimes makes ink marks(墨迹) on my clothes with her pen. These things always happen and she doesn't care about my feelings. I need your help. Can you let me have another deskmate?

Yours,

Celia

Dear Celia,

I'm sorry to hear that Lana has so many bad habits. And I'm glad that you discuss your problems with me.

I talked to Lana yesterday. She said she did these things because of her carelessness(粗心). She wanted to be polite with our help. She agreed to put the litter in a bag. She said she would do her own homework and be careful with her pen. She asked you to remind(提醒) her by saying "Would you mind returning my pencil?"

Would you mind not changing your deskmate? She is a nice girl. It's important for you to help each other and you will understand each other better.

Yours,

Scott

根据信件内容，完成表格。

Celia's problems with Lana	Lana's solutions(解决方法)
She drops the litter into my desk.	1. ________________
2. ________________	You can remind me by saying "Would you mind returning my pencil?"
3. ________________	4. ________________
5. ________________	I will be careful with my pen.

六、根据单词首字母填空。

Dear chairman,

We are writing to you about (1)p________ wild animals.

Tigers are big and (2)s________. They have very bright eyes. They are in danger because people like to hunt them for fur and make (3)m________ from their bones. Wolves have very good eyesight and (4)h________ and smell. They are usually friendly (5)t________ each other. They never hunt people. They do not kill for (6)f________. Wolves are also in danger because they have (7)n________ to live. If we do nothing for them. Soon their (8)n________ will be smaller and smaller and we won't see them in the near (9)f________.

We think we (10)s________ help these animals.

Yours sincerely,

Lucy King

Section Three

一、单项选择。

(　　)1. I ________ my watch, but I didn't ________ it at last.

A. looked for; found　　B. looking for; found

C. found; for　　D. looked for; find

(　　)2. The hard work made the woman ________ very tired.

A. feel　　B. felt　　C. fell　　D. to fell

(　　)3. — What ________ to the little baby a moment ago?

— He fell off the bed.

A. happens　　B. happened　　C. was happened　　D. is happening

(　　)4. — What should I do to ________ healthy?

— Try to eat a balanced diet.

A. have B. need C. stay D. take

(　　)5. — Who cooked lunch today?

— My father ______.

A. does B. did C. was D. is

(　　)6. — ______________

— When she was seventeen.

A. When was Liu Xuan born? B. Who do you admire?

C. How old was Liu Xuan? D. When did Liu Xuan win the medal?

(　　)7. — Jason got 80 in the math exam. What about you?

— I did ______ than he. I didn't pass it.

A. bad B. worse C. worst D. better

二、完形填空。

Long long ago, there was a swan(天鹅) with golden feathers(金羽毛). She lived in a lake. A woman lived in a small house __1__ the lake with her two daughters. They were very poor. They worked hard all year round, __2__ still, they lived a hard life and sometimes they even didn't have enough __3__ to buy food.

The swan was __4__ to see that. She said to herself, "I'll give one of my __5__ to them each day, then they can live a happy life with the money selling my feathers." That evening, she __6__ to the poor woman's house and left a golden feather on the table without saying __7__. From then on, the swam came every day and gave them a feather. The woman was very happy because their life was much __8__ than before.

But day after day, the woman became greedy(贪婪). She said to her __9__. "The swan may fly away one day. If so, we will be poor again. We should take all __10__ feathers when she comes next time."

"Oh, no, Mom!" cried the daughters, "This will __11__ the swan. She helps us a lot!" But the mother wouldn't listen. When the __12__ came as usual, the mother caught her and took all her feathers. But suddenly, the golden feathers __13__ chicken feathers.

Then, the Golden Swan said, "Poor Mother, I came to __14__ you, but you wanted to kill me. Now, I am leaving and will __15__ come back. Never be greedy!" With these words, the swan flew away.

(　　)1. A. above B. over C. near D. under

(　　)2. A. and B. but C. so D. or

(　　)3. A. money B. time C. room D. energy

(　　)4. A. happy B. surprised C. sad D. scared

(　　)5. A. presents B. golden coins C. feathers D. collections

(　　)6. A. flew B. ran C. climbed D. walked

(　　)7. A. something B. everything C. nothing D. anything

(　　)8. A. duller B. better C. busier D. harder

(　　)9. A. brothers B. sisters C. sons D. daughters

(　　)10. A. his B. her C. their D. our

(　　)11. A. hurt B. save C. protect D. refuse

( )12. A. woman B. daughter C. chicken D. swan
( )13. A. heard of B. changed into C. looked for D. came from
( )14. A. trouble B. help C. teach D. invite
( )15. A. sometimes B. always C. usually D. never

三、原文填空。

1. We travelled by train and boat. I hated the boat ________.
2. I also love the pubs, with their music and friendly ________.
3. Yesterday we went to a ________ in the middle of the island.
4. From 1552 the castle was the home of a ________ of Ireland, and it ________ a private home until 1976.
5. Many of the rooms are the same as they were in the past, with old ________ and paintings.

四、信息匹配。左栏是一些人物的假期计划，右栏是一些旅行社的广告，请将人物与其感兴趣的广告进行匹配。

( ) 1. Mary likes animals very much. She wants to see all animals can live in the wild happily. ( ) 2. Sally is going somewhere exciting. She wants to have fun with her friends. ( ) 3. Tony wants to go to a quiet place to relax himself. ( ) 4. Linda likes the famous writer Shen Congwen. And she wants to know more about him. ( ) 5. After watching the movie *Shaolin Temple*, Jim really wants to see what a real Shaolin Temple is like.	A. A 2-day trip around the Qinghai Lake. Enjoy the beautiful scenery of this salt lake in West China. B. Climb the Songshan Mountain in Henan and visit Shaolin Temple. C. Come to the Wolong Nature Reserve and see the lovely pandas. D. Have fun in the Happy Valley of Shenzhen. Many exciting games are waiting for you. E. A 2-day trip to the ancient town of Lijiang. Relax yourself and enjoy the peaceful life here. F. A 2-day trip to the ancient town of Phoenix. You can visit the hometown of Shen Congwen. G. Come to Kenya and you'll see many different kinds of animals in the wild.

Section Four

一、单项选择。

( ) 1. The ________ of living areas makes wild animals become fewer than before.

A. loss　　B. lost　　C. losing　　D. lose

(　　)2. — You can choose to go with us ________ with them.

— Well, I'd like to go with you.

A. but　　B. and　　C. or　　D. if

(　　)3. ________ workers in the factory ________ over two thousand.

A. The number of; is　　B. The number of; are

C. A number of; is　　D. A number of; are

(　　)4. It's not polite to ask a ________ question like "Are you married?"

A. good　　B. private　　C. silly　　D. honest

(　　)5. If you visit ________, you'll see the Eiffel Tower.

A. Paris　　B. Sydney　　C. Washington　　D. Tokyo

(　　)6. — Did you see a young man in black pass by just now?

— No, sir. I ________ a magazine.

A. read　　B. was reading

C. am reading　　D. would read

(　　)7. ________ weather it is!

A. What fine　　B. What a fine

C. How fine　　D. How a fine

(　　)8. The leaves ________ into the pot and ________ for a while and produced a pleasant smell.

A. jumped; kept　　B. fell; remained

C. dropped; stood　　D. blew; left

(　　)9. The teacher is coming. Please stop ________ and keep ________.

A. talking; quiet　　B. talking; quite

C. to talk; quiet　　D. to talk; quite

(　　)10. — Remember, don't play in the street. It's dangerous!

— ________

A. OK, I won't.　　B. Yes, I will.

C. Yes, I would.　　D. Yes, I do.

二、根据本单元课文的内容判断下列表述的正误。

(　　) 1. I am in Briton and I travelled to Dublin by plane.

(　　) 2. We were both very tired when we arrived.

(　　) 3. Leeds Castle was the home of six kings of England.

(　　) 4. Today the queen lives in the Leeds Castle.

(　　) 5. The castle and its beautiful gardens are open to the public all year round.

三、阅读理解。

Here are some tips on how to stay safe in earthquakes.

1. Stay inside and **duck** and cover. Get under a desk or table, or stand in a corner or under a doorway. Cover your head and neck with your arms.

2. Move against a wall if in a high building with no protective desk or table nearby. Cover your head and neck with your arms.
3. Try to get into an open area away from trees, buildings, walls, and power lines (电杆) if outdoors.
4. Pull over (停靠) to the side of the road away from overpasses (天桥) and power lines if driving. Stay in your car until the shaking ends.
5. Get away from shelves or other areas where objects may fall if in a crowded store or public area. Do not run for the door. Lower your body close to the ground and cover your head and neck with your hands and arms.
6. Stay in your seat if in a cinema or a theater. Get below the level of the back of the seat and cover your head and neck with your arms.
7. If you take cover (躲避) under a strong piece of furniture, hold on to it and be prepared to move with it.
8. Try to stay away from kitchens, where there are often many objects that might fall or get burnt.

(　　)1. The best title of the passage is ________.

A. How to protect yourself in an earthquake

B. Covering your head and neck with your arms can protect you in an earthquake

C. Advice for dangerous situations

D. How to stay calm in an earthquake

(　　)2. The underlined word "duck" in Tip 1 means ________.

A. a water bird with short legs

B. some kind of meat for eating

C. walk like a duck

D. lower your head or body very quickly

(　　)3. Which is the correct way to act in an earthquake?

A. Run downstairs and cover your head and neck with your arms.

B. Drive your car quickly through the overpass and get out of it.

C. When you stay under a strong piece of furniture, you should hold on to it and be prepared to move with it.

D. Climb over the back of the seat and cover your head and neck with your arms.

(　　)4. ________ should be the most important part(s) to be protected in an earthquake.

A. Your head and arms　　B. Your arms

C. Your neck and arms　　D. Your head and neck

(　　)5. Tip 3 and Tip 4 give you some advice (建议) on what you should do when you are ________.

A. inside a building　　B. outside a building

C. in your house　　D. in a store

四、句型转换。

1. He started to learn the piano when he was five years old.
   He started ________ the piano at ________ ________ ________ five.（同义句）
2. I took part in the school football team last year.（对画线部分提问）
   ________ ________ you ________ part in the school football team.
3. I went to Bali by air.（对画线部分提问）
   ________ ________ you ________ to Bali?
4. I had my lunch at school yesterday.（变一般疑问句）
   ________ you ________ your lunch at school yesterday?
5. It is sunny today.（对画线部分提问）
   ________ ________ ________ like today?

Section Five

一、听下面五段对话，每段对话后有一个小题，从题中所给的A、B、C三幅图片中选出最佳选项。

(　　)1. Which is the man's favorite animal?

A.  B.  C. 

(　　)2. What did Walter do yesterday?

A.  B.  C. 

(　　)3. What will people use in this city in ten years?

A.  B.  C. 

(　　) 4. Where does Mary want to go this summer vacation?

A. 

B.  C. 

( )5. What is Lucy going to be when she grows up?

A.

B.

C.

二、听对话回答问题。

( )1. Where is the woman?
A. She's in a stamps show. B. She's in a shoe shop.
C. She's in a police station.

( )2. What will Tom do when he leaves school?
A. He wants to go to the college. B. He must finish his homework first.
C. He has decided to go for a holiday in China.

( )3. What's the girl's uncle?
A. He's a taxi driver. B. He's an engineer.
C. He's a manager of a restaurant.

( )4. What happened to Tony?
A. Tony bought a new glass for Annie.
B. Annie borrowed a glass from Tony.
C. Tony broke Annie's glass.

( )5. How much are the sports shoes?
A. Eighteen dollars. B. Eight dollars. C. Eighty dollars.

三、听对话回答问题。

听第一段对话，回答第 1 ~2 题。

( )1. When will Jack go to the movies?
A. Tonight. B. Tomorrow. C. Tomorrow night.

( )2. What will happen if Ellen goes?
A. Her sister will go with her.
B. She won't finish the housework.
C. She won't finish her homework.

听第二段对话，回答第 3 ~5 题。

( )3. What would the girl do if she saw a big bicycle accident?
A. She would run away.
B. She would call the police.
C. She would help the people who can't see.

( )4. Which country would the girl fly to first if she could fly anywhere in the world?
A. England. B. Japan. C. Canada.

( )5. What famous person from history would the girl most like to meet?

A. Zhou Enlai. B. Yao Ming. C. Mao Zedong.

听第三段对话，回答第 6 ~ 8 题。

(　　)6. Who is Hector visiting?
A. His parents. B. His grandparents. C. His cousins.

(　　)7. Where is Susan going?
A. To the countryside. B. To Shanghai. C. To the Central Park.

(　　)8. When is Susan leaving?
A. On June 25. B. On July 25. C. On July 5.

听第四段对话，回答第 9 ~ 10 题。

(　　)9. Peter's mum asks him to ________.
A. turn off the radio B. turn down the radio
C. go to bed

(　　)10. What will Peter do?
A. Do some writing. B. Go to sleep. C. Do some reading.

四、短文理解。

(　　) 1. What does the mother say when the girl has something difficult to do?
A. I will help you. B. Do it yourself.
C. Ask the teacher for help.

(　　) 2. Who did the cleaning for the girl that day?
A. The girl herself. B. Her friends. C. Her mother.

(　　) 3. Whom does the girl see a dentist with?
A. Nobody. B. Her classmate. C. Her father.

(　　) 4. What's the girl like?
A. Friendly and sunny. B. Lazy and crazy.
C. Clever and hard-working.

(　　) 5. What does the girl think of her mother?
A. A busy mother. B. A good teacher.
C. A hard-working woman.

五、单项选择。

(　　)1. We started in different directions but ________ in the same place.
A. woke up B. ended up C. put up D. looked up

(　　)2. My friend Lisa is good at all the subjects at school, ________ English.
A. really B. mostly C. especially D. exactly

(　　)3. Neither they nor Tom ________ there.
A. has gone to B. have gone to
C. has gone D. have gone

(　　)4. There are few people in the room, ________?
A. are they B. aren't they C. are there D. aren't there

(　　)5. The old man lived ________ the river.
A. on B. by C. in D. about

(　　)6. He is the best ________ English in our class.

A. at　　B. in　　C. for　　D. to

(　　)7. Did John hit Bob ________ eye?

A. in the　　B. on the　　C. in his　　D. on his

(　　)8. There ________ a talk show on CCTV-1 at ten yesterday evening.

A. was　　B. is going to have　　C. will have　　D. had

(　　)9. — ________ did Jane exercise?

— Four times a week.

A. How soon　　B. What time　　C. How long　　D. How often

(　　)10. — What should I do to ________ healthy?

— Try to eat a balanced diet.

A. have　　B. need　　C. stay　　D. take

六、完形填空。

One day an old man went into a cafeteria (自助餐厅) to eat in America for the first time. He sat down at a table and __1__ for someone to take his order. Of course, __2__ did. Finally, a woman with a plate full of food sat down opposite him and told him __3__ a cafeteria worked. "Start out at that end," she said. "Just go along the line and __4__ what you want. At the other end, they'll tell you how much you have to __5__."

"I soon learned that's how everything __6__ in the US," the old man later told a friend. "Life is a cafeteria here. You can get anything you want __7__ you are willing to pay the price. You can even get success, but you'll never get it if you wait for someone to __8__ it to you. You have to get up and get it yourself."

In fact, __9__ everywhere is like a cafeteria. Don't wait for things to happen to you. Success lies in your own __10__.

(　　)1. A. asked　　B. left　　C. called　　D. waited

(　　)2. A. somebody　　B. everybody　　C. nobody　　D. anybody

(　　)3. A. how　　B. what　　C. where　　D. why

(　　)4. A. send out　　B. give out　　C. pick out　　D. look out

(　　)5. A. buy　　B. pay　　C. give　　D. choose

(　　)6. A. works　　B. takes　　C. needs　　D. keeps

(　　)7. A. if　　B. because　　C. though　　D. until

(　　)8. A. carry　　B. lend　　C. move　　D. bring

(　　)9. A. food　　B. life　　C. money　　D. success

(　　)10. A. work　　B. hands　　C. opinion　　D. books

七、完形填空。

It's never easy to admit(承认) you are in the wrong. We all __1__ to know the art of apology. Think how often you're done wrong. Then count how many __2__ you've expressed clearly you were __3__. You can't go to bed with an easy mind if you do __4__ about it.

A doctor friend, Mr. Lied, told me about a man who came to him with different kinds of signs: headaches, heart __5__ and insomnia(失眠). __6__ some careful exams, Mr. Lied found nothing __7__ with him and said, "If you don't tell me what's __8__ you, I can't help you." The man admitted he was cheating his brother of his inheritance(遗产). Then and there the __9__ doctor __10__ the man write to his brother and __11__ his money. As soon as the __12__ was put into the post box, the man suddenly cried. "Thank you," he said to the doctor, "I think I've got __13__."

An apology can not only save a broken relationship(关系) but also make it __14__. If you can think of someone who should be __15__ an apology from you. Do something about it right now.

( )1. A. decide B. have C. need D. try
( )2. A. mistakes B. people C. ways D. times
( )3. A. sorry B. weak C. sad D. wrong
( )4. A. something B. anything C. nothing D. everything
( )5. A. trouble B. matter C. illness D. problem
( )6. A. Before B. After C. Till D. Since
( )7. A. well B. wrong C. good D. bad
( )8. A. hurling B. changing C. touching D. worrying
( )9. A. clever B. silly C. good D. kind
( )10. A. made B. helped C. saw D. let
( )11. A. returned B. gave C. kept D. paid
( )12. A. paper B. box C. money D. letter
( )13. A. better B. well C. sick D. worse
( )14. A. never B. worse C. stronger D. harder
( )15. A. given B. received C. known D. forgotten

八、首字母填空。

About three years old, I felt very lonely. I didn't like my classmates, my parents or anyone else. My classmates didn't want to talk (1)________ me and my parents were always saying that other kids were better than me. I thought I was the (2)________ unlucky(不幸的) person in the world.

One day I had a big fight with one of my classmates. I was so angry (3)________ I hit(打) him in the face. Just at that moment, a boy stood up and (4)________ the fight. He was the monitor(班长) of our class.

After that, he often helped me and we became good (5)________. Whenever I got angry or sad, he would help (6)________ to cool down. My life began to change because of the boy, my best friend. We spent a lot of interesting days together. As (7)________ goes by, I have become happier with people and things. And people around me have changed, (8)________. My parents don't shout at me and my classmates become (9)________ to me.

But now I can't see my best friend because he is seriously (10)________ and is staying in hospital. How I miss the days when we were together! I hope he will be all right and come back to school soon.

Unit 11

Section One

一、用 be 动词的适当形式填空。

1. I ________ at school just now.
2. He ________ at the camp last week.
3. We ________ students two years ago.
4. They ________ on the farm a moment ago.
5. Sally ________ eleven years old last year.

二、写出下列年份。

1. 1099 ________________
2. 2001 ________________
3. 1998 ________________
4. 1970 ________________
5. 1800 ________________
6. 2010 ________________

三、句型转换。

1. It was exciting.（变否定句）

____

2. All the students were very excited.（变否定句）

____

3. They were in his pocket.（变一般疑问句）

____

4. There was a car in front of the house just now.（对画线部分提问）

____

5. Did you stay in America for long?（否定回答）

____

四、完成对话。

This is an interview with Andy Lau(刘德华).

A：Nice to meet you, Andy. May I have an interview with you?

B：Fine.

A：(1)________?

B：I was born in 1961.

A：Where（2）________？

B：I（3）________ in Hong Kong.

A：What did you use to be？

B：I（4）________ a worker.

A：When（5）________？

B：I became an actor in 1981.

A：When did you win the best leading actor of the Hong Kong Film Awards？

B：In 2000.

五、改错题。

1. How is Jane yesterday？ ____________________
2. He go to school by bus last week. ____________________
3. He often goes home at 6：00 last month. ____________________
4. I can fly kites seven years ago. ________
5. Did you saw him just now？ ____________________

六、看 Jason 上周的日记，写出问句和答句。

Sep. 28th
go to the Zhongshan Park

Sep. 29th
have dinner with Jacky

Sep. 30th
attend a lecture

Sep. 31st
go to the movies at night

Oct. 1st
go for an outing with family

Oct. 2nd
celebrate mothers birthday

eg：

On Sep. 29th

Did Jason have dinner with Mary？（negative）

No，he didn't. He had dinner with Jacky.

1. on Sep. 28th（affirmative）

____

____.

2. on Oct. 1st（affirmative）

____.

____.

3. on Oct. 2nd (negative)

____.

____.

七、用括号中词的适当形式填空。

1. He takes off his shoes and put them under the bed ________(quiet).
2. She ________(like) watching cartoons when she was a child.
3. There was a car accident yesterday and it ________(stop) all the traffic.
4. I ________ (see) the film *Alice in Wonderland* last week, while my sister ________ (study) at home.
5. —________ you ________ (travel) in England last summer holiday?
   —Yes, the trip ________ (be) great.

八、首字母填空。

1. The d________ is very important for him to get the job.
2. She worked as an a________ in the company.
3. Dr. Hawking had an i________ with the reporter on Channel 2.
4. What is the date of your b________?
5. Sally put on the c________ and acted on the stage.

Section Two

一、单项选择。

1. The boy stayed in the classroom ________ it got dark.
   A. before　B. until　C. since　D. while
2. —Who was on duty last Friday?
   —________
   A. I am.　B. I was.　C. Yes, I was.　D. No, I wasn't.
3. ________ you ________ TV last night?
   A. Do; watch　B. Did; watch　C. Did; watched　D. Do; watch
4. The ________ rope is mine.
   A. ten meters long　B. ten-meters long
   C. ten-meter-long　D. ten meter long
5. The man started ________ his own ________ in his book at twenty.
   A. write; experiences　B. writing; experiences
   C. to write; experience　D. writing; experience
6. ________ he was a little boy, he could take care of himself.
   A. Though　B. Because　C. When　D. As
7. I like to watch programmes ________ animals.
   A. with　B. on　C. against　D. in

8. It started ________ when I ________ home.
   A. to rain; arrived at　　B. raining; got
   C. to rain; got to　　D. raining; arrived
9. — Did you ________ the match?
   — Yes, we ________ them 4-2.
   A. win; beat　B. beat; win　C. beat; beat　D. win; win
10. — Could you show me how to use the computer?
   — Yes, I ________.
   A. could　B. will　C. shall　D. can

二、汉译英。

1. 美剧________　　2. 芝麻街________
3. 职责________　　4. 改变……的主意________
5. 拒绝________　　6. 教育某人________
7. 标题________　　8. 提供________

三、将下列动词归类并写出其正确的过去式形式。

fly　plant　drink　play　go　make　write　get　show　call　see　say
want　leave

regular（规则）	irregular（不规则）

四、用所给动词的适当形式填空。

1. He ________ (live) in Changsha two years ago.
2. The cat ________ (eat) a fish last night.
3. We ________ (have) a party last Halloween.
4. Nancy ________ (not leave) school early yesterday.
5. I ________ (make) a model ship with Mike yesterday.
6. They ________ (want) ________ (play) chess in the classroom at PE lesson last Thursday.
7. I ________ (try) ________ (cook) a nice meal the day before yesterday.
8. Einstein's mother ________ (educate) him at home.
9. It is time for supper now. Let's ________ (stop) ________ (have) it.
10. Could you give me a piece of paper ________ (write)?

五、原文填空。

1. Spinney ________ and knows that he has a responsibility to children ________.
2. He doesn't want children ________ Big Bird is ________ a man.
3. Once, ________, a child saw him as he ________.
4. She ________ at first, but changed her mind and ________ two years later.
5. She ________ it at thirteen and finished it ________ her sixteenth birthday.

六、句型转换。

1. She took some photos at the Sports meeting.（变一般疑问句）
   ____
2. Nancy went to school early.（变否定句）
   ____
3. He met the little boy at the entrance of the hall.（对画线部分提问）
   ____
4. Sarah moved to Oxford because she wanted to have further study.（对画线部分提问）
   ____
5. We provided some good books for the children in the countryside.（换一种说法）
   ____

七、句子翻译。

1. 他拒绝参加她的生日宴会。
   He ________ ________ join in her birthday party.
2. 她的父母问她是否愿意去上海度假。
   Her parents asked her ________ she ________ ________ spend a holiday in Shanghai.
3. 他在加拿大有一段美好的经历。
   He had a wonderful ________ in Canada.
4. Shirley 有责任保护她的安全。
   Shirley has a ________ to ________ her safe.
5. 这部电影太感人了，以致在场所有的人都哭了。
   The movie ________ so moving ________ all the people in the cinema ________.

Section Three

一、单项选择。

(　　) 1. America is a ________ country, but China is a ________ country.
   A. developing; developed　　B. developed; developing
   C. develop; developed　　D. developing; develop

(　　) 2. Betty ________ the chess club last week.

A. took part in　B. joined in　C. joined　D. take part in

(　　) 3. At that moment, the man ________ how serious the mistake was.

A. know　B. understand　C. understood　D. realised

(　　) 4. We all ________ the environment of our planet.

A. worried about　B. are worry about

C. were worried about　D. worry about

(　　) 5. Martin ________ Sally when they left the university.

A. married with　B. got married to

C. marry　D. got married with

二、根据课文内容判断正误。

(　　) 1. Rick Allen had a very bad accident and lost his right arm. So he couldn't play the drum any further.

(　　) 2. Carol Spinney, aged 57 started working with puppets when he was eight years old.

(　　) 3. The book written by Caitlin Moran was a sad story about a year in the life of a family who educate the children at home.

(　　) 4. Rick is unmarried and if he can't chop vegetables with one hand he simply uses his feet.

(　　) 5. Sesame Street is a British television series for children.

三、选词填空。

well-known　lose　chop　perform　climb　call　until　work

1. Carl Lewis is a ________ runner in the history of America.
2. The old man was ________ and he needed help to be sent home.
3. The carpenter ________ up the ladder to mend the roof of the house.
4. He can't ________ the trees with only one hand.
5. The movie ________ *The Lord of the Rings* interested us most.
6. He didn't arrive ________ the concert was over.
7. The clerk has a lot of ________ to do, so he can't leave now.
8. The ballet dancers ________ so well that we were all moved.

四、写出下列动词的过去式。

1. have ________	2. dance ________	3. worry ________
4. ask ________	5. become ________	6. eat ________
7. play ________	8. chop ________	9. throw ________
10. kick ________	11. pass ________	12. lose ________

五、句型练习。

1. Tom plays the piano <u>three times a week.</u>（对画线部分提问）

________ ________ does Tom play the piano?

2. Nick is a clever boy.(改为感叹句)

________ ________ Nick is!

3. Wendy was too tired to drive a car.(换一种说法)

Wendy was ________ ________ ________ ________ ________ drive a car.

4. He had a meeting last week.(否定句)

He ________ ________ a meeting last week.

5. The little girl finished reading the English novel yesterday.(对画线部分提问)

________ ________ the little girl ________ ________ yesterday?

六、翻译句子。

1. 尽管这个小男孩只有3岁,但是他会自己穿衣服。

________ the little boy is three years old, he can ________ himself.

2. 他的父母问他是否愿意和他们一起生活。

His parents ________ him if he ________ to live with them.

3. 她的生活在很多方面发生了变化。

Her life ________ in many ________.

4. 他有责任照顾这两个孩子。

He has a ________ to ________ ________ these two children.

5. 他直到晚上8点钟才到家。

He didn't ________ home ________ it was 8 at night.

七、完形填空。

Tom did not like doing his homework, because he liked to do some __1__ things after school. And his teacher always __2__ a lot of mistakes in his homework. Then one day, his maths teacher __3__ at Tom's homework and saw that he got all his answers right. He was very __4__ and surprised. The next morning before class, he called Tom __5__ his desk and __6__ to him, "You got all your homework right this time. Did your father help you?" Sometimes Tom's father helped him with his homework, __7__ this time he didn't help Tom because he __8__ at home. So Tom answered, "No, sir. He was busy last night, so I __9__ to do it __10__."

( )1. A. others B. another C. the other D. other

( )2. A. made B. found C. looked at D. looked

( )3. A. laughed B. knocked C. looked D. saw

( )4. A. please B. pleased C. pleasure D. sad

( )5. A. to B. for C. in D. at

( )6. A. talked B. asked C. told D. said

( )7. A. and B. but C. so D. or

( )8. A. isn't B. won't be C. wasn't D. can't be

( )9. A. wanted B. mustn't C. liked D. had

( )10. A. itself B. of them C. myself D. himself

Section Four

一、将下列字母重新排序成正确的单词。

1. c u o c a o t p n i ____________ 2. o r b n ____________
3. a u t h g t ____________ 4. c i c a e n d t ____________
5. d v e o e l p e d ____________ 6. l i b n d ____________

二、请用动词正确的形式填空。

1. I ________ (see) an exciting film last night.
2. — ________ she ________(practice)________(play) her guitar yesterday?
   — No, she ________.
3. Bellie's teachers ________(teach) all the subjects well.
4. Many people ________ (die) of SARS in 2003.
5. She ________(learn) ________ (speak) Spanish at the age of 13.
6. —When ________ you ________(write) this song?
   —I ________(write) it last year.
7. My friend, Carol, ________(decide) ________(be) a cook after he left school.
8. —________ Mr. Li ________(do) the project on Monday morning?
   —Yes, he ________.
9. —How ________(be) Tom's weekend? —It ________(be not) bad.
10. When ________ your mother ________(become) a sales assistant?

三、根据课文内容判断正误。

(　　) 1. Minnesota is a state in the west of the USA.
(　　) 2. It was Louis Braille who developed the writing system for the blind people.
(　　) 3. Louis Braille died in an accident.
(　　) 4. Louis Braille was born blind.
(　　) 5. She received education in Paris at the National Institute for the blind children.

四、阅读有关 **Diana Spencer** 的材料，选择单词，并用其适当的形式填空。

Diana Spencer
birthday—July 1st, 1961
Lady Diana Spencer—1975
first child—June 21, 1982
marriage—from July 29, 1981 to 1996
car accident—August 30, 1997

get　have　born　become　show　die　begin　divorce（离婚）

Diana Spencer was (1)________ on July 1st, 1961. She (2)________ Lady Diana Spencer after her father inherited the title of Earl Spencer in 1975. Although she was known for her shyness growing up, she (3)________ an interest in music and dancing. She moved to London. She (4)________ working with children, later she became a kindergarten teacher at the Young England School. She (5)________ married to Prince Charles, on July 29, 1981. On June 21, 1982, Diana and Charles (6)________ their first child: Prince William Arthur Philip Louis. They had two sons and later in 1996 (7)________. Diana (8)________ in a car crash after trying to escape the paparazzi in Paris on the night of August 30, 1997.

五、连词成句。

1. did / what / you / yesterday / do

____

2. watch / John / did / TV / weekend / last

____

3. went / I / to / park / my / bike

____

4. jumped / the / into / lake / he / and / the / to / swam / kite

____

5. did / how / she / go / yesterday / home

____

六、阅读理解。

Tom arrived at the bus station quite early for Paris bus. The bus for Paris would not leave until five to twelve. He saw a lot of people waiting in the station. Some were standing in line, others were walking around. There was a group of schoolgirls. Their teacher was trying to keep them in line. Tom looked around but there was no place for him to sit. He walked into the station cafe. He looked up at the clock there. It was only twenty to twelve. He found a seat and sat down before a large mirror on the wall. Just then, Mike, one of Tom's workmates came in and sat with Tom. "What time is your bus?" asked Mike. "There's plenty of time yet," answered Tom. "Well, I'll get you some more tea then," said Mike. They talked while drinking. Then Tom looked at the clock again. "Oh! It's going backward (倒行)!" he cried. "A few minutes ago it was twenty to twelve and now it's half past eleven." "You're looking at the clock in the mirror," said Mike. Tom was so sad. The next bus was not to leave for another hour. Since then Tom has never liked mirrors.

(　　)1. Tom went into the station cafe because ________.

A. Mike asked him to have a cup of tea

B. it was quite early and he could find a seat there

C. he didn't like to stay with the schoolgirls

D. he wanted to have a drink with his workmate there

( )2. What time was it in fact when Tom looked at the clock in the mirror?

A. Half past twelve. B. Twenty to twelve.

C. Half past eleven. D. Half past one.

( )3. From the story we know that when we look at a clock in a mirror, we will find ________.

A. the time is right B. it's going slower

C. it's going backward D. it's going faster

( ) 4. Which of the following is true?

A. Tom arrived in Paris on time.

B. The next bus would leave in half an hour.

C. After that Tom didn't like clocks any longer.

D. Tom looked at the clock in the mirror only once.

( )5. Which of the following is the title of the story?

A. The Mirror of the Station. B. Not a Careful Man.

C. Missing a Bus. D. The Clock in the Mirror.

Section Five

一、听句子，选择适当的应答语。

( )1. A. I'm Chinese. B. I'm not well. C. I'm a foreigner.

( )2. A. She walks much. B. She does every day. C. She walks to school.

( )3. A. What a pity! B. Help yourself. C. Watch out.

( )4. A. Not at all. B. Thank you. C. No, not so good.

( )5. A. Let's go. B. I'm ready. C. Yes, I have.

二、听对话，选择相应的图画。

( )1.

A

B

C

( )2.

A

B

C

( )3. 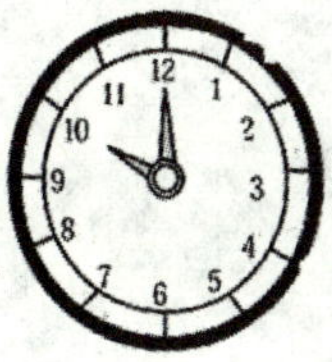  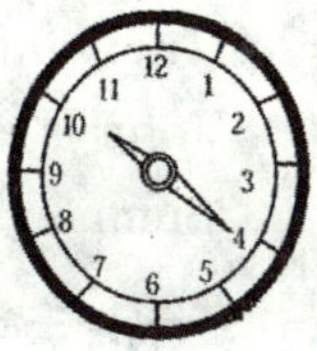

A B C

( )4. 

A B C

( )5.   

A B C

三、听五段对话和五个问题，选择正确答案。

( )1. A. Warm. B. Cold. C. Hot.

( )2. A. Yes, he is. B. No, he isn't. C. We don't know.

( )3. A. In 2005. B. Six years ago. C. In 2000.

( )4. A. He likes loud music.
B. The house here is too old.
C. He wants to live in a quiet place.

( )5. A. Fish. B. Chicken. C. Beef.

四、听一段长对话，选择正确答案。

( )1. What are the speakers mainly talking about?
A. Life. B. Camping. C. Plans.

( )2. What will the woman do in the city?
A. Work at a store. B. Attend a school. C. Have a picnic.

( )3. Who will the woman stay with?
A. The man. B. Her family. C. The man's brother.

( )4. What do they do in the morning when they camp?
A. Go swimming. B. Play basketball. C. Tell stories.

(　　)5. What can we learn from the conversation?
A. The woman has worked for four summers.
B. John is the man's brother.
C. Summer vacation is coming.

五、听短文，回答下面五个问题，选择正确答案。

(　　)1. When did this happen?
A. One afternoon.　　B. One night.　　C. One morning.

(　　)2. How many persons were there in the room when someone was knocking at the door?
A. One person.　　B. Two persons.　　C. Three persons.

(　　)3. What did the young man wear?
A. A white shirt.　　B. A pair of glasses.　　C. Long trousers.

(　　)4. Who was the young man?
A. He was a friend of the writer's.
B. He was a friend of the writer's brother's.
C. He was a strange man to them.

(　　)5. What was probably the end of the story?
A. The young man was taken away by the police.
B. The young man became their friend.
C. The young man ran away.

六、词义连线。

(　　) 1. responsibility　　A. teach or train sb.
(　　) 2. costume　　B. duty
(　　) 3. refuse　　C. a set of clothes that are typical or to make sb. look like sth.
(　　) 4. educate　　D. to say or show that you will not do sth.
(　　) 5. realize　　E. to start to know sth. that you had never noticed before

七、单项选择。

(　　) 1. He will be a drummer when he ______ up.
A. grow　　B. grew　　C. grows　　D. will grow

(　　) 2. He began to play the guitar ______ he was 11 years old.
A. since　　B. while　　C. when　　D. then

(　　) 3. Eton College ______ students ______ good education.
A. offers; to　　B. provides; with　C. provides; for　D. offers; for

(　　) 4. Rick Allen became a <u>well-known</u> drummer after playing for six years.
A. famous　　B. infamous　　C. popular　　D. interesting

( ) 5. The movie was ________ moving ________ almost everyone in the cinema cried.

A. too; to B. very; that C. /; enough D. so; that

( ) 6. You look ________. What do you ________?

A. worry, worry about B. worry; worried about

C. worried; worry about D. worried; worried about

( ) 7. The dinner didn't start ________ all the friends arrived.

A. when B. while C. until D. whether

( ) 8. My father had a busy day ________.

A. the day before yesterday B. tomorrow

C. next Saturday D. every day

( ) 9. Mrs. Clarke has a son ________ Bruno.

A. called B. calling C. calls D. to call

( ) 10. I saw an apple ________ into the water.

A. fall B. was fallen C. falls D. is fallen

( ) 11. I thought the news ________ important.

A. is B. was C. are D. were

( ) 12. —You're a very good student. —________.

A. No, not at all B. Yes, I am

C. Just so and so D. I'm glad to hear that

( ) 13. The old ________ the big tree down with two hands.

A. chop B. chopped C. chops D. was chopped

( ) 14. ________ it is getting dark, ________ the farmers are still working in the field.

A. Though; but B. But; though C. Though; / D. But; /

( ) 15. Don't let the children ________ in the reading room.

A. shout B. to shout C. shouting D. shouted

八、完形填空。

One Saturday morning John and his mother went __1__ a shoe shop __2__ John a pair of new shoes. Mrs. Lee put her bag on a chair __3__ she looked at some shoes. She could not see __4__ she liked and went away. Suddenly she said, "Oh, my bag, someone __5__ it away!" All the other people in the shop stopped __6__ and looked at her. John ran after the man at once. A few minutes __7__, John came back with __8__. He __9__ it to his mother. She opened the bag and had a look in __10__. Then she said, "Oh, god, nothing is lost."

( )1. A. by B. on C. to

( )2. A. to buy B. to give C. to take

( )3. A. so B. but C. when

( )4. A. some B. any shoes C. any bags

( )5. A. went B. had C. took
( )6. A. sitting B. thinking C. talking
( )7. A. after B. later C. next
( )8. A. the bag B. the shoes C. the man
( )9. A. give B. gave C. take
( )10. A. one B. it C. them

九、阅读理解。

Long, long ago, as the birds flew over the world, they saw that men had a beautiful thing. It was a bright, burning thing. Men cooked their food and kept themselves warm with it. The birds thought life would be better if they could have this thing, too. So they decided to send a messenger to humans(人类) to ask for a little piece of it. They thought Chicken was a good one to send because he was a good talker. So Chicken went.

He flew far over the forest until he came to the town of men. He went into a town and saw the burning thing. He learned that it was called "Fire". He did not ask for a piece of it to take back to the birds because there was so much food lying around men's houses that he started eating and forgot what he had come for.

Men liked Chicken because he crowed(啼叫) very early in the morning, and woke them up. They let him run in and out of their houses. They threw him food. So Chicken stayed with humans. He never went back to the birds. He even forgot how to fly.

( ) 1. When the birds flew over the world, they saw ________.
A. a beautiful lake B. a burning thing C. a messenger D. a chicken

( ) 2. The birds thought that if they too could have this thing life would be ________.
A. better B. safer C. longer D. brighter

( ) 3. The birds decided to send a messenger to ask men ________.
A. to come to the birds B. what the burning thing was
C. for food D. for a little piece of burning thing

( )4. The birds sent chicken to humans because they thought he ________.
A. was good at talking B. knew men in the town very well
C. could crow well D. could fly far over the forest

( )5. From this story we know that the burning thing was ________.
A. the sun B. the forest C. fire D. the house

十、用括号中词的适当形式填空。

1. Shelly ________ (can) already (ride) a horse when she was young.
2. — How often ________ she ________ (write) in her diary on weekdays?
   — Once a week. But she ________ (write) more when she was at home.
3. We all ________ (feel) very sad when we ________ (hear) of the death of Michael Jackson.

4. I ________ (hurt) my finger when I was ________ (cut) the meat.
5. She tried ______ (get) used to ______ (walk) home instead of ______ (drive)

十一、首字母填空。

1. Many people lead interesting and different l ________.
2. May I have your s ________, please?
3. He is disabled but he can play the d ________ well.
4. The man finally r ________ that he could be the same as others.
5. Jay is a w ________ singer, Many teenagers like him very much.

十二、句型练习。

1. She stayed at school for five days.(对画线部分提问)

____

2. Some people in Thailand moved away from their hometown because there was a terrible flood(水灾).(对画线部分提问)

____

3. The children joined the band last month. (换一种说法)

____

4. The man climbed up the mountain with the help of the local people. (变否定句)

____

5. Sally returned home late last night. (变一般疑问句)

____

6. Lang Ping was a volleyball player 15 years ago.(对画线部分提问)

____

7. Shakespeare was born in 1564.(对画线部分提问)

____

8. Her nickname was "toothpick" because she was very thin at that time.(对画线部分提问)

____

9. We had a great time in South America. (换一种说法)

____

10. Which film did you like best?(换一种说法)

____

Unit 12

Section One

一、读一读，连一连。

(　　) 1. draw　　　　A. mumps
(　　) 2. shut　　　　B. shopping
(　　) 3. buy　　　　C. a number
(　　) 4. catch　　　　D. your eyes
(　　) 5. go　　　　E. raffle tickets

二、首字母填空。

1. Red is my l ________ color. I love it. What about you?
2. —What's your n ________? —Eight.
3. I really want to see the movie. Can I have a t ________ for tomorrow, please?
4. I'm very hungry. Will you please give me a ________ piece of bread?
5. I've c ________ a bad cold. I want to have a rest.

三、单项选择。

(　　)1. The man ________ in 1992, he ________ for ten years.
A. died; was dead　　B. died; has been dead
C. was dead; has died　　D. was dead; has been died

(　　)2. They ________ in this school since they ________ to this city in 2000.
A. have studied; have come　　B. have studied; came
C. studied; came　　D. were studying; have come

(　　) 3. —How long can I ________ this book? — Two weeks.
A. borrow　　B. keep　　C. lend　　D. return

(　　)4. I have ________ a member of Greener China since three years ago.
A. become　　B. became　　C. been　　D. joined

(　　)5. — Have you finished your work ______? — Yes, I have ____ done it.
A. yet; yet　　B. already; already　　C. already; just　　D. yet; just

四、句型转换。

1. rulers, Tom, got, any, not, has（连词成句）

____

2. She has got some money.(改为一般疑问句)

______

3. They have got a ball of string and a kite.(改为否定句)

______

4. Mary has got many apples.(对画线部分提问)

______

5. —你学习英语多久了?　—我已经学了两年了。(汉译英)

—How long ______ you ______ English?

—I ______ ______ it for two years.

6. It is three years since he became a worker.(同义句)

He ______ ______ a worker ______ three years.

7. Mary has been to Beijing only twice.(对画线部分提问)

______

五、重点句型精练。

eg: father / nails / a hammer

Has father got any nails?　He's got some nails, but he hasn't got a hammer.

1. Tom / a headache / a temperature

______

2. They / strawberries / cream

______

eg: Sandy / a sandwich / a cake

Has Sandy had a sandwich yet? He's already had a sandwich, but he hasn't had a cake.

3. Sue / flu / mumps

______

4. They / a shave / a haircut

______

eg: What about some nails?　I've got some. Have you got any?

What about a money-box?　I've got one. Have you got one?

5. What about some steak?

______

6. What about a hammer?

______

六、根据上下文选用适当的句子补全对话。

A. Ahh... What's wrong, doctor?	B. All right. Thank you, doctor.
C. Since last night.	D. Do you feel well?
E. Two days ago.	F. What's the matter?
G. Have you taken your temperature?	

A: (1) ______

B：I don't feel very well. I've got a headache and a cough.

A：(2) ________________

B：Yes. But I haven't got a fever.

A：Open your mouth and say "Ahh".

B：(3) ________________

A：You've got a cold. How long have you been like this?

B：(4) ________________

A：Take this medicine and stay in bed for a few days. Then you'll be all right.

B：(5) ________________

Section Two

一、读一读，连一连。

( ) 1. play　　A. to the cinema

( ) 2. go　　B. like a Russian

( ) 3. see　　C. an usual hat

( ) 4. try on　　D. truant

( ) 5. look　　E. a lovely film

二、首字母填空。

1. Do you m ________ opening the window?
2. Thanks a lot. I am g ________ better.
3. The lights have a ________ been on for a whole night.
4. That boy played t ________ yesterday. His mother was very angry with him.
5. Look at that l ________ girl! She's very smart.

三、单项选择。

( )1. The Greens have ________ their hometown ________ 1990.

A. left; since　　B. left; for

C. been away from; after　　D. been away from; since

( )2. Where have you ________? I didn't see you just now.

A. been　　B. gone　　C. been to　　D. gone to

( )3. —Where's Bob? — He ________ Paris with his sister. He'll be back in two weeks.

A. has been to　　B. has gone to　　C. comes from　　D. went to

( )4. — ________ is it from here?

—It's about ten minutes' walk.

A. How long　　B. How soon　　C. How far　　D. How many

( )5. How long have you ________ this bike?

A. bought　　B. had　　C. borrowed　　D. got

四、句型转换。

1. Where have you been today?（用 the library 回答）
____
2. you, have, the park, to, been（?）（连词成句）
____
3. Has Mr. Wu been to the cinemas?（否定回答）
____
4. she's, to, been, just, the doctor's （.）（连词成句）
____
5. I have been here for two hours.（对画线部分提问）
____
6. I found my parcel a while ago.（用 already 改写画线部分）
I ________ ________ my parcel ________.
7. He did his lessons this morning.（改为一般疑问句）
____

五、重点句型精练。

eg: Did Sandy go to church in the morning?
No, he didn't. He hasn't been to church yet.
1. Did the children go to the library the other day?
____
2. Did you go to the watchmaker's last month?
____

eg: Has he ever been to Europe?（during the war）
Yes, he has. He's already been to Europe.
He was in Europe during the war.
3. Has she ever been to Asia?（last year）
____
____
4. Has he ever been to Russia?（a fortnight ago）
____
____
5. Have they been to the park?（last Sunday）
____
____

六、根据上下文选用适当的句子补全对话。

A. Don't you have some less expensive shirts?
B. Yes, I'd like to buy a shirt.
C. Good afternoon.
D. I'll take this one.
E. Goodbye.
F. Thirty-four.
G. How much is it?

A：Good afternoon, sir. May I help you?
B：(1) ______________________________
A：Yes, sir. What size, please?
B：(2) ______________________________
A：Here's one in your size. This is a very fine shirt.
B：(3) ______________________________
A：These are ninety-five each.
B：That's a little more than I wanted to pay. (4) ______________
A：Yes, I think I can find some for you. Here are some for eighty. And then we have some for seventy-five here.
B：This one looks nice. (5) ______________________________

Section Three

一、读一读，连一连。

( ) 1. suit A. to the chief
( ) 2. tread B. the floor
( ) 3. take off C. an usual hat
( ) 4. polish D. on the grass
( ) 5. speak E. that boy

二、首字母填空。

1. She often goes to that m ________ to buy some fresh vegetables.
2. It's an u ________ day for me today. I'll never forget it.
3. I like the coat very much. The color s ________ me well.
4. Would you like to s ________ me your photo? I want to have a look.
5. She hasn't been to the seaside s ________ the year before last.

三、单项选择。

( )1. Li Lei has ________ Guangzhou since he was 14.
A. come to B. gone to C. been to D. been in
( )2. The teacher isn't here. He ________ to the office.
A. went B. will go C. has gone D. is going
( )3. —________ you ________ the film yet? —Yes, I ________ it last Saturday.
A. Will, see; saw B. Did, see; saw
C. Have, seen; have seen D. Have, seen; saw
( )4. I ________ such an interesting book before.
A. was never reading B. will never read
C. had never read D. have never read
( )5. The old people ____ lonely at all since we began to visit them once a week.
A. don't feel B. hasn't felt C. haven't felt D. didn't feel

四、句型转换。

1. 1982, since, has, she, here, been(.)(连词成句)

____

2. Has he filled the basin?(否定回答)

____

3. I have posted the letter.(对画线部分提问)

____

4. They have lived here since two years ago.(对画线部分提问)

____

5. She has never surfed, ________ ________?(反义疑问句)

____

五、完形填空。

My life is always filled with sadness and little joy. However, no matter what happens, I can always face it bravely.

Last year, I couldn't believe the __1__ that I was allowed to enter the only key high school in my hometown. Then I rushed to my home and told my parents. But my father didn't seem as __2__ as I was. He just kept smoking without saying a word and my mother put her head down and couldn't help __3__.

I knew very well what my family was __4__. My mum had been ill in bed for 2 years. We lived a hard life and I couldn't continue my schooling. I felt so upset but I could say __5__ to my parents. I decided to help my father with his work __6__ my family.

To my surprise, things completely changed __7__ the beginning of the new term. My head teacher came to my family with some money, which had been __8__ by my schoolmates. He encouraged me, "Always have a dream." With tears in my eyes, I stepped into the key high school.

I have been studying hard since I entered the high school. Whenever I meet difficulties, I always __9__ my teacher and schoolmates. I have a college dream and I must work hard for it, no matter __10__ hard life is. Just as a great man says, "When one door shuts, another opens in life."

(　　)1. A. idea　B. story　C. news　D. thought

(　　)2. A. nervous　B. excited　C. interested　D. worried

(　　)3. A. crying　B. laughing　C. saying　D. shouting

(　　)4. A. about　B. before　C. against　D. like

(　　)5. A. nothing　B. something　C. anything　D. everything

(　　)6. A. support　B. to support　C. supporting　D. supported

(　　)7. A. after　B. since　C. before　D. on

(　　)8. A. raised　B. spent　C. planned　D. saved

(　　)9. A. dream of　B. think of　C. hear of　D. talk of

(　　)10. A. what　B. which　C. that　D. how

六、根据上下文选用适当的句子补全对话。

A. What size do you want?	B. Good morning.
C. What about those shoes over there?	D. Can I try them on, please?
E. What can I do for you?	
F. I'm afraid we haven't got any black shoes in that size at the moment.	
G. How many do you want?	

A: (1) ________________

B: I'm looking for a pair of black shoes.

A: (2) ________________

B: Size eight.

A: (3) ________________ But we've got some brown ones.

B: Hmm. Have you got any other kind?

A: (4) ________________

B: Well, that pair looks nice. How much does it cost?

A: Fifty yuan.

B: Hmm! That's a bit expensive. (5) ________________

A: Certainly.

Section Four

一、读一读,连一连。

( ) 1. park A. the cake
( ) 2. knock B. the soup
( ) 3. bake C. the car
( ) 4. answer D. at the door
( ) 5. stir E. the phone

二、首字母填空。

1. I'll be back in a w________.
2. May I speak to the C________ Inspector, please?
3. She is a very f________ singer. We all know her.
4. Tom wants to be a s________ in the future. He likes science very much.
5. Three bank r________ have happened lately in the city.

三、写出下列动词的过去式与过去分词。

1. count ______ ______	2. turn ______ ______	3. answer ______ ______
4. carry ______ ______	5. live ______ ______	6. knock ______ ______
7. visit ______ ______	8. open ______ ______	9. try ______ ______
10. play ______ ______	11. stop ______ ______	12. stir ______ ______

四、单项选择。

( )1. The musician hasn't been here ________.
A. three weeks B. since three weeks
C. for three weeks D. about three weeks

( )2. I have known him ________.
A. two years B. for over two years
C. two years ago D. last year

( )3. We haven't seen him ________.
A. last week B. for last week
C. since last week D. since a week

( )4. I ________ Tom since he was a little boy.
A. knew B. know
C. has known D. have known

( )5. He's finished his homework, ________?
A. isn't he B. hasn't he C. doesn't he D. wasn't he

五、句型转换。

1. Gloria left an hour ago (同义句)
Gloria ________ ________ ________ an hour ago.
2. Mr. Bean told them a story a moment ago. (对画线部分提问)
____
3. He has already finished his homework. (改为否定句)
He ________ finished his homework ________.
4. They have found the lost books already. (改为一般疑问句,并作否定回答)
________ they ________ the lost books ________? No, they ________.
5. Julia has not got home from school yet. (改为肯定句)
Julia ________ ________________ home from school.
6. I have finished my homework. (对画线部分提问)
____
7. 我们自从毕业后一直是朋友。(翻译成英语)
We ________ ________ friends ________ we left school.
8. They did their homework late last night. (改为否定句)
____

六、阅读理解。

Father's Day

Everyone celebrates Father's Day a bit differently, but if you are looking for something a bit different, here are some things or ways you might consider.

Flowers—Yes! How many ties does one dad need! If you know your dad has a special, then a bunch of flowers would be nice. If you are unsure what type of flowers, then a single rose will let him know your care.

Handmade Card/Picture—It doesn't matter if you're 8,28 or 48. A handmade card or note from the heart speaks more of your feelings than the things you bought from the store.

Home Cooking—Give mom the day off as well and invite them both over for a good home cooked meal. But remember today is not the day to test out that new recipe. Play it safe（慎重行事）and stick to（贴近）dad's taste.

Dinner—If you're not the home cooking type, then nothing is better than being treated（招待）to a tasty meal at a nice restaurant surrounded（围绕）by the ones you love. It doesn't have to be anywhere fancy（考究的）, depending on your dad, it could be the neighborhood dinner.

(　　) 1. Which of the following is NOT mentioned in the passage?

A. Flowers.　　B. A watch.　　C. A handmade note.　　D. A tie.

(　　) 2. According to the passage, we can infer（推测）________ might often cook at home.

A. son　　B. mom　　C. dad　　D. daughter

(　　) 3. What does the writer advice you to do on Father's Day?

A. You must take your father to a fancy restaurant.

B. You should test out a new recipe.

C. You have to buy a tie for your father.

D. You can buy your father a single rose to show your care.

(　　) 4. Which statement is NOT true?

A. If you are 38, you can't make a card for your father.

B. A handmade card expresses more your feelings than the things from the store.

C. It's a good idea to invite both of your parents for a home cooked meal.

D. You should cook the food your father likes best.

(　　) 5. If you are not home cooking type, you may ________.

A. buy some food from a restaurant

B. ask your mother to cook

C. treat your father at a restaurant

D. learn from a cook

Section Five

一、听写单词和短语。

1. ________　2. ________　3. ________　4. ________　5. ________

6. ________　7. ________　8. ________　9. ________　10. ________

二、对话理解。根据你所听到的对话及问题选择正确答案。

(　　) 1. A. My birthday.　　B. Thursday.　　C. Friday.

( )2. A. In the super market. B. In the classroom. C. In the cinema.

( )3. A. She watched a table tennis match.
B. She played table tennis. C. She saw a film.

( )4. A. She is reading. B. She is writing.
C. She is drawing.

( )5. A. The report on the radio. B. The war on Iraq(伊拉克).
C. The life of the president of Iraq.

三、短文理解。根据你所听到的短文内容及问题选择正确答案。

( )1. A. In America. B. In England. C. In Australia.

( )2. A. For one year. B. For two years. C. For three years.

( )3. A. Three. B. Four. C. Five.

( )4. A. England. B. Japan. C. China.

( )5. A. Because they won't have to move any more.
B. Because they will go to another new country.
C. Because they can see their friends all over the world.

四、单项选择。

( ) 1. How long ________ you ________ a party member?
A. have; become B. have; joined C. have; been D. have; worked

( ) 2. Jack has lived in Beijing ________ he came to China.
A. when B. since C. before D. for

( ) 3. I ________ here since I was born.
A. have lived B. have left C. have been to D. have arrived

( ) 4. He has ________ the watch for a year.
A. buy B. bought C. have D. had

( ) 5. Her brother ________ the Party since 1978.
A. joined B. has joined C. has been in D. was in

( ) 6. He has made a lot of friends ________.
A. in the past B. years ago C. since years ago D. just now

五、原文填空。

1. I want a boy to ________ a piece of paper out of this hat.
2. All the children bought raffle tickets. The first ________ was a bicycle.
3. What did you think, mum ? I didn't play ________.
4. Professor Boffin has been to lots of countries. He's showing Sandy some ________ hats.
5. Try it on, Sandy. It ________ you, Sandy.
6. That's funny. The library's ________. Let's climb in and see.
7. —What's happened, sir? —There's been a ________ at the library.
8. Don't ________ on my nice clean floor. I've just polished it.
9. Look at your ________ shoes, Sandy! Don't come into the kitchen.

10. Look, sir! There's a light ________ in the library.

六、用 never, ever, already, yet, for, since 填空。

1. I have ________ seen him before, so I have no idea about him.
2. Jack has ________ been away from here ________ an hour ago.
3. Mr. Wang has taught in this school ________ ten years.
4. —Have you ________ seen the film? —No, I have ________ seen it.
5. —Has the bus left ________? —Yes, it has ________ left.

七、时态填空。

1. Every student ________ (see) the film already.
2. Kent and I ________ (write) a song before.
3. Dick ________ (do) the work already.
4. The people in the mountains ________ never ________ (see) films.
5. Patty ________ (buy) a magazine about the school life before.
6. The actress ________ (live) here all her life.
7. The glass is broken. Who ________ (break) this glass?
8. The workers ________ (not finish) that job yet.
9. ________ you ________ (borrow) the book we talked about last time?
10. There's no more wine in the bottle. They ________ (drink) all of it.
11. Tom ________ (leave) a message for you. He ________ (call) last night.
12. I ________ (see) the movie once before. I ________ (love) it a lot.
13. —________ (you/hear) the news? —Yes, I ________.
    —Who ________ (tell) you the news? —Li Ming ________ (do).
    —When ________ (he/tell) you? —Two hours ago.

八、句型转换。

1. You have never been to Shanghai before, ________ ________?（改为反义疑问句）
2. —他找到他的钢笔了吗？ —还没找到。（汉译英）
   —________ he ________ his pen yet? —No, he ________ ________ his pen yet.
3. Mr. Wang began to teach English in this school in 1999.（改为同义句）
   Mr. Wang ________ ________ English in this school since 1999.
4. He has lunch at home.
   He ________ ________ lunch at home.（否定句）
   ________ he ________ lunch at home?（疑问句）
5. They have lived here since 3 years ago.（对画线部分提问）
   ____?
6. 你去过上海，是吗？（汉译英）
   You ________ ________ Shanghai, ________ ________?
7. I have posted the letter.（对画线部分提问）
   ____?

九、汉译英。

1. 吉姆已经做完了作业,他现在有空了。

____

2. 他已经收到了那封信。

____

3. 我父亲以前到过长城。

____

4. 她还没有看过那部新电影。

____

5. 她去过上海。

____

6. 他这些天上哪儿去了?

____

十、根据上下文选用适当的句子补全对话。

A. OK. Just a minute.	B. You're welcome. Goodbye.
C. All right. I'll give him the message.	D. Thanks.
E. Can I leave a message?	F. Yes, I think so.
G. Can I take a message?	

A: Hello. May I speak to Larry?

B: I'm afraid Larry isn't here right now. (1)________

A: This is Bob, his friend speaking. Would you please ask Larry to bring a few bottles of soda to the party tonight?

B: (2)________ I'm writing it down. "Bob called. You should bring a few bottles of soda to the party tonight." Is that right?

A: (3)________ You might ask him to call me back if he has a chance.

B: (4)________

A: Thanks very much.

B: (5)________

A: Goodbye.

十一、完形填空。

Mr. Green works in an office in Chicago. __1__ Saturday, he went to the office to do some work. When he got on the elevator, it stopped between the __2__. Mr. Green could not get out of the elevator. He started to __3__, but no one __4__ him. Then Mr. Green remembered that it was a holiday in America. No one was going to come to work __5__ Tuesday.

There was __6__ for him to do. He had to wait. With nothing to eat __7__ drink, Mr. Green slept for most of the time. Early Tuesday morning, his __8__ came to work and found the elevator was not working. When the elevator was __9__, Mr. Green came out.

He was cold, weak, and tired. He had been in the elevator for about sixty-four __10__! Now Mr. Green says, "I will only use elevators if they have a telephone in them."

( )1.	A. On	B. One	C. All	D. None
( )2.	A. buildings	B. rooms	C. steps	D. floors
( )3.	A. speak	B. say	C. shout	D. laugh
( )4.	A. saw	B. heard	C. came	D. talked
( )5.	A. until	B. on	C. by	D. since
( )6.	A. something	B. nothing	C. everything	D. anything
( )7.	A. and	B. for	C. or	D. but
( )8.	A. wife	B. teachers	C. parents	D. workmates
( )9.	A. closed	B. opened	C. clean	D. empty
( )10.	A. hours	B. days	C. minutes	D. weeks

十二、阅读理解。

This is a song millions of Americans will hear this New Year's Eve. It is called *Auld Lang Syne*（《友谊地久天长》）. It is the traditional music played during the New Year's celebration. *Auld Lang Syne* is an old Scottish poem. It tells about the need to remember old friends.

The words "auld lang syne" mean "old long since". No one knows who wrote the poem first. However, a version by Scottish poet Robert Bums was published (出版) in 1796. The words and music we know today first appeared in a songbook three years later.

The song is played in the United States mainly on New Year's Eve. The version (译文) you are hearing today is by the Washington Saxophone Quartet. As we end our program with *Auld Lang Syne*. I would like to wish all our radio friends a very Happy New Year! This is Buddy Thomas.

( ) 1. This passage is from ________.

A. newspaper　　B. a magazine

C. a TV program　　D. a radio program

( ) 2. ________ is introducing *Auld Lang Syne* to us.

A. Robert Bums　　B. The Washington Saxophone Quartet

C. Buddy Thomas　　D. The passage doesn't tell us

( ) 3. From the passage, we know that the song *Auld Lang Syne* mainly played in the USA ________________.

A. on New Year's Eve　　B. on Christmas Eve

C. on weekends　　D. on holidays

( ) 4. The words and music of *Auld Lang Syne* we know today first appeared ________.

A. in 1790　　B. in 1793　　C. in 1796　　D. in 1799

( ) 5. The song *Auld Lang Syne* is about ________.

A. the history of Scotland　　B. an old Scottish poet

C. the need to remember old friends　　D. the wishes to the radio friends

Unit 13

Section One

一、读一读，连一连。

(　　) 1. light	A. the newspaper
(　　) 2. play	B. a parcel
(　　) 3. waste	C. time
(　　) 4. read	D. a fire
(　　) 5. make	E. a trick on him

二、写出下列动词的过去式与过去分词。

1. say ______ ______	2. get ______ ______	3. light ______ ______
4. find ______ ______	5. tell ______ ______	6. hear ______ ______
7. meet ______ ______	8. set ______ ______	9. spend ______ ______
10. read ______ ______	11. cut ______ ______	12. shut ______ ______
13. put ______ ______	14. hit ______ ______	15. have ______ ______

三、首字母填空。

1. He died in a car a ________ years ago.
2. Be careful! Don't t ________ on the grass.
3. The road was s ________ after the rain.
4. He p ________ his glasses with a handkerchief before answering.
5. You mustn't play games in the street. It's d ________.

四、时态填空。

1. He ________ (bring) some flowers yesterday.
2. —What are you doing? —We ________ (repair) our bicycles.
3. —Where is my apple? —Sorry, I ________ (eat) it.
4. All my birds ________ (fly) away. I don't have them any more.
5. Who ________ (take) my cheese away? It was here a moment ago.

五、单项选择。

(　　)1. —________ he ________ at this school last term? —Yes, I think so.

A. Did; study　　B. Has; studied　　C. Was; study　　D. Did; studied

(　　) 2. —Have you mended your shoes, Bob?
—Yes, I ________ them twenty minutes ago.
A. have mended　B. mend　　C. had mended　D. mended

(　　) 3. —I'm sorry you have missed the bus. It ________ five minutes ago.
—What a pity!
A. was leaving　B. has left　　C. left　　D. leaves

(　　) 4. Have you met Mr. Li ________?
A. just　　B. ago　　C. before　　D. a moment ago

(　　) 5. The famous writer ________ one new book in the past two years.
A. is writing　　B. was writing　　C. wrote　　D. has written

六、句型转换。

1. The factory opened ten years ago.（同义句）
The factory ________ ________ ________ for ten years.
2. They have cleaned the room twice this week.（对画线部分提问）
________ ________ ________ ________ they ________ the classroom this week?
3. I've spoken to your mother on the phone.（用 yesterday 改写句子）
____
4. He's just taken off the hat.（同义句）
He ________ off his hat a few minutes ________.

七、重点句型精练。

eg: What's Sandy done?　cut his finger / a while ago
Sandy's just cut his finger. He cut his finger a while ago.
1. What's mother done?　shut the window / a few minutes ago
____
2. What's Sue done?　set the table / at six o'clock
____

eg: What's happened?　the boys / break the window / yesterday
The boys have just broken the window.
When did they break the window?　They broke the window yesterday.
3. What's happened?　the children / wake up / at seven
____
____
4. What's happened?　the girl \ see a movie \ this evening
____
____

八、根据上下文选用适当的句子补全对话。

A. About a quarter to six, OK?	B. Yes. I think so. Why?
C. Sorry, I'm busy.	D. Are you OK?
E. Is it OK?	F. Oh, thank you. I would love to.
G. What time shall I come?	

A: Meimei, are you free next Tuesday evening?

B: (1)____________

A: Would you like to have supper with me?

B: (2)____________ But I must ask my parents first. (3)____________

A: We'll have our supper at about a quarter past six. Will you come a little earlier?

(4)________________

B: I have a lot of homework to do. I must finish that first. But I think I can be free at six.

(5)________________

A: Sure.

Section Two

一、读一读，连一连。

( ) 1. blow up	A. on the phone
( ) 2. speak	B. ill
( ) 3. throw away	C. a kite
( ) 4. fly	D. the waste paper
( ) 5. feel	E. a balloon

二、写出下列动词的过去式与过去分词。

1. give ______ ______	2. do ______ ______	3. see ______ ______
4. begin ______ ______	5. run ______ ______	6. come ______ ______
7. go ______ ______	8. set ______ ______	9. rise ______ ______
10. wake ______ ______	11. speak ______ ______	12. break ______ ______

三、首字母填空。

1. My father likes reading n________. Now He is reading it every day.
2. It was cold yesterday. We l________ a fire to get warm.
3. She n________ a map. She didn't know the way.
4. It's April 1st today. We played t________ on each other during playtime.
5. B________ out the candles and say "Happy birthday!"

四、单项选择。

(　　) 1. —________ you ________ your homework yet? —Yes. I ________ it a moment ago.

A. Did; do; finished　　B. Have; done; finished

C. Have; done; have finished　　D. will; do; finish

(　　) 2. —How long have you ________ here? —About two months.

A. been　B. gone　C. come　D. arrived

(　　) 3. ________ you just ________ breakfast?

A. Did; have　B. Have; had　C. Do; have　D. Will; have

(　　) 4. His uncle ________ for more than 9 years.

A. has come here　　B. has started to work

C. has lived there　　D. has left the university

(　　) 5. The Greens ________ many places of interest since they came to China.

A. will visit　B. visited　C. have visited　D. visit

(　　) 6. —How long ________ you ________ your dictionary? —About two months.

A. did; buy　B. have; get　C. have; had　D. have; bought

五、句型转换。

1. My father bought the car half a year ago.（同义句）

My father ________ ________ the car ________ half a year.

2. I have already finished my homework.（变一般疑问句）

____

3. My friend has just bought a piano.（对画线部分提问）

____

4. What has Sandy got?（用 an old coat 回答）

____

5. Mr. Bean told them a story a minute ago.（对画线部分提问）

____

6. They have cleaned the room twice this week.（对画线部分提问）

________ ________ ________ ________ they ________ the classroom this week?

六、重点句型精练。

eg: Blow up some balloons!　(before the party)

We've already blown up some balloons. We blew up them before the party.

1. Throw away the waste paper!　(after the lesson)

____

2. Ride your bicycles!　(during the day)

____

eg: What have they done?　fly kites / a while ago

They've just flown kites.

When did they fly kites? They flew kites a while ago.

____

3. What have they done? draw pictures / at lunch time

____

____

4. What have they done? take off shoes / in the evening

____

____

七、根据上下文选用适当的句子补全对话。

A. Sure. How about Monday?	B. I don't know.
C. Let's meet at the gate of the park.	D. Me, too.
E. Well, let's get together soon.	F. See you.
G. Are you free on Wednesday?	

A: I'd love to talk with you, but I really have to go now.

B: (1)______________________

A: OK. Could we have lunch together some day next week?

B: (2)______________________

A: Hmm. I'm afraid I can't make it on Monday. I've to fly to Chicago.

(3)______________________

B: Wednesday sounds good. Where should we meet?

A: (4)______________________

B: Fine.

A: See you then.

B: (5)______________________

Section Three

一、读一读，连一连。

( ) 1. ring — A. the ladder

( ) 2. think about — B. a pair of shoes

( ) 3. hold — C. a math problem

( ) 4. fight — D. in the war

( ) 5. wear — E. the bell

二、首字母填空。

1. I went home late yesterday. My mom was very c ________ with me.

2. Lucy is wearing a l ________ hat today.
3. That naughty boy k ________ an old bottle all his way to school.
4. D ________ the break, my teacher read his newspaper today.
5. Please t ________ away the waste paper on your desk and make your desk tidy.

三、写出下列动词的过去式与过去分词。

1. ring ______ ______	2. write ______ ______	3. sing ______ ______
4. feel ______ ______	5. wear ______ ______	6. stand ______ ______
7. sleep ______ ______	8. shine ______ ______	9. sit ______ ______
10. hold ______ ______	11. think ______ ______	12. fight ______ ______

四、单项选择。

(　　) 1. Once you ________ a promise, you must carry it out.
A. have made　B. had made　C. made　D. is making

(　　) 2. The May 4th movement ________ in 1919.
A. had taken place　B. was taking place
C. was taken place　D. took place

(　　) 3. The house is dirty. We ________ it for weeks.
A. didn't clean　B. hadn't cleaned
C. don't clean　D. haven't cleaned

(　　) 4. I've ________ here for only one day.
A. got　B. arrived　C. reached　D. been

(　　) 5. China ________ the WTO last year and ________ a new member of it.
A. joined; has become　B. join; become
C. will join; become　D. has joined; has become

五、句型转换。

1. Daddy has read Sue's report.（对画线部分提问）
____

2. —火车已经开走了吗？—是的。—什么时候开走的？—半小时以前。（汉译英）
—________ the train ________? —Yes, it ________.
—When ________ it ________? —It ________ half an hour ago.

3. He's never been to Mount Tai, ________ ________?（反义疑问句）

4. I joined the Party ten years ago.（同义句）
I ________ ________ a Party member ________ ten years.

5. The boy said goodbye to his mother just now.（对画线部分提问）
____?

6. My father has lived in Tianjin since 1993.（对画线部分提问）
____?

六、根据上下文选用适当的句子补全对话。

A. Great!	B. How about 7:00?
C. Would you be able to come?	D. Yes. We hope you'll be able to join us.
E. I'm very happy to see you again.	F. We'll be looking forward to meeting you.
G. Sorry to hear that.	

A: We'd like to ask you and your wife to have dinner with us this Saturday evening.
(1) ______

B: This Saturday evening?

A: (2) ______

B: It's very kind of you. We'd be very happy to come.

A: (3) ______

B: What time should we plan to arrive?

A: (4) ______

B: 7:00? That's fine. (5) ______

七、完形填空。

Now satellites are __1__ to forecast(预报)the weather. They are in space, and they can __2__ any part of the world. The satellites take pictures of the atmosphere(大气), __3__ this is where the weather forms(形成). They send these __4__ to the weather stations. So meteorologists(气象学家)can see the weather of any part of the world. From the pictures, the scientists can often say __5__ the weather will change.

Today, nearly five hundred weather stations in sixty countries receive satellite pictures. When they receive new pictures, the meteorologists compare them with earlier __6__. Perhaps they may find that the clouds have changed during the last few hours. This may mean that the __7__ on the ground may soon change, too. In their next weather forecast, the meteorologists can say this.

So the weather satellites are a great __8__ to the meteorologists. __9__ satellites were invented, the scientists could forecast the weather for about 24 or 48 hours. Now they can make good forecasts for three or five days. Soon, perhaps, they may __10__ forecast the weather for a week or more ahead(提前).

(　　) 1.	A. help	B. to help	C. helped	D. helping
(　　) 2.	A. reach	B. arrive	C. get	D. go
(　　) 3.	A. so	B. because	C. even	D. and
(　　) 4.	A. satellites	B. pictures	C. weather	D. space
(　　) 5.	A. that	B. for	C. where	D. how
(　　) 6.	A. it	B. one	C. ones	D. them
(　　) 7.	A. clouds	B. weather	C. pictures	D. trees
(　　) 8.	A. report	B. luck	C. helpful	D. help
(　　) 9.	A. Before	B. After	C. Since	D. If

(　　) 10. A. can　　B. be　　C. be able to　　D. could

Section Four

一、读一读，连一连。

(　　) 1. run　　A. the window
(　　) 2. break　　B. the table
(　　) 3. set　　C. a story
(　　) 4. tell　　D. a finger
(　　) 5. cut　　E. round the field

二、首字母填空。

1. It's warm inside. You can t ________ off your coat.
2. She bought some flowers for my teachers a w ________ ago.
3. Open the p ________, and you can see a beautiful box in it.
4. I called my mother a m ________ ago.
5. Write on your name on this s ________ of paper.

三、写出下列动词的过去式与过去分词。

1. say	______	______	2. get	______	______	3. light	______	______
4. find	______	______	5. run	______	______	6. come	______	______
7. go	______	______	8. set	______	______	9. sit	______	______
10. hold	______	______	11. think	______	______	12. fight	______	______

四、单项选择。

(　　)1. The bookshop ________ for eight years.
A. has been open　B. has been opened　C. has opened　D. has open

(　　)2. I ________ this book for two weeks. I have to return it now.
A. borrowed　B. have borrowed　C. kept　D. have kept

(　　)3. Have you ever ________ to the Great Wall? It's very beautiful.
A. gone　B. been　C. went　D. go

(　　)4. I'm sorry, I ________ your name.
A. had forgotten　B. forgot
C. have forgotten　D. forgotten

(　　)5. —How do you like Beijing, Mr. Black? —Oh, I ________ such a beautiful city.
A. don't visit　B. didn't visit
C. haven't visited　D. hadn't visited

五、用过去时或现在完成时填空。

1. —________ you ________ (have) lunch ? —Yes.

—When ________ you ________ (have) it? —I ________ (have) it at 12:00.

2. —________ you ________ (write) a letter to your aunt yet?

—Yes, I ________. I ________ (write) one last week.

3. —________ he ________ (finish) his homework? —Not yet.

4. —________ they ever ________ (be) abroad? —Yes, just once.

5. Your father ________ just ________ (finish) his work.

6. Your father ________ (finish) his work just now.

7. Last term I ________ (learn) many English words.

8. They ________ (not read) the interesting books yet.

9. He ________ never ________ (go) to the science museum.

10. ________ you ever ________ (drink) coke?

六、句型转换。

1. They came to China five years ago.（同义句）

They ________ ________ ________ China for five years.

2. I've already done my homework.（改为否定句）

____?

3. Professor Boffin came here two weeks ago.（同义句）

Professor Boffin has ________ here ________ ________ ________.

4. He saw the doctor because he caught a bad cold.（对画线部分提问）

____

5. —你看过这本故事书吗？ —看过，我去年看的。（汉译英）

—______ you ______ ______ the story book? —Yes, I ______ it last year.

七、阅读理解。

Katy Ross was eighteen-year-old in Nepal, a small country in North India. Katy left school 8 months ago and soon she will go to university. She loves travelling and decides to visit Asia before she goes to university.

Katy is living with a family in the capital of Nepal. She has learnt a lot about the country since she arrived 4 months ago. The family has two children but many uncles and cousins live with them in their big house. They have taken Katy to many parties.

Katy teaches for four hours a day at a small school. All the classes are in English and the pupils have spoken English since the age of six. The older children speak English very well. Katy has taught writing, grammar and art, all in English. She enjoys art most. And she thinks the children like the lessons best, too.

Katy has not a lot of time to see Nepal, but soon she will stop teaching and travel around Nepal with a friend. "After that," Katy says, "we will visit more countries in Asia. We're not sure which ones yet."

(　　)1. Why is Katy in Nepal?

A. She is studying there.

B. She wants to take some pictures there.

C. She wants to learn more about the country.

D. She is an exchange student.

(　　)2. Which of the following is TRUE about the family Katy is living with?

A. They are friendly.

B. There are three people in their house.

C. They are strange.

D. They have never taken Katy to the parties.

(　　)3. How long has Katy been in Nepal?

A. Eight months. B. Six months.

C. Four months. D. One month.

(　　)4. When did the children begin to speak English?

A. When they are 5 years old. B. When they are 6 years old.

C. When they are 7 years old. D. When they are 8 years old.

(　　)5. According to the passage, Katy ________.

A. likes travelling very much

B. doesn't want to live with a family

C. only teaches writing in English

D. will go back to school after she leaves Nepal

Section Five

一、听写单词和短语。

1. ________ 2. ________ 3. ________ 4. ________ 5. ________

6. ____________ 7. ____________ 8. ____________

9. ____________ 10. ____________

二、对话理解，根据对话内容选择问题的正确答案。

(　　) 1. A. Some books. B. A T-shirt. C. A jacket.

(　　) 2. A. In 1874. B. In 1931. C. In 1847.

(　　) 3. A. Climb hills. B. Stay at home. C. Go shopping.

(　　) 4. A. Lily. B. Lily's mother. C. Lily's grandmother.

(　　) 5. A. 809621. B. 809612. C. 806912.

三、短文理解，根据短文内容选择问题的正确答案。

(　　) 1. A. In a middle school. B. In different places.

C. In the same school all his life.

(　　) 2. A. Once a month. B. Every day.

C. Once a week.

(　　) 3. A. He wanted to do more work. B. He wanted to teach the woman.

C. A better teacher will take his place.

( ) 4. A. Mr. Green wouldn't be as good as the next teacher.
B. Mr. Green was the best teacher of all the teachers.
C. Mr. Green would be better than the next one but is worse than the last one.

( ) 5. A. Mr. Green was the last dance teacher there.
B. Mr. Green was so bad that he had no students to teach.
C. Mr. Green was the sixth dance teacher in that city.

四、单项选择。

( ) 1. We have lived here ________ five years ago.
A. when B. since C. before D. after

( ) 2. Li Mei is only a ten-year-old girl, but she ________ to draw for about five years.
A. learns B. learned C. would learn D. has learned

( ) 3. How long has he ________?
A. kept the book B. had the car
C. been in the club D. All the above

( ) 4. Have you eaten my food ________?
A. already B. ever C. just D. yet

( ) 5. He hasn't finished his word, ________?
A. has her B. has he C. hasn't he D. hasn't him

五、原文填空。

1. —What can we do? —You can ________ a fire in the living room.
2. Let's play a ________ on the girls, Sandy.
3. We can put the trick on this ________ of paper and make a parcel.
4. We've just found this ________. We found it a moment ago.
5. You've both very lazy this morning. You mustn't ________ time.
6. —Why don't you make a ________? —We've already done so.
7. This morning Sandy ________ his new shoes to school.
8. ________ playtime Sandy played football with Billy.
9. After school Sandy went home. Mother was ________ with him.
10. You've only ________ them for a few hours, and they're already old!

六、选择正确的介词填空。

around	between	during	to	in	for	after	with	before	at

1. Come under my umbrella. Don't stand ________ the rain.
2. We held a party for Helen the day ________ yesterday.
3. Every morning I run ________ the playground for half an hour.
4. She had sat ________ her desk for three hours.

5. Mum was cross ________ me when she saw my poor school report.
6. We have a ten-minute break ________ classes.
7. ________ school we went home.
8. ________ the summer holidays, we went swimming everyday.
9. He ran all the way ________ school, but was still late.
10. My father bought a camera ________ me last Sunday.

七、用 have/has been to/in, have gone to 及 go (to) 的各种形式填空。

1. —Where is Jack? —He ________ his country.
2. David ________ the park just now.
3. John ________ England since he came back.
4. How long ________ they ________ this village?
5. The Smiths ________ Beijing for years.
6. —________ you ever ________ America? —Yes, I ________ there many times.
7. I ________ this school since three years ago.
8. —Where is Jim? —He ________ the farm.
9. —When ________ he ________? —He ________ an hour ago.
10. —Would you like to ______ the zoo with me? —Yes, but I ______ there before.

八、用适当的时态填空。

1. She ________ (live) here ever since she was ten.
2. Both of them ________ (be) in Hongkong for ten days.
3. Both of them ________ (come) to Hongkong ten days ago.
4. Half an hour ________ (pass) since the train ________ (leave).
5. Mary ________ (lose) her pen. ________ you ________ (see) it here and there?
6. ________ you ________ (find) your watch yet?
7. —Are you thirsty? —No, I ________ just ________ (have) some orange.
8. We ________ already ________ (return) the book.
9. ________ they ________ (build) a new school in the village?
10. I ________ (not finish) my homework . Can you help me?
11. My father ________ (read) the novel twice.
12. I ________ (buy) a book just now.

九、句型转换。

1. 从上星期三以来，我没见过他。（汉译英）
   I ________ ________ him since ________ ________.
2. He has learnt Japanese <u>since he came to his company</u>.（对画线部分提问）
   ____
3. Mr. Bean told them a story <u>a minute ago</u>.（对画线部分提问）
   ____
4. My father went to England in 2003 and 2005.（同义句）

My father ________ ________ ________ England ________.

5. He's gone to Beijing, ________ ________?（改为反义疑问句）

十、根据上下文选用适当的句子补全对话。

A. Is it far from here?	B. Can you tell me where it is, please?
C. Or you can walk there if you like.	D. How far is it?
E. You're welcome.	F. How can I get there, please?
G. Excuse me!	

A: Excuse me. This is the first time for me to visit this city. I want to go to the nearest Xinhua Bookstore. (1)________

B: It's on the Pingan Street.

A: Pingan Street? (2)________

B: No, not far from here. It's only a mile away from here.

A: (3)________

B: Well, you can take the No. 4 bus. The bus stop is just over there. (4)________

A: All right. Thank you.

B: (5)________

十一、完形填空。

Who designed (设计) the first helicopter (直升机)? Who __1__ of the most famous pictures in the world? Who knew more about the human body than most __2__? There is an answer __3__ all these questions—Leonardo de Vinci (达·芬奇).

Leonardo may have been the greatest genius (天才) __4__ have ever known. He lived in Italy around the year 1500, but many of his inventions seem modern to us today. For example, one of his notebooks has drawings of a helicopter. Of course, he couldn't __5__ a helicopter with the things he had. But scientists say his idea would have worked.

But Leonardo __6__ an inventor. He was one of the greatest artists of his day. By the time he was twenty years old, he was called a master (大师) painter, and as he got older he became __7__ more famous. Sometimes he drew a hand ten different ways __8__ he was ready to paint.

Many of Leonardo's wonderful paintings are still with __9__, today. You may know one of his most famous works the __10__ woman known as the *Mona Lisa*.

(　　)1. A. took　B. made　C. painted　D. invented

(　　)2. A. artists　B. doctors　C. painters　D. people

(　　)3. A. to　B. of　C. for　D. from

(　　)4. A. the scientists　B. the artists　C. the world　D. people

(　　)5. A. draw　B. paint　C. work　D. build

(　　)6. A. was just　B. wasn't just　C. wasn't　D. was no longer

(　　)7. A. less　B. no　C. even　D. very

( )8. A. before B. after C. because D. when
( )9. A. him B. us C. them D. you
( )10. A. interesting B. crying C. smiling D. surprising

十二、阅读理解。

Musician Wanted Can you play the drums or the guitar? Would you like to make some money this vacation? We need two new band members for our group. Are you interested? Then come for an audition (试演) on Saturday afternoon at 2：00 p. m. , Hopewell Center Auditorium.	New T4 Music Show We are looking for a number of people to come down and be part of our camera audience, age range 12—15, to dance and have fun. If you love music, dancing and look good, we would love to hear from you. Choice of time: 12：45 p. m. or 7：45 p. m. Call the Nokia Green Room at 556-3826.
Conversation Tutor Wanted Can you speak English? Do you like kids? I need someone to help my daughters learn English during their vacation. It doesn't matter if your English isn't perfect, just as long as you can hold a conversation. Please call Mrs. Johansson at 555-3721. The pay is good.	Part-time Cleaning Help Are you looking for a vacation job? Can you clean house and cook? Then, I need you. The work is boring, but the pay is good. I need you from 2：00—5：00, Monday to Saturday. Please call Emily Martin at 393-7741.

( ) 1. If you want to be a tutor, you can call ________.
A. 293-7742 B. 555-3721 C. 667-8973 D. 556-3826

( ) 2. People who like dancing can come at ________.
A. 7：45 p. m. B. 11：45 a. m. C. 12：15 p. m. D. 2：00 p. m.

( ) 3. Ms. Martin really needs a ________.
A. tutor B. musician C. cleaner D. dancer

( ) 4. Julia can ________, she wants to be a band member.
A. dance B. speak English
C. play the violin D. play the guitar

( ) 5. Who will the tutor help?
A. Mrs. Johansson. B. Emily.
C. Mrs. Johansson's daughters. D. Mrs. Johansson's sons.

Unit 14

Section One

一、根据中文意思完成句子。

1. 你想去哪里度假？
   ________ go on vacation?
2. 我想去放松的地方。
   I'd like to go ________.
3. 我想让你帮我拿个毛巾来。
   I ________ for me.
4. 你能给我一些建议吗？
   ________ some suggestions?
5. 你愿意和我一起去野餐吗？
   ________.

二、根据对话内容，用方框中所给词语的适当形式填空。

travel, sound, to go, exciting, about, relax

A: Look at those travel posters. I'd love to go on a vacation.
B: Where would you like (1)________, Sam?
A: I'd love to (2)________ in the Amazon jungle in Brazil.
B: You would?
A: Sure. I like (3)________ vacations.
B: Wouldn't that be dangerous?
A: No, not really. How (4)________ you, Gina? Where would you like to go?
B: Oh, I don't know. I'd just like to (5)________ on a beach... you know, a beautiful beach in Florida. That is (6)________ peaceful.

三、"would like"句型转换。

1. Do you want to have some water?（改为同义句）
   ________ you ________ ________ some water?
2. We'd like to buy some oranges.（改为一般疑问句）

________ you like to buy ________ oranges?

3. I'd like to go to the Great Wall this weekend. (对画线部分提问)

________ ________ you ________ to go this weekend?

4. Would you like to go out for a walk with me? (作肯定回答)

Yes, ________ ________ ________.

四、根据短文和表格所给的信息,回答下列问题。

Visitors to the United States

Many people come to the United States on vacation(度假). Some go to the big, exciting cities like New York, Miami and Los Angeles. Others want to see the beautiful, uncrowned places like the Rocky Mountains and the Arizona Desert.

Country	Number of visitors in 1995	Total amount spent	Amount each person spent
Mexico	8,083	$2,853,299	$353
Germany	1,848	$4,023,096	$2,177
United Kingdom	2,888	$6,422,912	$2,224
Canada	14,663	$6,202,449	$423
France	922	$1,830,170	$1,985
Japan	4,598	$11,186934	$2,433

1. Which country sent the most tourists to the United States?

____

2. Which visitors spent the most per person?

____

3. Which country had more than 10,000 visitors?

____

4. Which country had less than 1,000 visitors?

____

5. Where would you like to go on vacation?

____

五、选出不属于该组的一个单词。

1.	tiring	exciting	fascinating	interesting	belonging
2.	trip	vacation	travel	chicken	journey
3.	dinner	farm	meals	supper	lunch
4.	Hawaii	Boston	Washington	Paris	Los Angels

5. butter　gravy　potatoes　bread　glasses

六、连词成句。

1. book / you / did / recently / read / what ?

____

2. have / got / you / plans / any/ for / evening / this?

____

3. afraid / am / I / that / I / can't / come / tonight

____

4. to / far / we / don't / have / go

____

5. John's / to / somewhere / likes / and / clean / grandmother / quiet / go

____

Section Two

一、单项选择。

(　　) 1. There is not ________ meat in my bowl. There is ________ chicken in it.
A. some; any　B. any; some　C. any; any　D. some; some

(　　) 2. —Is there ________ tea in that green cup? —Yes, there is ________.
A. the; some　B. any; any　C. some; any　D. any; some

(　　) 3. Will you buy me ________ stamps?
A. some　B. any　C. a little　D. no

(　　) 4. —Have you any ink? —Yes, I have ________ in my bottle.
A. few　B. a few　C. little　D. a little

(　　) 5. Thirty years ago, only ________ people were interested in the computer and knew how to use it.
A. little　B. a little　C. a few　D. few

(　　) 6. The young people worked in the small village ________ the year of 1972.
A. during　B. on　C. for　D. by

(　　) 7. Study hard, ________ you'll not catch up with your friends.
A. but　B. and　C. or　D. so

(　　) 8. There must be ________ reason for what they have done.
A. any　B. many　C. some　D. much

(　　) 9. His father went to his doctor for ________ about his trouble.
A. an advice　B. some advice　C. advices　D. the advices

(　　) 10. I'll tell you ________.
A. a good news　B. good a news
C. a piece of good news　D. some piece of good news

二、看下面这张邀请卡，回答相关问题。

1. When is the party?

____.

2. What is the party for?

____.

3. How do people contact them?

____.

4. Where is the party held?

____.

三、根据句意及首字母提示填空。

1. I'd like to i ________ her to my birthday party.
2. Here is his r ________ to your letter.
3. Many boys say they would like to be a f ________ in the future.
4. Would you like to go out for a p ________ tomorrow?
5. Your d ________ will come true if you study hard.

四、看下面三幅图片，哪一个是正确的。

(　　)1. Which picture shows the right way of setting the table?

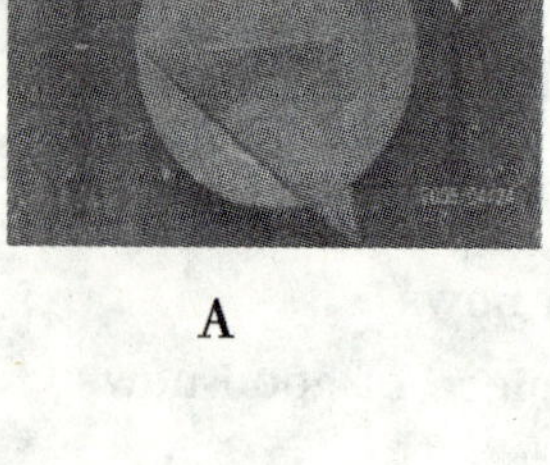
A

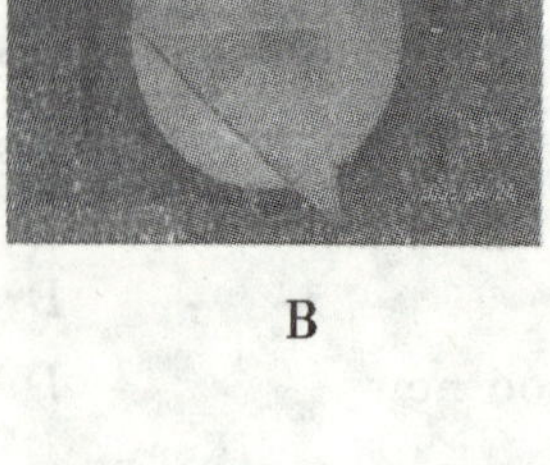
B

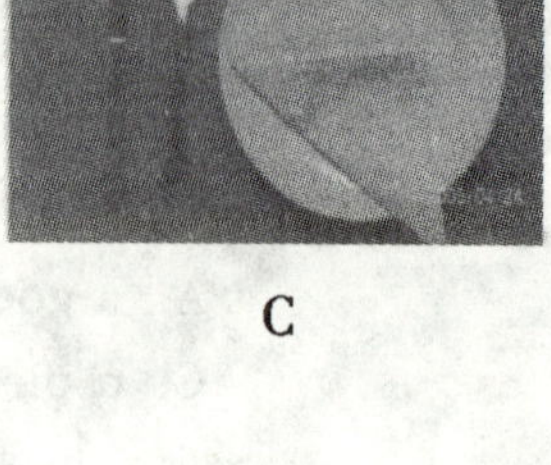
C

根据图片将下面这段文字补充完整。

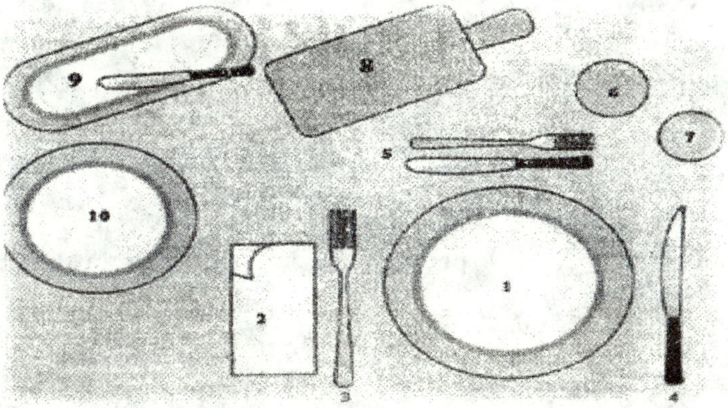

For example: Put the big plate in the middle.

put the (2)________ on the left of the big plate and the (3)________ on the right. (4)________ at the top are for dessert. The small plate (5)________ is for bread. There is (6)________ beside the big fork (7)________ are the for the drinks.

五、阅读下面这封信，完成邀请卡的填写。

For:(1)________________

Date:(2)________________

Time:(3)________________

Place: Lincoln-Belmont YMCA
3333 North Marshfield

Type of Party:
(4)________________

R.S.V.P.
(5)________________

Lincoln-Belmont
YMCA
3333 North Marshfield
June 23,2011

Dear Professor Smith,

My wife and I would be very happy if you could come to dinner on Monday, June 28, at 6 : 30 in the evening. We are having a wedding anniversary party. We do hope you can join us. Please contact me at 3445902334.

Sincerely yours
Albert Shaw

Section Three

一、单项选择。

( )1. The boy ________ in bed when his mother ________ into his room.

A. lied; came B. lay; was coming
C. was lying; came D. was laying; came

( )2. Please wait to ________.
A. sit in B. seat C. sitting D. be seated

( )3. The little boy ________ his mother ________ some sweets as his birthday present.
A. wants; for B. asked; for C. wanted to; give D. asks; from

( )4. There were ________ people and ________ noise in the street.
A. many; many B. much; much
C. much; many D. many; much

( )5. — Have you any ink?
— Yes, I have ________ in my bottle.
A. few B. a few C. little D. a little

( )6. Wansongyuan Road is cool and quiet, there are many trees on ________ side of the roads.
A. either B. left C. both D. all

( )7. A big fire broke out ________ the night of October 29.
A. at B. in C. on D. by

( )8. There are three windows ________ the wall.
A. on B. in C. against D. at

( )9. — Where are the students?
— They ________ in the dining hall at the moment?
A. have a test B. having a dinner
C. had dinner D. are having dinner

( )10. He will finish all the assignments ________ next Monday.
A. on B. by C. by the end of D. after

二、用所给词的适当形式填空。

1. Would you like ________(have) dinner with me?
2. Do you usually do some ________(clean) on Sundays?
3. Neither my sister nor my brother ________(help) me.
4. If it ________(not rain) tomorrow, we'll have a picnic.
5. You'd better ________(ask) the policeman over there.
6. It's important for you ________(learn) English well.
7. They had to work for hours to stop the ship from ________(go) down.
8. What ________ you ________(do) when the bell rang?
9. Do you know the boy ________(call) Jack?
10. How did Lily make the baby ________(stop) crying?

三、换一种说法。

1. I think it's wrong. = I ________ ________ it's ________.

2. I often go to America for holiday by air. = I often ________ ________ America for my holiday.
3. I want some tea, please. = I ________ ________ some tea.
4. He is too old to work now. = He ________ ________ ________ to work now.
= He is ________ old ________ he can't work now.
5. There is a police station on left side of our school.
=Our school is ________ ________ ________ ________ of the police station.

四、首字母填空。

On the evening of October 7, Li Feng was watching TV while his mother was (1) b ________ cooking supper in the kitchen. (2) S ________ the telephone rang. Li Feng (3) q ________ picked it up to (4) a ________ the call. It was from a good friend of his (5) m ________. She wanted to say "Happy Birthday" to his mother. "Today is Mother's birthday, but I (6) f ________ all about it. Mother gives me a lot of (7) l ________ and care while I didn't care for her (8) e ________. From now on, I must always (9) r ________ this, (10) s ________ my love to her and care for her enough," Li Feng thought to himself, feeling a little ashamed(惭愧的).

五、完形填空。

How much do you know about manners(礼仪)? Different countries have __1__ manners. In __2__ Asian countries, it is good manners to take off your __3__ before you go into a house. __4__ in European (欧洲) countries, even if they sometimes become very dirty, this is not done. If you are a __5__ in a Chinese house, when you have a meal, you usually do not __6__ the food. You often leave a little to __7__ that you have had enough. But in England, a visitor always finishes food to show that he has __8__ it. We must know the customs (风俗) of other __9__, so that they will not think __10__ bad-mannered. People all over the world __11__ that a well-mannered person should be kind and __12__ to others. If you __13__ this, at least you will not go very far wrong. __14__ likes a person with good manners, but no one likes a person with bad manners. __15__ your manners.

( )1. A. same B. different C. some D. interesting
( )2. A. some B. any C. other D. few
( )3. A. bags B. shoes C. coats D. hats
( )4. A. And B. So C. But D. Or
( )5. A. stranger B. traveller C. visitor D. man
( )6. A. need B. finish C. choose D. have
( )7. A. say B. see C. understand D. show
( )8. A. finished B. enjoyed C. taken D. drunk
( )9. A. countries B. villages C. cities D. places
( )10. A. them B. me C. us D. him

(　　)11. A. find　B. know　C. guess　D. agree
(　　)12. A. careful　B. helpful　C. hardworking　D. healthy
(　　)13. A. forget　B. remember　C. learn　D. study
(　　)14. A. Somebody　B. Anybody　C. Nobody　D. Everybody
(　　)15. A. Take　B. Make　C. Mind　D. Keep

Section Four

一、单项选择。

(　　)1. — ________ can I keep this storybook?
— For two weeks.
A. How soon　B. How long　C. How often　D. How many

(　　)2. My brother takes ________ in the gym every day.
A. exercises　B. exercise　C. exercising　D. an exercise

(　　)3. Could you tell me ________ about your hometown?
A. anything　B. something　C. nothing　D. somethings

(　　)4. John eats ________ food and he is much too fat.
A. much too　B. many too　C. too many　D. too much

(　　)5. You must not read ________ the sun.
A. under　B. in　C. at　D. on

(　　)6. I learn English by ________, and my twin sisters teach ________ Japanese.
A. mc; them　B. myself; themselves
C. myself; them　D. me; themselves

(　　)7. — I'm sorry, I can't go to the concert. I must do some housework.
— ________
A. What shame!　B. What a pity!
C. What a nice concert!　D. You're so nice!

(　　)8. We shouldn't spend ________ watching TV.
A. much too time for　B. too much time on
C. too much time in　D. much too time on

(　　)9. I see him ________ football almost every day.
A. play　B. to play　C. playing　D. plays

(　　)10. Would you like ________ to have?
A. anything else　B. else something
C. something else　D. else anything

二、阅读并排序。

Read the following instruction of making Homemade Orange Marmalade. Then put the instructions into the right order.

Ingredients: five or six oranges, some sugar, water and Orange Jello(果冻) and two canning jars to put them in.

(　　) Let this cook for thirty minutes stirring often.

(　　) In a saucepan add the oranges and juice, zest, one cup of sugar or more to your taste and about two cups of water.

(　　) In another pot, place two cups of water and the Orange Jello on low heat. Taste it and add more sugar if needed.

(　　) Wash the Oranges with a little soap. Cut the oranges into quarters and peel and slice them thinly. Then grate(干燥) the zest(橙皮) of three oranges and place them with the oranges.

(　　) Let cool and place the mixture in jars. Then put in refrigerator.

(　　) Taste and enjoy the Homemade Orange Marmalade Jelly on buttered toast the next day!

(　　) Then add to the orange mixture(混合物) and stir well.

三、看图描述。

A

B

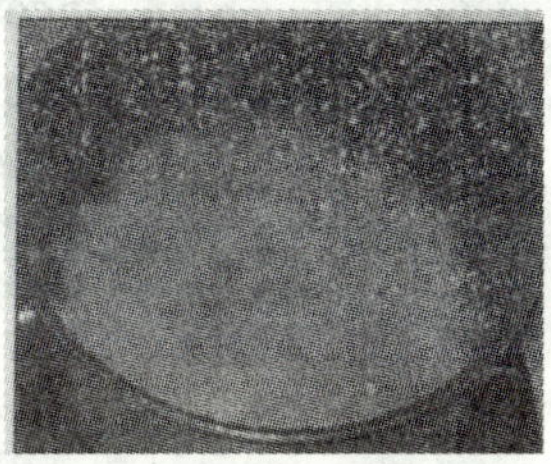

C

D

E

Picture A: get some rice into a ________

Picture B: ________ the rice

Picture C: ________ some water into the pot and ________ it

Picture D: ________ the lid (锅盖) on and ________ for 20 minutes

Picture E: serve the cooked rice with a ________

四、阅读理解。

Many animals hide to stay alive. They hide in many ways. Some animals hide in leaves; some animals hide in snow. Usually their colors or shapes help protect them. It's hard to see an Arctic bear in snow. Its white fur helps protect it. Chameleons(变色龙) can hide by changing colors. Their skin turns the same color as what is around them. Some chameleons can change colors in five minutes. Many animals try to look bigger than they are to stay alive. Some animals can make other animals think they are very big. If they look very big, animals that are looking for food will run away. Bears can walk on two legs. They look very, very scary. Some animals will run away from them.

Many animals try to stay around other animals. This helps them stay alive. Zebras stay close together so that they can help each other look out of danger. Seeing many stripes at once can also confuse animals that want to eat them. Some birds stay in a circle, each toward a different direction. In this way they can also help each other stay alive by looking around for animals that want to eat one of them.

( ) 1. Animals have ways to stay alive. How many of them are mentioned in the passage?

A. One. B. Two. C. Three. D. Five.

( ) 2. Why do animals hide?

A. Because they like to play hide-and-seek.

B. Because they are shy.

C. Because they want to catch other.

D. Because they want to protect themselves.

( ) 3. How do Chameleons hide?

A. They change colors. B. They change shapes.

C. They hide in snow. D. They hide in leaves.

( ) 4. How do zebras protect themselves?

A. Become good friends. B. Talk to each other.

C. Help each other look out for danger. D. Eat and play together.

( ) 5. Why do animals try to look bigger than they are?

A. They want other animals to run away from them.

B. They want other animals to follow them.

C. They want other animals to see them.

D. They want other animals to like them.

Section Five

一、根据听到的句子，从所给的 A、B、C 三个选项中选择符合题意的图画。

( ) 1. A.  B. 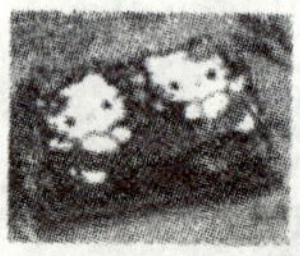 C. 

( ) 2. A.  B.  C. 

( ) 3. A. 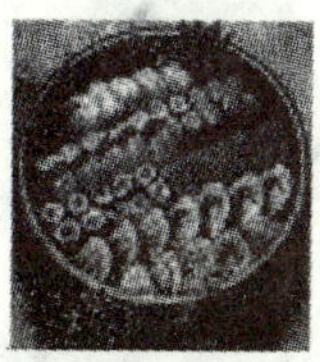 B.  C. 

( ) 4. A. 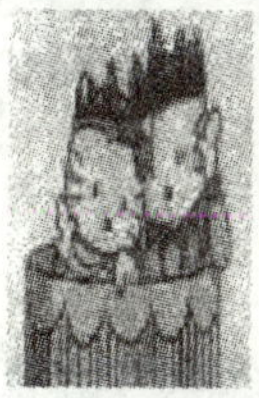 B.  C. 

( ) 5. A. 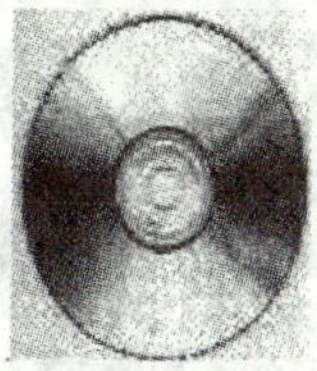 B.  C. 

二、听对话，回答问题。

( )1. When does the library close?

A. At 5∶45. B. At 5∶15. C. At 5∶50.

( )2. How many students haven't got the books?

A. 40. B. 15. C. 25.

( )3. Who is the tallest of the three?

A. Kate. B. Sam. C. Lucy.

( )4. What are they talking about?

A. About yesterday. B. About weather. C. About school.

( )5. What kind of clothes does the girl like to wear?

A. Blouse. B. Sweater. C. Skirt.

三、听下面四段对话，从题中所给 A、B、C 三个选项中选出最佳答案。

听第一段材料，回答第 1 ~2 题。

( )1. Where does the woman want to go ?

A. The bus station. B. The supermarket. C. The museum.

( )2. Which bus can take the woman there?

A. The No. 16 bus. B. The No. 17 bus. C. The No. 70 bus.

听第二段材料，回答第3~4题。

(　　)3. Has Mrs. Green ever visited Dalian?

A. No, never.　B. Yes, but only twice.　C. Yes, many times.

(　　)4. What does she think of Dalian?

A. It's beautiful.　B. It's a big city.　C. Both A and B.

听第三段材料，回答第5~7题。

(　　)5. How does Mary look today?

A. Not well.　B. Very well.　C. Beautiful.

(　　)6. What's wrong with her?

A. She is tired.　B. She is worried.　C. She is ill.

(　　)7. What will Mary do next?

A. Visit a doctor.　B. Have a good rest.　C. Sleep all day.

听第四段材料，回答第8~10题。

(　　)8. Where does the conversation happen?

A. In a hotel.　B. In a shop.　C. In a restaurant.

(　　)9. Which floor will the man stay on?

A. The third floor.　B. The fourth floor.　C. The seventh floor.

(　　)10. How much should the man pay for two nights?

A. 40 dollars.　B. 160 dollars.　C. 80 dollars.

四、你将听到一段短文，然后你将看到五个问题，每个问题有三个供选择的答案，请你根据短文内容选择适当答案。

(　　)1. Where does Li Lei live?

A. In a big house.　B. In a small house.　C. In a garden.

(　　)2. What does Li Lei's mother grow in the garden?

A. Vegetables and flowers.

B. Rice and wheat.

C. Apples and peas.

(　　)3. Where is the park?

A. Near Li Lei's house.

B. Near the center of the town.

C. Near the bus stop.

(　　)4. How does Li Lei go to town?

A. By car.　B. By bike.　C. By taxi.

(　　)5. What does Li Lei like doing in summer?

A. Going shopping.　B. Going fishing.　C. Going swimming.

五、单项选择。

(　　) 1. — Must I go now?

— ________________.

A. Yes, you must. B. No, you must.

C. Yes, you mustn't. D. Yes, you needn't.

( ) 2. — Would you like me to carry the box for you?

— ______

A. Yes, please. B. Yes, you would.

C. No, please. D. That's all right.

( ) 3. Don't worry. There is ______ time to go.

A. any B. few C. a little D. may

( ) 4. — You won't take part in the sports meet, will you?

— ______

A. Yes, I won't. B. No, I will.

C. Yes, I do. D. No, I won't.

( ) 5. — I'm taking my math exam tomorrow.

— ______

A. Well done! B. Good luck! C. Never mind! D. Congratulations!

( ) 6. Nothing in the world is ______ if you try your best to do it.

A. impossible B. wonderful C. interesting D. necessary

( ) 7. How nice the dress is! You look ______ today.

A. health B. happily C. beautiful D. tired

( ) 8. Please write about ______ last week.

A. what happened to him B. what he happened

C. he happened what D. what did he happen

( ) 9. Look! The little boy is ______ the plate like a driver.

A. watching B. turning C. flying D. throwing

( ) 10. — If you make a lot of noise, Lily can't sleep well. Would you please keep quiet?

— ______

A. It doesn't matter. B. You're welcome.

C. Thank you. D. I'm sorry.

六、完形填空。

As a student, you must __1__ a lot of interesting books. Most of the books come from the school __2__, I am sure. Perhaps you also get books from the public library in your town . Then books are sometimes given to you as presents by your parents or friends, I think. Besides, if you like reading and want to learn __3__, I am sure that you buy books __4__. Do you know __5__ books are made? Well, after a book is written, it passes __6__ the hands of many different workers. Each one __7__ very carefully, for there must not be any __8__ in the book. Different people read many times before it is finished. Millions of books are printed(印刷) in our country every year. So people can get __9__ to read. Now may I ask you a __10__? How well do you take __11__ of books? What have you learned about the care of books ? Perhaps you bought yourselves some __12__ books. Do you put paper on them ? Do you open __13__ ? Sometimes new books break along the back if you open __14__ suddenly in the middle. I hope that you don't __15__ the pages carelessly. If you do, you may tear them.

(　　)1. A. read	B. watched	C. looked	D. seen
(　　)2. A. headmaster's office	B. classroom	C. teacher's office	D. library
(　　)3. A. much	B. more	C. most	D. few
(　　)4. A. all	B. yourself	C. also	D. either
(　　)5. A. what	B. why	C. which	D. how
(　　)6. A. through	B. to	C. in	D. from
(　　)7. A. does	B. is work	C. work	D. works
(　　)8. A. mistakes	B. questions	C. wrong	D. thing
(　　)9. A. much	B. enough	C. a lot	D. great
(　　)10. A. matter	B. thing	C. word	D. question
(　　)11. A. careful	B. after	C. out	D. care
(　　)12. A. more	B. new	C. well	D. nicer
(　　)13. A. always	B. the books	C. it	D. carefully
(　　)14. A. them	B. carefully	C. it	D. book
(　　)15. A. break	B. throw	C. write	D. turn

七、阅读理解。

A

American schools begin in September after a long summer holiday. There are two terms in a school year. The first term is from September to January, and the second is from February to June. Most American children begin to go to school when they are five years old. Most students are seventeen or eighteen years old when they finish high school.

High school students take only four or five subjects each term. They usually go to the same classes every day, and they have homework for every class. After class they do many interesting things.

After high school, many students go to college. They can go to a small one or a large one. They usually have to give a lot of money. So many college students work after class to get the money for their studies.

(　　)1. How many terms are there in a school year in America?

A. Four.　　B. One.　　C. Three.　　D. Two.

(　　)2. The first term is ________.

A. from February to June　　B. from January to September

C. from June to February　　D. from September to January

(　　)3. When a child is ________ years old he or she can go to school.

A. five　　B. four　　C. seven　　D. six

(　　)4. How many subjects do the high school students take each term?

A. As many as they like.　　B. Five.

C. Four.　　D. Four or five.

(　　)5. Why do many college students have to work after class?

A. Because some work is helpful to their studies.

B. Because the teachers ask them to do so.

C. Because they like to work very much.

D. Because they need to get money for their studies.

B

Strong Museum: Hours and Admission(入场券)

Hours: Monday—Thursday: 10 : 00 a. m. —5 : 00 p. m.

Friday: 10 : 00 a. m. —8 : 00 p. m.

Saturday: 10 : 00 a. m. —5 : 00 p. m.

Sunday: 11 : 00 a. m. —5 : 00 p. m.

Closed on Thanksgiving Day and Christmas Day.

The Museum Shop is open during regular museum hours. Admission to the shop is always free.

The Museum Library is open Monday—Friday 10 : 00 a. m. —5 : 00 p. m.

The Skyliner Restaurant is open during regular museum hours Monday through Saturday, and from 11 : 30 a. m. to 5 : 00 p. m. on Sunday.

Admission: Adults(成年人): $7.00

The teenagers and students with ID: $6.00

Children aged 2 to 7: $5.00

Children younger than 2: free

Strong Museum members : free

Strong Museum offers a 50% discount(打折) to groups of 20 or more.

(　　)6. Strong Museum usually opens ________.

A. Monday through Thursday　　B. every day except Wednesday

C. from Monday to Friday　　D. every day of the week

(　　)7. You can have dinner in Strong Museum ________ on Fridays.

A. from 10 : 00 a. m. to 8 : 00 p. m.　　B. from 10 : 00 a. m. to 5 : 00 p. m.

C. from 11 : 30 a. m. to 5 : 00 p. m.　　D. at any time of the day

(　　)8. If you are a group of 30 students with ID visiting Strong Museum, how much should you pay for the admission ?

A. $105.　　B. $90.　　C. $210.　　D. $180.

(　　)9. According to the advertisement above, which of the following is true?

A. Children to Strong Museum are free.

B. An adult visiting Strong Museum should pay $7.00.

C. The museum is open all the year round.

D. The teenagers are free to Strong Museum.

(　　)10. Which is the best title that can be used in the advertisement for Strong Museum?

A. Strong Museum—An Exciting Place for Adults.

B. Strong Museum—Children's World for Fun.

C. Welcome to Strong Museum for a Long Holiday.

D. Strong Museum—The Best Place to Spend Your Day.

八、首字母填空。

1. She can't s ________ Mike. He is always borrowing money from her.
2. There's n ________ to eat at home. Let's go to the restaurant.
3. I know a secret r ________ of making the roast beef.
4. How do you l ________ the table in your country?
5. Mr. Black isn't used to eating with the c ________.
6. I received an i ________ to Tom's house-warming party.
7. The mountaineers finally reached the t ________ of the Himalayas.
8. She noted down the m ________ points of the speech.
9. Please read the i ________ before you take the medicine.
10. Mother's p ________ onions, no wonder it seems that she is crying.

九、句型转换。

1. I'd like to cook myself at home.（对画线部分提问）

____.

2. How about going for a walk in the park?（换一种说法）

____.

3. There is a lot of orange juice in the jar and some water in the bottle.（变为否定句）

____.

4. There is a big hole at the bottom of the bucket.（对画线部分提问）

____.

5. He likes talking with others with mouth full of food.（对画线部分提问）

____.

Unit 15

Section One

一、单项选择。

(　　) 1. It's about ten minutes ________ bus.
A. on　　B. for　　C. by　　D. in

(　　) 2. — ________ to get to the museum?
— Go along the street.
A. What　　B. Which　　C. Where　　D. How

(　　) 3. — ________ is it from the city center to the farm?
— Thirty minutes' drive.
A. Where　　B. How long　　C. How soon　　D. How far

(　　) 4. — Excuse me. Is there a post office near here?
— Yes, please go ________ the bridge and you will see it.
A. off　　B. from　　C. across　　D. beside

(　　) 5. Please take the ________ turning ________ the right.
A. second; on　　B. second; in　　C. two; on　　D. two; in

(　　) 6. There is ________ in rush hours.
A. many buses　　B. much traffic　　C. lot traffic　　D. enough buses

(　　) 7. He ________ for Seattle in a week.
A. leaves　　B. is leaving　　C. has left　　D. left

二、请根据图案及提示的词语完成下面的句子。

1. cinema/ corner
—Is there ____ ____ near here?
— It's ____ ____ ____.

2. hospital/ traffic lights
—Could you tell me how to ____ ____ ____ ____?
—Turn left ____ ____ ____ ____.

3. car park/ square

— Excuse me. Where ______ ______ ______?

— It is right ______ ______ ______.

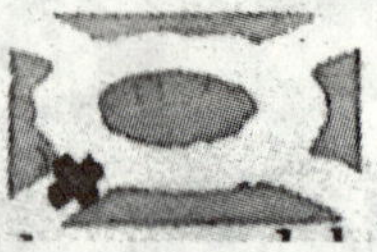

4. van/ roundabout

— Did you see the accident?

— Yes. A ______ broke down ______ ______ ______.

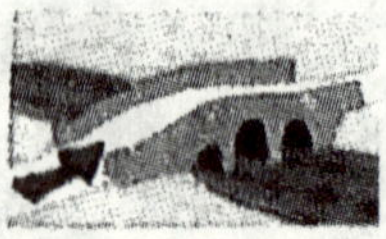

5. petrol station/ bridge

—How can I ______ ______ ______ ______?

— Just go ______ ______ ______.

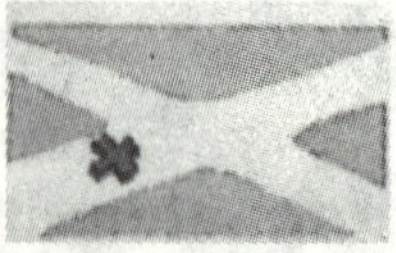

6. bus station/ crossroads

— Could you tell me where the nearest ______ ______ ______?

— It's ______ ______ ______.

三、看图并完成下面的对话。

1. A: How do you go to school every day?

   B: ______________.

   A: How long does the trip take?

   B: ______ ______ me twenty minutes.

2. A: ______________?

   B: It's on in Maple Street.

   A: ______________?

   B: You can take a train.

3. A: ______________?

   B. Yes. There's one on the corner.

   A: __________?

   B: No. It's quite near.

4. A: __________?

   B: You can go there by subway.

   A: __________?

   B: The station is a hundred meters away.

四、句型练习。

1. near, a, is, museum, here（连词成句）

   ______________________________________.

2. could, way, tell, the, you, me(连词成句)

____?

3. far, traffic lights, far, here, are, from, the(连词成句)

____.

4. There is a sports center down the road.(变成否定句)

____

5. She can show you the way.(变成一般疑问句)

____

6. It's about ten minutes' walk.(对画线部分提问)

____

Section Two

一、单项选择。

( ) 1. — How far is the Lost Property Office from here?

— It's ________.

A. one and a half miles B. one and a half mile

C. one miles and a half D. one mile and half mile

( ) 2. Those signs are for people ________ foot.

A. by B. with C. on D. for

( ) 3. There is one train at 11:30 and another at 12:05. ________ train will take you to Oxford in time for the meeting.

A. Either B. Both C. All D. None

( ) 4. — How do you like the scenery here?

— ________________.

A. Have fun. B. It's interesting.

C. I don't think so. D. The same to you.

( ) 5. You can walk ________ the road now.

A. crossing B. across C. cross D. crossly

( ) 6. — Where can I go for my vacation?

— Why not ________ Paris?

A. to go B. go to C. to consider D. considering

( ) 7. — How do you like the trip ________ Rome?

— Well, it's ________.

A. from; pleased B. to; interesting

C. at; amazed D. in; loving

二、看图并做出适当的回答。

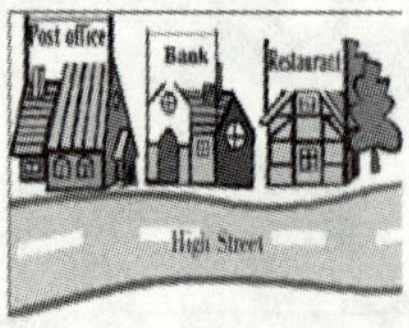

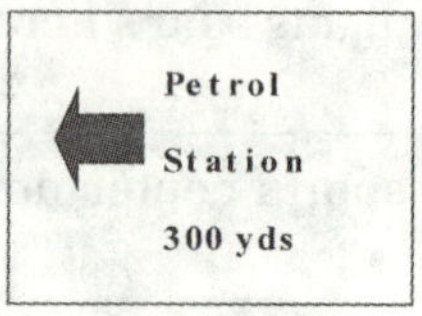

1. Is there a bank near here?

____

2. Where is the bank?

____

3. Is there a petrol station near here?

____

4. How far is it?

____

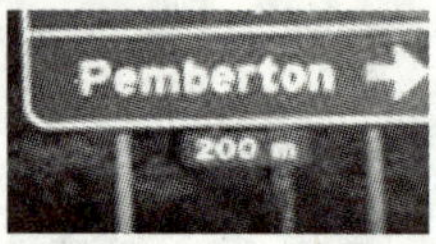

5. How far is Pemberton from here?

____

6. How may we get there?

____

7. Is there an airport down the street?

____

8. Where is the airport?

____

三、圈出能在城市里找到的另九处地方。

A	L	I	B	R	A	R	Y	S	G
P	O	S	T	O	F	F	I	C	E
O	A	T	L	J	S	A	Q	H	C
I	L	A	E	A	U	G	E	O	T
N	N	T	F	T	Z	R	E	O	H
N	C	I	E	W	P	K	B	L	E
S	H	O	S	P	I	T	A	L	A
T	U	N	O	A	M	L	N	C	T
L	C	P	N	R	X	N	K	T	R
R	R	U	L	K	R	I	Y	A	E
O	H	M	U	S	E	U	M	B	D

四、补全下面的情景对话，每空填一个词。

A：Excuse me!

B：(1)________ ?

A：Can you tell me the (2)________ to the Lost and Found Office, please?

B：Of (3)________ . Go along Bridge Street (4)________ about two kilometers and (5)________ the first turning on the right. There you will see some traffic lights. (6) ________ left at the lights. Walk on until you reach the corner. The office is

(7)________ your left.

A: Is it quite far?

B: Well, a little bit. It's about 20 minutes' (8)__________. Or you can go there (9)________ a bus.

A: Which bus should I take?

B: (10)________ No. 22 or No. 63 goes there.

A: It's so nice of you. Thank you very much.

B: You are welcome.

Section Three

一、单项选择。

( ) 1. In Britain, cars drive on the ________ side of the road.
A. left-hand B. right-hand C. both D. all

( ) 2. — What does this sign mean?
— You mustn't ________ here.
A. to talk B. talk C. talking D. talked

( ) 3. Haven't you seen the sign? It ________ "NO PARKING".
A. reads B. speaks C. says D. both A and C

( ) 4. — The songs are wonderful, I like them.
— I'm glad to hear that. I ________ the CD last week.
A. buys B. bought C. have bought D. had bought

( ) 5. — Do you know ________?
— Maybe they're talking about the latest film.
A. what are they talking about B. what they are talking
C. what they are talking about D. they are talking what

( ) 6. Walk ________ the bank and you will find the museum on your right.
A. passed B. past C. passing D. to past

( ) 7. Don't get off the train ________ it ________.
A. till; will stop B. until; stops C. if; stops D. if; will stop

二、请根据图片和例句写出相应的句子。

eg: Don't honk.

1. __________

2. ________

3. ________

4. ________

5. ________

6. ________

7. ________

三、阅读理解。

Our Family Bulletin Board

Family Movie Theater Movie: *The Lion King III* Time: 7:30 this Saturday night Place: The living room Everyone of the family is welcome!! Any questions, talk to me! Dad	Fiona's Art Show Our sister, Fiona, is showing her drawings this Sunday night from 7:00 to 9:00. There are 10 wonderful pieces to show. Orders are welcome!!
To Mom: Next Thursday is the day of our trip to Beijing Zoo. Don't forget to prepare lunch for me. I accept anything except sandwiches. Thanks! Ben	Riddles-Just for fun I have a friend. It has a big mouth, two long hands. It likes eating books. What is it? He has four legs in the morning, two legs at noon, and three legs in the evening. Guess a living thing. Chip

( ) 1. The family has at least ________ people.

A. four B. five C. six D. seven

( ) 2. Ben will go to Beijing Zoo next ________.

A. Saturday B. Sunday C. Tuesday D. Thursday

(　　) 3. The answer of the first riddle is ________.

A. an eraser　　B. a pen　　C. a ruler　　D. a schoolbag

(　　) 4. From the passage, we can know ________.

A. Ben is going to see an art show next Thursday

B. Chip can order a picture at Fiona's art show

C. the family plan to go shopping on Saturday night

D. only those who solve the riddles can watch the movie

(　　) 5. Which of the following is TRUE?

A. Ben likes eating sandwiches.

B. The family will watch the movie at a movie theater.

C. A bulletin board is a place where people can stick their notices.

D. The second riddle talks about a kind of food.

四、根据句子内容补全单词。

1. T ________ reaches a peak between 8 and 9 in the morning.
2. There was a stone b ________ over that river.
3. The sign says"NO R ________" as the floor is quite slippery.
4. You should c ________ enough information before starting a report.
5. The boy seemed to be lost. He was asking a policeman for d ________ to his way back.
6. He earns money by w ________ stories for a newspaper.

Section Four

一、单项选择。

(　　) 1. He often ________ to the market ________ fresh vegetables when he was in his forties.

A. goes; to buy　　B. went; to buy

C. went; bought　　D. goes; bought

(　　) 2. It's a ________ from the cafeteria to the dorm.

A. ten minute's walk　　B. ten-minutes-walk

C. ten minutes' walk　　D. walk in ten minutes

(　　) 3. The officials didn't give ________ information about their conference.

A. many　　B. a lot of　　C. much　　D. some

(　　) 4. — ________ rush across the road, ________?

— Are you kidding? The road is too busy.

A. Let's; shall we　　B. Let's; will you

C. Let's not; can we　　D. Let us; would you

(　　) 5. — David, many thanks for helping me ________ when I lost my job.

A. on　　B. off　　C. out　　D. in

(　　) 6. — We need to make ________ for the future

—Yeah, and then we can manage out life well.

A. suggestions　　B. replies

C. plans　　D. ideas

(　　) 7. — Fred, you are leaving your school. How do you like it?

— Very much. I ________ this school since I moved here.

A. came to　　B. have been in

C. has gone　　D. have been to

二、仿照例句完成句子。

eg: How can I get to the police station?

Could you tell me how to get to the police station?

Could you tell me how I can get to the police station?

1. How can we get to the National Gallery?

Could you tell us ________________?

Could you tell us ________________?

2. Which bus can he take?

He doesn't know ________________.

He doesn't know ________________.

3. What presents shall I buy?

Can you tell me ________________?

Can you tell me ________________?

4. Where will we go?

We don't know ________________.

We don't know ________________.

三、用所给词语的适当形式填空。

1. The first *A to Z* ________(be) in the shops in 1936 and ________(sell) very well.
2. When he ________(fall) down and ________(hurt) his ankle, we sent for a doctor immediately.
3. Why not ________(think) about their suggestions?
4. Please don't ________(make) a noise.
5. What about ________(travel) to Asia this time?
6. He ________(buy) this new laptop the day before yesterday.
7. Jason ________(smoke) a lot but he finally gave it up.
8. Has he ever considered ________(move) to Hainan?
9. The volunteers helped the elders ________(clean) their rooms.
10. The representatives ________(put) off the meeting because it rained so heavily.

四、完形填空。

Hong Kong was once covered by a thick forest. As more and more people came to __1__ in Hong Kong, the trees were cut down and burnt. Now there is __2__ forest left, though there are still some small areas covered with trees. We call these woods.

Elephants, tigers and many __3__ animals were living in the thick forest. When people began to settle down in Hong Kong, the __4__ began to die out. Early farmers grew rice and __5__ pigs and chickens in the valleys. They cut down the trees and burnt them. They needed __6__ to keep themselves warm in winter, to cook their food and to keep away the dangerous animals. Elephants quickly disappeared because there was not enough food for them to eat. __7__ did most of the wolves and tigers. Monkeys and many other animals soon died in the __8__ way.

You might think that there are no longer any animals in Hong Kong except in the zoos. But there are still about 36 different animals __9__ there, though their number is getting smaller. So it is important for people to __10__ wild animals.

( ) 1. A. work B. study C. live D. spend

( ) 2. A. many B. a few C. no D. not

( ) 3. A. other B. others C. the other D. another

( ) 4. A. people B. animals C. plants D. things

( ) 5. A. grew B. made C. got D. raised

( ) 6. A. fire B. hot C. heat D. light

( ) 7. A. So B. Too C. As D. Nor

( ) 8. A. same B. different C. hard D. pain

( ) 9. A. live B. to live C. lived D. living

( ) 10. A. protect B. look at C. find D. cage

五、下面的每个句子都有一个错误的地方，请把它们找出来并改正。

1. The sign says, "No spiting."

____.

2. Jerry sended the letters for them yesterday.

____.

3. I want a room has a great view of the sea.

____.

4. Would you like me making a booking for you?

____?

5. It's my job help the seniors cross the roads.

____.

6. He saw a boy knocked into the lamppost.

____.

Section Five

一、听录音完成句子。

1. Please turn left ________ Zhongshan Road and drive ________.

2. Now turn right at the ________.
3. There is a tourist ________ centre on the first floor.
4. Go straight ahead at the ________.
5. Could you tell me the way to the town ________?

二、听句子，选出与之相关的回答。

( ) 1. A. A couple of hours ago. B. To Wuhan. C. It's comfortable.
( ) 2. A. Two years ago. B. Since a month ago. C. Once a year.
( ) 3. A. James did. B. Beijing. C. I like Chinese.
( ) 4. A. They are magnificent. B. Ten times. C. Eight.
( ) 5. A. At seven o'clock. B. By tube. C. It's convenient.
( ) 6. A. Let's go and see it. B. Great. C. I will drop by you.

三、听一段对话，根据内容选择对应的答案。

( ) 1. Which means of transport does he often choose?

A. 

B. 
C. 
D. 

( ) 2. At what time does he often get to work?
A. 8:00. B. 8:05. C. 7:55. D. 7:45.

( ) 3. What happened this morning?
A. He was sick. B. He had a car accident.
C. He was late for work. D. He made a joke.

( ) 4. What may the lady be?
A. A doctor. B. A waitress. C. A housewife. D. A manager.

四、听一段独白，回答问题。

( )1. What do you think this is?
A. An ad. B. A report. C. A story. D. A letter.

( ) 2. At what time will they start the party?
A. 2 a. m. B. 12 p. m. C. 2 p. m. D. 8 p. m.

( ) 3. If you go there this Saturday, what may you NOT see?

A. 
B. 

C. 
D. 

( ) 4. Who does Jack invite?
A. Betty. B. Amy.
C. Cindy. D. Both Betty and Amy.

5. 根据独白内容填写所缺词语。

Her home is not ________ from our school. If you come, you may go ________ ________ Dreams Road for ten ________, and then you'll find a studio on the ________. Amy's home is just ________ it. Hope to see you at the ________.

五、听几段小对话，完成下列各题。

( ) 1. What are they talking about?

A. An interview. B. Shopping. C. A nice suit.

( ) 2. Whose suit is it?

A. It's Patrick's. B. It's Patrick's parents'.

C. It's from Patrick's friend.

( ) 3. What is the boy going to do?

A. He's going to play with the girl.

B. He's going to do his homework.

C. He's going to play badminton with Frank.

( ) 4. How long might it take to get there if you go on foot?

A. Less than 10 minutes. B. About 20 minutes.

C. More than 2 hours.

( ) 5. What are they going to do?

A. They are going to watch a movie.

B. They are going to move to a new house.

C. They are going to a book shop.

( ) 6. When is the boy's birthday?

A. On January 19. B. On January 20. C. On January 21.

六、听一首英语诗歌，完成下列各题。

Just for You

I (1)________ the reddest apple from the tree.
It was the finest one that I could (2)________.
I (3)________ it all except a bite or two. Just for you.
I (4)________ home the groceries from the store.
I (5)________ to be helpful with a chore.
I (6)________ them all away except a few.
Just for you.

七、单项选择。

( ) 1. — When ________ you ________ my missing wallet?

— I ________ a similar one last night.

A. did; see; saw B. have; seen; see

C. do; see; saw D. will; see; had seen

( ) 2. Japan lies ________ the east of China.

A. in B. from C. against D. to

( ) 3. The road is quite ________. Do you see the cars lining up?

A. busy B. heavy C. thick D. slow

( ) 4. Look ________! The vase is falling down.

A. at B. out C. for D. into

( ) 5. — There's a kite ________ the tree. Can you get ________ for me?

— I will try.

A. in; one B. on; it C. in; it D. on; one

( ) 6. Please ________ before you cross the road.

A. look yourself B. look up C. look around D. look again

( ) 7. It ________ me two days to go sightseeing in Kyoto.

A. spent B. took C. used D. paid

( ) 8. — ________ ?

— I caught a bad cold.

A. What do you do? B. What did you catch?

C. Why are you here? D. What's wrong with you?

八、把下列句子改为一般过去时。

1. Why won't you join us?

____.

2. He turns off the lights when he is out.

____.

3. Shirley cuts the watermelon into halves.

____.

4. They turn right at the crossroads and then walk on.

____.

5. How does he achieve this?

____.

九、完形填空。

Some years ago, Chinese high school students would show their new schoolbags, new clothes or new pens to their classmates when the new term started. Today, however, it has __1__. If you still come back to school __2__ only these things, you are out-of-date. Students in big cities like to take the latest high-tech(高科技) things to school, and feel happy and __3__ to show off these things to __4__. Cell phones, MP4 players, electronic dictionaries, the list is endless.

Young people __5__ that living in the 21st century, they must keep up with the times. They don't want to fall __6__. Besides, they think that they __7__ to keep in touch with their classmates, so they need cell phones. They also like to __8__ the pop music, so they want CD players. They explain that, __9__ like electronic dictionaries, these can be __10__ in their study, __11__. They think that their parents should understand ___12___ they want these things.

Foreign students will also bring some latest high-tech things when they ___13___ to school at the beginning of a new term. ___14___, they often use the money which they made by themselves during the holiday to ___15___ these high-tech things that they want.

( )1.	A. changed	B. come	C. joined	D. stopped
( )2.	A. over	B. from	C. of	D. with
( )3.	A. wrong	B. luckily	C. well	D. pleased
( )4.	A. other	B. the other	C. others	D. other student
( )5.	A. think	B. wonder	C. hate	D. see
( )6.	A. down	B. off	C. behind	D. back
( )7.	A. need	B. should	C. can	D. must
( )8.	A. hear	B. listen to	C. read	D. play
( )9.	A. look	B. just	C. feel	D. nothing
( )10.	A. new	B. rich	C. latest	D. useful
( )11.	A. also	B. too	C. either	D. then
( )12.	A. where	B. which	C. what	D. why
( )13.	A. return	B. return back	C. reach	D. arrive
( )14.	A. If	B. However	C. So	D. Still
( )15.	A. borrow	B. buy	C. lend	D. steal

十、阅读短文填词。从下列动词中选出五个符合情境的词语并用其适当的形式填空。

answer, ask, tell, do, explain, wait

I was going to meet my boyfriend the other day but I was feeling a little under the weather. I wanted to give my boyfriend a call to(1)________ him that we should call off our plans for the evening.

When I called the number, a woman(2)________ the phone. "Hello," she said. I had not counted on a woman answering Mike's phone. I was a little surprised.

I asked, "Is Mike there?" The woman said, "He(3)________ some washing right now." Then I asked, "Can you tell him to call his girlfriend?" I hung up the phone without waiting for the woman's answer.

Thirty minutes later, Mike had not called me back. I went on(4)________ for an hour before I called Mike again. A man answered the phone. "Hello," he said. The voice was strange. Suddenly I knew that I had the wrong phone number. I said, "You're not Mike!" The man said, "And you're not my girlfriend. I(5)________ that to my wife for over an hour."

Unit 16

Section One

一、首字母填空。

1. The Martins are having a p________ in the park.
2. Tom will s________ his holiday in Tahiti.
3. There is a small v________ in the valley.
4. Sarah borrowed her books from the school l________.
5. People usually go to c________ on Sundays in Christian countries.
6. Let's go to the c________ to watch *Mission Impossible IV*.

二、用所给动词的一般将来时填空。

1. I ________(leave) in a minute. I ________(finish) all my work before I ________(leave).
2. —How long ________ you ________(study) in our country?
   —I ________(plan) to be here for about one more year. I ________(hope) to visit the other parts of your country.
   —What ________ you ________(do) after you ________(leave) here?
   —I ________(return) home and ________(get) a job.
3. I ________(be) tired. I ________(go) to bed early tonight.
4. Mary's birthday is next Monday, her mother ________(give) her a present.
5. It is very cold these days. It ________(snow) soon.

三、单项选择。

(　　)1. There ________ a meeting tomorrow afternoon.
A. will be going to　　B. will going to be
C. is going to be　　D. will go to be

(　　)2. Charlie ________ here next month.
A. isn't working　　B. doesn't working
C. isn't going to working　　D. won't work

(　　)3. He ________ very busy this week, he ________ free next week.
A. will be; is　　B. is; is
C. will be; will be　　D. is; will be

(　　)4. There ________ a dolphin show in the zoo tomorrow evening.

A. was　　B. is going to have

C. will have　　D. is going to be

(　　)5. —________ you ________ free tomorrow?

— No. I ________ free the day after tomorrow.

A. Are; going to; will　　B. Are; going to be; will

C. Are; going to; will be　　D. Are; going to be; will be

(　　)6. Mother ________ me a nice present on my next birthday.

A. will gives　　B. will give　　C. gives　　D. give

(　　)7. — Shall I buy a cup of tea for you?

—________(不,不要。)

A. No, you won't.　　B. No, you aren't.

C. No, please don't.　　D. No, please.

四、阅读理解。

Hi! Have you ever suddenly felt that someone you knew was in trouble — and was he? Have you ever dreamed something that came true later? Maybe you have ESP (超感觉知觉).

ESP stands for Extrasensory Perception. It may be called a sixth sense. It seems to let people know about events before they happen, or events that are happening some distance away.

Here's an example. A woman was ironing clothes. Suddenly she screamed, "My father is dead! I saw him sitting in the chair!" Just then, a telegram came. The woman's father died of a heart attack. He died sitting in a chair.

There are thousands of stories like this one on record. Scientists are studying them to find out what's behind these strange mental messages. Here's another example—one of hundreds of dreams that have come true.

A man dreamed he was walking along a road when a horse and carriage came by. The driver said, "There's room for one more." The man felt the driver seemed dead, so he ran away. The next day, when the man was getting on a crowded bus, the bus driver said, "There's room for one more."

Then the man saw that the driver's face was the same face he had seen in the dream. He wouldn't get on the bus. As the bus drove off, it crashed and burst into flames. Everyone was killed!

Some people say stories like these are **coincidences**. Others, including some scientists, say that ESP is real. From studies of ESP, we may someday learn more about the human mind.

(　　)1. According to the passage, the author believes that the sixth sense is ________.

A. in existence　　B. imaginative

C. not real　　D. impossible

(　　)2. ESP lets people know about ________.

A. events before they happen　B. events after they happen

C. events happening some distance away　D. A and C

(　　)3. By studying ESP, scientists may get to ________.

A. learn how people tell lies　B. know more about human dreams

C. know more about human mind　D. learn how strange things happen

(　　)4. In the last paragraph the underlined word "coincidences" probably means ________.

A. things that may not happen　B. things that happen in a dream

C. things that must happen　D. things that happen by accident

Section Two

一、将下列国家和对应的首都连线。

Russia	Warsaw
Nigeria	Athens
Greece	Tokyo
Brazil	Lagos
Japan	Moscow
Poland	Brasilia

二、根据语境和所给的首字母填空。

1. We have many famous p ________ in our university.
2. Our factory uses r ________ to do dangerous work instead of men.
3. S ________ the table is a suitable housework for children.
4. B ________ of the bad weather, we can't enjoy the beautiful view in Hawaii.
5. Don't stand in f ________ of a car.

三、句型转换。

1. They are going to Tahiti to spend summer holiday.（改为一般疑问句）

____

2. I shall arrive at Prague in 24 hours.（改为否定句）

____

3. Steven will join us in <u>New Hampshire</u>.（对画线部分提问）

____

4. The journey will take us <u>two months</u> to finish.（对画线部分提问）

____

四、单项选择。

(　　) 1. — Where is the morning paper?

— I ________ it for you at once.

A. get B. gets C. to get D. will get

( ) 2. ________ a concert next Saturday?

A. There will be B. Will there be

C. There can be D. There are

( ) 3. If they come, we ________ a meeting.

A. have B. will have C. had D. would have

( ) 4. He ________ her a beautiful hat tomorrow as a prize.

A. gives B. gave C. will give D. is going to giving

( ) 5. He ________ to us as soon as he gets there.

A. writes B. has written C. will write D. wrote

( ) 6. He ________ in three days.

A. coming back B. will come back

C. came back D. is going to coming back

五、阅读理解。

Man, a land animal. But he is also closely tied to the sea. Throughout history the sea has served the needs of man. The sea has provided man with food and a convenient way to travel to many parts of the world. Today, nearly two-thirds of the world's population live within 80 kilometers of the sea coast.

In the modern technological world, the sea offers many resources to help mankind survive. Resources on land are beginning to be used up. The sea, however, still can be hoped to supply many of man's needs.

The list of riches of the sea yet to be developed by man's technology is big. Oil and gas explorations have been carried out for nearly 30 years. Valuable amounts of minerals exist on the ocean floor ready to be mined.

Fish farming promises to be a good way to produce large quantities of food. The culture of fish and shellfish (贝类动物) is an ancient skill practised in the past mainly by **Oriental people**, including people in China.

Besides oil and gas, the sea may offer new sources of energy. Experts believe that the warm temperature of the ocean can be used in a way similar to the steam in a steamship. Ocean currents and waves offer possible use as a source of energy.

Technology is enabling man to explore ever more deeply under the sea. The development of strong, new materials has made this possible.

The technology to harvest the sea continues to improve. Experts believe that by the year 2020 the problems that prevent us from exploiting(开发) fully the food, minerals, and energy sources of the sea will be largely solved.

( ) 1. The major things that the sea offers man are ________.

A. fish and oil B. minerals and oil

C. warm temperature and ocean currents

D. the food, energy sources, and minerals

( ) 2. The underlined words "Oriental people" in the fourth paragraph probably mean ________.

A. Asian people B. African people

C. European people D. American people

( ) 3. The best title for this passage is ________.

A. Sea Harvest B. Sea Food

C. Technology for Exploiting the Sea D. Man and the Sea

Section Three

一、结合语境，用适当的动词填空。

1. Without your help, I can't ________ the exam.
2. Let me ________ some coffee for you.
3. It's your turn to ________ the floor this week.
4. It's a bit cold. Would you please ________ the window?
5. The TV is too loud. You should ________ it down a little bit.

二、用所给动词的适当时态填空。

1. —________ you ________ (be) here this Saturday?

—No. I ________ (visit) my teacher.

2. —________ I ________ (get) you a copy of today's newspaper?

—Thank you.

3. I am afraid there ________ (be) a meeting this afternoon. I can't join you.
4. Sandra ________ (love) the story, and she ________ (read) it countless times.
5. Most of us don't think their team ________ (lose).
6. Sanya ________ (go) to Italy last year, and she ________ (fly) to Switzerland next year.
7. Mike ________ (believe, not) this until he ________ (see) it with his own eyes.
8. I believe that AC Milan ________ (win) this year's Euro Champion.

三、单项选择。

( ) 1. Who ________ we ________ swimming with tomorrow afternoon?

A. will; goes B. do; go C. will; going D. shall; go

( ) 2. We ________ the work this way next time.

A. do B. will do C. going to do D. will doing

( ) 3. Tomorrow he ________ a kite in the open air first, and then ________ boating in the park.

A. will fly; will go B. will fly; goes

C. is going to fly; will goes D. flies; will go

( ) 4. The day after tomorrow they ________ a volleyball match.

A. will watching　　B. watches

C. is watching　　D. are going to watch

(　　) 5. There ________ a birthday party this Sunday.

A. shall be　　B. will be

C. shall going to be　　D. will going to be

四、参照例句造句。

eg：They / Mrs. Fisher's / in a short time

They will go to Mrs. Fisher's in a short time.

1. They/Mr. Wang's/in three minutes

____

2. Tom and Jerry/Mr. Yao's/in a moment

____

3. Sheila/Texas/in a month

____

4. We/Tahiti/next week

____

5. He/the fun fair/in one hour

____

五、完形填空。

There was __1__ a rich man named Steve. One day he asked his friend Jack __2__ and buy a bottle of wine __3__ him, without giving him any __4__. Jack asked, "Steve, how can I buy wine without money?"

"Anyone can buy wine with money," Steve said. "A person who can buy wine without money is really an able man."

Jack __5__ to go to the street to buy wine. "What __6__ I do?" He thought as he went. After a while, Jack came __7__ with an empty bottle. Steve __8__ happy about this and said, "__9__ do you want me to drink?"

Jack answered, "Anyone can drink from a bottle with wine in __10__. A person who can drink from an empty bottle is really an able man!"

(　　) 1. A. once　B. before　C. ago　D. long time

(　　) 2. A. go　B. goes　C. to go　D. went

(　　) 3. A. to　B. with　C. for　D. from

(　　) 4. A. bottle　B. money　C. shopping list　D. shopping basket

(　　) 5. A. had　B. went　C. would　D. begin

(　　) 6. A. did　B. shall　C. am　D. may

(　　) 7. A. back　B. to　C. late　D. over

(　　) 8. A. didn't　B. wasn't　C. not　D. was

(　　) 9. A. How　B. Where　C. When　D. What

(　　) 10. A. one　B. it　C. them　D. him

Section Four

一、选出下列各组单词中不属于同一类的词。

(　　) 1. A. professor　B. student　C. teacher　D. soldier

(　　) 2. A. policeman　B. Frenchman　C. Englishman　D. American

(　　) 3. A. grape　B. tomato　C. pear　D. apple

(　　) 4. A. sister　B. brother　C. aunt　D. friend

(　　) 5. A. October　B. summer　C. autumn　D. spring

二、阅读下面的对话，从7个选项中选择5个恰当的选项完成此对话，使其意思完整。

(D = Daniel; L = Linda)

D: Hello, Linda. Nice to meet you.

L: Hello, Daniel. (1) ________________.

D: You see, summer holiday is coming. (2) ________________

L: I'm going to travel to the Shanghai Expo Garden.

D: (3) ________________. By the way, will you go there alone?

L: (4) ________________. My cousin will go with me.

D: (5) ________________.

L: We'll start on July 8.

D: I think you will enjoy yourselves there.

A. How do you do?　B. It's a good place to travel.
C. What's your plan for it?　D. When will you go?
E. No, I won't.　F. Nice to meet you, too.
G. I'll go there by train.

三、单项选择。

(　　) 1. ________ your brother ________ a magazine from the library?
A. Are; going to borrow　B. Is; going to borrow
C. Will; borrows　D. Are; going to borrows

(　　) 2. — Shall I come again tomorrow afternoon?
— ________ (好的。)
A. Yes, please.　B. Yes, you will.
C. No, please.　D. No, you won't.

(　　) 3. It ________ the year of the horse next year.
A. is going to be　B. is going to
C. will　D. will is

(　　) 4. ________ open the window?
A. Will you please　B. Please will you

C. You please　　　　　　　　D. Do you

(　　) 5. — Let's go out to play football, shall we?

— OK. I ________.

A. will coming　　　　　　　　B. be going to come

C. come　　　　　　　　　　　D. am coming

四、句型转换。

1. The CEO will make a speech at the meeting next week.（改为否定句）

____

2. There will be some sea fish served at the buffet.（改为一般疑问句）

____

3. Sylvia will go on a business trip <u>to Alabama</u>.（对画线部分提问）

____

4. Samuel will be back from Hong Kong <u>in two weeks</u>.（对画线部分提问）

____

五、阅读短文，根据短文内容判断句子的正误。

The favorite food in the United States is the hamburger. The favorite place to buy a hamburger is a fast food restaurant. At a fast food restaurant people order their food, wait a few minutes, and carry it to their tables themselves. People also take their food out of the restaurant and eat in their cars or in their homes. At some fast food restaurants, people can order their food, pay for it and pick it up without leaving their cars.

There are many kinds of fast food restaurants in the United States. The most numerous sell hamburgers, French fries and milkshakes. They are traditionally popular food among Americans. Fast food restaurants also serve Chinese food, Mexican food, Italian food, Chicken, seafood and ice cream.

Fast food restaurants are very popular, and many American people like them. First, people can wear any type of dress when they go to a fast food place. Second, they are fast. Finally, most food in the restaurant is not expensive.

(　　) 1. Most American people like hamburgers.

(　　) 2. People must eat the fast food at the fast food restaurant.

(　　) 3. People can order their fast food and pick it up in their cars.

(　　) 4. People can get many kinds of food in the fast food restaurant.

(　　) 5. Americans like to go to fast food restaurant because the restaurants are fast, not formal, and not expensive.

Section Five

一、情景应答，根据听到的内容选择正确的答语。

(　　)1. A. Really? Wonderful!　　　　B. I go to school at seven.

C. It's time to go to school.

( )2. A. She is better now. B. She likes dancing.
C. She is tall and pretty.

( )3. A. No, I don't agree. B. That's all right.
C. Yes, I think so.

( )4. A. What a pity. B. You are unlucky.
C. Congratulations!

( )5. A. Yes, I do. B. No, I didn't.
C. Yes, I play it every day.

二、听对话，选择正确的答语。

听下面五段对话，每段对话后各有一个问题，请选择正确的答语。

( )1. A. At home. B. In the hospital. C. In the classroom.

( )2. A. To the factory. B. To the store. C. To the hospital.

( )3. A. Tom's friend. B. Tom. C. Tom's uncle.

( )4. A. In a hospital. B. At fourth street. C. On a bus.

( )5. A. He'll buy another kind.
B. They'll get some more tea.
C. They don't have any more tea.

听下面一段对话，回答第6~7题。

( )6. What does John want to be when he grows up?
A. He wants to be a teacher.
B. He wants to be a football player.
C. He wants to be an astronaut.

( )7. What would John like to do if he wants to be stronger?
A. He'd like to have more healthy food.
B. He'd like to play football every day.
C. He'd like to do morning exercise.

听下面一段对话，回答第8~10题。

( )8. Who is Mr. Smith?
A. He's Miss Lin's friend. B. He's Miss Lin's classmate.
C. He's a science teacher.

( )9. What did Tom want to borrow from Miss Lin?
A. He wants to borrow a VCD. B. He wants to borrow a book.
C. He wants to borrow a magazine.

( )10. What do Tom's classmates think about the life on Mars?
A. They think it very interesting. B. They find it a little boring.
C. They hope they could go to Mars.

三、听短文，根据短文内容选择正确答案。

( )1. What was the husband like?

A. He was small and thin. B. He was large and fat.

C. He was tall and strong.

(　　)2. How often did the man get his pay?

A. Every month. B. Every day.

C. Every week.

(　　)3. What was his wife doing when he hurried into the living room?

A. She was listening to the radio and eating apples.

B. She was watching TV and waiting for her husband.

C. She was listening to the radio and cleaning the room.

(　　)4. How did he get the ten thousand dollars?

A. He saved the money little by little.

B. He bought the lottery tickets(彩票).

C. He found the money in his office.

(　　)5. How did his wife feel when she heard the news?

A. She was happy. B. She was angry.

C. She was happy at first. Then she got angry.

四、根据中文提示,在空格内填入适当的单词,使句子意思完整。

1. He tried a ________ (第五) time, but without luck, he failed again.
2. Two bridges were ________ (建造) across the Ganjiang River a few years ago.
3. The boy drew a big elephant ________ (用) his pencil.
4. The glass is ________ (满) with hot water.
5. Have you ________ (收到) from your boyfriend?

五、用所给单词的适当形式填空。

1. Jim can play football very well. He's a good ________ (play).
2. There isn't any cloud in the sky. What a ________ (sun) day!
3. Will you go ________ (skate) with me?
4. You should be ________ (care) when you cross the street.
5. Do you think Lucy is a ________ (forget) girl?

六、单项选择。

(　　) 1. If it ________ tomorrow, we'll go roller-skating.

A. isn't rain B. won't rain C. doesn't rain D. doesn't fine

(　　) 2. — Will his parents go to see the Terra Cotta Warriors tomorrow?

— No, ________________.

A. they willn't B. they won't C. they aren't D. they don't

(　　) 3. ________ you ________ free next Sunday?

A. Will; are B. Will; be C. Do; be D. Are; be

(　　) 4. He ________ there at ten tomorrow morning.

A. will B. is C. will be D. be

(　　) 5. They ________ an English evening next Sunday.

A. are having　　B. are going to have

C. will having　　D. is going to have

七、句型转换。

1. The Obamas will come home soon.（改为否定句）

____

2. They have lived here for ten years.（改为一般疑问句）

____

3. Jenny didn't finish her homework until the day before yesterday.（对画线部分提问）

____

4. We shall have a big party on the beach at night.（对画线部分提问）

____

5. Johnny is going to join the army next month.（对画线部分提问）

____

八、完形填空。

Many animals use some kinds of "language". They use signals and the signals have meanings. For example, __1__ a bee has found some food, it goes __2__ its home. __3__ is difficult for a bee to tell __4__ bees where the food is by speaking to them, but it can do a little dancing. This tells the bees where the food is and __5__ it is.

Some animals show __6__ they feel by making sounds. It is not difficult to tell if a dog is angry because it barks. Birds make several different sounds and __7__ has its meaning. Sometimes we humans make sounds in the same way. We make sounds like "Oh" to __8__ how we feel about __9__ or we __10__ something on our feet.

We humans have languages. We have words. These words have meaning of things, action, feeling or ideas. We are able to __11__ each other information, to tell other people __12__ we think or we feel. By writing down words, we can remember what has happened or __13__ messages to people far away.

Languages, like people, live and die. If a language is not used by people, it is called a dead language. This language cannot live and grow because __14__ speaks it.

A living language, of course, is often spoken by people today. It grows and changes with time. New words are created, and some old words have __15__ meanings.

(　　)1. A. because　B. since　C. when　D. as

(　　)2. A. out of　B. back from　C. away from　D. back to

(　　)3. A. It　B. This　C. That　D. He

(　　)4. A. each other　B. another　C. the other　D. others

(　　)5. A. how long　B. how far away　C. how many　D. how old

(　　)6. A. why　B. which　C. how　D. what

(　　)7. A. each　B. every　C. all　D. some

(　　)8. A. show　B. say　C. talk　D. speak

(　　)9. A. everything　B. something　C. nothing　D. anything
(　　)10. A. put　B. drop　C. fall　D. set
(　　)11. A. give　B. put　C. show　D. take
(　　)12. A. that　B. which　C. what　D. why
(　　)13. A. send　B. bring　C. push　D. get
(　　)14. A. someone　B. no one　C. anyone　D. everyone
(　　)15. A. new　B. right　C. real　D. good

九、阅读理解。

After The Super Girl was shown on TV, it was loved by millions of people, especially the young people. It becomes a hot topic among people. Here are some of their opinions:

China is a developing country and women now show their abilities as freely as men do. The modern world is a stage for them to show who they are and what they want.

—Nancy, 14

One of the girls looks like Jolin Tsai. In Singapore, a show of this kind is called Superstar. I think the competition like this is a good chance for the young girls with the dreams of stage. As for The Super Girl, I hope I can see one international super star coming out from this year's competition.

—Linda, 16

I am worried about these super girls. They are educated in different ways. At their ages, they should be spending more time at school, not on the stage. What are they learning? And for what?

—John, 15

(　　)1. What do people think about The Super Girl ?
A. It was loved by all the people.
B. Different people have different ideas.
C. All the young people enjoyed it very much.
D. It is not popular among people.

(　　)2. ________ is one of the famous super girls.
A. Li Yuchun　B. Jolin Tsai　C. Song Zuying　D. Zhang Huimei

(　　)3. Nancy thinks that ____________.
A. men could do better than women
B. women can show their abilities as freely as men do
C. women can do much better than men now
D. the modern world is a stage for women to show where they go

(　　)4. John worries about the super girls because these girls ____________.
A. don't spend enough time studying at school
B. spend too much time studying at school
C. show their abilities in their free time
D. are educated in the same way

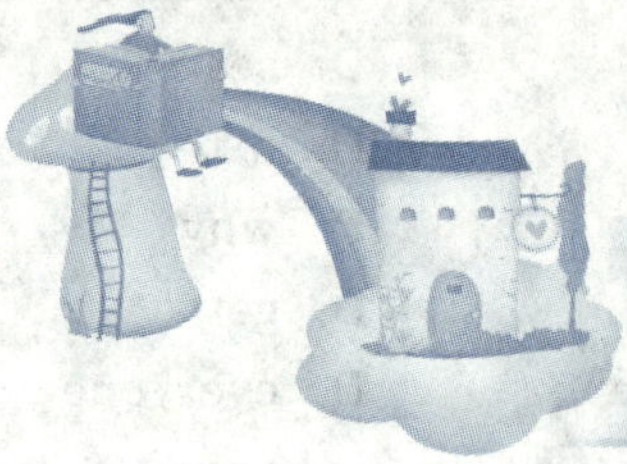

Unit 17

Section One

一、用所给词的正确形式填空。

1. Whose ________(be) these cakes?
2. Mr. Brown and Mrs. Brown ________(work) at school.
3. Miss Brown ________(like) English very much.
4. Mary ________(study) at No. 9 Middle School.
5. Do you like ________(play) football?
6. ________(finish) the homework before you go home.

二、用正确的介词填空。

Example: I'm in Class Five.

1. Can I borrow a book ________ biology?
2. This prize is ________ Tom.
3. He goes to work ________ car.
4. We study ________ No. 5 Middle School.
5. Billy looks ________ his father.
6. He arrives ________ school at 8 every morning.
7. Hubei is ________ the south of China.
8. He works ________ a nurse in a hospital.

三、从 B 栏中找出与 A 栏相对应的答语。

A	B
( ) 1. Can you speak more slowly, please?	A. Go along this street to the end.
( ) 2. I don't feel well today.	B. Thanks, but I am full.
( ) 3. Help yourself to some dumplings.	C. Sorry, I thought you can follow me.
( ) 4. Excuse me, how can I go to the Bank of China?	D. OK, it's a piece of cake.
( ) 5. Can you repair my watch?	E. You had better see a doctor.

四、翻译。

1. 请问，去火车站怎么走？

____

2. 这本书很畅销。

This kind of book ________.

3. 这本字典的价格至少50元。

________ the dictionary is ________ 50 yuan.

4. 在过去，伦敦被人们看做雾城。

________, London was known ________ a city of fog.

5. 据说他去过英国两次。

________ that he has ________ England twice.

6. 我们相信他迟早会回来的。

We believe he will be back ________.

五、阅读理解。

Robert is fifteen now. Two and a half years ago he came to the city and began to study in a middle school. He studies hard and gets on well with his classmates. And he often helps his friends with their lessons. But as he comes from a village, the headmaster who was born in a rich family is bad to him and does his best to make excuses to punish him. The boy knows it and takes precautions against(提防) it.

One afternoon all the students went to have lunch and he bought a piece of bread. He was reading a book under a big tree, while a dog was standing near him. At that moment the headmaster came out and saw it. He became angry and said, "Don't you know we don't let anybody rear (饲养) dogs in the school?"

"Yes, I do, sir," said the boy.

"Why have you brought your dog to school, then?"

"It isn't my dog."

"Why is it following you, then?"

"You're following me now, sir," said the boy. "Can you say you are mine?"

请根据以上短文在改写后短文的空白处填入适当的词，使其完整。

Robert is fifteen. He is in a (1) ________ school now. He studies hard and his classmates are (2) ________ to him. And he often helps his friends to (3) ________ their lessons. But as he was (4) ________ in a farmer family, the headmaster from a (5) ________ family is bad to him and does (6) ________ he can to punish him.

One day in the (7) ________, all the students went (8) ________ lunch and he bought a piece of bread, reading a book under a tree. At the moment a dog was standing near him. (9) ________ the headmaster saw this, he wanted to (10) ________ him. But he failed that day again.

Section Two

一、用所给动词的适当形式填空。

1. Please ________ (tell) me about your favorite subject.

2. Where ________ Michael Owen ________ (come) from?
3. He ________ (want) ________ (look) for a job in town.
4. Let us ________ (give) them our best wishes. ________ (go) for it, Steal Roses!
5. Would you like ________ (be) a professional football player?
6. I am afraid of ________ (swim), but Tom often ________ (teach) me ________ (swim).
7. What ________ he ________ (go) to do this weekend?
8. Here ________ (be) the flowers for Mom.
9. The woman often ________ (take) a look at her cat to eat things.
10. Look! The cats ________ up the trees. (climb)

二、用所给词的适当形式填空。

1. Sandy is very ________ (sleep) today, so he is soon ________ (sleep) in the bed.
2. China is developing ________ (it) own fast food industry.
3. Fast food is part of ________ (every day) life for many people.
4. Nowadays, people enjoy fast ________ (serve).
5. Mother's Day falls on ________ (two) Sunday in May.
6. I'm going to ________ (travel) abroad next week.
7. For many Americans, the last night of the old year will be a loud, ________ (live) celebration.
8. Many Americans go to a hotel or eating place ________ the night of December 31st.

三、单项选择。

(　　) 1. Now the air in our city is ________ than it used to be. Something must be done to stop it.
A. very good　B. much better　C. rather bad　D. even worse

(　　) 2. We love to go to the country in spring as the flowers smell so ______.
A. well　B. nice　C. wonderfully　D. nicely

(　　) 3. —Oh. I'm hungry. Mum, can I have the hamburger on the plate?
—No. It tastes ________.
A. terribly　B. terrible　C. good　D. well

(　　) 4. —What do you think of your English teacher?
—I love her. She is really ______. She always has a smile on her face.
A. outgoing　B. funny　C. friendly　D. serious

(　　) 5. —Tim, do you think time is money?
—Yes, but I think money is ______ time.
A. more important than　B. very important as
C. the same as　D. not important as

四、情景对话。

A：Hi, David! (1)______________?

B：Hi, Sarah! I am going to see Anna. She is in hospital.

A：(2)__________________?

B：She had a traffic accident on her way to school and was hurt.

A：(3)____________. Is there anything serious?

B：Yes, there is something wrong with her head.

A：Oh, my God! (4)________________.

B：I hope so, too.

A：(5)______________?

B：Sure. Let's go!

五、阅读理解。

Tokyo may be one of those places that you love and hate at the same time. In Tokyo, there are always too many people in the places where I want to go. There are also too many cars. Tokyo drivers often spend a long time in the busy street, just like drivers in London, Paris and New York.

Tokyo also has a lot of people on foot, and sometimes it is really difficult to walk in the street. The worst time in the street is at 11:30 at night. That is because the nightclubs are closing at that time and everybody wants to go home then. There are 35,000 nightclubs in Tokyo, and usually none of them is empty at night.

During the day, most people go to work by train. Six million train tickets are sold every year in Tokyo. At most stations, trains arrive every two or three minutes, but at certain hours it is not enough at all. Although trains are always crowded, they are very good in many ways. They always leave and arrive on time. In London trains, you may see everybody reading a newspaper. But in Tokyo trains, everybody seems to be sleepy, no matter whether his journey is long or short. If you stand outside the station for five minutes, there will be three fire engines(消防车) going past you. They are on the way to one of the fires that Tokyo has every day. Tokyo has so many surprises that none of them can really surprise me now.

(　　)1. In London, Paris and New York, there are ______ in the street.

A. a few trains　　B. many trains

C. too many cars　　D. no cars

(　　)2. Japanese trains ______________________.

A. don't often leave and arrive on time

B. are not crowded

C. are good for sleep

D. are the important traffic tools for Japanese

(　　)3. The business of the nightclubs in Tokyo is ______________.

A. very bad　　B. just so so

C. not too good D. very good

(　　)4. From the passage, we can know ________.

A. the writer likes Tokyo more than he hates

B. the writer hates Tokyo more than he likes

C. the writer wants to leave Tokyo as soon as possible

D. the writer has got used to the life in Tokyo

Section Three

一、根据句意，结合提示填空（每空一词）。

1. I'm used to ________(处理) with matters of this sort.
2. There is something wrong with our computer. It needs ________(修理).
3. The Fashion Show will be ________(举行) from 12th to 20th May.
4. What is his speech ________(主要) about?
5. I believe you have made a good ________(decide).
6. Look! The dogs are looking for food ________(careful) in the street.

二、用动词的适当形式填空（每空一词）。

1. She ________(wash) her hands before dinner every day.
2. They ________(drive) to the party yesterday.
3. You are welcome to let us know what you are not ________(satisfy) with at any time.
4. The students were made to ________(realize) where the gravity is by the teacher.
5. Nick was ________(make) to write five compositions by his teacher last week.
6. The film star has been ________(die) for years.
7. Nobody told me when to ________(leave).

三、从四个选项中选出一个能替换句子画线部分的词或短语。

(　　)1. The woman doesn't change her mind because she thinks she is right.

A. way B. idea C. life D. sound

(　　)2. When she is unhappy, I am unhappy.

A. feel the same B. am different C. feel happily D. feel same

(　　)3. Buses are usually full of people in the morning.

A. many B. busy with C. hard for D. filled with

(　　)4. Look out! There is a car coming fast.

A. Look up B. Look out of the window

C. Be careful D. Be careful with

(　　)5. John is one of the top students in our class.

A. tallest B. best C. highest D. good

四、单项选择。

(　　) 1. Don't worry, sir. I'm sure I can run ________ to catch up with them.
A. slowly enough　　B. enough slowly
C. fast enough　　D. enough fast

(　　) 2. —Where do you think ________ he ________ the computer?
—Sorry, I have no idea.
A. /; bought　　B. has; bought
C. did; buy　　D. does; buy

(　　) 3. —Is there anything wrong with my son, doctor?
—________.
A. Do it, please.　　B. I don't mind.
C. I don't feel very well.　　D. Nothing serious.

(　　) 4. —Can you tell me why ________?
—Because I want to help the people there.
A. do you go to Tibet　　B. did you go to Tibet
C. are you going to Tibet　　D. you are going to Tibet

(　　) 5. Sandy and Sue are at the seaside. They are ________ holiday now.
A. in　　B. on　　C. at　　D. with

五、阅读并判断正误。

Inventions arrive every day. When people invent great new things, we get ideas about the future. What will the future be like? It's possible that we may often fly up into space! Out of all the coolest inventions of the year, Space Ship One is thought to be the best.

Space Ship One is a 6-metre-long white spaceship. On June 21, 2004, American pilot Mike Mclville flew it to space and back—about 100 kilometres up into the sky. Some might say it's not a big deal. You know, people went to the moon years ago. Well, Space Ship One is special because it is the first spaceship that wasn't made by the government(政府). It was built and sent up by a private(私人的) US company.

Lots of people went to travel in space. But it's too expensive. American millionaire (百万富翁) Dennis Tito paid almost US $20 million to become the first space tourist to visit the International Space Station in 2001. So private companies began to think of making their own spaceship to take other tourists up into space. The success of Space Ship One is a good start. "The flight opens a new page in history, putting space within the reach of ordinary people," said Patti Smith, an official at US Federal Aviation Administration(联邦航空管理局).

In the next 10 to 15 years, if you pay $20,000 to $100,000 you could fly high above the earth. What about having your own spaceship in your garage(车库) and taking it to space at the weekend?

(　　) 1. Of all the coolest inventions from which people can get ideas about the future of the year, Space Ship One was chosen as the best one.

(　　) 2. From the passage, we know that only government has the right to build the spaceship.

(　　) 3. If you want to fly to the Space Station, you'd better eat more food to be strong.

(　　) 4. People have known things well about the space since 1960.

(　　) 5. The successful flight of Space Ship One opens a new page in history, because it puts space near to the ordinary people.

Section Four

一、用所给动词的适当形式填空。

1. Here ________ (be) your exercise-books, class.
2. He always ________ (get) up late and he ________ (be) always in a hurry.
3. The family usually ________ (spend) a quiet day at home.
4. What ________ we ________ (do) tomorrow?
5. Let's ________ (listen) to the radio first.
6. The computer ________ (not work). I ________ (take) it to the shop tomorrow.
7. They ________ (go) to the cinema next evening.
8. Here ________ (be) the weather forecast for tomorrow.
9. Mother ________ (travel) by train next week.
10. The Smiths ________ (go) to the cinema tomorrow night.

二、单项选择。

(　　) 1. — I'll plan a visit to Hong Kong if it ________ tomorrow.
— Really? I think I ________ with you.
A. don't rain; go　　B. won't rain; go
C. isn't rain; will go　　D. doesn't rain; will go

(　　) 2. He was sure that he ________ his wallet in the office.
A. left　　B. would leave
C. had left　　D. has left

(　　) 3. When she ________ at the door, my mother ________ some washing.
A. knocked; did　　B. was knocking; did
C. knocked; was doing　　D. knocks; is doing

(　　) 4. — ________ you ever ________ Tom before?
— No, I ________ him just two minutes ago.
A. Have, known; met　　B. Have, known ; have met
C. Did, know; met　　D. Did, know; had met

(　　) 5. Mr. Smith ________ short stories, but he ________ a TV play these days.
A. is writing; is writing　　B. is writing; writes

C. writes; is writing　　　　D. writes; writes

(　　) 6. — How did the accident happen?

— You know, it ____ difficult to see the road clearly because it ______.

A. was; was raining　　　　B. was; had rained

C. is; is raining　　　　D. was; rained

(　　) 7. — How long ________ you ________ England, Sue?

— Since two years ago.

A. have; been to　　　　B. have; gone to

C. have; been in　　　　D. have; moved to

(　　) 8. It ________ two years since he ________ the Party.

A. is; has joined　　　　B. was; joined

C. has been; joined　　　　D. had been; joined

三、补全对话：选出正确的句子填入空格处。

A: Excuse me. Could you tell me where the nearest museum is?

B: Well, it's a bit far. You can go along the street, then take the first turning on the right, walk on and you'll find one there. (1)________.

A: Oh, thanks. (2)________.

B: It should be open now. It opens at 8:00 am.

A: Good. (3)________.

B: Which bus? I don't know. You may ask the policeman over there. (4)________.

A: OK. By the way, where is the nearest McDonald's, do you know?

B: Right behind you, sir. See that sign?

A: Oh, thanks a lot.

B: (5)________.

A. And can you tell me which bus I should take?

B. Do you know at what time it opens?

C. He must know that.

D. You're welcome.

E. What's wrong with you?

F. You can't miss it.

G. Let me help you.

四、在短文的空格内填入适当的词，使其内容通顺，首字母已给。每空格限填一词。

Bedtime stories are one of the delights (喜悦) of early childhood. But (1)a ________ to Dr. Julie Spreadbury from Queensland, parents (2)s ________ not speed up reading to their children after they enter primary school. She says listening to, reading and (3)d ________ the stories help children's relaxation.

"My theory (理论) is that when children can read (4)t ________, most parents stop reading to them," Dr. Spreadbury says. That may be at the end of the Year 1, which is far too informal.

Dr. Spreadbury says bedtime reading (5) n ________ only gives children a good (6) b ________ at school, but also brings parents and their children closer. This makes it funnier for them to open up and talk to parents about things that are worrying them, (7) o ________ things they are reading in their everyday life.

Section Five

一、情景反应。听问句，选出恰当的答语。

(　　)1. A. I'm afraid you can't.　B. That's great.　C. It doesn't matter.
(　　)2. A. Good idea.　B. At 7 o'clock.　C. Not at all.
(　　)3. A. No, please do it.　B. Yes, you can do it.　C. It's very kind of you.
(　　)4. A. She is better now.　B. She likes dancing.　C. She is tall and pretty.
(　　)5. A. Since last year.　B. September.　C. Six o'clock.

二、对话理解。根据对话内容选择问题的正确答案。

(　　)1. A. Football.　B. Basketball.　C. Volleyball.
(　　)2. A. Going to a picnic.　B. Doing homework.　C. Going fishing.
(　　)3. A. By bus.　B. By bike.　C. By plane.
(　　)4. A. He has to take a lesson.
B. He has to do homework.
C. He has to see a friend.
(　　)5. A. By learning grammar.
B. By listening to the radio.
C. By memorizing words.

听下面一段小对话，完成第 6～7 题。

(　　)6. A. At 1:30 .　B. At 1:45 .　C. At 2:00.
(　　)7. A. With soldiers.　B. With friends.　C. With classmates.

听下面一段较长对话，完成第 8～10 题。

(　　)8. A. Because she doesn't know the language.
B. Because she has never been abroad.
C. Because she doesn't know the culture there.
(　　)9. A. Watches.　B. Time.　C. Culture.
(　　)10. A. She can't be late.　B. She should buy a present.
C. She should take some flowers.

三、短文理解。根据短文内容选择问题的正确答案。

(　　) 1. A. A teacher.　B. A farmer.　C. A worker.
(　　) 2. A. She is tall and beautiful.　B. She is tall and fat.　C. Her hair is brown.
(　　) 3. A. Fishing.　B. Swimming.　C. Planting flowers.

( ) 4. A. Her friends. B. The teacher. C. The father.

( ) 5. A. Playing. B. Studying. C. Surfing the Internet.

四、用所给词的适当形式填空。

1. Paul is a ________ (France) boy.
2. Billy makes a lot of mistakes. He is really a ________ (care) boy.
   But Simon's always ________ (care). His work is always neat and tidy.
3. There are four terms in a school year. The ________ (two) term is the Winter term.
4. The wind often blows in ________ (east) Britain.
5. — Who are they? Are they Mr. and Mrs. Clark and their children?
   — Yes, they are the ________ (Clark).
6. It's so ________ (quiet) in the classroom, we walk ________ (quiet).

五、从方框中选择合适的词,并用其正确的形式填空。

parent, tell, call, celebrate, together, why, start, after, shop, newspaper

Most people buy lots of presents just before Christmas. But some people think we buy too much. They have started a special day (1) ________ Buy Nothing Day. They don't want anyone to go (2) ______ on that day. Buy Nothing Day is on November 29. It is (3) ________ Thanksgiving. Often, before Christmas we see many ads in (4) ________ and on TV (5) ________ us to "buy, buy, buy!" The idea for Buy Nothing Day (6) ________ in Vancouver, Canada. Now people all over the world (7) ________ Buy Nothing Day. In California, the U. S., (8) ________ and children get (9) ________ to read stories, sing songs, and draw pictures. The children talk about (10) ________ they don't need a lot of toys.

六、单项选择。

( ) 1. The boy has breakfast ________ home.
A. on B. from C. in D. at

( ) 2. We must keep the classroom ________.
A. clean B. to clean C. cleaning D. cleaned

( ) 3. She ________ know the answer, but I'm not sure.
A. maybe B. may be C. may D. must

( ) 4. There is ________ in today's newspaper.
A. nothing new B. anything new
C. new anything D. new something

( ) 5. —You look rather tired. ________ stop to take a rest?
—All right. But I'll have to work for a few more minutes.
A. Why not B. Do you C. What about D. How about

( ) 6. I've ________ the word in several dictionaries, but I can't ________ how to use the word correctly.

A. looked in; find out　　B. looked up; find out

C. looked up; find　　D. looked for; find

(　　)7. My father will have a ________ holiday next month. He'll take me to Qingdao.

A. ten days　　B. ten days'

C. ten-days　　D. ten day's

(　　)8. —Hi, Tom! Can you tell me when ________ for London?

—Yes, tomorrow afternoon.

A. leaving　　B. leaves　　C. to leave　　D. are you leaving

(　　)9. —Will you please write a short passage on "Meteor Garden" and ________ it to me this evening?

—What about tomorrow? My computer doesn't work okay now.

A. give　　B. e-mail　　C. take　　D. bring

(　　)10. There will be a volleyball match in our school, ________?

A. be there　　B. is there　　C. will there　　D. won't there

七、根据汉语提示将句子补充完整。

1. 还是孩子时她就对表演产生了兴趣。

She ________ acting ________ she was a child.

2. 在过去的十年里，中国发生了巨大变化。

Great changes ________ in China ________.

3. 他非常聪明，总想到一些好主意。

He is ________ to ________ some good ideas.

4. 我认为父母在日常生活中一定要严格要求孩子们。

I think parents must ________ their children ________.

5. 参加篮球比赛能给我们提供学习团队精神的机会。

Playing basketball games can ________ with chances ________.

八、完形填空。

People from different cultures sometimes do things that make each other uncomfortable __1__ realizing it. Americans who have never been out of their country have very little experience with people of other cultures. But they are usually open and friendly. They enjoy meeting new people, __2__ guests and bringing people together formally or informally. They use __3__ in most situations and speak casually（随意地）about __4__. So if your American host does something that makes you __5__, let him know __6__ you feel. Most people will be __7__ for your honesty. And you'll learn something about a new culture.

Americans may invite you to their homes __8__ they really get to know you. Sometimes they are said to be superficially（表面的）friendly. Perhaps it __9__ so, but they are probably just having a good time. As __10__, it takes time to become good friends with people in the U. S.

( )1. A. on B. after C. with D. without
( )2. A. making B. make C. having D. have
( )3. A. surnames B. first names C. family names D. full names
( )4. A. they B. themselves C. theirs D. them
( )5. A. unpleasant B. comfortable C. happy D. enjoyable
( )6. A. what B. whatever C. how D. however
( )7. A. thankful B. sorry C. nervous D. pleased
( )8. A. before B. after C. when D. until
( )9. A. looks B. being C. exits D. seems
( )10. A. anywhere B. everywhere C. nowhere D. elsewhere

九、阅读理解。

In the time it takes you to read this sentence, the population of the world will have grown by ten people. That may not sound much, but it is 9,000 people in an hour, 1.5 million a week, or 79 million a year. That is the same as adding most of the population of Germany to the world every year.

Most of these new people were born in developing countries. These countries are found in much of Africa, South America and parts of Asia. In the developed countries of Europe and North America, the population is growing very slowly. This is because women in these countries have, on average, only one or two children. In the developing countries, many women have five or more children. In 1950, around one quarter of the world's population lived in the developed countries. By 2050, these countries will be home to only around one tenth of the world's people.

In the developing countries, more than one billion people already live below the poverty（贫困）line. These people do not have enough food to eat and they live in poor housing; children get little or no time at school and people suffer（遭受痛苦）from many kinds of diseases.

At the beginning of the 21st century, the world's population was around six billion people. The UN has said that the world's population will level off at 12.5 billion people by the year 2100. Other groups think the world's population will continue to grow, reaching 14 billion people before it becomes stable（稳定的）, or even falls.

1. How many people are added to the world's population an hour?

____

2. Where can developing countries be found?

____

3. In 1950, what percentage of the world's population lived in developing countries?

____

4. What are examples that show people are living below the poverty line?

____

Unit 18

Section One

一、单项选择。

( ) 1. Where ________ you ________ this weekend?
A. were; go B. will; go C. did; went D. are; gone

( ) 2. — Would you like to have a cup of coffee with me after school?
— ________. Sorry.
A. I'd love to B. Thanks
C. I'm afraid I must go home right now
D. No, I am busier than you

( ) 3. — ________ jump on the bed. Be a good boy.
— OK. I won't.
A. Not B. Don't C. No D. Doesn't

( ) 4. — What are you doing tomorrow?
— Well, I ________.
A. have a rest B. am going camping
C. was sick D. ask for a leave

( ) 5. Let's ________ on Saturday.
A. to go fishing B. go fish C. going fishing D. go fishing

( ) 6. They plan ________ a movie after the exam.
A. seeing B. to see C. saw D. should see

( ) 7. Who ________ to buy the tickets?
A. offers B. plays C. order D. provide

二、请根据对话内容排序。

1. A. You won't believe it. It's very cheap.
B. Really? Do you think it looks good on me?
C. What a beautiful jersey!
D. Yes, I wish I could find one just like that.
E. Actually I can't wait to do so.
F. Why not try it on?

正确顺序：____ ____ ____ ____ ____ ____.

2. A. Take care.
   B. I keep coughing a lot.
   C. What's wrong with you?
   D. You should see a doctor.
   E. Thanks! I will.

正确顺序:____ ____ ____ ____ ____.

3. A. So would you like to go hiking with us?
   B. Thank God the rain will stop.
   C. It's reported that the weather will be fine this weekend.
   D. I'd love to! Is there anything I should bring?
   E. Well, I have prepared everything. Just grab your backpack.

正确顺序:____ ____ ____ ____ ____.

三、请仿照例句完成句子,回答需完整。

eg: A: What are you doing this evening?
    B: I'm staying at home. (stay)

1. A: What are they doing this holiday?
   B: ____________. (go to Peru)
2. A: What are her parents doing this weekend?
   B: ____________. (come to see her)
3. A: What is Jane doing next Monday?
   B: ____________. (go to the dentist's)
4. A: Where is Sophie heading tomorrow?
   B: ____________. (head for Prague)
5. A: Which train is he taking tomorrow?
   B: ____________. (6 p. m. train)

四、根据意义及首字母写出对应的单词。

1. p________: to think carefully about something you want to do in the future
2. o________: to say that you are willing to do something
3. c________: a building in which films are shown
4. g________: a place where motor vehicles are repaired
5. r________: the cause or explanation for something
6. v________: to go and spend time in a place or with someone

五、句型练习。

1. is, he, sitting, the, tree, under (连词成句)

____.

2. tickets, who, to, the, offers, buy(连词成句)

____?

3. afraid, they, can't, tomorrow, there, I'm, go(连词成句)

____.

4. Let's fix a time.（变成否定句）

____.

5. He is working on the farm right now.（变成一般疑问句）

____?

6. The Simons are doing some cleaning for the vacation.（对画线部分提问）

____?

Section Two

一、单项选择。

(　　) 1. — Have you seen Tony?

— Oh, he's ________ at present.

A. ordering tickets　　B. booking tickets

C. booked ticket　　D. ordered ticket

(　　) 2. There ________ enough furniture ________ the guestroom.

A. is; in　　B. are; on　　C. is; on　　D. are; in

(　　) 3. This carpet is not expensive. You can buy it ________ $30.

A. in　　B. at　　C. on　　D. for

(　　) 4. — What about ________ in Cambridge this July?

— That's a good idea.

A. go travelling　　B. going travel

C. going travelling　　D. to go traveling

(　　) 5. —Who cleaned the classroom yesterday?

—Jessie ________.

A. cleaned　　B. do　　C. did　　D. was

(　　) 6. — ____________________?

— It's interesting. I'd like to read it again.

A. Why not read the book?　　B. What do you think of the book?

C. How do you get the book?　　D. What's the book about?

(　　) 7. — Would you like ________ some lasagna?

— Thanks, but ________.

A. to have; it's awful　　B. to have; I'm full

C. having; it's delicious　　D. having; I'm hungry

(　　) 8. The film is very ________ and all of us ________ in it.

A. interesting; interested　　B. interested; are interesting

C. interesting; are interested　　D. interested; interesting

二、看图补全对话。

A：Good afternoon. (1)________?

B：I'd like three tickets for *The Nutcracker* on Thursday evening.

A：For Thursday evening? Sorry, (2)________.

B：(3)________ Wednesday night?

A：Yes, we have.

B：(4)________?

A：Well, we have got tickets at six dollars and eight dollars. (5)________?

B：The latter one. Here is the money. Thank you.

A：Your change. Thanks.

三、选择词语对应的解释。

(　　)1. drama　　A. a person whose job is to find out information about criminals

(　　)2. earn　　B. a piece of writing to be performed by actors, play for the theater, TV, radio

(　　)3. programme　　C. causing fear

(　　)4. detective　　D. a show or performance

(　　)5. frightening　　E. to get money by working

四、下面每句有一处错误，请找出并改正。

1. I'm writting to tell you about my new flat.
____.
2. Lieing on the grass, he finds it pleasant to relax a little bit.
____.
3. Why don't you to tell me the truth?
____.
4. Lillie is visitting her grandparents this Spring Festival.
____.
5. Where shall we going tomorrow morning?
____.

五、用所给词语的适当形式填空。

1. Look! It's snowing! What about ________(make) some snowmen in the garden?
2. Your baggage is really heavy. Let me ________(help) you with those bags.
3. — Could I ________ (have) a word with you?
   — ________ (come) into my office, please.
4. — Would you like ________(go) window shopping with me?
   — Sorry, I ________(be) quite busy.

5. She ____(wear)school uniforms every day before she graduated from that college.
6. Julia doesn't want to work in her father's company. She is interested in ________ (start) her own business.
7. Why not ________ (do) some shopping online?
8. Listen! Jennifer ________(sing) happily in the bathroom.
9. Be quiet! The babies ________(sleep).
10. Don't ________(break) any dishes again, okay? You ________(break) ten in all last week. Can you ________(be) more careful?

六、现在进行时也可表示将来的安排。试用现在进行时改写下列句子。

1. I will take the dance lessons next year.
____.
2. My classmates are going to put up the posters here.
____.
3. Shall we meet Aeron at 11:00 tomorrow morning?
____?

Section Three

一、单项选择。

( ) 1. There ________ only one desk and three chairs in that room last night.
A. was B. were C. will be D. are
( ) 2. — You came here at ten? You're late again!
— I'm sorry and I ________ next time.
A. won't B. don't C. wasn't D. am not
( ) 3. — ________________?
— I caught a bad cold.
A. What do you do? B. What did you catch?
C. Why are you here? D. What's the matter?
( ) 4. — The extra-curriculum activity sounds terrific.
— Why not ________ us?
A. to join B. joining in C. join D. to join in
( ) 5. — What are you talking about?
— I just want all of them ________ at the gate.
A. get together B. gather C. to gather D. to get down
( ) 6. I'd ________ go over the lessons tonight.
A. rather to B. like C. like to D. better to
( ) 7. He ________ in 1915 and ________ in 2002.
A. born; was dead B. was born; was dead
C. was born; died D. was born; is dead

二、选择词语对应的解释

( )1. violent A. to give new or different sound effects to, or change the original spoken language of (a film, radio show or TV show)

( )2. workshop B. just; really

( )3. exactly C. a room or an area in a factory where heavy repairs and jobs on machines are done

( )4. dub D. an official paper giving a statement that affect is true

( )5. certificate E. acting with damaging physical force

三、根据图片，选择方框中合适的词语补全对话。

would like	why not	what about
do you mind	would you like	why don't you

Linda: (1)________ to have some tea?

Joana: Actually, I (2)________ some coffee.

Linda: Okay, (3)________ get some coffee instead? Here it is!

Joana: Thanks! (4)________ add some milk ?

Linda: I don't really like it.

Joana: (5)________ a little sugar?

Linda: Oh, no, thanks. I prefer the way it is.

Joana: Yep! Black it is. Oh, my phone is ringing. (6)____ my answering it right now?

Linda: Of course not!

四、完形填空。

Air is all around us. It is around us __1__ we walk and play. From the time we are born air is around us on every side. When we sit down, it is around us. When we go to bed, air is also around us. We live __2__ air.

All __3__ things need air. We __4__ live without food or water for a few days, but we can't live for more than a few minutes __5__ air. We take in __6__. When we are working hard or running fast, we need __7__ air. However, when we are asleep, we need __8__ air.

We live in air, but we can't see it. We can only feel it. We can feel it when it is moving. Moving air is called wind. How can we make air __9__?

Here is one way. Hold an open book in front of your face. Close it quickly. What can you feel? __10__ you feel is air.

( )1. A. as B. after C. because D. since

( )2. A. under B. in C. below D. with

( )3. A. live B. living C. alive D. with
( )4. A. can B. won't C. can't D. lively
( )5. A. out of B. with C. without D. out
( )6. A. water B. air C. food D. wind
( )7. A. more B. most C. many D. few
( )8. A. least B. much C. no D. less
( )9. A. move B. to move C. movingly D. moved
( )10. A. What B. That C. Where D. Which

五、根据句子内容补全单词。

1. You can pay either in c ________ or by credit card.
2. Do you like the magicians' p ________ at the party?
3. I hate seeing all kinds of a ________ before a film starts.
4. They arrived at e ________ the same time.
5. The famous actress e ________ a lot of money by playing this role.
6. What's your name and a ________? I can't read it!

六、用另一表述方式改写画线部分并使句子保持相同含义。

1. Why not have a second thought on this plan?
____?
2. He is returning home next Tuesday.
____.
3. What about booking the room on the Internet at a lower price?
____?

Section Four

一、单项选择。

( ) 1. — You did a good job!
— ________.
A. You're so kind. B. Thanks a lot.
C. You did better than me. D. I'm not so well.

( ) 2. — How are you getting along ________ your classmates?
— Very well.
A. for B. with C. by D. from

( ) 3. Mr. Lee often plays tennis when he ________.
A. has free B. is free C. was free D. has free times

( ) 4. — You'd better ________ when you are sick.
— Thanks for your concern.
A. to rest B. rested C. resting D. rest

( ) 5. Lucy can't go shopping, because she has ________ work to do.

A. much too B. too many C. too much D. a lot

( ) 6. There is ________ else in the box. It's empty.

A. something B. anything C. nothing D. everything

( ) 7. I had a ________ sleep last night. Did you sleep ________, Gina?

A. good; well B. good; good C. well; well D. well; good

( ) 8. — Would you like a smoothie?

— ________________.

A. Sorry, I won't. B. Yes, give me a cup of tea.

C. Yes, please. D. That's nothing.

二、按照图片内容完成对话。

1. What did you do just now?

____

2. ________________?

It cost me $3.99.

3. ________________?

I will go and watch a movie with Tad.

4. How does Max go to work every day?

____

三、句型练习。

1. is, holiday, he, in, spend, going, to, the, Greece（连词成句）

________________.

2. trees, who, over, planting, are, there（连词成句）

________________?

3. They'd like to stop for a moment.（变成一般疑问句）

________________?

4. She'd better drop that stupid topic.（变成否定句）

________________.

5. He is going to help us with our project.（对画线部分提问）

________________?

6. I'd like to have my hair dyed.（对画线部分提问）

________________?

四、阅读理解。

Some children wish to be writers when they grow up. They mean that they want to write stories or books. They would be happy if many people read their stories or books some day, but I would like to tell these children that they will need to be good readers and read a lot before they become good writers.

Nearly all great writers listened to others tell stories long before they started school. They also kept on reading for hours and hours for years. Even when they have become writers, they spend much of their time reading books instead of watching TV in the evening.

If you are a good reader, it won't take you long to do the reading homework your teacher asks you to do. Then you will have time to read other books for fun. You read so well that you always want to look for more books to read.

If you want to be a writer, reading is very important. When you decide to become a writer, you had better tell yourself, "I must read more and more if I really want to become a good writer."

(　　)1. Some children want to be writers because they ________.
A. want to make money　　B. want to practice their handwriting
C. like reading books　　D. want people to read their books

(　　)2. Many great writers ________ before they became writers.
A. watched TV every day　　B. were good at telling stories
C. read a lot　　D. learned from some famous teachers

(　　)3. If you are good at reading ________.
A. your teacher's reading homework will be easier for you
B. you will spend a lot of time on your homework
C. the teacher will ask you to read more
D. the school will offer you more books

(　　)4. From the passage we can know that ________.
A. children like reading
B. reading helps to make one a good writer
C. good readers are good writers
D. it's good to be a good writer

(　　)5. Which is the best title of this passage?
A. Great Writers.　　B. How to Become a Writer.
C. How to Be a Good Reader.　D. Books and Stories.

Section Five

一、选出你听到的单词。

(　　)1. A. playing　B. planning　C. planet　D. please
(　　)2. A. could　B. should　C. would　D. found
(　　)3. A. go skating　B. go skiing　C. go shopping　D. go swimming
(　　)4. A. offer　B. order　C. often　D. author
(　　)5. A. learn　B. burn　C. hen　D. Ken

(　　)6. A. dubbing　　B. dumb　　C. dark　　D. dam

二、听句子,选出与之相关的回答。

(　　)1. A. I'm glad to.　　B. I should come earlier.　　C. I'd give it to charity.

(　　)2. A. Twenty dollars.　　B. Thirty kilos.　　C. Ten minutes.

(　　)3. A. No problem.　　B. Don't worry. I can introduce them to you.

C. You are brave enough.

(　　)4. A. Because I will have an exam.

B. Because it's sunny.

C. Because I like reading.

(　　)5. A. He went there by plane.

B. Here are many cars.

C. A traffic accident.

三、听几段对话，根据内容选择意义相近的答案。

(　　) 1. A. Games on the Ipad are beautiful.

B. The girl hates playing games.

C. Games on the Ipad are interesting.

(　　) 2. A. She hasn't heard the name of Nikko.

B. She didn't receive any letter from Nikko recently.

C. Nikko is not very busy.

(　　) 3. A. She wants some coffee.

B. She never drinks tea.

C. She chooses to drink cola.

四、听一段独白,在图片右侧写上代表其顺序的数字并补全句子。

________: Boil ________________.

________: Choose ________________.

________: Put ________________.

________: Get ________________.

五、听三段小对话,完成下列各题。

听第一段对话,完成第 1 ~2 题。

(　　) 1. How many children does the man have?

A. One.　　B. Two.　　C. Three.

(　　) 2. How much does the man have to pay?

A. \$18.　　B. \$14.　　C. \$21.

听第二段对话,完成第 3 ~5 题。

(　　) 3. How do I go to school?

A. Take a bus.　　B. Ride a bike.　　C. Walk.

(　　)4. How many classes do I usually have in the morning?

A. One.　　B. Two.　　C. Four.

(　　)5. Where do I usually go after my classes?

A. To a bank.　　B. Home.　　C. To the club.

听第三段对话,完成第 6 ~8 题。

(　　) 6. Where will the woman go?

A. To a party.　　B. To the doctor's.　　C. To work.

(　　) 7. What's wrong with the man?

A. He is tired.　　B. He is sick.　　C. He doesn't like parties.

(　　) 8. What's the woman's advice?

A. Stay at home.　　B. See a doctor at once.

C. Make an appointment with the doctor.

六、听一段短文,回答问题。

(　　)1. For whom did James do some shopping?

A. For his son.　　B. For himself.

C. For his wife.　　D. For his daughter.

(　　) 2. What did he choose?

A. A woolen pair of gloves.　　B. A leather pair of trousers.

C. Some flowers.　　D. Large-sized, purple gloves made of wool.

(　　) 3. Did James choose the present carefully?

A. Yes.　　B. No.

C. At first, he was careful.　　D. We can't tell from the story.

(　　) 4. What can you infer from the story?

A. James Lee doesn't know much about gloves. He has a poor taste.

B. Mrs. Lee doesn't need gloves at all.

C. James Lee doesn't like his wife at all.

D. Mrs. Lee often dislikes his presents and changes them.

七、听一首英语诗歌 *Friends Lullaby*,完成下列各题。

The stars out, the moon is up. It's time to go to (1)________.

I'm so (2)________ you have a place to lay your little head.

Have a deep and peaceful (3)________. Dream away the hours.

When you wake the sun will come, to smile upon the (4)________.

Go to sleep my little (5)________, beneath the evening star.

You will always have a friend, no matter (6)________ your are.

八、单项选择。

(　　) 1. — Let's go skating this afternoon.

— ________________.

— That's too bad. Another time, then.

A. I'd like to, but I have a lot of things to do.

B. You just need this football.

C. The sports car is very expensive.

D. Great, skating is my favorite sport.

(　　) 2. — When you finish ______ your novel, remember ______ me a call, OK?

— All right.

A. to write; gave　　B. writing; to give

C. read; to send　　D. reading; giving

(　　) 3. — It's very late. ______ take a taxi?

— Good idea.

A. Would you like　　B. How about

C. What about　　D. Why not

(　　) 4. Cecily and I go to school ______ eight thirty ______ every Saturday morning.

A. at; on　　B. in; in

C. at; /　　D. on; in

(　　) 5. — How was your weekend?

— ________________

A. I'd like to visit my uncle this weekend.

B. It was wonderful.

C. Did you have a nice weekend?

D. I used to spend it in the countryside.

(　　) 6. How about ______ with us to the hall right now?

A. going　　B. to go　　C. will go　　D. go

(　　) 7. Stop ______! Our boss is at the door and it's time for work.

A. talking　　B. to talk　　C. not to talk　　D. not talking

(　　) 8. — What do you think of Ms. Seeger?

— She is kind and always ______ her help to others.

A. buys　　B. offers　　C. makes　　D. receives

九、请将下列动词的过去式和现在分词填入表格。

arrive	arrived	arriving	eat		
stop			lie		
write			set		
rise			take		

十、完形填空。

In the doctor's waiting-room, the patients, __1__, old and young, were sitting quietly on the chairs. Billy, a schoolboy, was sitting there, too. They all looked very sad __2__ Billy. He was reading an interesting story in a magazine, and there was a __3__ on his face.

Just then the __4__ came in to say he was ready __5__ the next patient. Billy jumped up and ran into __6__ room.

"Good morning. Doctor."

"Good morning. What is your trouble, young man?" asked the doctor. Before Billy could answer a word, the doctor made him lie down on a bed. "Now, let me listen to your heart." Billy tried to speak, but the doctor told him __7__ anything. "I'll __8__ your temperature." Billy tried to sit up, but the doctor stopped him. "Now open your mouth— Mm, good." After a moment, the doctor said, "Well, my boy, you haven't got a fever. It's __9__ — Mm, in fact, there's nothing wrong with you." "I know there isn't," said the boy. "I just came here to get some __10__ for my grandfather."

(　　)1. A. men and woman　　B. men and women
　　C. women and man　　D. man and woman

(　　)2. A. except　　B. besides　　C. excepting　　D. for

(　　)3. A. sad　　B. sorry　　C. smile　　D. happy

(　　)4. A. worker　　B. doctor　　C. teacher　　D. conductor

(　　)5. A. to　　B. at　　C. for　　D. with

(　　)6. A. a doctor　　B. doctor　　C. the doctor's　　D. the doctors

(　　)7. A. not saying　　B. to not say　　C. not to say　　D. not say

(　　)8. A. have　　B. make　　C. take　　D. bring

(　　)9. A. serious nothing　　B. nothing serious
　　C. serious something　　D. something serious

(　　)10. A. message　　B. medicine　　C. things　　D. magazines

十一、阅读理解。

Are you looking for something fun and would you like to help others in your spare time? Then join us to be a volunteer（志愿者）! We're a non-profit（非营利的）organization. We have volunteer jobs of all ages. Anyone, from twelve-year-old children to people in their seventies can become a volunteer.

You can help people in many ways. Schools need help with taking care of children while parents are working. Hospitals need volunteers to look after children while their parents are seeing a doctor. Animal lovers can help take care of those dogs and cats without homes. There is something for everyone.

"As a volunteer, I don't want to get anything. Seeing the children's happy faces, I'm happy, too," said Carlos Domingo, an old woman of 62. "I often played computer games in my spare time before. Now I help older people learn how to use computers," said another volunteer at the age of 18.

If everyone helps out a bit, we'll have a better world to live in. Interested? Call us at 800-555-5756 or visit our website: www. activol. com.

( )1. When do the volunteers help others?

A. In their spare time. B. At weekends.

C. On weekdays. D. In the evenings.

( )2. ________ can be a volunteer.

A. Children B. Old women

C. Anyone aged 12-70 D. Young people

( )3. Volunteers want to get ________ when they help others.

A. money B. computers C. everything D. nothing

( )4. Carlos Domingo does volunteer work for ________.

A. animals B. children C. computers D. older people

( )5. We can read such a passage ________.

A. in a newspaper B. in a storybook

C. in a picture book D. in a textbook

期末考试(一)

卷面分值:100 分　考试时间:100 分钟

第一部分

（80 分）

一、听力理解部分（30 分）

第一节（共 6 小题，每小题 1 分，满分 6 分）

听下面 6 个问题。每个问题后有三个答语，从题中所给 A、B、C 三个选项中选出最佳选项。听完每个问题后，你都有 5 秒钟的时间来作答和阅读下一小题。每个问题仅读一遍。

(　　)1. A. It's Monday.　　B. It's January 2nd.
C. It's a nice day today.

(　　)2. A. I have been to England.　　B. Just fine.
C. I have tried my best.

(　　)3. A. Jazz.　　B. Very much.
C. I like it a lot.

(　　)4. A. He works hard.　　B. I think they are interesting.
C. I know little.

(　　)5. A. It's 50 Yuan.　　B. Sorry, I am busy.
C. It's two o'clock.

(　　)6. A. I answer telephones.　　B. I'm a teacher.
C. By car.

第二节（共 6 小题，每小题 1 分，满分 6 分）

听下面 6 段对话。每段对话后有一个小题，从题中所给 A、B、C 三个选项中选出最佳选项。听完每段对话后，你都有 10 秒钟的时间来作答和阅读下一小题。每段对话仅读一遍。

(　　)7. Which book will the man borrow?
A. The cookbook.　　B. The storybook.　　C. A picture book.

(　　)8. Where do you think the man and the woman are talking now?
A. In the market.　　B. In the classroom.　　C. In the cinema.

(　　)9. How often does the woman go swimming?
A. Sometimes.　　B. Never.　　C. Every day.

( )10. How many people are there in the girl's family in Wuhan?
A. 5. B. 7. C. 8.

( )11. What did they decide to do?
A. They decided not to meet.
B. They would meet at 11:00.
C. They would not have the meeting in the classroom.

( )12. What is the boy going to do this Saturday morning?
A. Swim with Bob.
B. Plant trees with Linda.
C. Have a picnic with Linda.

第三节(共18小题,每小题1分,满分18分)

听下面4段对话或独白。每段对话或独白后有几个小题,从题中所给的A、B、C三个选项中选出最佳选项。听每段对话和独白前,你将有时间阅读各个小题,每小题5秒钟;听完后,各小题将给出5秒钟的作答时间。

听第13段材料,完成第13~15题。

( )13. What is Lucy going to do?
A. She is going to send some postcards.
B. She is going to meet her Chinese teacher.
C. She is going to do some shopping.

( )14. What day is it the day after tomorrow?
A. Mother's Day. B. Teachers' Day. C. Women's Day.

( )15. What is Lucy going to buy for Miss Zhao?
A. A postcard. B. A pen. C. Some flowers.

听第14段材料,完成第16~18题。

( )16. The woman is a ________ in the city.
A. policeman B. visitor C. cleaner

( )17. Where does the woman want to do?
A. Visit the city. B. Catch a bus.
C. Go to No. 1 Middle School.

( )18. What does Julie Brown do?
A. She is a new student.
B. She is an English teacher.
C. She is a history teacher.

听第15段材料,完成第19~21题。

( )19. Who is answering the phone?
A. Sally. B. Jim. C. Dave.

( )20. When did Jim go out?
A. Half an hour ago. B. An hour ago. C. We don't know.

( )21. Which statement is NOT true?
A. Jim is going to get some paint.

B. Jim may stop at the pub on the way back.

C. Dave won't call again.

听第16段材料，完成第22~25题。

(　　)22. Who traveled to America besides Columbus?

A. The Vikings.　　B. The Red Indians.　　C. Both A and B.

(　　)23. When did Columbus discover America?

A. In 1942.　　B. In 1492.　　C. We don't know.

(　　)24. Who invented the electric light bulb?

A. Columbus.　　B. Mars.　　C. Edison.

(　　)25. Which statement is true?

A. Mars will be visited by men soon.

B. It's certain who visited America first.

C. They are asking each other questions about general knowledge.

听第17段材料，完成第26~30题。

(　　)26. Who really invented the first car?

A. A German.　　B. An American.　　C. A Frenchman.

(　　)27. From this story we can know the car was invented ________.

A. more than 100 years ago

B. less than 100 years ago

C. just 100 years ago

(　　)28. How many brothers and sisters did Henry Ford have?

A. Six.　　B. Five.　　C. Four.

(　　)29. How many dollars did young Ford earn(挣) every week?

A. 2.5 dollars.　　B. 3.5 dollars.　　C. 3 dollars.

(　　)30. Which statement is NOT true?

A. The first car was invented in 1893.

B. He met with a lot of difficulties in the invention.

C. He repaired watches in the evenings for fun.

请同学们将试卷翻到第二部分，完成听写部分的试题。

二、单项选择（15分）

(　　)31. We often go to work by taxi ________ rainy mornings.

A. on　　B. in　　C. of　　D. at

(　　)32. — ________ did you go to the shopping mall?

— Hardly ever.

A. How long　　B. How far　　C. How often　　D. How soon

(　　)33. This machine is used ________ the dishes and it's very convenient.

A. to washing　　B. wash　　C. washed　　D. for washing

(　　)34. Our school is having a football match with the students from ________ country.

A. other　B. another　C. others　D. the other

(　)35. There's only ________ milk left. We'd better go to the supermarket and get some.

A. a little　B. many　C. a few　D. much

(　)36. The tour guide ________ the safety of the tourists.

A. have a responsibility to　B. has responsibility with

C. is responsible of　D. is responsible for

(　)37. James Smith ________ the dancing club since he ________ his 50th birthday party.

A. has join; has　B. has taken part in; has

C. has been in; had　D. joined; had

(　)38. Those foreign friends left Paris ________.

A. since last week　B. since a week ago

C. for a week　D. a week ago

(　)39. — Where is Lily?

— She ________ Shanghai.

A. has gone to　B. has been to　C. went to　D. goes to

(　)40. With a ________ look on her face, she said the song was very ________.

A. relaxing; relaxed　B. relaxed; relaxing

C. relaxing; relaxing　D. relaxed; relaxed

(　)41. My English teacher always tries to instruct us ________ in correct ways.

A. to study　B. study　C. studying　D. studied

(　)42. Shougang Institute of Technology (SGIT) ________ the city of Beijing, occupying an area of about 201,000 square meters.

A. situate in　B. is situated in

C. is situating in　D. situates

(　)43. Andy's mother always ________ us ________ their house to have dinner.

A. invite; to go　B. invite; to

C. invites; to　D. invites; to go

(　)44. — ________ is it from your home to your school?

— About ten minutes' walk.

A. How far　B. How long　C. How often　D. When

(　)45. China is famous for many different types of folk dances, ________ the dragon dance and the lion dance.

A. included　B. to include　C. including　D. being included

三、完形填空（15 分）

Do you know how to study better and make your study more effective? We all know that Chinese students usually study very hard for long __46__. This is very good, but it doesn't help __47__, for an effective student must have enough sleep, enough food, enough rest and exercise. Every day you need __48__ out for a walk or visit some friends or some nice places. It's good for __49__.

Then, when you return to your studies, your mind will be refreshed（清醒）and you'll learn more __50__ study better. Psychologists（心理学家）__51__ that learning takes place this way. Here take English learning __52__ an example. First you make __53__ progress and you feel happy. Then your language study seems __54__ at the same level for a long time. So you will think you're learning __55__ and you may __56__. This can last for days or even weeks, yet you needn't give up. At some point your language study will take __57__ big jump again. If you get enough sleep, food, rest and exercise. __58__ English can be very effective and __59__. Don't give up along the way. Learn it gradually and you're sure __60__ a good result.

(　　)46.	A. seconds	B. weeks	C. days	D. hours
(　　)47.	A. a little	B. a lot	C. a few	D. many
(　　)48.	A. go	B. to go	C. take out	D. to take
(　　)49.	A. study	B. fit	C. eyes	D. healthy
(　　)50.	A. after	B. or	C. and	D. to
(　　)51.	A. have taught	B. have thought	C. have found	D. say
(　　)52.	A. to	B. at	C. in	D. as
(　　)53.	A. a lot	B. a great number	C. a lot of	D. many
(　　)54.	A. to have	B. to make	C. to stay	D. to take
(　　)55.	A. something	B. anything	C. everything	D. nothing
(　　)56.	A. give in	B. give up	C. give out	D. give off
(　　)57.	A. another	B. other	C. others	D. the other
(　　)58.	A. Speaking	B. Studying	C. Writing	D. Using
(　　)59.	A. possible	B. interesting	C. hard	D. difficult
(　　)60.	A. to get	B. to catch	C. to make	D. to form

四、阅读理解（20分）

A

Strange things happen to time when you travel because the earth is divided into twenty-four zones, one hour apart（相间隔）. You can have days with more or fewer than twenty-four hours, and weeks with more or fewer than seven days.

If you make a five-day trip across the Atlantic Ocean, your ship enters a different time zone every day. As you enter each zone, the time changes one hour. Traveling west, you set your clock back, traveling east, you set it ahead. Each day of your trip has either twenty-five or twenty-three hours.

If you travel by ship across the Pacific Ocean（太平洋）, you cross the International Date Line. By agreement, this is the point where a new day begins. When you cross the line, you change your calendar one full day, backward or forward. Traveling east, today becomes yesterday. Traveling west, it is tomorrow.

(　　)61. Strange things happen to time when you travel because ________.

A. no day really has twenty-four hours

B. no one knows where time zones begin

C. the earth is divided into time zones

D. in some places one day always has twenty-five hours

(   )62. The difference in time between zones is ________.

A. one hour B. more than seven days

C. seven days D. twenty-four hours

(   )63. If you travel across the Atlantic Ocean, going east, you set your clock ________.

A. one hour ahead in each time zone

B. one hour ahead for the whole trip

C. one full day back for each time zone

D. one hour back in each time zone

(   )64. From this passage, it seems true that the Atlantic ________.

A. is in one time zone

B. is divided into twenty-four zones

C. is divided into five time zones

D. is in four time zones

(   )65. The International Date Line is the name for ________.

A. the beginning of any new time zone

B. any point where time changes by one hour

C. the point where a new day begins

D. the end of any new time zone

B

John is twelve years old. He had a bad cold and coughed day and night. He went to see a doctor. The doctor gave him some cough medicine. Here are the instructions on the bottle of the medicine.

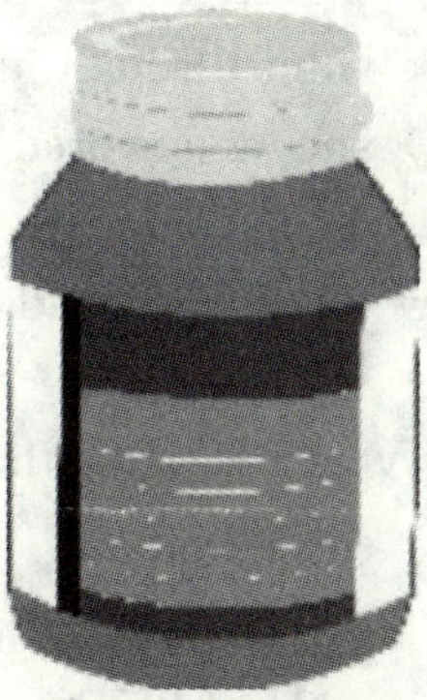

Cough Medicine

Shake it well before use.

Take it three times each day before meals.

Dose (药量):

Age: Over 14 2 teaspoonfuls

8—13 1 teaspoonful

4—7 1/2 teaspoonful

Not right for children below the age of three.

Put it in a cold place. Use it before November 1st, 2012.

(   )66. John should take ________ a day.

A. 2 teaspoonfuls B. 3 teaspoonfuls

C. 4 teaspoonfuls D. 1 teaspoonful

(   )67. The medicine should be kept in ________.

A. a fridge　　B. hot water
C. any place　　D. the sun

(　　)68. John should ________ before he takes it.
A. shake the medicine well　　B. eat nothing
C. do some exercise　　D. drink a cup of tea

(　　)69. When people are ________ years old, they cannot take this medicine.
A. eighty　　B. thirty
C. two　　D. twelve

(　　)70. John will ________ the medicine when it is left after Nov. 2nd, 2012.
A. shake　　B. stop to take
C. take once　　D. take six times more

C

Hank Stram was on vacation traveling through Europe by train with his two children, Tina and Max. Their seats were in the last carriage of the train.

After they had eaten their lunch, Hank got up. "I'm just going down to the dinner car to get a coffee. I'll be back soon. We won't get to the station till five this afternoon."

The dining car was near the front of the train. As the train was traveling fast and moving from side to side. Hank decided to drink his coffee there and not to carry it back to his seat. Soon he got talking to another person who happened to be from America, too. They found that they had a lot in common and got on well. There was an announcement in German when the train stopped and started moving again. But Hank paid no attention.

Finally they said goodbye to each other and Hank started to walk through the carriage when he found he couldn't go on further. He was in the last carriage.

Meanwhile, his children were enjoying their trip. They looked out of the window and talked happily. They thought their father was on the same train. At about three o'clock Tina decided to see what their dad was up to. But when she went through just a few carriages, she found herself at the front of the train. Finally she discovered the truth. The train had divided in the station where they had stopped. The front part was going to Frankfort and the other part was going to Bonn. Then they knew they had lost their dad.

At five o'clock their train stopped in Bonn Station. But Hank was not with them. Where was he?

(　　)71. Where were Hank and his two children traveling to?
A. Frankfort.　　B. Bonn.　　C. Berlin.　　D. Europe.

(　　)72. Why did Hank leave his children?
A. He was going to get himself a coffee.
B. He was going to have lunch in the dining car.
C. He wanted to have a talk with somebody else.

D. He was going to buy his children each a coffee.

(　　)73. Why didn't Hank get back to his seat immediately after the announcement?

A. Hank couldn't hear a single word of the announcement.

B. He didn't know German.

C. He was having his coffee.

D. He didn't pay any attention to the announcement.

(　　)74. When did the two children realize (意识到) that they had lost their dad?

A. When the train stopped in a station.

B. Two hours after their father left them.

C. By the time the train stopped in Bonn Station.

D. After they found the train had divided.

(　　)75. From the passage we can conclude(推断) that Hank ________.

A. went home alone

B. was in Bonn with his children

C. was in Frankfort

D. was still drinking coffee in the dining car

D

My name is Hyo Jin Kang and I am from South Korea. I have been here for six months and I am taking the General English Course. Life in Boston is wonderful for me.

First of all, my friend said that this city is a good place to study English and visit some places. Before coming here, I didn't know that Boston is such an attractive city. Boston is the oldest city in USA, so there are a lot of places to hang out with friends. There are many museums which are free on specific days. When I visited Harvard, it was crowded with many people because it is said that if you touch the foot of John Harvard, your grandchild will go to Harvard. In addition, Boston is famous for sports. Last week, I went to watch the Celtics game, which is the basketball team and I had a lot of fun!

Second, when I arrived in the USA, everything was new. I didn't know what to do so I was confused. Nowadays I am taking "Language through Music". It is my favorite because the teachers are kind and patient. They really helped me a lot.

Thirdly, the best thing is the homestay. I live with my host family with two lovely kids! We all have homemade dinner every day unless I have an appointment with my friends. On weekends, after dinner we spend time together playing board games or watching movies. There are many neighbors near my host family so sometimes we have parties such as Super Bowl or block parties. These are good opportunities to experience American cultures and spirits.

The more I enjoy life in Boston, the more valuable this time is. My life in Boston is full of experiences I will never forget.

(　　)76. Why is Hyo Jin Kang in Boston now? Because ________.

A. she wants to visit some famous places in Boston.

B. her host family invited her to Boston.

C. she wants to know American music and culture.

D. she wants to learn English there.

(　　)77. How did she feel when she first came to Boston?

A. Puzzled.　B. Lonely.　C. Wonderful.　D. Interesting.

(　　)78. Which of the following things doesn't she do in her spare time?

A. She attends parties in the neighbourhood.

B. She goes to different places with her friends.

C. She goes back to her hometown now and then.

D. She visits the museums sometimes.

(　　)79. Which is true according to the passage?

A. Boston is famous for its football team.

B. She wants to have dinner with her friends rather than with the host family.

C. All museums in Boston are free.

D. She will never forget the days in Boston.

(　　)80. Which is the best title for this passage?

A. Learn English in Boston.　B. My Favourite English Course.

C. On the Way to Harvard.　D. My Homestay.

第二部分

（20 分）

一、听写，听一篇文章并根据所听内容补全所缺单词（5 分）

Hey Bill. This is Hank. I'm just __1__ to let you know that I'll be a little late to the game tomorrow night. I have to work a few extra hours at work to finish a __2__. I should wrap things up sometime __3__ seven and eight though. Oh, then I'm planning on __4__ by Lisa's house for about an hour since she's been sick recently. And, uh, one more thing. I'll swing by my house to __5__ up some food for the game. See you then.

1. ________ 2. ________ 3. ________ 4. ________ 5. ________

二、将单词与符合的意思匹配（5 分）

(　　)1. delay　A. a document showing that you have competed a course of study or part of your education

(　　)2. villa　B. to move to a later time

(　　)3. instructor　C. pleasant country house in its own garden, often used only part of the year for holidays

(　　)4. cutlery　D. knives, forks and spoons used for eating food

(　　)5. diploma　E. a person whose job is to teach somebody a practical skill or sport

三、用所给词的适当形式填空(5 分)

1. I'd like ________ (drink) a glass of milk before going to bed.
2. I'm used to ________ (teach) in a high school.
3. The little boy spends two hours ________ (do) his homework every day and he can study very well.
4. Either you or Frank ________ (be) going to take part in the after-class activity.
5. — Are you thirsty?
   — No, I ________ just ________ (have) some orange.
6. Teachers should be ________ (responsibility) to all the students in their classes.
7. We gladly accepted their ________ (invite) to the open ceremony.
8. Lucy hopes ________ (get) a job overseas.
9. Could you ________ (deliver) this package for me, please?
10. What about ________ (dig) some sweet potatoes this morning?

四、句型转换(5 分)

1. Father was able to fix the clock. (改成否定句)
____
2. Lillian has already been to some foreign countries. (改成否定句)
____
3. Sam cut his finger in the kitchen. (改成一般疑问句)
____
4. Tina left her hometown when she was 16. (改成一般疑问句)
____
5. I would like <u>two bottles of</u> shampoo. (对画线部分提问)
____
6. I could play <u>the violin</u> when I was young. (对画线部分提问)
____
7. It's <u>about a fifteen-minute drive</u> from the city park to our school. (对画线部分提问)
____
8. James went to the theatre <u>an hour ago</u>. (对画线部分提问)
____
9. Jason used to listen to the music on every Sunday afternoon last year. (换一种说法)
____
10. It took Tom three hours to finish all his homework. (换一种说法)
____

期末考试(二)

卷面分值:100 分　考试时间:100 分钟

第一部分

（70 分）

一、听力理解部分（25 分）

第一节　（共 10 个小题,每小题 1 分,满分 10 分）

第一部分　（5 分）

听下面 5 个小对话,从题中所给的 A、B、C 三个图片中选出最佳选项。听完每个对话后,你有 5 秒钟的时间来作答和阅读下一小题。每个问题仅读一遍。

(　　)1. What's the weather like in Wuhan today?

A. 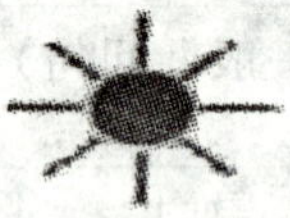　B. 　C. 

(　　)2. How does David usually go to school?

A. 　B. 　C. 

(　　)3. What will Tony give his father?

A. 　B. 　C. 

(　　)4. Where is the boy's soccer?

A. 　B. 　C. 

(　　)5. Which sign is mentioned in the conversation?

A.  B.  C. 

第二部分(5 分)

听下面 5 段对话。每段对话后有一个小题,从题中所给的 A、B、C 三个选项中选出最佳选项。听完每段对话后,你有 10 秒钟的时间来回答有关小题和阅读下一小题。每段对话仅读一遍。

(　　) 6. Who gives Tom the birthday present?

A. May.　　B. His father.　　C. His mother.

(　　) 7. Where does she like living?

A. Other countries.　　B. City center.　　C. Countryside.

(　　) 8. Which country is the man from?

A. America.　　B. Germany.　　C. England.

(　　) 9. Where is his dictionary?

A. He doesn't know.　　B. In his schoolbag.　C. He can't find it.

(　　) 10. What's the weather like today?

A. It's rainy.　　B. It's sunny.　　C. It's snowy.

第二节　(共 15 个小题,每小题 1 分,满分 15 分)

听下面 4 段对话或独白。每段对话或独白后有几个小题,从题中所给的 A、B、C 三个选项中选出最佳选项。听每段对话和独白前,你将有时间阅读各个小题,每小题 5 秒钟;听完后,各小题将给出 5 秒钟的作答时间。每段对话或独白读两遍。

听第 11 段材料,回答第 11～13 题。

(　　)11. When is Mary allowed to watch TV?

A. On school nights.　　B. On weekends.　　C. On Monday evening.

(　　)12. Who buys clothes for Mary?

A. Herself.　　B. Her father.　　C. Her mother.

(　　)13. What does Mary think of her parents' rules?

A. Useless.　　B. Good for her.　　C. Not strict enough.

听第 12 段材料,回答第 14～16 题。

(　　)14. What nationality is the woman?

A. England.　　B. English.　　C. We don't know.

(　　)15. What does the woman need for making fruit salad?

A. Two apples, one pear and one banana.

B. Two pears, two bananas and one apple.

C. One apple, one pear and two bananas.

(　　)16. How much yogurt does the woman need when she wants to make fruit salad for her husband?

A. One cup.　　B. Two cups.　　C. Three cups.

听第 13 段材料,回答第 17～20 题。

(　　)17. How many languages does the woman speak?

A. 2.　　B. 3.　　C. 4.

(　　)18. Which language can't the woman speak?

A. English.　　B. French.　　C. Japanese.

(　　)19. Which language can't the woman write?

A. English.　　B. French.　　C. Hindi.

(　　)20. Which of the following is TRUE according to the dialogue?

A. The woman can speak Hindi but she can't speak English.

B. The woman can write a little French but she can't speak it at all.

C. Japanese and English belong to different language systems.

听第 14 段材料，回答第 21～25 题。

(　　)21. Who saw the thieves in the house?

A. The writer.　　B. The writer's wife.　C. The police.

(　　)22. What did the writer do after he found there were some thieves in his house?

A. He shot them.　　B. He called the police.

C. He caught the thieves.

(　　)23. How many times did the writer call the police?

A. One time.　　B. Two times.　　C. Three times.

(　　)24. Why did the police go to the writer's house quickly?

A. Because they want to catch the thieves.

B. Because they thought the thieves killed the writer.

C. Because they thought the writer shot the thieves.

(　　)25. Which of the following is NOT true according to the passage?

A. The writer and his wife went to their best friend's birthday party last night.

B. The writer is very clever.

C. There weren't any policemen in the area when the writer first phoned the police.

请同学们将试卷翻到第二部分，完成听写部分的试题。

二、单项选择（15 分）

(　　)26. She ________ us English two years ago.

A. teached　　B. taught　　C. has taught　　D. teaches

(　　)27. Don't worry, we still have ________ time left.

A. a little　　B. little　　C. a few　　D. few

(　　)28. I don't think the job ________, I can learn a lot from it.

A. is bored　　B. is boring

C. is interested　　D. is interesting

(　　)29. Owen didn't feel ________ after the game.

A. enough well　　B. enough good

C. well enough D. good enough

( )30. Cifer's shoes are out of shape. I want to buy her ________.

A. a pair of new shoe B. a new pair of shoes

C. a big pair of shoe D. a pair of big shoes

( )31. There ________ a basketball game ________ Class One and Class Eight tomorrow afternoon.

A. will have; with B. will be; between

C. has; from D. will have; between

( )32. Steve still ________ find his exercise book now. He ________ it.

A. can; lose B. couldn't; lost C. can't; has lost D. could; lose

( )33. You may go and ask Kathy for help. She knows ________ about French.

A. a few B. few C. a little D. little

( )34. This kind of old cloth ________ usually ________ the decoration of the room in the ancient China, but now we can only see it in the museum.

A. were; used to B. was; using for

C. were; used for D. was; used for

( )35. There are five foreign students in my class. One is from America and ________ are from Canada.

A. another B. the other C. the others D. other

( )36. — What are your mother and your sister doing?

— My mother is ________ the soup and my sister is ________ the vegetables.

A. stir; chop B. stiring; chopping

C. stirring; chopping D. stirred; chopped

( )37. Another soap opera ________ will be on TV this week.

A. serie B. serious C. seriousness D. series

( )38. What ________ me most is that the director had never received any college education.

A. interest B. interests C. interesting D. to interest

( )39. — Have you got any plans ________ this summer vacation?

— Yes. I plan ________ in the summer camp in America.

A. for; to take part B. to; taking part

C. with; to join D. at; joining

( )40. The poor man ________ since he ________.

A. was very sad; become blind B. has been very sad; went blindly

C. was very sad; went blind D. has been very sad; went blind

三、完形填空(10 分)

As soon as he finished his homework, Eric jumped onto his bicycle and rode off in the direction of the beach. While he was __41__ along, he thought about the whales. He hoped he would see them again today. After he got to the beach, Eric __42__ his bicycle behind a bush so that no one could see it from the road. Then he ran down onto the sand. ___43___ it was only four in the afternoon, the sky was already growing dark. Eric frowned（皱眉）, if it ___44___ he wouldn't be able to see the whales because they would stay in deeper water. He hurried along the beach ___45___ the rocks. They were the best place to watch the whales because of their ___46___. Before Eric reached the rocks he felt a drop of water on his head. "Oh no!" he thought. "Now the whales will stay in the deep water and I won't be able to ___47___ them!" But just then he saw a large shape on the beach, it was a young whale! The whale had come too close to the shore（海岸）and got stuck（搁浅）on the ___48___! At first the whale didn't move at all and Eric thought it was ___49___. Then he saw its tail move weakly. Eric turned and ran through the rain as fast as he could back to his bicycle. He had to get ___50___! Unless they got the whale back in the water soon, it would die and Eric couldn't let that happen.

(　　)41. A. riding　B. running　C. getting　D. walking
(　　)42. A. sent　B. hid　C. look　D. got
(　　)43. A. As　B. Since　C. Because　D. Although
(　　)44. A. shone　B. snowed　C. rained　D. blew
(　　)45. A. down　B. off　C. to　D. from
(　　)46. A. length　B. size　C. height　D. shape
(　　)47. A. watch　B. kill　C. catch　D. save
(　　)48. A. soil　B. beach　C. grass　D. water
(　　)49. A. dead　B. pretty　C. lovely　D. alive
(　　)50. A. care　B. oil　C. medicine　D. help

四、阅读理解（20分）

A

The Same Song Comes to Dabieshan
Want to spend a wonderful evening?
Want to see your favourite pop singer?
Come on!
PLACE: Dabieshan People's Square
TIME: 7:00 p. m.　Nov. 7th
TICKET: ￥180

Welcome to Our Club
Do you want to be an artist?
Just come and have a try!
Music lesson　Price: ￥100
Dance lesson　Price: ￥50
Art lesson　Price: ￥60

Airplane History Museum
Opened on October 25th, 1986
You should use the floor plan to find your way around. If you are with your children, stay close to them. The museum is very big and it is easy to get lost.
Open: 8:30 a. m.—12:00 a. m. and 2:00 p. m.—5:00 p. m.
Admission: ￥4; children under 5 years old get in for free

(　　)51. You can see your favourite pop singer ________.
A. in Dabieshan People's Square
B. in the club

C. in Airplane History Museum

D. in Dabieshan people's cinema

(　　)52. We can NOT learn ________ in the club.

A. music　　B. art　　C. English　　D. dance

(　　)53. If you want to have music and dance lessons, you will pay ________.

A. ￥100　　B. ￥150　　C. ￥160　　D. ￥180

(　　)54. People can visit the museum at ________ every day.

A. 1∶00 p. m.　　B. 3∶00 p. m.　　C. 7∶00 p. m.　　D. 8∶10 p. m.

(　　)55. ________ can get into the museum for free.

A. An adult　　B. A student

C. A child under 5 years old　　D. Children about 5 years old

B

Charlie was spending his summer holidays by the sea. One day he climbed over some rocks. He was looking for some crabs (螃蟹) for supper. He took off his shorts and put them on a rock.

The afternoon went quickly. Time was flying by. Look! The sea was coming in fast. It was over some of the rocks now.

Charlie looked up. "It's getting late. Oh dear! Look at the sea. Where are my shorts now?" he thought. He saw them on a rock.

Oh dear! The rock was an island! Now he must swim and get them.

Charlie jumped into the sea and started swimming. He reached the rock and put his shorts on his head. Then he started swimming back. Oh no! The sea was too strong for Charlie. It was pulling him away from the beach.

"Help!" he called. "I can't get back."

Luckily, a boat was coming by. The people in the boat saw Charlie and heard his call for help.

"Are you all right?" asked the woman in the boat.

"No! I can't swim back. The sea is too strong."

The woman stopped the boat and she and a girl pulled Charlie into the boat. He threw his shorts into the boat, too. Then they turned the boat bound and took Charlie back to the beach.

"That was lucky," said the woman.

"Thank you very much," said Charlie.

"Be careful next time," said the woman. "The sea is usually very strong near these rocks."

"Next time, I'm going to keep my shorts in my bag," said Charlie. "Better safe than sorry!"

(　　)56. Where did the story take place?

A. In the hills.　　B. By the sea.

C. On the river.　　D. In the town.

(　　)57. What was Charlie doing that day?

A. He was watching the sea. B. He was looking for seafood.
C. He was lying on the beach.
D. He was helping the people in the boat.

( )58. Before looking for crabs, Charlie put ________.
A. his shirts in a bag B. his shoes on a rock
C. his shorts in a bag D. his shorts on a rock

( )59. Charlie cried for help because ________.
A. the sea was carrying him away from the beach
B. the sea was pulling Charlie onto the rocks
C. the sea was getting lower
D. the sea was going out

( )60. Who saved Charlie?
A. A man and a girl. B. Two men.
C. A woman and a girl. D. A man and a boy.

C

My mum says my head is too expensive, because all my operations(手术) have cost millions of dollars. I am sick with hydrocephalus. That means "water in the head". Water runs through the body like a river, but sometimes it won't leave my head. That water gives me bad headaches and lots of other problems. So, doctors put a small tube (管子) in me to take away the water from my head.

I stay in the hospital most of the time. Sometimes the doctors let me go out to play. But sometimes if I play too much, my tube has problems. I have to go back to the hospital.

My doctor, Dr. Beck, is the greatest. He takes good care of me, and he's a lot of fun, too. My illness is hard to understand, but Dr. Beck always takes time to teach me about it by drawing pictures or telling stories. I draw cartoons for him, too, to make him laugh when he gets tired.

When I grow up, I dream of becoming a doctor so that I can take care of the kids like me. I have been in the hospital a lot, and my mum is a nurse, so I have learned a lot by wathing and asking questions. When I'm a doctor, I'll tell sick kids my story to make them feel better when they're afraid.

( ) 61. The best title of this reading is ________.
A. Where I spend the Time B. A Very Expensive Head
C. Why I Want to Be a Doctor D. My Doctor, Dr. Beck

( ) 62. My head aches ________.
A. when I play too much
B. if I go back to school
C. before the tube in my head drops
D. When there's water in my head

( ) 63. I stay in the hospital most of the time ________.
A. because my mum is a nurse in the hospital

B. so I know something about how to look after sick people

C. but I have no chance to meet other doctors

D. and I don't have to pay for anything here

( ) 64. I draw cartoons for ________.

A. Dr. Beck B. the nurse

C. my mother D. the doctors

( ) 65. From the passage we know that ________.

A. Dr. Beck is very good at drawing cartoons

B. the sick child has many funny stories for doctors

C. hydrocephalus can also cause some other problems

D. nobody can understand the illness well

D

World Laughter Day was started in Mumbai, India in 1998 by Dr. Madan Kataria, organizer of the worldwide Laughter Yoga activity.

The celebration of World Laughter Day is for world peace and is a plan to make good friends through laughter. Now more and more people are joining the Laughter Yoga movement. On the 9th of January, 2000, more than 10,000 people gathered in Denmark to celebrate the third World Laughter Day. It was very successful.

World Laughter Day is now celebrated on the first Sunday of May every year. Hundreds of people all over the world laugh together on that day. No one thinks that laughing doesn't make us feel good.

Today, some people in the world still face war. Laughter is a good way to deal with world problems. When different groups laugh together, they can get along better. Many difficult problems can become easier to be solved if people feel good.

Laughter is a world language, which is the same in every country. We should believe that only laughter can bring the world together and help people become good friends.

The famous writer, Mark Twain said, "Mankind has only one really effective weapon, and that is laughter."

( ) 66. World Laughter Day was started ________.

A. in 1998 B. in 2000

C. in America D. in China

( ) 67. The celebration of the third World Laughter Day was held ________.

A. in India B. in Denmark

C. in Mumbai D. by Mark Twain

( ) 68. The meaning of the underlined sentence is ________.

A. laughing doesn't make us feel good

B. laughter makes us feel happy

C. nobody thinks it is good to laugh

D. everyone thinks laughing together makes us feel sad

( ) 69. The Laughter Yoga movement tells us ________.

A. laughter can stop war

B. people should laugh at each other while doing Yoga

C. laughter is the best way to deal with world problems

D. laughing together can help people get along well

(　　)70. What's the best title of the passage?

A. World Laughter Day.

B. Successful Laughter.

C. The First World Yoga Day.

D. The Celebration of World Yoga Day.

第二部分

（30 分）

一、听写，听一篇文章并根据所听内容补全所缺单词（5 分）

Coin collection is one of the oldest __1__. In the past it was often enjoyed by kings and scholars. It is also a pleasant way of saving.

The __2__ on coins tell many stories. The coins of a country often are a record of its history and geography. Some ancient coins tell us all we know about a country or a period of history. They bring us portraits of rulers who would be otherwise unknown. Coins tell us about the art, religion, dress and hairstyle of people who lived long ago.

Your special __3__ will help you decide the kind of coin collection you would like to have. You may wish to collect the coins of one country or one part of the world. Or you may want your collection to contain coins from all over the world in a __4__ period of time.

To get the most enjoyment from your hobby of coin collecting, read as much as you can on the subject. Try to form a group of collector friends. If you have an old or foreign coin, find out where and when it was made, its name and __5__, and what you could have bought with it when it was in use.

1.________ 2.________ 3.________ 4.________ 5.________

二、将单词与符合的意思匹配（5 分）

(　　) 1. atmosphere　　A. (of an activity, etc.) worth doing; that makes you happy because you think it is useful or important

(　　) 2. royal　　B. at the present time, in contrast with the past

(　　) 3. rewarding　　C. a set of instructions that tells you how to cook sth.

(　　) 4. recipe　　D. the feeling or mood that you have in a particular situation, a feeling between two or more people

(　　) 5. nowadays　　E. connected with or belonging to the king or queen of a country

三、根据所给首字母及句意完成以下句子（10 分）

1. Everyone kept ________ (silence) after the manager finished his speech.

2. Thank you for ________ (visit) our school today.
3. Have you finished ________ (prepare) for the world of adults?
4. Going out late at night may be very ________ (frightened) for a child.
5. Many boys in my class enjoy ________ (play) basketball on Friday afternoons.
6. The Eiffel Tower is one of ________ (attract) tourist attractions in the world.
7. I ________ (collector) most of albums of Mariah Carey since 2007.
8. I don't know ________ (exact) what time Sunny will come.
9. Ariel ________ (plan) to travel around the world the other day.
10. Mr. Hu is one of the most ________ (experience) teachers in our school.

四、句型转换(5 分)

1. Bungee jumping started on Pentecost Island. (改成否定句)

____

2. She'd like to visit Greece one day. (改成一般疑问句)

____

3. Tom has been away from home <u>for about 2 months</u>. (对画线部分提问)

____

4. It took me three hours to clean the room. (换一种说法)

____

5. What a handsome boy John is! (换一种说法)

____

五、翻译(5 分)

1. 一天,镇上起了一起大火。

____

2. 如果你们不带上你们的雨衣,你们将会后悔的。

____

3. 你才穿了这双鞋几个小时,它们就已经旧了。

____

4. 他对看这个节目的孩子负有责任。

____

5. 在英国,车辆在道路的左边行驶,司机坐在车的右边。

____

Tapescripts

Unit 1

Section Five

一、听写单词。

1. stir 2. sticking-plaster 3. my goodness 4. February 5. store-room
6. nasty 7. beard 8. bake a cake 9. terrible 10. money-box

二、选出相对应的答语。

1. Can I ask you some questions? 2. What's your matter?
3. How are you felling today? 4. What should we do to fight bird flu?
5. How long do you sleep every night?

三、听短对话，选出最佳答案。

1. W: Do you know about Chinese history?
M: Yes, I am interested in it.
W: I have been studying it for three years.
Q: What are they talking about?
2. M: Look at the old buildings. They are special.
W: Yes, they are in European style.
M: I don't agree. They are in Russian style.
Q: Are the old buildings in European style or in Russian style?
3. W: Hi, Mr. Smith. Are you enjoying yourself in China?
M: Yes, I am. I like Chinese culture and Chinese history.
W: How do you like the food here?
M: A little. It's too hot.
Q: What does Mr. Smith think of the food here?
4. W: Tom, you won't collect kites. We don't have any room to store them.
M: No, Mom. I'll use the living room to store them.
W: Oh, my god!
Q: Where would Tom put his kites?
5. M: Alice, congratulations to you! You are the first to pass the finishing line.
W: Thank you. I have been running for 2 hours.
M: You are great! You are the winner among the 20 runners.
Q: How many runners took part in the game?

Unit 2

Section Five

一、听写单词。

1. what a rush 2. go to school 3. photograph 4. parcel 5. balloon
6. interesting 7. tourist 8. heavy shower 9. terrible gossip 10. weighing machine

二、选出相对应的答语。

1. What's this in English? 2. How do you spell it?
3. How old are you ? 4. What class are you in?
5. What's your phone number? 6. Who's that?
7. Where are you from?

三、听对话，选出正确答案。

1. W：What's that?
   M：It's a yellow bag.
2. W：This is Mary. She is Nick's good friend.
   M：Nice to meet you, Mary.
3. W：How many students are there in your class, Jim?
   M：There are twenty boys and twenty-two girls.
4. W：Excuse me, where is the reading room?
   M：It's in front of the teaching building.
5. W：Is this sweater yours?
   M：No, it's Jim's.

Unit 3

Section Five

一、听写单词。

1. institute　2. excellent　3. activity　4. calendar　5. break
6. concert　7. midnight　8. situated　9. casual　10. routine

二、听问题选答案。

1. What's the time now?
2. What date is it today?
3. What day is it today?
4. When do you usually go to school?
5. How often does Mike go to the supermarket?
6. Where is Millie from?

三、听对话并回答问题。

1. W：Time to get up, Bob.
   M：Hum, I want to sleep a little longer.
   W：It's already seven o'clock. Be quick, or you will be late.
   M：OK. I am getting up.
   Q：What's the time now?
2. W：What is your father?
   M：He is a professor.
   W：And what is your mother's job?
   M：She is a writer.
   Q：What is the man?
3. M：Shall we go to play football?
   W：No. I don't like it at all.
   M：Do you like tennis?
   W：Yes, I do. I like it a lot. But I am not a very good player.
   Q：Which sport does the woman like?
4. M：What's the time by your watch, Mom?
   W：It is six o'clock.
   M：Oh, this clock is three minutes slow.
   Q：What time is it now?
5. M：What is the date today, Betty?
   W：Today is May the thirty-first.
   Q：What date is tomorrow?
6. W：May I help you, sir?
   M：No, thank you. I'm just looking.

W: Well, please let me know if you need assistance.

Q: Where does this conversation happen?

7. W: Come on, James! You don't have to study tonight. Let's go swimming!

M: Leave me alone! I've got an exam tomorrow.

Q: What will James do next?

四、听下面几段对话并完成每段对话后的几个小题。

听对话,回答第 1 ~3 题。

W: Hello.

M: Hello, Cathy! This is Mike.

W: Hi, Mike! Nice to hear from you again.

M: Listen. I'm phoning to invite you to a party at our new house.

W: New house? Really?

M: Yes. We've moved. Can you come?

W: Well, that depends. When is it?

M: This Saturday evening.

W: All right. I'll come. I'm looking forward to seeing you and your new house. Um ... when does the party start?

M: Come any time after eight. All right?

W: OK.

M: Bye! See you on Saturday evening.

W: Wait a moment, Mike. You haven't ... Mike? Are you still there? You haven't given me your new address. Hello? Mike? Hello?

听对话,回答第 4 ~7 题。

W: Where are you going for your holidays this year, Jim?

M: I don't know yet. My wife's going to her mother's for a couple of weeks. She lives by the sea, you know.

W: Oh, does she? That's convenient.

M: Yes, but I want to go to the country.

W: Don't you like the sea?

M: Yes, very much. But I need peace and quietness when I'm on holiday. What are you going to do, Mary?

W: I'm going to stay at home.

M: Aren't you going to have a holiday abroad this year?

W: No, I want to buy a car, and that's going to take every penny I've got.

五、听短文并填空。

Spring Festival is usually in late January or early February. It is the first day of the Chinese year. This is a very special festival for all Chinese people. Before the festival, people are busy. They clean their houses and go shopping for food, presents and new clothes.

In Guangzhou people go to the flower markets to look at all the beautiful flowers. Many people buy flowers, too. On the evening before Spring Festival, people usually have a big supper with their family. After supper, they watch TV or go out. At Spring Festival people go and visit their friends and family. They eat nice food. The children love this time. They can get "lucky money".

Unit 4

Section Five

一、把你所听到的句子写在下面的横线上。

1. Have some vegetables.
2. Let's have a holiday.

3. They are having a fight.
4. Father is smoking.
5. Don't make a noise.
6. He must drink some medicine.
7. She has got an earache.
8. Don't ask him the way because he is a tourist.

二、听下面一段短文，根据短文内容，判断下列句子的正误，将 T 或 F 填入题前的括号内。

Bob is studying in a village school. There are two hills not far from his home. There is a valley between the two hills. The school is in the middle of the valley. He walks to school every day. There is a small river next to the school. There is a stone bridge over the river. There is a big playground in front of the teaching building. There are some big trees behind the classroom building and the children often read and play under the trees after school. There are many fields near the school. When autumn comes, all the teachers and students will help farmers with their harvest.

三、听下面五段小对话，根据对话内容选择最佳答案。

1. W: David, how do you often go to school?
   M: I took a bus before, but now I often go to school on foot.
2. M: Excuse me. Do you mind if I sit here?
   W: No, of course not.
3. M: Would you like a cup of coffee?
   W: Well, I'd rather have a cup of tea if you don't mind.
4. W: Do you know what time the concert begins?
   M: At 9 : 15.
   W: Oh, I got here at nine. It's a little early.
5. M: I hear you are going boating tomorrow?
   W: No, I'm going fishing with my friends.

Unit 5

Section Five

一、听写句子。

1. Where was father yesterday afternoon?
2. Were Sandy and Sue at the library last night?
3. Mother and father were at the cinema last night.
4. They weren't at home a short time ago.
5. He was in Washington last week.
6. They were in France last month.

二、听下面五段小对话，选择正确的答语。

1. M: Can you tell me when I can come to see the dentist, nurse?
   W: Let me see. Today is Wednesday. Maybe it is OK two days later from now. Oh, no, three days, I think.
2. M: I must catch the 9 : 15 flight to Japan. It's nearly 8 o'clock now. Can you drive me there?
   W: No hurry. I'll try to drive you there in 10 minutes.
3. M: Which box is the better of the two?
   W: Er … I prefer the smaller one to the bigger one.
   M: So do I.
4. M: What does your sister do?
   W: She was a teacher 3 years ago, but now she is a reporter, and she wants to be a doctor.
5. M: How's the weather in Wuhan today? I'm going to visit my aunt there.
   W: It's windy and cloudy.

M: That's too bad. Here in Tianjin there's no cloud at all.

三、听下面一段对话，选择最佳答案。

Mr. Lee will work in the city. The Lees are discussing the problem of moving to the city.

M: I will work in the city and we had better live in the city as well.

W: I really don't want to. A flat in the city is as expensive as a house here.

M: It is good for you and our daughter. The local shops have convenient opening hours. The flat is near a very good school.

W: That may be true. But the air in the city is not so fresh as that here. The running water there is not so clean as it is here.

M: I don't care about these. The city offers restaurants, theatres and cinemas. There is also a barbecue and picnic area in the housing estate.

W: I don't like them. I like watching TV or reading a novel at home.

M: Let's leave the matter to your father then.

四、听下面一段短文，选出正确的选项。

Have you ever seen an animal without a head? There is such an animal! It has no tail or legs. Its body is full of holes. It eats and breathes but never moves. It lives under water. The water brings the animal air. The water brings the animal little plants and animals to feed on. What animal is it? It is the sponge! The sponge is a water animal. Some sponges are found in shallow water. Other sponges live on the floor of the sea. Sponges grow in many sizes, shapes, and colours. Men dive for sponges. Animal sponges are needed for many things. But most sponges sold in the stores are not animals. They are made by man. How are the sponges used?

Unit 6

Section Five

一、听写单词。

1. cartoon　2. creative　3. fitness　4. gardening　5. nature
6. photograph　7. relaxing　8. running-track　9. pottery　10. aerobics

二、听问题选答案。

1. What do you always do in your spare time?　2. What kind of programme do you like?
3. Where are they going to take a vacation?　4. When does the shop open?
5. Why don't you like playing badminton?
6. How many hours a week do you stay with your grandparents?

三、听对话并回答问题。

1. M: Is Bob's telephone number 85791038?
   W: Oh, no. It's 85781088.
   Q: What is Bob's telephone number?
2. M: How many people are there in your family?
   W: Three of them are in India. In fact, there are too many to count.
   M: What about here in Wuhan?
   W: Oh, there's my dad and mom, and my two brothers and I.
   Q: How many people are there in the girl's family in Wuhan?
3. W: Do you chat online every day?
   M: No, I only chat online on Saturday and Sunday.
   Q: How often does the man chat online?
4. W: I'm afraid I can't meet you at 10 at the school gate.
   M: Then we'd better make it an hour later in the classroom.

W：That's all right.

Q：What will they do?

5. M：How much is your T-shirt?

W：It's 300 Yuan.

M：300 Yuan for a T-shirt like that? I can't believe it!

Q：What does the man think of the T-shirt?

6. M：Hi，Linda. Are you going to have a picnic this Saturday?

W：No，we aren't. We're going to plant trees this Saturday morning. Will you join us?

M：That's good. But Bob asked me to go to swim with him. I'll tell him I won't go.

Q：What is the boy going to do this Saturday morning?

7. W：How long can I keep this book?

M：One month. You must renew it if you don't finish it in time.

Q：Where does the conversation probably happen?

四、听下面几段对话并完成每段对话后的几个小题。

听第一段对话，回答第1～3题。

W：Hello，332440.

M：Oh hello，Sally. This is Dave Thomson here. Could I speak to Jim，please?

W：I'm afraid he's not in at the moment，Dave. He went out about an hour ago and he's not back yet.

M：Any idea when he might be back?

W：Well，he shouldn't be long. He said he was just going to get some paint. But I wouldn't be surprised if he's stopped off at the pub on the way back.

M：OK，well，please tell him I've called，and I'll try again later.

W：All right. Goodbye，Dave.

M：Thanks then，Sally. Goodbye.

听第二段对话，回答第4～7题。

M：Excuse me! Could you please tell me the way to the No. 1 Hospital?

W：Sure. Go along this road and turn left at the second crossing. You'll see a tall building on the right. It's the Bank of China. The No. 1 Hospital is just behind it. You can't miss it.

M：Thanks. By the way，is there a flower shop near the hospital?

W：No，there isn't. At the first crossing，you'll see a flower shop at the corner.

M：Thank you very much.

W：That's all right.

五、听短文并填空。

There are many kinds of TV programs on TV. I like to watch cartoons，game shows and comedies. But cartoons are my favorite. I usually watch TV for thirty minutes a day and the program I watch is a cartoon called *Doraemon*. It is on TV from six thirty to seven o'clock，Monday to Friday. A lot of people watch it at that time. It's an interesting cartoon. *Doraemon* is drawn by a Japanese cartoonist. *Doraemon* is a smart robot and the star of the cartoon. He can do many incredible things. For example，he can go traveling everywhere or make people smaller or bigger. *Doraemon* is a good TV program. It is my favorite TV show.

Unit 7

Section Five

一、听下面五段对话，选出与对话意思相符的图片。

1. W：Jim，what are you going to do next Sunday?

M：I'm going skiing. Would you like to go with me?

2. M: Do you mind my smoking here?
   W: Sorry. Please look at the sign. It says "no smoking" here.
3. M: I like listening to music when I have a walk by the river.
   W: That's good. Why not buy a radio first?
   M: A good idea!
4. W: What's your father?
   M: He's a doctor and he is very kind to his patients.
5. W: I'm interested in Beijing Opera. Can you teach me?
   M: No problem!

二、听下面五段对话，选择正确答案。

1. M: I hear today is your birthday.
   W: No, yesterday was my birthday. It's Christmas Day today.
2. M: I know you're from England. But did you live in America for some time?
   W: Yes, we did. We lived there for five years, and then we came to Beijing because my father found work here last year.
3. W: Jim, does the bus go to the Children's House?
   M: Yes. Let's get on it.
4. W: They say Lucy runs very fast.
   M: I don't think so. I think Lily runs faster.
   W: You're right. But she doesn't run as fast as Kate.
5. M: Why were you late for school this morning?
   W: I went to the bus stop at 6 : 30, but the early bus left just five minutes earlier.

三、听下面几段对话，选择正确答案。

听下面一段对话，回答第1~2题。

M: Hi, Maria, What a nice photo! Who is the boy on your right?
W: Oh, he is my young brother, Tom.
M: But, he is much taller and stronger than you, isn't he?
W: Yes, he is.

听下面一段对话，回答第3~4题。

W: Excuse me. Which is the way to the nearest supermarket?
M: Go down the street, then turn left at the second crossing. At the end of the road, you will find it.
W: Can I get there by bus?
M: Certainly. You can take the No. 7 bus.
W: Thank you very much. Byebye.
M: Bye.

听下面一段对话，回答第5~7题。

W: Are you going to the zoo tomorrow?
M: Yes, but I am not going there by bus tomorrow.
W: Oh, why not?
M: I am staying at my uncle's house tonight. He is driving me to the zoo after breakfast.
W: Oh, good. But are you joining us at the gate at 9 : 00 am ?
M: Yes, of course. We are leaving his house at 8 : 00 am, so I won't be late! I am taking the bus back to school with you in the afternoon. Will you have lunch there?
W: Oh, yes. Mr. Wu will bring sandwiches for everyone.
M: Oh, that's good. See you tomorrow.

四、听短文，完成信息表。

Good morning, boys and girls,

Our school basketball team is in the final of the basketball competition. Here is the plan of the day.

At 9 am, we will meet at the cinema gate on Sunny Street. The bus leaves at 9.25 am. Then we'll arrive at South Hill School at 10 am. The match starts at 10 : 30 am. After the match finishes, there is the presentation of the cup and medals at 11 : 45 am. After lunch, you must get on the bus in front of Wildlife Restaurant. It will leave at 1 : 15 pm to bring you back to school.

Please come and support our team.

Unit 8

Section Five

一、将你听到的单词或短语写在下面的横线上。

1. grocer	2. chemist's	3. stationary	4. restaurant	5. steak
6. course	7. cream	8. station	9. wait	10. flute
11. pistol	12. share	13. bunch	14. thief	15. donkey
16. traffic	17. question	18. kick a goal	19. round	20. iodine

二、选出你所听到的句子。

1. Shall we meet at the theatre?
2. They are going to go to the art gallery on Tuesday.
3. Let me show you around the park.
4. Mrs. Black often meets her friends for tea.
5. My little brother always counts on his fingers.

三、听句子，并选择正确的答语。

1. What's the matter with Mr. Smith?
2. How long does it take you to go to school?
3. Can you tell me how to get to the nearest bank?
4. What is the cat like?
5. Let me show you the way to the supermarket.
6. What happened to the little boy?
7. How far is the shopping centre from here?
8. How often do you work in the garden?
9. What's wrong with this roller-coaster?
10. How will they feel after the football match?

四、听句子，选出一个与你所听到的句子意思相近的选项。

1. Football is a very popular game in China, but not in America.
2. Mary wants another one, but she is full.
3. I'm your new teacher, so I don't know all your names.
4. Both Dick and Jones like basketball.
5. Peter's work starts at half past seven and finishes at a quarter past six.

Unit 9

Section Five

一、将你所听到的单词写在下面的横线上。

1. during	2. Europe	3. breakfast	4. untidy	5. lunch
6. uniform	7. along	8. message	9. wastepaper-basket	10. midnight
11. string	12. out of sight	13. indoors	14. heavily	15. puppet
16. sheet	17. cork	18. busily	19. paint	20. carefully

二、根据你所听到的问题选出正确的答语。

1. Excuse me, could you please tell me the way to the nearest hospital?
2. What will he do?
3. Do you mind my smoking?
4. How often do you go to your grandpa's?
5. What do you think of the new film?
6. Who is over there?
7. What is your sister?
8. How does your brother go to school everyday?
9. You are both very late this morning.
10. When did he move to Beijing?

三、根据你所听到的对话选择正确答案。

1. M: What do you think of London?
   W: Wonderful. I feel at home.
   Q: What does the woman mean?
2. M: I hear you are moving to a new house soon, Maria.
   W: I have to. Because the man in the next room is singing all the time and I can't sleep.
   Q: Why is Maria moving?
3. W: Did you listen to the weather report this morning?
   M: Yes, the radio says it will stop raining and be clear up soon, but it seems that we still have to wait.
   Q: How is the weather when they are talking?
4. M: How was your dinner at the Pizza Hut?
   W: Much better than I expected though I'm not very interested in Italian food. For that price, it should have been better.
   Q: What does the woman mean?
5. M: How do you like the film, Ellen?
   W: Well, the story is not so good. The music is just so-so. Anyway, the dialogue is humorous.
   Q: What does the woman think of the film?

四、根据你所听到的短文选择正确答案。

Every week, Peter and Linda get five dollars from their parents. This money is their weekly income. It is not a gift. Peter and Linda must work for the family to earn the money. Peter takes out the garbage and cleans the garden. He should do it every day, but sometimes he forgets. Linda helps her mother with the cooking. She also washes the dishes after dinner. Peter and Linda don't have to use their money for food. They use it for their hobbies. Sometimes they go to the movies. Sometimes they buy CDs. Each week they can save some of their money.

期中考试(一)

一、听力理解部分(25 分)

第一节(共 6 小题,每小题 1 分,满分 6 分)

听下面 6 个问题。每个问题后有三个答语,从题中所给的 A、B、C 三个选项中选出最佳选项。听完每个问题后,你都有 5 秒钟的时间来作答和阅读下一小题。每个问题仅读一遍。

1. What can I do for you?
2. What's the weather like today?
3. Where is my new pencil-case?
4. What's the matter with you?
5. How did you go to New York last week?
6. What do you like to do in your spare time?

第二节（共5小题，每小题1分，满分5分）

听下面5段对话。每段对话后有一个小题，从题中所给的A、B、C三个选项中选出最佳选项。听完每段对话后，你都有10秒钟的时间来回答有关小题和阅读下一小题。每段对话仅读一遍。

7. M：What time will the match begin?
   W：At 9 o'clock. Andt it's a quarter to 9 now.
   Q：What time is it now?
8. W：May I have a look at the magazine?
   M：Yes, of course. It's about taking pictures.
   Q：What are the two persons talking about?
9. W：Is your mother a doctor, Peter?
   M：No, she's a very good nurse.
   Q：Where does Peter's mother work?
10. W：Why are you in a hurry?
    M：Oh, I'm going to the airport.
    Q：Where is the man going?
11. M：Mom, are there any cakes in the fridge?
    W：No, but there is some oranges in it.
    Q：What does the boy want?

第三节（共14小题，每小题1分，满分14分）

听下面4段对话或独白。每段对话或独白后有几个小题，从题中所给的A、B、C三个选项中选出最佳选项。听每段对话和独白前，你将有时间阅读各个小题；听完后，各小题将给出5秒钟的作答时间。每段对话或独白读两遍。

听第12段材料，回答第12～14题。

M：Hello. This is South Airline. What can I do for you?
W：Hello. I want to book one ticket to New York next Monday, the 8th of March.
M：Do you want a morning or an afternoon flight?
W：A morning flight, please.
M：Can you tell me your name, please?
W：Susan, S-U-S-A-N, Susan.
M：And your telephone number?
W：7865456.
M：That's OK.
W：Thank you.

听第13段材料，回答第15～17题。

W：Hello, Sam. When is the best time to visit Hong Kong?
M：Well, most people come in July and August, but I think the best month is May.
W：Why?
M：Because it's warm and not too hot.
W：What can travellers do in Hong Kong?
M：Lots of things, like visiting Hong Kong Disneyland, eating delicious food, going shopping and walking on the beach.
W：What's the sea like?
M：It's nice there, warm and usually clean.
W：Great! I can't wait to go there now.

听第14段材料，回答第18～20题。

W：Good morning. May I take your order?

M: Yes, I'm a vegetarian, so I don't want to eat any meat. Do you have any vegetarian dishes?

W: Yes, we do. We have onion soup and two kinds of salads. We also have spicy tofu and vegetarian burgers.

M: Well, I like spicy food. Maybe I'll try the tofu. You said you had two kinds of salad. What are they?

W: We have a house salad and a tomato salad.

M: What's the house salad?

W: It's made of tomatoes, onions, potatoes and beans.

M: That sounds great. I'd like a house salad, please.

W: OK, so spicy tofu and one house salad. What would you like to drink?

M: Orange juice, please.

听第15段材料,回答第21~25题。

Last summer, I went to Miami, Florida where I stayed for two weeks. My friend John and I flew to Miami from New York in three hours. It was the first time for both of us to travel by air. We sat in deep armchairs and enjoyed the unusual sight of the world. We stayed at a hotel on the beach. We slept late every morning and then had breakfast outdoors. When the weather was not hot, we used to go sight-seeing in the morning. We visited the science museum. In the afternoon, we used to go swimming, lie in the sun or go water-skiing. After dinner in the evening, we used to go dancing in the disco. The weather was very good every day and the time went by only too quickly. We were both very sorry when we had to leave.

请同学们将试卷翻到第二部分,完成听写部分的试题。

一、听写,听一篇文章并根据所听内容补全所缺单词。短文读两遍(5分)

With the development of the Internet, a great number of people do shopping on the Internet. Shopping online becomes more and more popular.

People have different opinions on shopping on the Internet. Some think it's convenient. You don't need to spend a lot of time choosing something from shop to shop. You can just sit in front of the computer, and search on the Internet for the things you like.

However, some people don't like shopping online. They think it's not safe, and once cheated, people will have nowhere to complain about. What's more, people can't see the goods. If clothes are bought online, they can't be tried on personally.

I am convinced that shopping online would be a better way than the traditional one. All you need to do is to sit in front of your computer and click the mouse. The goods come in all shapes, sizes and colors on the Internet. If you feel unsure about those, you can have a chat with the sellers online till you are certain on the things you will buy.

期中考试(二)

一、听力理解部分(25分)

第一节(共6小题,每小题1分,满分6分)

听下面6个问题。每个问题后有三个答语,从题中所给的A、B、C三个选项中选出最佳选项。听完每个问题后,你都有5秒钟的时间来作答和阅读下一小题。每个问题仅读一遍。

1. How is your father?
2. What time did David finish his homework?
3. Where are they from?
4. Who's over there?

5. What color is your backpack?

第二节（共 5 小题，每小题 1 分，满分 5 分）

听下面 5 段对话。每段对话后有一个小题，从题中所给的 A、B、C 三个选项中选出最佳选项。听完每段对话后，你都有 10 秒钟的时间来回答有关小题和阅读下一小题。每段对话仅读一遍。

6. W：I think that math is not as interesting as English. What about you, Jim?
   M：I really can't agree with you. I prefer math.
7. M：Is Jack in the office? I want to see him.
   W：He is on the way here.
8. M：Look! The room is full of smoke. I can hardly breathe.
   W：I quite agree. Smoking should not be allowed here in the office.
9. M：How much is the bag, please?
   W：Two for $2.99, sir. How many are you going to buy?
10. W：Are you going straight home after school today, Bob?
    M：No, I have a class until one o'clock and I'm going to spend three hours at the reading room before going home.

第三节（共 14 小题，每小题 1 分，满分 14 分）

听下面 4 段对话或独白。每段对话或独白后有几个小题，从题中所给的 A、B、C 三个选项中选出最佳选项。听每段对话和独白前，你将有时间阅读各个小题；听完后，各小题将给出 5 秒钟的作答时间。每段对话或独白读两遍。

听第 11 段材料，回答第 11～13 题。

W：What's your trouble, young man?
M：I've got a headache and a bad cough. I feel terrible.
W：When did it start?
M：Last Friday.
W：Have you got a fever?
M：Yes, the temperature is a bit high.
W：Oh, I see. Just a cold. Don't worry. Nothing serious. You'd better stay in bed. Take this medicine and you'll be all right soon.

听第 12 段材料，回答第 14～16 题。

W：Can I help you?
M：Yes. I want to buy a coat.
W：What kind of coat do you want to buy?
M：It's getting warmer and warmer. I'd like a cotton coat for spring.
W：What color would you like? Yellow or green would be a good color for you.
M：Oh, I want a white coat.
W：Are you sure? It's not a popular color this year. It gets dirty so easily.
M：I know. But I don't like other colors.

听第 13 段材料，回答第 17～20 题。

M：Jane, what's the matter? You look pale. Are you ill?
W：I just had a terrible experience.
M：I'll find a place for you to sit for a while.
W：No, thanks, Bill. I'll be fine in a minute.
M：What happened just now?
W：While I was crossing the street, I was almost hit by a car.
M：Were you hurt?

W: No. I jumped back in time.

M: How terrible! I hope you have got the number of the car, so you can tell it to the policeman.

W: But the driver went away.

M: Drivers like that should have their licenses taken away.

W: I agree. And I'll remember not to read a newspaper or enjoy music while crossing the street.

M: Oh, my God! You were reading at that time! Don't do it again.

W: I won't. Thank you, Bill.

听第 14 段材料,回答第 21 ~25 题。

On a cold Saturday morning last autumn, I went to town to do some shopping, and as I was walking through the park, it suddenly began to rain. I ran into a nearby phone box quickly since I didn't have an umbrella. It was raining heavily, but it was one of those short autumn showers that don't last long, so I decided to stay in the phone box until it stopped.

A few minutes later, I saw a young man walk up to the phone box, wearing a yellow raincoat and holding a tool box. I didn't want to go out into the rain. So I picked up the phone and pretended I was talking to someone. I thought the man would go away, but he didn't. He just waited patiently in the rain, watching me wave my hands and act as if I were deep in conversation.

Luckily, after ten minutes, the rain began to stop. "OK, Mum," I said loudly into the phone. "I'll see you later. Bye!" I put the phone down, picked up my shopping bag and stepped out of the phone box. "I'm sorry I use the phone so long," I said to the man.

"Oh, I didn't want to use the phone," he replied with a smile. "I've just come to repair it. It's out of order, you see." I felt myself go bright red in the face and I hurried away with my head down, feeling a complete fool.

请同学们将试卷翻到第二部分,完成听写部分的试题。

一、听写,听句子并根据所听内容补全所缺单词(5 分)

1. I wrote a letter to my friend Jane and looked forward to her letter then.
2. It's very difficult to get rid of bad habits.
3. He is always late. It isn't worth waiting for him.
4. The wedding was magnificent. So many people crowded to see it.
5. It is said that the storm caused serious damage. A lot of people died and hundreds of people became homeless.

Unit 10

Section Five

一、听下面五段对话,每段对话后有一个小题,从题中所给的 A、B、C 三幅图片中选出最佳选项。

1. W: Tom, what animals do you like?
   M: I love many animals like elephants and penguins, but I like pandas best.
2. W: Did you watch TV yesterday morning, Walter?
   M: No, I didn't. I went to buy some food for lunch.
3. M: Will people use bikes or buses in this city in ten years?
   W: Neither. They will use cars.
4. M: Have you ever been to Shanghai, Mary?
   W: No, never. But I want to go there this summer vacation.
5. M: What are you going to be when you grow up, Lucy?
   W: I want to be a singer.

二、听对话回答问题。

1. M：Can I help you?
   W：Yes, please. I'd like a pair of sports shoes.
2. W：Tom, what are you going to do when you leave school?
   M：I plan to go on to the college.
3. M：Does your uncle work in Japan?
   W：Yes, he works as an engineer in a car factory.
4. M：I'm sorry, Annie. I broke your glass just now. But I'll buy you a new one tomorrow.
   W：Oh, never mind, Tony. I wouldn't let you do that.
5. W：Have you got a pair of sports shoes in my size?
   M：I think so. How about these?
   W：Oh, I like them very much. How much are they?
   M：Eighty dollars.

三、听对话回答问题。

听第一段对话，回答第1~2题。

M：Hello!
W：Hello! This is Ellen!
M：This is Jack. Would you like to go to the movies with me?
W：When is it?
M：Tonight.
W：I'd love to, but I can't. If I go, I won't finish my homework.

听第二段对话，回答第3~5题。

M：I'm doing a survey. Can I ask you some questions?
W：Sure.
M：What would you do if you saw a big bicycle accident?
W：I would call the police.
M：What would you do if you could be a famous doctor?
W：I would help the people who can't see.
M：What would you do if you could fly anywhere in the world?
W：Mm. That's hard. There're lots of places I'd like to see. I'd go to Canada first.
M：Good. One more question. What famous person from history would you most like to meet?
W：I would most like to meet Zhou Enlai.
M：Good answer. That's all my questions.

听第三段对话，回答第6~8题。

W：Hey, Hector! What are you doing for the summer vacation?
M：I am visiting my grandparents in the countryside. I am leaving on June 25th. How about you, Susan?
W：I am going to Shanghai with my cousins.
M：Oh, cool! Are you going to visit the Shanghai World Expo Park?
W：Of course, we are. It's a good place to go sightseeing.
M：Have you ever been there before?
W：Not yet. A great vacation! I can't wait.
M：When are you leaving then?
W：On July 5th.
M：Well, have a great time!

听第四段对话，回答第9~10题。

W：Peter, would you mind turning down the radio? Your father is sleeping.
M：Sorry, Mum. I'll do some reading instead.

W: Good boy!

四、短文理解。

When I have something difficult to do, I always ask my mom, "Could you help me?" But she always says, "Do it yourself, dear." Then I get so sad. I think she is a lazy mother.

For example, one day, I invited some friends to my home. My bedroom was out of order. Books were all over the table and the ground. I forgot to make my bed. So I asked my mother to help me clean it. But she said seriously, "Do it yourself, girl." So I did it myself.

Because of my "lazy" mom, I am supposed to wash my clothes and clean my room. I have to help my parents do some housework. I even have to go to the dentist's by myself if I have a toothache. It's really hard to do everything on my own, but I have learned a lot.

From now on, I understand my mother. It's her "laziness" that makes me clever and hard-working. Just as my mom always says, "A lady can't be lazy or she'll be crazy. Work can make you sunny."

Unit 11

Section Five

一、听句子，选择适当的应答语。

1. What's the matter with you, Jack?
2. How does your daughter go to school every day?
3. I missed the football game on TV last night.
4. The shirt looks smart on you.
5. We are leaving for London now. Have you taken the air plane tickets?

二、听对话，选择相应的图画。

1. W: Mike, your watch is very nice.
   M: Thank you, Lucy. It's my birthday present from my aunt.
2. M: Where do you live?
   W: I like living in the countryside. I drive a car to work every day.
3. W: Will you be here at ten o'clock?
   M: No, I'll be there thirty minutes later.
4. W: Do you have books about computers?
   M: Yes, we do. Here is one about the ABC of computers.
   W: Thanks. How long may I keep it, please?
   M: Two weeks.
5. M: What are you going to do this afternoon?
   W: I've no idea.
   M: Shall we play basketball?
   W: No. Let's go to the movies.
   M: OK. That's a good idea.

三、听五段对话和五个问题，选择正确答案。

1. M: This heat is killing me!
   W: Me too!
   M: I would like a cold drink. What about you, Linda?
   W: Why not? I'll get you one.
   Q: What is the weather like now?
2. W: What is that man near the door? Is he a doctor?
   M: No, he is a policeman.
   Q: Is that man a policeman?

3. M：The Smiths have gone back to New York.
   W：Really? How long have they lived there?
   M：For six years.
   Q：When did Mr. Smith move there?
4. W：I hear you are going to move to a new house, aren't you?
   M：Yes, it'll be a bit expensive, but the man upstairs always plays music loudly.
   Q：Why is the man going to move to a new house?
5. M：How about food? Which do you like best—beef, fish, or chicken?
   W：Well, I like them all, but I'd say I like chicken the best. It's healthy…and I know a lot of different ways to cook chicken.
   Q：What is the woman's favorite?

四、听一段长对话，选择正确答案。

M：What are you going to do after you return from Washington?
W：I'm going to stay in the city.
M：What will you do all day?
W：I'm going to work with my father at the store. In the evening, I'll read books. On the weekends, I'll go to beach with my family.
M：Have you ever worked?
W：No, but I can learn. What are you going to do this summer?
M：I'm going to camp. I've gone to camp for four summers.
W：I've never done that. What do you do there?
M：We do many things. In the morning, we go swimming. In the afternoon, we play basketball or tennis. We sit around a fire at night. We sing or tell stories.
W：That sounds wonderful.
M：It is wonderful. What's John going to do this summer?
W：I think he's going to the mountains with his parents.
M：Well, so long, Mary. Have fun.
W：You too, Peter. Give my regards to John. I'll see you in September.

五、听短文，回答下面五个问题，选择正确答案。

It was quite late at night. I was reading a newspaper alone in my room when I heard someone knocking at the door. I opened it and saw a young man with glasses standing there. He said that he was a friend of my brother's and wanted to have a talk with him. I didn't know if my brother had such a friend, but I had to let him in.

As we talked, I found that he knew nothing about my brother. Then I came to know that his words were not true. Suddenly my brother rushed in and the young man was so surprised that he didn't know what to do for a moment. We caught the man and called the police at the same time.

Unit 12

Section Five

一、听写单词和短语。

1. unusual　2. suit　3. robbery　4. slippery　5. accident
6. draw another number　7. quite a while
8. play truant　9. a famous scientist
10. a few moments ago

二、对话理解。根据你所听到的对话及问题选择正确答案。

1. M：What day was it yesterday?

W: It was Thursday.

Q: What day is it today?

2. M: May I use your dictionary? I forgot to bring mine.

W: Certainly, here you are.

Q: Where do you think the man and the woman are talking now?

3. M: Did you watch the table tennis match on TV last night, Jenny?

W: No, I went to the cinema.

Q: What did Jenny do last night?

4. M: Don't read in bed, Mary. It's bad for your eyes.

W: OK, Dad.

Q: What is Mary doing?

5. M: When did the war on Iraq break out?

W: It broke out on March 20, 2003.

M: Where is the president of Iraq? Has he died?

W: Yes, hc has been killed.

Q: What are they talking about?

三、短文理解。根据你所听到的短文内容及问题选择正确答案。

Jim Green is a 15-year-old English schoolboy. His sister Kate is 14. At present, Jim and Kate are at a school in Sydney, one of the biggest cities in Australia. They have been there for two years. They like the school, but they know that soon they will leave and return to England with their parents. Jim and Kate have also been to schools in America, France, Japan and China. This is because their father, Mr. Green, works for a very big international company. The company has sent him to work in many different countries. Mr. Green usually stays in one country for about two years. Then the company moves him again. His family always goes with him. The Greens are a happy family and love seeing the world. Jim and Kate have learned to speak French, Japanese and a little Chinese. The two children have friends all over the world. But they are glad that they are going to return to England. Recently, the children told their parents, "We want to stay in England. We don't want to move again." Their father agreed and he asked his company to keep him in England. The company has agreed. Jim and Kate are very happy about this.

Questions:

1. Where are Jim and Kate now?
2. How long have they been in that country?
3. How many languages can Jim and Kate speak?
4. Which country are the Greens going to return to?
5. Why are Jim and Kate very happy?

Unit 13

Section Five

一、听写单词和短语。

1. waste 2. parcel 3. ground 4. lovely 5. match
6. play a trick on 7. throw away 8. blow up
9. light a fire 10. knock at the door

二、对话理解。根据对话内容选择问题的正确答案。

1. M: Hi, Lucy. Have you seen my jacket?

W: Oh, yes. I saw it on your desk just now.

Q: What's the boy looking for?

2. M：Have you read the story about Thomas Edison?
W：Yes, I have. He was a great inventor. He was born in 1847 and died in 1931.
Q：When was Edison born?
3. M：Would you like to climb hills or stay at home this Saturday?
W：Neither. I prefer shopping.
Q：What would the woman like to do this Saturday?
4. M：Lily, why didn't you come to school yesterday? Were you ill?
W：No. My mum asked me to stay at home to take care of my granny. She was ill.
Q：Who was ill yesterday?
5. W：Hello. 809612.
M：This is Tom.
W：I'm afraid you got the wrong number.
M：Sorry. I want … I want 809621.
Q：What's the number the man called?

三、短文理解。根据短文内容选择问题的正确答案。

Mr. Green was a dance teacher. He was a nice man and always had a lot of students. They came to his classes every week. Every year, he moved to a new town, and was soon teaching a lot of students in the dance school there, but then he decided to move again to a big city. He said that he would have more work there. A woman came to his classes quite often. When the woman heard that he was going to leave, she said, "A new teacher will take your place, won't he? But I don't think he will be as good as you are." Mr. Green was happy when he heard this, but he said, "Oh, no! I'm sure he'll be as good as I am—even better." The woman said, "No, five teachers have come and gone while I've been here, and each new one was worse than the last."

Questions:
1. Where did Mr. Green teach dancing?
2. How often did his students come to his classes?
3. Why did Mr. Green move to a big city?
4. What did the woman think of Mr. Green?
5. Which is wrong from this story?

Unit 14

Section Five

一、根据听到的句子，从所给的A、B、C三个选项中选择符合题意的图画。

1. My mother bought a Hello Kitty clock for me. It's very lovely.
2. Last summer my parents and I went to Italy for our holiday.
3. I like Japanese food especially sushi.
4. We were clapping our hands when we saw the parade.
5. The CD-Room is designed by Nancy Jackson.

二、听对话，回答问题。

1. M：Can I come to your library and borrow some books?
W：Sure. We are open until 5 : 50.
2. W：How many students are there in your class?
M：Forty.
W：But how many of them have got the books?
M：Twenty-five.
3. W：Lucy is taller than Kate.

M: Yes, but Sam is taller than Lucy.

4. W: It's cloudy today, isn't it?

M: Yes, it is. It was cloudy yesterday, too.

5. M: What kind of clothes do you like to wear?

W: I like to wear a blouse but my brother likes to wear a sweater.

三、听下面四段材料，从题中所给 A、B、C 三个选项中选出最佳答案。

听第一段材料，回答第 1 ~2 题。

W: Excuse me. Which is the way to the nearest supermarket?

M: Go down the street, then turn left at the second crossing. At the end of the road, you will find it.

W: Can I get there by bus?

M: Certainly. You can take the No. 17 bus.

W: Thank you very much. Byebye.

M: Bye.

听第二段材料，回答第 3 ~4 题。

M: Have you ever visited Dalian this spring?

W: Yes, many times.

M: How do you like Dalian?

W: Very much, it's a big city, and it is beautiful.

M: I think so.

听第三段材料，回答第 5 ~7 题。

M: Hello! Mary! You don't look well. Are you feeling all right?

W: Not really.

M: I'm sorry to hear that. What's the matter?

W: Nothing serious. I just have a cold.

M: I'm sorry to hear that. You'd better go to see a doctor.

W: No, I took some medicine just now. I'll be OK soon.

M: All right. Have a good rest.

W: Thanks. I will.

听第四段材料，回答第 8 ~10 题。

W: Good morning. Can I help you?

M: Yes, I'd like to have a room for two nights.

W: Well, we still have rooms on the third, the fourth and the seventh floor.

M: OK. I'd like to live on the third floor. How much should I pay for one night?

W: 80 dollars.

M: Do you have hot water in the room?

W: Yes, 24 hours.

M: What time are the meals served?

W: Breakfast begins at 7 : 00, lunch 11 : 30 and supper 5 : 30 p. m.

M: Can anyone show me to my room?

W: Look, that boy over there will.

M: Thanks.

四、你将听到一段短文，然后你将看到五个问题，每个问题有三个供选择的答案，请你根据短文内容选择适当答案。

Hello, my name is Li Lei, I am going to show you around my hometown. First, here is my house. It's a small house. We have a garden. My mother grows vegetables and flowers in the garden. Outside the garden is a bus stop. It takes about ten minutes to get to the nearest town. There are lots of buildings there. There is a shopping center and a cinema. There is also a park near the center of the town. I like going into town on my bike. The town is near the sea. I often go swimming in summer when it's warm and sunny. There is not much pollution in the town because cars are not allowed to go into the center of the town.

I have lots of friends here. I think it's a wonderful place to live. I hope you'll like it.

Unit 15

Section Five

一、听录音完成句子。

1. Please turn left into Zhongshan Road and drive along.
2. Now turn right at the lights.
3. There is a tourist information centre on the first floor.
4. Go straight ahead at the crossroads.
5. Could you tell me the way to the town hall?

二、听句子,选出与之相关的回答。

1. When did the last train leave?
2. How long have you been in Germany?
3. Who helped you with your Chinese?
4. How many bridges are there across the Yangtze River in Wuhan?
5. How did you go to school yesterday?
6. What did you think of the movie *Avatar*?

三、听一段对话，根据内容选择对应的答案。

W: How do you come here every day?

M: I usually take a bus.

W: Then how long does the trip take you?

M: Well, you know, it always takes me twenty-five minutes and I leave at half past seven so that I can arrive at the office five minutes earlier than the others. I'm terribly sorry but the bus broke down half way and I did run so quickly.

W: It doesn't matter since it's the first time and you are just ten minutes late. Remember to be on time tomorrow.

M: I will. Thank you.

四、听独白,回答问题。

Dear Betty,

July 6th is Amy's birthday. We'll hold a party at Amy's home at two o'clock this afternoon. We'll dance and sing, and we'll also eat a big cake. We'll be very happy if you can come to join us. If you don't come, Amy will feel unhappy.

Her home is not far from our school. If you come, you may go straight along Dreams Road for ten minutes, and then you'll find a studio on the left. Amy's home is just beside it. Hope to see you at the party.

Yours,

Jack

五、听几段小对话,完成下列各题。

听第一段对话,完成第 1 ~2 题。

W: Hi, Patrick. The suit is gorgeous. When did you buy it?

M: I didn't buy it. I borrowed it from a friend as I had an interview.

听第二段对话,完成第 3 题。

W: Frank and James are plying badminton. Let's go and play with them.

M: I'd love to, but I have to do my homework first.

听第三段对话,完成第 4 题。

W: Is the Science Museum far away from here?

M: No, it takes only 10 minutes by bike.

听第四段对话,完成第 5 题。

M: When shall we move into the new house?

W: Tomorrow afternoon. Pack your books this morning!

听第五段对话,完成第 6 题。

W: Today is January 20. It's your birthday. Happy birthday to you!

M: Oh, thank you very much, but my birthday is tomorrow.

六、听一首英语诗歌,完成下列各题。

Just for You

I picked the reddest apple from the tree.
It was the finest one that I could see.
I saved it all except a bite or two. Just for you.
I carried home the groceries from the store.
I wanted to be helpful with a chore.
I put them all away except a few. Just for you.

Unit 16

Section Five

一、情景应答,根据听到的内容选择正确的答语。

1. We don't have to go to school tomorrow, do you know?
2. What does she look like?
3. Do you think they should also be treated with kindness?
4. The organizers chose me to be the host of the charity show.
5. Did you use to play the piano?

二、听对话,选择正确的答语。

听下面五段对话,每段对话后各有一个问题,请选择正确的答语。

1. W: I feel very tired. I can't go to work.
   M: Let me have a look. It's nothing serious. Take this medicine three times a day.
   W: Thank you, sir.
   Q: Where are they?
2. W: I'm going to do some shopping.
   M: Get me a toothbrush. OK?
   W: OK.
   Q: Where is the woman going?
3. W: Tom, there's a telephone call for you half an hour ago.
   M: Oh, who was it?
   W: It was your uncle.
   Q: Who made a telephone call half an hour ago?
4. W: This bus goes to the hospital, doesn't it?
   M: Yes, it does.
   W: Where should I get off?
   M: At Fourth Street.
   Q: Where are they?

5. W：Shall we make another cup of tea?
   M：Why not?
   Q：What does the man mean?

听下面一段对话，回答第6～7题。

W：What do you want to be when you grow up, John?
M：I want to be an astronaut, Mum.
W：Why do you think so?
M：Because I think it must be interesting to watch Earth from space.
W：But you have to be strong and healthy if you want to be an astronaut.
M：You're right, Mum. If you let me play football every day, I'll be stronger.

听下面一段对话，回答第8～10题。

M：Excuse me, Miss Lin. Have you got any VCDs about the life on Mars?
W：Yes, Tom. I've got some.
M：That's great. Could I borrow one, please?
W：Of course, you can. Why do you need it?
M：The science teacher Mr. Smith asked us to read books or watch VCDs to know more about Mars. He said you had some VCDs.
W：Are you interested in the life on Mars?
M：Yes, and so are my classmates.
W：Oh, I see. Here it is. I hope it can be helpful to you.
M：Thank you, Miss Lin.
W：You are welcome.

三、听短文，根据短文内容选择正确答案。

There was once a large, fat woman. She had a small, thin husband. He worked in a big office and got his weekly pay every Friday evening. As soon as he got home on Fridays, he had to give his wife all his money, and his wife gave him back only enough to buy his lunch in the office every day.

One day the small man came home very happily. He hurried into the living room. His wife was listening to the radio and eating apples there.

"You'll never guess what happened to me today, dear," he said. He waited for a few seconds and then said again, "I won ten thousand dollars buying the lottery tickets!"

"That's wonderful!" shouted his wife. Happily. But then she thought for a few seconds and said angrily, "But wait a minute! How could you have enough money to buy the tickets?"

Unit 17

Section Five

一、情景反应。听问句，选出恰当的答语。

1. I'm sorry I'm late.
2. Shall we go hiking this afternoon?
3. Would you mind if I open the window?
4. What does she look like?
5. How long have you been there?

二、对话理解。根据对话内容选择问题的正确答案。

1. M：Lucy, what's your favorite sport?
   W：Football. I like playing football best.
   Q：What's Lucy's favorite sport?
2. M：Did you go hiking last Sunday?

W: Yes, what about you?
M: I went fishing. That's my hobby, you know.
Q: What's the man's hobby?

3. M: Linda, how are you going to the library today?
W: Oh, I'm going there by bike.
Q: How is Linda going to the library today?
4. M: When is your birthday?
W: Tomorrow. Can you come to my party, Bob?
M: I'd love to. But I'm afraid I will be a little late. I must have a guitar lesson first.
Q: Why will the boy be late for the party?
5. W: Your English is pretty good, Tom. How do you usually study it?
M: There're many ways of learning. I study it by listening to the radio. It really helps.
Q: How does Tom learn English?

听下面一段小对话,完成第6~7题。

M: What time does our football match start on Sunday?
W: The game begins at 2 : 00.
M: Cool! Who are we going to play with?
W: A team of soldiers, surprised?
M: Wow, they must be very strong and have excellent foot skills.
W: Maybe. But soldiers usually give a good game.
M: I'll try my best.
W: Don't hurt your feet these days.
M: Don't worry. See you then.
Questions:
6. When will the match start?
7. Who are they going to play with?

听下面一段较长对话,完成第8~10题。

W: I'm going to Switzerland, but I am a little nervous.
M: Why are you nervous?
W: Because I don't know the culture there.
M: Take it easy! I'm glad to tell you what you should do. Above all, don't be late! Being on time is very important there, because they care about time.
W: I know their watches are very famous.
M: I'd like to buy such a famous watch for my father as a Father's Day present.
W: That's a nice idea.
Questions:
8. Why does the girl feel nervous before going to Switzerland?
9. What are famous in Switzerland?
10. What should the girl do if she goes to a party in Switzerland?

三、短文理解。根据短文内容选择问题的正确答案。

Every mother is great, so is my mother. My mother is a common worker. But I love her very much. She is tall and of medium build. She has two big eyes. Her hair is black and curly. I think she is very beautiful.

My mother is hard-working like many other mothers. Whenever she is at home or at work, she is always busy. On weekends, she often cleans our house and she likes planting flowers, too. She often says, "Flowers can make the air fresh and keep the house beautiful." She often gives flowers to her friends.

She is strict in my study. She often says to me, "Study is the most important thing to a student. You must study hard. Then you can do more and better for others and yourself. " And she is also kind to me. When I have trouble, I'd like to ask her for help.

Questions:

1. What does the mother do?
2. What is the mother like?
3. What does the mother like doing?
4. Who does she often give flowers to?
5. What is important to a student from the passage?

Unit 18

Section Five

一、选出你听到的单词。

1. planning 2. would 3. go skiing 4. offer 5. learn 6. dubbing

二、听句子，选出与之相关的回答。

1. Would you like to come with me?
2. How much pork do you want?
3. Can you help me with the heavier box?
4. Why do you go over all the textbooks?
5. How did he go there?

三、听几段对话，根据内容选择意义相近的答案。

1. M: Have you played games on the Ipad?
   W: Of course! They are pretty fun.
2. M: Have you heard from Nikko?
   W: No, not recently. She is quite busy.
3. M: Would you like some coffee or tea?
   W: Neither. Thanks. I prefer diet-cola.

四、听一段独白，回答问题。

Do you know how to make perfect tea? First, choose the tea leaves. You can get some of your favorite tea, either black or green. Then, use your tea-spoon to get enough tea. If you like a strong flavor or a sleepless night, you can take a full teaspoonful or even two. Or usually, half a teaspoonful is okay if you want a sound sleep. The third step is to boil water. It's easy for you, isn't it? And here comes the last. Put the tea and boiling water into a cup and let it stew for about two minutes. See? A perfect cup of tea is ready! Enjoy it!

五、听几段小对话，完成下列各题。

听第一段对话，完成第1～2题。

W: Where are you going tomorrow?

M: I will take Jason, Irene, Mata together with their mum to the cinema tomorrow.

W: Is the new Three-D movie on?

M: Yes, and they want to see the IMAX. You know it's 6 dollars for an adult and half the price for a kid.

听第二段对话，完成第3～5题。

W: Wow! Nice bicycle!

M: Yeah. It takes me to school every day.

W: You guys are having busy days for your science lessons, right?

M: Not really. Normally we have two classes which last three hours in the morning. And in the afternoon, we spend two hours doing experiments.

W: So what are you killing times?

M: Well, I often go and play the guitar with our band in a club after school.

听第三段对话，完成第 6 ~ 8 题。

W: Would you like to go to the party?

M: Well, I feel under the weather. I guess I will go there next time.

W: What's the matter with you? Did you see the doctors?

M: No. There is a pain in my back and I just think I will be fine soon.

W: You'd better make an appointment with the doctor at once.

M: OK. Thanks.

六、听一段短文，回答问题。

One day, James Lee went to a mall to buy a pair of gloves for his wife as her birthday present. "We have woolen gloves, cotton gloves and the gloves made of leather," the salesgirl said. "What material does your wife prefer?" Mr. Lee didn't even have a look and replied, "Woolen." The salesgirl then took out several pairs and went on asking, "What color do you want?" Mr. Lee was a little bothered and said, "Purple. Whatever." "Do you know her size? Medium or large?" the girl continued. Mr. Lee got angry and shouted, "Just give me a pair. Any size is OK. It is certain that she will come here with the gloves tomorrow and get them changed anyway."

七、听一首英语诗歌 *Friends Lullaby*，完成下列各题。

The stars out, the moon is up. It's time to go to bed.
I'm so glad you have a place to lay your little head.
Have a deep and peaceful sleep. Dream away the hours.
When you wake the sun will come, to smile upon the flowers.
Go to sleep my little friend, beneath the evening star.
You will always have a friend, no matter where you are.

期末考试(一)

一、听力理解部分(30 分)

第一节(共 6 小题，每小题 1 分，满分 6 分)

听下面 6 个问题。每个问题后有三个答语，从题中所给 A、B、C 三个选项中选出最佳选项。听完每个问题后，你都有 5 秒钟的时间来作答和阅读下一小题。每个问题仅读一遍。

1. What day is it today?
2. How have you been these years?
3. What's your favorite kind of music?
4. How much do you know about the works of Henry?
5. Excuse me, what's the time by your watch, please?
6. What do you do?

第二节(共 6 小题，每小题 1 分，满分 6 分)

听下面 6 段对话。每段对话后有一个小题，从题中所给 A、B、C 三个选项中选出最佳选项。听完每段对话后，你都有 10 秒钟的时间来作答和阅读下一小题。每段对话仅读一遍。

7. M: Jessica, I'm going to the library. I need a picture book.
   W: Can you help me return the cookbook and the storybook?
   M: Sure.
8. M: May I use your dictionary? I forgot to bring mine.
   W: Certainly, here you are.
9. M: How often do you exercise?

W：I keep running every day，sometimes I go swimming，but I never play ball games.

10. M：How many people are there in your family?

W：Three of them are in India. In fact，there are too many to count.

M：What about here in Wuhan?

W：Oh，there's my dad and mom，and my two brothers and I.

11. W：I'm afraid I can't meet you at 10 in the library.

M：Then we'd better make it an hour later in the classroom.

W：That's all right.

12. M：Hi，Linda. Are you going to have a picnic this Saturday?

W：No，we aren't. We're going to plant trees this Saturday morning. Will you join us?

M：That's good. But Bob asked me to go to swim with him. I'll tell him I won't go.

第三节(共18小题,每小题1分,满分18分)

听下面4段对话或独白。每段对话或独白后有几个小题,从题中所给的A、B、C三个选项中选出最佳选项。听每段对话和独白前,你将有时间阅读各个小题,每小题5秒钟;听完后,各小题将给出5秒钟的作答时间,每段对话或独白读两遍。

听第13段材料,完成第13~15题。

W：Hi，Mike.

M：Hi，Lucy. Are you free this afternoon?

W：I'm afraid not. I'm going to the shop to buy some presents for Mrs. Zhao，our Chinese teacher.

M：Oh，I see. The day after tomorrow will be Teachers' Day. What are you going to buy?

W：I'm going to buy a postcard or a pen for her.

M：But I know she likes flowers very much，why not buy some flowers?

W：That's a good idea.

听第14段材料,完成第16~18题。

M：Excuse me. How can I get to No. 1 Middle School?

W：Sorry，I'm also new in this city.

M：Thank you all the same. Do you come to visit the city?

W：Not the city，but my daughter. She's working at No. 1 Middle School.

M：That's fun. What's her name?

W：Julie Brown.

M：Oh，she teaches my son English.

听第15段材料,完成第19~21题。

W：Hello，332440.

M：Oh hello，Sally. This is Dave Thomson here. Could I speak to Jim，please?

W：I'm afraid he's not in at the moment，Dave. He went out about an hour ago and he's not back yet.

M：Any idea when he might be back?

W：Well，he shouldn't be long. He said he was just going to get some paint. But I wouldn't be surprised if he's stopped off at the pub on the way back.

M：OK. Well，please tell him I've called，and I'll try again later.

W：All right. Goodbye，Dave.

M：Thanks then，Sally. Goodbye.

听第16段材料,完成第22~25题。

W：When was America discovered，Tony?

M：I'm not certain. Do you know?

W：America was discovered by Christopher Columbus in 1492.

M：In a way that's right. But the Vikings travelled there long before Columbus. And what about the

Red Indians?

W: All right. Ask me a question now.

M: Who invented the electric light bulb?

W: That's easy. It was invented by Edison.

M: Correct. Now a harder question. Who will be the first men on Mars?

W: I can't answer that. But I think Mars will be visited by men before the end of this century.

听第 17 段材料,完成第 26 ~30 题。

The car was invented just a century ago. You may know all kinds of cars' names, but many people don't know who was the inventor of the first car. The first car was invented not by a German, but by an American. His name was Henry Ford. Henry was born in a poor family. He was the eldest of six children. When he was a boy, he became interested in mending watches and machines. When he was twelve years old, his mother died. Soon he had to work in a machine shop for two dollars and fifty cents a week. In the evenings he repaired watches for another dollar a week. The hard life made him strong and able. At that time there was another interest in the life of the young Ford. He dreamed to make a machine. It could run without a horse, so named "horseless carriage." He overcame a lot of difficulties and in April 1893, the "horseless carriage" was finally finished. It was the first car. Later Henry Ford founded the Ford Motor Company. He was really the first inventor of the car in the world.

请同学们将试卷翻到第二部分,完成听写部分的试题。

一、听写,听一篇文章并根据所听内容补全所缺单词 (5 分)

Hey Bill. This is Hank. I'm just calling to let you know that I'll be a little late to the game tomorrow night. I have to work a few extra hours at work to finish a report. I should wrap things up sometime between seven and eight though. Oh, then I'm planning on dropping by Lisa's house for about an hour since she's been sick recently. And, uh, one more thing. I'll swing by my house to pick up some food for the game. See you then.

期末考试(二)

一、听力理解部分(25 分)

第一节(共 10 个小题,每小题 1 分,满分 10 分)

第一部分(5 分)

听下面 5 个小对话,从题中所给的 A、B、C 三个图片中选出最佳选项。听完每个对话后,你有 5 秒钟的时间来作答和阅读下一小题。每个问题仅读一遍。

1. W: How is the weather in Wuhan today?
   M: Oh, it's sunny and pretty hot.
2. W: How do you usually go to school, David?
   M: On foot. Because walking is a good way to exercise.
3. W: Hi, Tony. It's Father's Day tomorrow. What will you give to your father?
   M: I will buy him a tie.
4. M: Hey, where's my soccer?
   W: Look! It's under your desk.
5. W: Wow, cool! What a wonderful picture!
   M: Why, Lisa? Stop touching it. Look at the sign.

第二部分(5 分)

听下面 5 段对话。每段对话后有一个小题,从题中所给的 A、B、C 三个选项中选出最佳选项。听完每段对话后,你有 10 秒钟的时间来回答有关小题和阅读下一小题。每段对话仅读一遍。

6. W：Tom，your watch is very nice.
   M：Thank you，Mary. It's my birthday present from my mother.
7. M：Where do you live?
   W：I like living in the countryside. But I live in the city now.
8. W：You speak English very well. Are you from America?
   M：No，I'm from Germany. Now I'm studying English in a language school.
9. W：What's the matter，Jim?
   M：I can't find my dictionary. Oh，it's here，in my schoolbag.
10. W：What's the weather like today?
    M：The radio says it's snowy. But look，it's rainy outside.

第二节(共15个小题,每小题1分,满分15分)

听下面4段对话或独白。每段对话或独白后有几个小题,从题中所给的A、B、C三个选项中选出最佳选项。听每段对话和独白前,你将有时间阅读各个小题,每小题5秒钟;听完后,各小题将给出5秒钟的作答时间。每段对话或独白读两遍。

听第11段材料,回答第11～13题。

M：Hi，Mary. Are you going to the party tonight?
W：No，I'm not allowed to.
M：You aren't allowed to go to parties，are you?
W：No. There are lots of things I can't do.
M：Like what?
W：Well，I'm not allowed to watch TV on school nights.
M：Really? But there are lots of good shows. You can learn a lot.
W：I'm not allowed to shop for clothes，either. My mother buys them.
M：Do your parents do everything for you?
W：No，but they have lots of rules.
M：Are you allowed to have a pet?
W：No，I'm not allowed to have a pet.
M：What are you allowed to do?
W：My parents say I'm allowed to study all night. Their rules make me a good student.

听第12段材料,回答第14～16题。

M：How do you make fruit salad?
W：First，cut up some bananas，pears and apples.
M：How many?
W：Two bananas，one pear and one apple. Then put the fruit in a bowl.
M：What else do you need?
W：I need a little sugar，some yogurt or cream. Finally mix them up.
M：But how much yogurt do you need?
W：Just one cup of yogurt is enough for me，but my husband likes one more cup.
M：Oh，I know. Thank you very much. Do you eat any other kind of salad in your country?
W：Yes. In England we also like salad with meat and vegetables.

听第13段材料,回答第17～20题。

M：Right. How many languages do you speak? Apart from English，of course.
W：I speak Hindi.
M：Ah. How well do you speak it?
W：Very well. I can write it，too.
M：Any other languages?

W: I can speak a little French. But I can't write it at all.

M: A little French. Can't write it. That's it?

W: Yes.

M: And you want to join our beginners' class in Japanese?

W: Yes, please.

M: Well, it's not going to be easy, you know. It's very different from English, Hindi or French.

W: I know. But I want to do it.

听第14段材料,回答第21~25题。

My wife and I went home from our best friend's birthday party last night. When I was going to open the door with the key, my wife told me that the light was on in the bedroom. As I looked for myself, I saw that there were people in the house taking things.

I phoned the police, but they told me that no one was around in the area to help at that time. They said they would send someone over as soon as they were free. I said OK and waited a minute. Then I phoned the police again. "Hello. I just called you a minute ago because there were people in my house. Well, you don't have to worry about them now because I've shot them all."

Within five minutes there were several police cars in the area. Of course, they caught the thieves in my house.

One of the officers said, "I thought you said that you had shot them!"

"I thought you said there was no police around!" I replied.

请同学们将试卷翻到第二部分,完成听写部分的试题。

一、听写,听一篇文章并根据所听内容补全所缺单词(5分)

Coin collection is one of the oldest hobbies. In the past it was often enjoyed by kings and scholars. It is also a pleasant way of saving.

The designs on coins tell many stories. The coins of a country often are a record of its history and geography. Some ancient coins tell us all we know about a country or a period of history. They bring us portraits of rulers who would be otherwise unknown. Coins tell us about the art, religion, dress and hairstyle of people who lived long ago.

Your special interests will help you decide the kind of coin collection you would like to have. You may wish to collect the coins of one country or one part of the world. Or you may want your collection to contain coins from all over the world in a certain period of time.

To get the most enjoyment from your hobby of coin collecting, read as much as you can on the subject. Try to form a group of collector friends. If you have an old or foreign coin, find out where and when it was made, its name and value, and what you could have bought with it when it was in use.

图书在版编目(CIP)数据

外语学校初中英语综合运用能力等级教程. Learn It. 二级/武汉实验外国语学校组编;钱晶晶,徐佳主编. —武汉:武汉大学出版社,2012. 10

武汉实验外国语学校校本课程/丛书主编:李茵　丛书副主编:王永汉　外语类总主编:徐涛　蔡文静

ISBN 978-7-307-09933-3

Ⅰ. 外…　Ⅱ. ①武…　②钱…　③徐…　Ⅲ. 英语课—初中—教材　Ⅳ. G634.411

中国版本图书馆 CIP 数据核字(2012)第 130856 号

责任编辑:叶玲利　　责任校对:刘　欣　　版式设计:韩闻锦

出版发行:**武汉大学出版社**　(430072　武昌　珞珈山)

(电子邮件:wdp4@ whu. edu. cn 网址:www. wdp. com. cn)

印刷:湖北恒泰印务有限公司

开本:880×1230　1/16　印张:20.5　字数:504 千字　插页:1

版次:2012 年 10 月第 1 版　　2012 年 10 月第 1 次印刷

ISBN 978-7-307-09933-3/G・2552　　定价:87.00 元(含磁带 2 盘)

Keys

Unit 1

Section One

一、1. D 2. C 3. A 4. B 5. C 6. B 7. C 8. D 9. C 10. D

二、1. first 2. find 3. never 4. shop 5. gym

三、1. My name is Li Lixin. 2. Nice to meet you, too.
3. See you! 4. It's September 5th.
5. My birthday is on February the 19th.

四、1. Bring those spoons to me. 2. Give that parcel to him.
3. Read the poem to her. 4. Show the film to them.
5. I am going to tell you the news. 6. Can you turn it off?
7. Show them to us. 8. Can you try it on?
9. Pass it to him. 10. I am going to give it to you.

五、1. Does; do 2. doesn't
3. How excited 4. When
5. Who

Section Two

一、1. D 2. A 3. C 4. B 5. A 6. C 7. D 8. A 9. D 10. D

二、1. Mr. Li is giving her class a lesson.
2. Don't look out of the window.
3. What can you see in the pond?
4. There are two children playing on the playground.
5. I can see a plane flying in the sky.

三、④,②, ①, ⑤,③

四、1. There are some boys sitting beside a tree.
2. I can see a girl swimming across the river.
3. Is there a cat lying under the chair?
4. I can't see a boy listening to the radio in the dorm.
5. Where is the UFO flying?

五、1. enjoying himself 2. usually visit
3. How often does; meet
4. Lisa always goes to see her grandmother on Sundays.
5. goes, on foot

六、1. What's wrong with you/ What's the matter with you
2. Why don't you go to see a doctor
3. how are you feeling

Section Three

一、1. D 2. D 3. B 4. A 5. C 6. C 7. B 8. D 9. C 10. D

二、1. on 2. in 3. on 4. for 5. by; through 6. with 7. in 8. with; for/at

三、1. B 2. C 3. A 4. B 5. A 6. B 7. A 8. C 9. A 10. C

四、1. Sam and Bob don't want to make a toy car.
2. They don't usually get up early every day.

3. I don't always stay at home at the weekends.
4. Does Jim live in Paris?
5. Do Diana and Maria begin work at 8 o'clock?
6. Do you like eating fresh fruit?
7. When does she usually read English?

Section Four

一、1. B 2. A 3. A 4. D 5. D 6. D 7. A 8. C 9. B 10. C

二、1. She is a terrible gossip.
2. I am going to weigh myself on this weighing machine.
3. My grandparents live next to me.
4. Mr. Li usually leaves home at 7.
5. Can you tell me the way to the railway station?

三、1. C 2. C 3. A 4. C 5. C

四、1. Does Mrs. Green do the housework every day?
2. Sandy isn't riding his bicycle.
3. ①How often does he go to school by bus? ②How does he usually go to school?
4. We are going to go to the library tomorrow.

Section Five

一、1. stir 2. sticking-plaster 3. my goodness 4. February 5. store-room
6. nasty 7. beard 8. bake a cake 9. terrible 10. money-box

二、1. C 2. A 3. E 4. B 5. D

三、1. C 2. C 3. C 4. A 5. B

四、1. A 2. C 3. C 4. B 5. B 6. A 7. C 8. C 9. A 10. C 11. A 12. A 13. B 14. D 15. B

五、1. known 2. caused 3. hardly 4. wear 5. cloud 6. worst 7. became
8. lift 9. result 10. stopped

六、1. B 2. D 3. A 4. A 5. C 6. A 7. A 8. B 9. C 10. B

七、1. B 2. B 3. A 4. D 5. D

八、1. Pass it to him. 2. There is a dog playing in the garden.
3. Tim doesn't come from Australia. 4. What do you often do in the afternoon?
5. When does she usually get up? 6. He won't go to work on foot next week.

九、1. what will you do for your 2. we will go hiking in the mountains
3. going boating 4. What about you? / Do you have any plans?
5. Have a good time

Unit 2

Section One

一、1. A 2. B 3. B 4. D 5. B 6. C 7. B 8. D 9. A 10. B

二、1. healthy 2. study 3. difference 4. favourite 5. exercise 6. telephone
7. class 8. friends 9. test 10. your

三、1. She doesn't have many books. 2. They don't have much glue.
3. There isn't much jam in the can. 4. I can't see any rice in the bowl.

5. Do you want an orange?　　6. Are there many shoes in the locker?
7. Does his daughter eat an apple every day?
8. How much ink does she have?
9. How many sandwiches are there in the basket?
10. How much cake do you need?

四、1. here 2. message 3. hope 4. inviting 5. when

Section Two

一、1. B 2. B 3. D 4. C 5. D 6. C 7. C 8. C 9. A 10. C

二、1. February 2. June 3. October 4. three 5. five 6. twelve 7. twenty 8. second 9. Wednesday 10. Monday

三、1. D 2. B 3. A 4. C 5. B 6. A 7. B 8. D 9. B 10. D

四、1. How much tea has Mr. Grant/does Mr. Grant have?
2. ①How many bicycles do you have?　②What do you have?
3. I need 2 pieces of paper.
4. It wants 3 bones.

五、1. What, the matter 2. Why not give 3. didn't find, anywhere 4. What were you doing 5. Where was

Section Three

一、1. A 2. D 3. A 4. D 5. A 6. A 7. C 8. C 9. A 10. B

二、1. You can make some glue with flore and water.
2. How much money does he have?
3. Her schoolbag is full of books.
4. I am going to hang this picture here.
5. What's the weather like outside?
6. My umbrella leaks.
7. What do you think of the music?
8. What is the cup made of?

三、1. cooks 2. teaches 3. is introducing 4. goes 5. is sleeping 6. am waiting 7. are 8. touch 9. is repairing 10. is studying

四、1. It's February the 21st.　It's April the 18th.
It's August the 17th.　It's March the 2nd.
It's October the 3rd.　It's July the 31st.
2. ①The bag made of plastic is expensive.
②It's cloudy today.
③How does it look outside?
3. How does my hairstyle look?

五、1. D 2. A 3. C 4. D 5. B 6. A 7. B 8. C 9. D 10. B

Section Four

一、1. C 2. D 3. D 4. C 5. C 6. A 7. A 8. B 9. C 10. C

二、1. How does the chocolate taste?
2. The strong policeman have big feet.
3. Does it feel like silk?
What does it feel like?

4. Jake doesn't like playing football very much.
   Does Jake like playing football very much?
5. What is Jessie doing in the park?
6. How many tourists are there on the tour bus?
7. Where is the bank?

三、1. A 2. D 3. B 4. A 5. C

Section Five

一、1. what a rush 2. go to school
3. photograph 4. parcel
5. balloon 6. interesting
7. tourist 8. heavy shower
9. terrible gossip 10. weighing machine

二、1. G 2. D 3. A 4. B 5. F 6. C 7. E

三、1. B 2. A 3. C 4. A 5. B

四、1. C 2. B 3. A 4. B 5. C 6. B 7. A 8. A 9. C 10. D 11. A 12. D 13. A 14. C 15. B

五、1. B 2. C 3. B 4. A 5. D

六、1. three 2. number 3. How 4. an 5. same 6. not 7. cake 8. Where 9. that 10. these

七、1. There aren't many tomatoes in the fridge.
2. That man is not going to sing a song.
3. Does it sound nice?
4. Does she need much bread?
5. How much toothpaste does your father want?

八、1. My mother is a math teacher. 2. Jill's birthday is on April 15th.
3. Don't smoke in the classroom. 4. I come from Paris.

Unit 3

Section One

一、1. D 2. C 3. C 4. B 5. D 6. D

二、1. It's seven o'clock. 2. It's twenty-eight past one.
3. It's two past two. 4. It's a quarter to one.
5. It's twenty-five to twelve. 6. It's three to five.
7. It's half past five. 8. It's a quarter past nine.

三、1. It's twenty to three. 2. It's ten past six.
3. It's three thirty. 4. It's four forty-five.
5. It's eight thirty-five. 6. It's twelve fifteen.

四、1. × 2. the 3. an 4. the;the 5. × 6. × 7. a;The 8. × 9. × 10. the 11. the

五、1. My work starts at seven thirty.
2. When do you usually arrive at the cinema on Sundays?
3. The TV programme is going to be over at half past eleven.
4. Mike goes to work on foot.
5. I usually do my homework after school.

六、1. What time does Mr. Lee usually go to work?
Mr. Lee usually goes to work at 8:15.
2. What time do you usually go shopping?
I usually go shopping at 2 p. m.
3. What time does Kate usually go to sleep?
Kate usually goes to sleep at 9 : 50.
4. When do the students usually have classes?
The students usually have classes in the morning.
5. When does Alan usually watch TV?
Alan usually watches TV at noon.
6. When does Lily usually play tennis?
Lily usually plays tennis in the afternoon.

Section Two

一、1. D 2. C 3. B 4. D 5. A 6. A
二、1. at 2. like 3. at; at 4. in 5. by 6. at 7. in 8. by 9. on 10. in
三、1. It's Tuesday. 2. It's July 26th.
3. It's July 27th. 4. It's Monday.
四、1. seven o'clock in the evening 2. three o'clock in the morning
3. half past eight in the morning 4. a quarter to five in the afternoon
5. six to three in the afternoon 6. five to twelve in the morning
7. eighteen past one in the morning 8. a quarter past nine in the evening
五、A. always B. usually C. often D. sometimes E. seldom F. hardly G. never
六、1. Does Mike often get up at 6 : 30?
2. Do your family always go to Brighton in summer?
3. The plane doesn't leave at 15 : 00.
4. We haven't any Brazilian coffee.
5. What time does Mike often go to bed? 6. Where does Steffen work?
7. How does your uncle usually travel? 8. What time is it?
9. What's the date today?
七、略

Section Three

一、1. D 2. C 3. A 4. D 5. C
二、1. likes 2. watches 3. don't like 4. is 5. finishes 6. go 7. comes; begins
三、1. casual clothes 2. international community 3. mean 4. social activities 5. in the evening
6. in the library 7. sporting events 8. get up 9. rise
四、1. play 2. have 3. make 4. do 5. make 6. go 7. do 8. do 9. have 10. go 11. do
12. play
五、1. Monday 2. Friday 3. Wednesday 4. Sunday 5. Tuesday 6. Thursday 7. Saturday
六、1. Does the cat often chase the mouse?
2. She lives in a small town near Paris.
3. British people have tea at about four o'clock.
4. That businesswoman goes to work by train every morning.
5. Jack does not do his homework at school.
6. I have a break in the cafeteria at ten.

七、1. B 2. A 3. C 4. A 5. D 6. A 7. B 8. D 9. C 10. A 11. B 12. D 13. A 14. D 15. B

Section Four

一、1. B 2. D 3. A 4. C 5. C 6. A 7. B

二、1. calendar 2. quarter 3. smart 4. forward 5. aerobics 6. possible 7. secretary

三、1. introduction 2. British 3. companies 4. closed 5. flies 6. teaches

四、1. A 2. D 3. A 4. C 5. D

五、1. It isn't often hot in summer.
2. How many students are there in this college?
3. How often does her mother work at home?

六、1. D 2. A 3. B 4. C

七、Dear Sir/Madam,

I'm writing to ask for information about your winter courses in King's College. My name is Andy. I'm a student at St. Mary Secondary School and I'm 13 years old now. I would like to take a course in your college in winter. Please send me information about dates and fees as soon as possible. Thank you!

Yours faithfully,

Andy

Section Five

一、1. institute 2. excellent 3. activity 4. calendar 5. break 6. concert 7. midnight 8. situated 9. casual 10. routine

二、1. C 2. A 3. A 4. B 5. B 6. C

三、1. A 2. C 3. B 4. B 5. C 6. C 7. A

四、1. C 2. B 3. C 4. A 5. B 6. C 7. C

五、1. special 2. presents 3. markets 4. evening 5. lucky

六、1. C 2. C 3. B 4. B 5. D 6. C 7. B 8. A 9. A 10. D

七、1. B 2. D 3. A 4. C 5. B 6. A 7. C 8. C 9. B 10. A 11. C 12. D 13. A 14. D 15. B

八、1. A 2. C 3. B 4. D 5. A

九、1. I wouldn't like any vegetables. 2. What time does the film start?
3. When is your birthday? 4. Jason goes to school on foot every day.
5. Tim usually takes a taxi to work.

十、1. from 2. to 3. at 4. on 5. in 6. with 7. at 8. in 9. with 10. between

Unit 4

Section One

一、1. Monday, Tuesday, Wednesday, Thursday, Friday 2. Saturday and Sunday 3. strong 4. ill 5. awful 6. healthy

二、

1. 9:05	nine o five	five past nine
2. 10:15	ten fifteen	a quarter past ten
3. 12:30	twelve thirty	half past twelve
4. 1:15	one fifteen	a quarter past one

5. 4:45 four forty-five a quarter to five
6. 6:55 six fifty-five five to seven
7. 11:35 eleven thirty-five twenty-five to twelve

三、2. What's Sue like?
She looks neat and tidy. She has a pretty skirt.
3. What's Billy like?
He looks naughty. He has dirty hands.
4. What's Peter like?
He looks strong. He has great muscles.
6. How does Lucy feel?
She feels hot. She has a temperature.
7. How does Sandy feel?
He feels terrible. He has a toothache.
8. How does Frank feel?
He feels sick. He has a stomachache.
9. How does Tony feel?
He feels awful. He has measles.
11. What's the matter with Mother?
She feels bad.
She has an earache, so she must call the doctor.
12. What's the matter with Mike?
He feels sick.
He has a stomachache, so he must drink some medicine.
13. What's the matter with Simon?
He feels ill.
He has mumps, so he must remain in bed.

四、1. D 2. B 3. D 4. B 5. B 6. D 7. D

Section Two

一、1. D 2. B 3. A 4. B 5. B 6. A

二、1. No Parking 2. No Smoking 3. No Drink
4. No Food 5. No Stepping 6. No Photograph

三、1. Don't put a penny in the slot. 2. The machine doesn't work.
3. Don't drink this medicine. 4. It doesn't taste awful.
5. Must Mother finish the work at once? 6. Can't we talk in the library?
7. Will he go to the concert this Friday? 8. Do you need a piece of paper?

四、1. Isn't he lucky? / He is so lucky! 2. What's the matter with Sandy?
3. Father has got flu. 4. What's the time? / What time is it?
5. He has got a bad cold. 6. Why does he drink this medicine?
7. It tastes like poison.
8. They feel weak, so they must remain in bed.
9. Billy is sitting on the back seat.
10. He is fast asleep in the sofa.
11. You can't park your car here.
12. Don't play with matches!

Section Three

一、1. medicine 2. stay 3. tongue 4. temperature 5. dentist's

6. remain 7. strawberry 8. poison 9. aspirin 10. matter

二、1. A 2. A 3. B 4. A

三、1. How does he look? 2. How does Simon feel?
3. When is she going to see me? 4. What must Billy do?
5. Where must they stay? 6. What should Peter do?
7. How is Billy? 8. Why mustn't I park here?
9. How do I look today? 10. What can Mr. Black do?

四、1. What do you think of the music? 2. It tastes funny.
3. No smoking or spitting here! 4. How is the weather going to be tomorrow?
5. Because Sandy has measles, he can't go to school.
6. How many books does she have? 7. What can I do for you?
8. Where do you come from? 9. It is like metal.
10. The children are swimming.

五、1. D 2. B 3. A 4. B 5. C 6. D 7. A 8. D 9. A 10. C

Section Four

一、1. himself 2. herself 3. myself 4. ourselves 5. itself
6. yourself 7. themselves 8. strawberries 9. libraries 10. potatoes
11. sandwiches 12. heroes 13. photos

二、1. tongue 2. he must drink this medicine
3. You mustn't park here 4. The police take away the car
5. Help yourself 6. Pour it over yourself
7. You must have a haircut 8. I want to have a shave
9. They're having a fight 10. Because you have a black eye
11. nasty 12. poison

三、1. C 2. A 3. A 4. B 5. B 6. A 7. D 8. D

四、1. A 2. A 3. C 4. D 5. D

Section Five

一、1. Have some vegetables. 2. Let's have a holiday.
3. They are having a fight. 4. Father is smoking.
5. Don't make a noise. 6. He must drink some medicine.
7. She has got an earache.
8. Don't ask him the way because he is a tourist.

二、1. F 2. F 3. T 4. T 5. F 6. F 7. T

三、1. A 2. A 3. B 4. B 5. C

四、1. C 2. B 3. D 4. E 5. A

五、1. funny 2. well 3. waste 4. will finish; leave 5. will leave
6. begin 7. calls 8. rises; sets 9. is running 10. will snow

六、1. When must you see Tom? 2. What must I do?
3. Why can't I park here? 4. How is Simon?
5. Who has a headache

七、1. D 2. A 3. B 4. C 5. B 6. B 7. D 8. B 9. C 10. A 11. C 12. C
13. D 14. B 15. A

八、1. C 2. A 3. B 4. D 5. D

九、1. D 2. A 3. G 4. C 5. F 6. B

十、H→G→E→D→A→B→C→F→I

Unit 5

Section One

一、1. was 2. were 3. was 4. came 5. went 6. sat 7. found 8. told 9. wrote 10. said 11. bought 12. made

二、1. funfair 2. Yesterday 3. library 4. key 5. prison 6. bathroom 7. barber's 8. diary 9. dentist's 10. stationer's 11. greengrocer's 12. butcher's

三、2. Was Sandy in bed last night?
When was Sandy in bed?
Where was Sandy last night?
3. Was Sue at the funfair this morning?
When was Sue at the funfair?
Where was Sue this morning?
4. Was the baby in the pram the night before last?
When was the baby in the pram?
Where was the baby the night before last?
5. Was mother at the grocer's two hours ago?
When was mother at the grocer's?
Where was mother two hours ago?

四、1. Father wasn't in the country yesterday evening.
2. There weren't any pictures in the parcel last night.
3. Sue didn't fold her clothes last night.
4. Were the children at the barber's the night before last?
5. Did Sandy have breakfast yesterday morning?
6. Was there any snow on the mountains last winter?
7. What did Tony have last term?
8. Where was the horse the day before yesterday?
9. How long ago were Sandy and Sue at home?
10. When was mother in the village?
11. Who went to the cinema just now?

五、1. A 2. B 3. C 4. A 5. A 6. D 7. D

Section Two

一、1. Washington D. C. 2. Berlin 3. London 4. Paris 5. Rome 6. Tokyo 7. Dublin 8. Athens 9. Madrid

二、1. D 2. A 3. D 4. D 5. C

三、1. You are always careless.
2. Were you at school the day before yesterday?
3. What's the matter with you?
4. I'm writing in my diary.
5. Perhaps the cat is under the bed.
6. She was here a few minutes ago.

四、2. We were in Sydney six months ago.

3. They were in Paris in 2005.
4. He was in New York the year before last.
5. Peter was in Japan last week.

五、1. D 2. C 3. B 4. E 5. A

Section Three

一、1. B 2. C 3. A 4. C 5. C

二、1. bar 2. jars 3. bottles/tins 4. packets 5. tube
6. packet 7. boxes 8. tin 9. bar 10. bowl

三、1. He felt happy.
2. There were four kinds of animals in the field.
3. The weather was fine / sunny that day. The bird was in the sky.
4. They were in hospital. One was a doctor and the other was a patient.

四、1. B 2. C 3. C 4. D 5. A 6. A 7. B 8. C 9. A 10. B

Section Four

一、1. diary 2. Scientists 3. dentist's 4. restaurant 5. were
6. January 7. long 8. to 9. Perhaps 10. interesting

二、1. arrived 2. didn't go 3. posted 4. was 5. clean
6. visit 7. had 8. weren't 9. didn't do 10. didn't watch
11. Did; go 12. did; get 13. was 14. Were 15. Was

三、1. D 2. C 3. D 4. A 5. D

四、1. There was a lot of snow on the mountains last year.
2. There were lots of cakes in the cupboard yesterday, but there aren't any more today.
3. How long ago were the children at the funfair?
4. Mother went to the greengrocer's just now.

Section Five

一、1. Where was father yesterday afternoon?
2. Were Sandy and Sue at the library last night?
3. Mother and father were at the cinema last night.
4. They weren't at home a short time ago.
5. He was in Washington last week.
6. They were in France last month.

二、1. B 2. A 3. B 4. B 5. C

三、1. B 2. C 3. B 4. A 5. D

四、1. B 2. B 3. C 4. A

五、1. church 2. baker's 3. butcher's 4. stationer's 5. greengrocer's 6. dentist's

六、1. What did Tom buy last week?
2. How did she drive the car?
3. When did they light a fire?
4. Where is he going to have a birthday party this Sunday?
5. Which girl is your sister?

七、1. C 2. B 3. D 4. A 5. C 6. C 7. A 8. C 9. A 10. A

八、1. A 2. D 3. A 4. D 5. B

九、B→D→C→E→A

Unit 6

Section One

一、1. D 2. D 3. A 4. A 5. B 6. C 7. B

二、1. basketball 2. collecting stamps 3. swimming 4. gardening 5. fishing 6. golf 7. riding 8. photography 9. tennis 10. music 11. reading 12. cooking

三、1. carrying 2. going 3. laying 4. making 5. spending 6. having 7. passing 8. hitting 9. coming 10. watching 11. swimming 12. flying 13. lying 14. riding 15. writing 16. teaching 17. beginning 18. shopping 19. seeing 20. skiing

四、1. Sandy doesn't like taking photos but he likes collecting stamps.
2. The Clarks don't like playing chess but they like playing cards.
3. Lucy and Lily don't like swimming but they like playing hopscotch.
4. My brother doesn't like studying but he likes playing computer games.
5. Those boys don't like playing basketball but they like playing football.
6. The cat doesn't like eating mice but it likes eating fish.

五、1. likes 2. is drawing 3. swimming 4. smoking 5. has 6. does 7. watch 8. goes 9. listening 10. reading 11. is looking

六、1. D 2. C 3. A 4. B 5. B 6. A

Section Two

一、1. C 2. B 3. B 4. D 5. B 6. C

二、1. chat shows 2. comedies 3. opera 4. horror movie 5. tragedies 6. news 7. cartoons 8. nature programme

三、1. What are you doing? I'm going sightseeing.
2. What are you doing? We are playing tennis.
3. What is the baby doing? It is drinking milk.
4. What are the girls doing? They are skipping.
5. What is Kate doing? She is doing aerobics.
6. What are your parents doing? They are baking a cake.

四、1. Lily is learning to speak French.
2. It is snowing now.
3. They are watching a basketball match on TV.
4. He is closing the window.
5. Look! The dog is barking.
6. Listen! The baby is crying.
7. They are having a meeting at eleven o'clock.
8. She is smiling to herself in the mirror now.

五、1. Is Frank climbing the hill?
2. Are you having a Chinese lesson now?
3. He isn't drinking a cup of coffee.
4. We aren't picking apples on a farm these days.
5. What are you doing?

Section Three

一、1. C 2. D 3. C 4. A 5. C 6. D 7. C

二、1. Everything is fine.
2. Watching videos is really good fun.
3. I like playing golf now.
4. I was surprised to learn that he was taking drugs.
5. Do you think the graph is correct for people of your age?

三、1. B 2. D 3. C 4. A 5. B 6. C 7. D 8. C 9. A 10. B

四、1. in 2. on 3. on 4. in 5. in 6. in 7. with 8. for; at

五、1. play 2. isn't eating 3. writing 4. to fly 5. sitting 6. sells 7. watering 8. to clean 9. spends; playing 10. is raining

六、1. Does Elsa like watching sport and films?
2. Don't look at these horses.
3. The girl isn't living with her grandparents at present.
4. Where is Grace reading?
5. What kind of programme doesn't your teacher like?
6. Why does Andy like fishing?
7. Norman comes from Scotland.

Section Four

一、1. A 2. B 3. B 4. D 5. C

二、1. The population of the world is still growing now.
2. I listen to the BBC world service every day.
3. They are playing on a squash court.
4. Look! Jack and his monkey are playing flying disk together in the garden.
5. People write to me from all over the world.
6. I am looking for a jacket for my son.

三、1. Are; reading 2. are playing 3. works 4. are singing 5. likes; drawing 6. is cooking 7. are having 8. is brushing 9. lives

四、1. T 2. F 3. F 4. T 5. F 6. T

五、1. Are you sending an e-mail?
2. The students aren't planting any trees now.
3. Who is sleeping right now?
4. Where is the boy playing squash?
5. It is really very interesting.

六、1. soaps 2. creative 3. detail 4. be good for 5. favourite programme 6. running track 7. fitness training 8. nature programme 9. questionnaire 10. yours faithfully 11. squash court 12. sports centre 13. for all ages 14. watch the baby 15. chat shows

Section Five

一、1. cartoon 2. creative 3. fitness 4. gardening 5. nature 6. photograph 7. relaxing 8. running-track 9. pottery 10. aerobics

二、1. C 2. A 3. C 4. C 5. B 6. A

三、1. C 2. A 3. B 4. A 5. B 6. B 7. A

四、1. A 2. B 3. C 4. B 5. B 6. A 7. C

五、1. cartoons 2. minutes 3. Friday 4. smart 5. everywhere

六、1. A 2. C 3. D 4. B 5. A 6. A 7. B

七、1. envelope 2. training 3. photography 4. famous 5. creative 6. relaxing 7. track

8. pottery 9. drama 10. gardening

八、1. A 2. C 3. B 4. D 5. B

九、1. A 2. D 3. C 4. B 5. D 6. A 7. A 8. C 9. D 10. B

Unit 7

Section One

一、1. B 2. A 3. A 4. A 5. B 6. A 7. C

二、1. John can play computer games a little.
2. John can't swim at all.
3. Lily and Lucy can play badminton very well.
4. Lily and Lucy can dance a little.
5. Lily can't play tennis at all. Neither can Lucy.

三、1. me 2. her 3. us; it 4. him

四、1. to take 2. reading 3. to finish 4. to work 5. to watch 6. walking

五、1. I can type something because there is a typewriter.
2. I can take photos because there is a camera.
3. I can send him a fax because there is a fax machine.

六、1. to have 2. doesn't have 3. good at 4. How often does; go 5. Don't

七、1. doing 2. to go 3. dancing 4. visiting 5. flies

Section Two

一、1. C 2. B 3. C 4. B 5. D 6. C

二、Ocean Museum is open between nine and half past five.
Ocean Museum is open from nine to half past five.
Health Centre is open between nine and half past six.
Health Centre is open from nine to half past six.

三、答案符合常理即可。

四、1. space and time 2. He uses a wheelchair
3. he had only two years to live 4. to think in pictures
5. *A Brief History of Time*

五、1. C/ look at 2. C/ to type 3. C/ running 4. A/ switch them on 5. B/ something different

Section Three

一、1. A 2. B 3. A 4. A 5. C 6. C 7. D

二、1. B 2. A 3. C 4. D 5. C 6. A 7. D 8. B 9. B 10. C

三、1. lifestyles 2. band 3. inventor; invent 4. creative 5. without 6. practice

四、1. Don't speak 2. worries 3. ring 4. is chasing 5. didn't hunt 6. to share 7. telling 8. to knock 9. thought

五、1. him 2. him 3. us 4. them 5. you

六、1. What do; looking 2. favorite 3. works as 4. doesn't eat 5. Do; enjoy 6. Where is
7. What has 8. Would; like

七、1. show 2. age 3. during 4. leave 5. sang 6. stopped 7. would 8. money 9. song
10. laughed

Section Four

一、1. D 2. B 3. A 4. C 5. B 6. B 7. D 8. C 9. A 10. B

二、1. to chat 2. running 3. hers 4. shelves 5. not eat 6. Without 7. Cross 8. visiting 9. giving 10. Children's 11. flies 12. first 13. are cooking

三、1. F 2. F 3. F 4. F 5. T

四、1. B 2. C 3. A

五、1. government 2. private 3. advertisement 4. inventions 5. opening hours 6. public 7. relaxation

Section Five

一、1. A 2. C 3. A 4. B 5. B

二、1. A 2. C 3. B 4. C 5. A

三、1. A 2. B 3. B 4. A 5. B 6. A 7. A

四、1. B 2. C 3. C

五、1. A 2. B 3. C 4. B 5. B 6. C 7. A 8. C 9. C 10. B 11. A 12. B 13. B 14. B 15. A

六、1. B 2. D 3. C 4. A 5. B 6. C 7. A 8. C 9. A 10. D

七、1. B 2. B 3. C 4. C 5. A

八、1. true 2. possible 3. arm(s) 4. herself 5. more
6. back 7. spends 8. smile 9. receive 10. remember

Unit 8

Section One

一、1. Mrs. Boffin: Go to the grocer's and get some eggs and some matches please, dear.
Professor: Good morning. May I have some eggs and some matches, please?
2. Mrs. Boffin: Don't hit your pocket like that! Oh! Look at those eggs!
3. Mother, father and Sue had some soup. Sandy didn't want any.
4. They all had strawberries, sugar and cream, "Yum! Yum!" Sandy said.
5. "Did you all have a nice meal?" father asked.
"Yes, thank you, Dad," Sue answered. "It was a lovely treat," Sandy said.

二、1. There wasn't any snow on the mountain last month.
There was some snow in the tree last month.
2. There weren't any students on the playground 5 minutes ago.
There were some students in the classroom 5 minutes ago.
3. The baker didn't have any hamburger yesterday, but he has some today.
4. The stationer didn't have any colour pencil yesterday, but he has some today.
5. Did Miss Green have lunch?
She didn't have lunch, but she had supper.

三、1. hit 2. got 3. asked 4. had 5. saw
6. going 7. had 8. Don't play 9. use; go 10. drive

四、1. D 2. C 3. D 4. B 5. A 6. D 7. B

五、1. Tony didn't keep in bed the day before yesterday.
2. Don't give him a carrot!

3. You'd better not stay at home all day.
4. Will you draw those animals on the wall?
5. Did you go to the station with grandpa today?
6. Did mom put any sticking-plaster around Sandy's finger?
7. What did father and Sandy have?
8. When did you go to the dentist's?
9. Get me some eggs, please.
10. Show the newspaper to me, please.

Section Two

一、1. Grandmother and grandfather arrived this morning.
They are going to stay with us for six days.
2. We waited for them at the station.
They travelled by train. The train arrived at five o'clock.
3. "What lovely flowers!" Mrs. Boffin said.
"Many happy returns, dear," Professor Boffin said.
4. "It's the 27th of February today. I remembered your birthday this year."
5. Mrs. Boffin smiled.
"My birthday was the day before yesterday," She answered.
"But thank you all the same. Better late than never."

二、1. Grace wanted a flute. She didn't want a water-pistol.
2. Sam wanted a shave. He didn't want a haircut.
3. Did you taste the cake last night?
No, I didn't taste the cake last night.
I tasted the cake this evening.
4. Did you pay the bill this afternoon?
No, I didn't pay the bill this afternoon.
I paid the bill this morning.
5. Sue didn't pour gravy over her food this morning.
She poured gravy over her food this evening.
6. The children didn't copy their exercises last night.
They copied their exercises the night before last.

三、1. B 2. A 3. D 4. C 5. D 6. C 7. A

四、1. There wasn't any cream in the bowl.
2. He didn't play basketball after class.
3. There weren't many vegetables in the refrigerator yesterday.
4. Did you have a nice dinner last night?
5. Does she have to finish her homework before dinner?
6. Did you live in Wuhan?
7. Would you like to have a cup of tea?
8. When did the new term begin?
9. Whose dictionary was it?
10. Where were they the night before last?

五、1. Many happy returns!
2. Better late than never!
3. Simon didn't go to school yesterday. He had a cold.
4. Father paid the bill the day before yesterday.

Section Three

一、1. I flew the kite with my parents and my sister last month.
2. I had a birthday party with my parents and my sister yesterday afternoon.
3. Alice didn't draw a picture last night.
4. Alice didn't listen to music this evening.

二、1. D 2. C 3. A 4. B 5. C 6. A 7. B

三、1. C 2. B 3. D 4. C 5. A

Section Four

一、1. They went home today and we went to the station with them.
On the way we noticed farmer Gimbel's donkey in a field.
"He's very quiet today," grandpa said.
2. Yesterday it was Friday, 13th March. It was Sandy's unlucky day.
In the morning he cut his finger with the bread-knife.
3. In the evening we both had lots of homework, but Sandy didn't mind at all.
"I can't do my homework," he said, and he didn't write a word!

二、1. was 2. cut 3. asked 4. put 5. arrived 6. met 7. shut 8. slept 9. lit 10. read 11. said 12. spent

三、1. B 2. D 3. E 4. A 5. C

四、1. A 2. C 3. B 4. A 5. C 6. D

五、1. My cotton shirt doesn't feel as smooth as the silk one.
2. Did he buy any flowers for his wife yesterday?
3. What didn't you finish?
4. What did he like doing when he was young?
5. Why didn't you go out?

六、1. B 2. C 3. A 4. B 5. D 6. C 7. B 8. A 9. D 10. C 11. D 12. A 13. C 14. B 15. D

Section Five

一、1. grocer 2. chemist's 3. stationary 4. restaurant 5. steak
6. course 7. cream 8. station 9. wait 10. flute
11. pistol 12. share 13. bunch 14. thief 15. donkey
16. traffic 17. question 18. kick a goal 19. round 20. iodine

二、1. B 2. C 3. B 4. A 5. C

三、1. B 2. C 3. A 4. B 5. B 6. A 7. A 8. A 9. C 10. B

四、1. C 2. B 3. B 4. C 5. A

五、1. C 2. D 3. C 4. C 5. B 6. B

六、1. afraid 2. pocket 3. restaurant 4. presents 5. bunch
6. stopped traffic 7. cross 8. carrot 9. station 10. iodine

七、1. I can't go to school by bike.
2. Did you have maths lesson an hour ago?
3. When did mom cut her finger?
4. Where did Sandy have lunch?
5. Give a carrot to him, please.

八、1. B 2. B 3. A 4. A 5. C 6. D 7. C 8. A 9. D 10. B

九、1. C 2. A 3. C 4. B 5. D

Unit 9

Section One

一、1. During the night Sandy heard a strange noise and woke up.
He sat up in bed and listened.
2. We both went downstairs. The light was on in the kitchen. We were both afraid.
3. Then we saw father. "I was hungry," father said. "So I made some sandwiches. Do you want one?"
4. This morning mother got up early and went into the kitchen.
The kitchen was very untidy and the light was still on!
5. Then father, Sandy and I went downstairs as well.
"What do you want for breakfast?" mother asked.
"We don't want any breakfast," father answered.

二、1. Did father sit at his desk during the lesson?
He didn't sit at his desk during the lesson.
He sat at his desk during the day.
2. Did Sue make a snowman during the game?
She didn't make a snowman during the game.
She made a snowman this morning.
3. Did the sun shine every day during March?
The sun didn't shine every day during March.
The sun shone every day during August.
4. Did the children come home this evening?
The children didn't come home this evening.
The children came home this afternoon.
5. Did the children wear their uniform on Friday?
The children didn't wear their uniform on Friday.
The children wore their uniform on Monday.

三、1. brought 2. bought 3. fought 4. thought 5. held
6. made 7. stood 8. told 9. shone 10. drank
11. drove 12. ate 13. gave 14. went 15. came
16. wore 17. took 18. forgot

四、1. did; spend; to go 2. drive 3. swimming 4. was; is flying 5. like; likes 6. Were 7. are; were; are having 8. dress; is putting 9. has; will go 10. visiting

五、1. A 2. B 3. A 4. B 5. D 6. B 7. C

六、1. We were both late yesterday.
2. He saw father drinking some tea in the kitchen last night.
3. I saw mother walking across the park this morning.
4. Mother brought them some steak during the meal.
5. We are both afraid to stay at home alone.

Section Two

一、1. Liz wrote a message during the lesson and passed it to Lillie.
2. Lillie read it and passed it to me.

3. I didn't read it because Mr. May saw me and took the piece of paper.
He threw it into the wastepaper-basket.
4. During play time Liz took the message out of the basket and showed it to me.
It said: Pass it along! "That's a silly message!" I said.

二、1. They had some bananas during lunch as well.
When did they have some bananas?
2. She went shopping in the afternoon as well.
When did mother go shopping?
3. She went to school by bus on Friday as well.
When did she go to school by bus?
4. Did Sandy and Sue run to school this morning?
They didn't run to school this morning.
They ran to school yesterday morning.
5. Did a thief break the window this evening?
He didn't break the window this evening.
He broke the window at midnight.
6. Did Sandy show his water-pistol to his friends during the lesson?
Sandy didn't show his water-pistol to his friends during the lesson.
Sandy showed his water-pistol to his friends during playtime.

三、1. wrote 2. ran 3. rang 4. sang 5. rode
6. woke 7. spoke 8. broke 9. showed

四、1. C 2. C 3. D 4. B 5. A 6. D

五、1. keeps 2. ahead 3. but 4. on
5. spent 6. edge 7. weak 8. serious

六、1. The classroom was very untidy and the lights were still on.
2. Professor Boffin forgot to take the umbrella again in the afternoon.
3. Mother had some coffee with friends in the afternoon as usual.

Section Three

一、1. Did the sun set very early in October?
The sun didn't set very early in October.
The sun set very early in December.
2. Did father begin work very late on Tuesday morning?
Father didn't begin work very late on Tuesday morning.
Father began work very late on Monday morning.
3. Did Sue hurt her head very much an hour ago?
Sue didn't hurt her head very much an hour ago.
Sue hurt her head very much a few minutes ago.
4. She drew a picture this evening as well.
When did Miss Smith draw a picture?
5. They went to the funfair after school as well.
When did the children go to the funfair?
6. She gave a speech on Friday as well.
When did sue give a speech?

二、1. B 2. C 3. B 4. D 5. B 6. B

三、1. C 2. A 3. B 4. C 5. D

Section Four

一、1. The other day it rained heavily, so we stayed indoors.
2. We made a puppet.
3. We used a sheet of paper, some large corks and some string.
4. We worked busily for two hours.
5. At last the puppet was ready.
6. We painted his face carefully.
7. Then Sandy pulled the strings and our puppet danced.
8. He danced very well.

二、1. D 2. B 3. C 4. C 5. C 6. A

三、1. didn't write 2. received 3. was singing 4. forgot 5. didn't say
6. like 7. learned 8. to drive 9. lent 10. will go

四、1. Cathy wasn't writing a letter at 9 pm yesterday.
2. Were you having a shower when the postman knocked at the door?
3. Did John have breakfast at 7 : 30 this morning?
4. How often does Henry go to the library?
5. How did the children work this morning?

五、1. C 2. D 3. A 4. B 5. C 6. C 7. A 8. B 9. A 10. C 11. B 12. C 13. A 14. C
15. C

Section Five

一、1. during 2. Europe 3. breakfast 4. untidy
5. lunch 6. uniform 7. along 8. message
9. wastepaper-basket 10. midnight 11. string 12. out of sight
13. indoors 14. heavily 15. puppet 16. sheet
17. cork 18. busily 19. paint 20. carefully

二、1. C 2. A 3. B 4. A 5. B 6. A 7. C 8. C 9. C 10. A

三、1. C 2. A 3. A 4. B 5. C

四、1. C 2. B 3. C 4. A 5. A

五、1. blew 2. knew 3. threw 4. flew 5. drew
6. swam 7. rose 8. set 9. began 10. hurt

六、1. dug 2. were 3. eating; go 4. broke; hurt 5. lying
6. doing 7. keep; entering 8. using 9. fell; hurt 10. waiting

七、1. She didn't have to look after her younger brother.
2. This cake doesn't taste delicious.
3. You'd better not have any drink.
4. Can you go skating tomorrow?
5. Did he take his children to the seaside yesterday?
6. Must he stay at home because of the heavy snow?
7. Why didn't you finish your homework?
8. How much did this dress cost her?

八、1. C 2. D 3. B 4. A 5. D 6. B 7. A 8. B 9. A 10. D 11. B 12. C 13. B 14. A
15. A

九、1. C 2. B 3. A 4. A 5. D

期中考试(一)

第一部分

1—5 ABCBB 6—10 CCABC 11—15 CAACC 16—20 BACCA 21—25 ABCBC
26—30 ACAAD 31—35 AABAA 36—40 ACCBB 41—45 BCACD 46—50 CBABC
51—55 CCBDA 56—60 BCDBD 61—65 DACDB

第二部分

一、1. popular 2. convenient 3. bought 4. better 5. shapes

二、1—5 BEADC

三、1. Lucy didn't have to clean her bedroom this afternoon.
2. Did Sandy get a fever?
3. How does the music sound?
4. How's the weather today?
5. When was the thief in prison?

四、1. situated 2. reading; playing 3. to do 4. have 5. cut

期中考试(二)

第一部分

1—5 CBACB 6—10 BACAC 11—15 CABBC 16—20 BACAA 21—25 CACBC
26—30 ABDCB 31—35 CABAD 36—40 CCBDB 41—45 ACDBD 46—50 BCDBA
51—55 DABCD 56—60 ACBAA 61—65 BCBDD

第二部分

一、1. wrote 2. habits 3. worth 4. magnificent 5. serious

二、1—5 EDAHC 6—10 FJGBI

三、1. swam 2. slept 3. rose 4. lost 5. are going to fly 6. Have ... got; hurts 7. weren't
8. was; isn't 9. inventor; inventing; has ... ; Invented 10. take

四、1. Did he hurt his leg the other day?
2. Did you eat any mooncakes and drink any tea on Mid-Autumn Festival?
3. Has she got a wonderful idea?
4. Don't wash your hands quickly.
5. The children didn't sing songs to celebrate the New Year's Day.
6. What did Tom buy last week?
7. How did she drive the car?
8. When did they light a fire?
9. Where is he going to have a birthday party this Sunday?
10. pay; for

Unit 10

Section One

一、1. B 2. C 3. D 4. A 5. B 6. B 7. B

二、1. I bought a magazine yesterday morning.
2. Mr. Black missed the train and was late for work the day before yesterday.
3. Jessica spent much money on her clothes last year.
4. Steven gave up learning Chinese because he thought it was too difficult last month.
5. My PE teacher was a professional tennis player 5 years ago.

三、1. old 2. bigger 3. Nobody 4. pleased 5. money
6. rich 7. take 8. more 9. received 10. wonderful

四、1. brought 2. homeless 3. not to forgive 4. didn't notice
5. would come 6. heard 7. were writing 8. read
9. to clean 10. (to) cook 11. wrote 12. will leave
13. died 14. playing 15. looking

五、1. ran 2. had 3. listened 4. read
5. sent 6. saw 7. left 8. found
9. stood 10. sat 11. came 12. bought
13. thought 14. thanked 15. studied

Section Two

一、1. A 2. A 3. D 4. C 5. B 6. A 7. B

二、1. to play 2. don't put 3. bought 4. were playing 5. watched

三、1. Where; when were; born 2. didn't do
3. begins working 4. How long did
5. What time did; go

四、1. She enjoyed skating two years ago.
2. They had dinner yesterday.
3. She was ill and took some medicine yesterday evening.
4. We visited Great Wall happily last year.

五、1. I will put the litter in a bag.
2. She doesn't return my pencil.
3. She copies my homework.
4. I'll do the homework by myself.
5. She sometimes makes ink marks on my clothes with her pen.

六、1. protecting 2. strong 3. medicine 4. hearing 5. to /towards
6. fun 7. nowhere 8. number 9. future 10. should

Section Three

一、1. D 2. A 3. B 4. C 5. B 6. D 7. B

二、1. C 2. B 3. A 4. C 5. C 6. A 7. D 8. B 9. D 10. B 11. A 12. D 13. B 14. B 15. D

三、1. journey 2. atmosphere 3. temple 4. governor; remained 5. furniture

四、1. G 2. D 3. E 4. F 5. B

Section Four

一、1. A 2. C 3. A 4. B 5. A 6. B 7. A 8. B 9. A 10. A

二、1. F 2. T 3. F 4. F 5. T

三、1. A 2. D 3. C 4. D 5. B

四、1. learning; the age of 2. When did; take 3. How did; go 4. Did; have

5. What's the weather

Section Five

一、1. A 2. C 3. C 4. A 5. B

二、1. B 2. A 3. B 4. C 5. C

三、1. A 2. C 3. B 4. C 5. A 6. B 7. B 8. C 9. B 10. C

四、1. B 2. A 3. A 4. C 5. B

五、1. B 2. C 3. C 4. D 5. B 6. A 7. A 8. A 9. D 10. C

六、1. D 2. C 3. A 4. C 5. B 6. A 7. A 8. D 9. B 10. B

七、1. C 2. D 3. A 4. C 5. A 6. B 7. B 8. D 9. A 10. D 11. A 12. D 13. B 14. C 15. A

八、1. with/ to 2. most 3. that 4. stopped 5. friends
6. me 7. time 8. too 9. friendly/ kind 10. ill/ sick

Unit 11

Section One

一、1. was 2. was 3. were 4. were 5. was

二、1. one thousand and ninety-nine/ten ninety-nine
2. two thousand and one
3. nineteen ninety-eight
4. nineteen seventy
5. eighteen hundred
6. two thousand and ten

三、1. It wasn't exciting. 2. None of the students were very excited.
3. Were they in his pocket?
4. Where was the car just now?
5. No, I didn't.

四、1. When were you born?
2. Where were you born?
3. was born
4. used to be
5. did you become an actor

五、1. is → was 2. go→ went 3. goes→ went 4. can→ could 5. saw→ see

六、1. Did Jason go to the Zhongshan Park? Yes, he did.
2. Did Jason go for an outing with his family? Yes, he did.
3. Did he celebrate his father's birthday? No, he didn't.

七、1. quietly 2. liked 3. stopped 4. saw; studied 5. Did; travel; was

八、1. diploma 2. assistant 3. interview 4. birthday 5. costumes

Section Two

一、1. B 2. B 3. B 4. C 5. B 6. A 7. B 8. A 9. A 10. D

二、1. American television series 2. Sesame Street 3. responsibility 4. change one's mind
5. refuse 6. educate sb. 7. headlines 8. provide

三、regular: planted, showed, called, wanted, played

irregular: flew, drank, went, made, wrote, got, saw, left, said

四、1. lived 2. ate 3. had 4. didn't leave 5. made 6. wanted; to play 7. tried; to cook 8. educated 9. stop; to have 10. to write

五、1. loves his work, watching the programme
2. to know that; really
3. though; climbed out of his costume
4. refused; left school
5. started writing; soon after

六、1. Did she take any photos at the Sports meeting?
2. Nancy didn't go to school early.
3. Where did he meet the little boy?
4. Why did Sarah move to Oxford?
5. We provided the children with some good books in the countryside.

七、1. refused to 2. if; wanted to 3. experience 4. responsibility; keep 5. was; that; cried

Section Three

一、1. B 2. C 3. D 4. C 5. B

二、1. F 2. T 3. F 4. F 5. F

三、1. well-known 2. lost 3. climbed 4. chop 5. called 6. until 7. work 8. performed

四、1. had 2. danced 3. worried 4. asked 5. became 6. ate 7. played 8. chopped 9. threw 10. kicked 11. passed 12. lost

五、1. How often 2. How clever 3. so tired that she couldn't 4. didn't have 5. What did; finish doing

六、1. Although; dress 2. asked; wanted 3. changed; ways 4. responsibility; look after 5. arrive; until

七、1. D 2. B 3. C 4. B 5. A 6. A 7. B 8. C 9. D 10. C

Section Four

一、1. occupation 2. born 3. taught 4. accident 5. developed 6. blind

二、1. saw 2. Did; practise playing; didn't 3. taught 4. died 5. learned; to speak 6. did; write; wrote 7. decided; to be 8. Did; do; did 9. was; wasn't 10. did; become

三、1. T 2. T 3. F 4. F 5. T

四、1. born 2. became 3. showed 4. began 5. got 6. had 7. divorced 8. died

五、1. What did you do yesterday?
2. Did John watch TV last weekend?
3. I went to park my bike.
4. He jumped into the lake and swam to the kite.
5. How did she go home yesterday?

六、1. B 2. D 3. C 4. D 5. D

Section Five

一、1. B 2. C 3. A 4. B 5. C

二、1. B 2. A 3. B 4. B 5. C

三、1. C 2. A 3. B 4. C 5. B

四、1. C 2. A 3. B 4. A 5. C

五、1. B 2. A 3. B 4. C 5. A

六、1. B 2. C 3. D 4. A 5. E

七、1. C 2. C 3. B 4. A 5. D 6. C 7. C 8. A 9. A 10. A 11. B 12. D 13. B 14. C 15. A

八、1. C 2. A 3. C 4. B 5. C 6. C 7. B 8. A 9. B 10. B

九、1. B 2. A 3. D 4. A 5. C

十、1. could; ride 2. does; write; wrote 3. felt; heard 4. hurt; cutting 5. to get; walking; driving

十一、1. lives 2. surname 3. drum 4. realized 5. well-known

十二、1. How long did she stay at school?
2. Why did some people in Thailand move away from their home town?
3. The children took part in the band last month.
4. The man didn't climb up the mountain with the help of the local people.
5. Did sally return home late last night?
6. What was Lang Ping 15 years ago?
7. When was Shakespeare born?
8. Why was her nickname "toothpick"?
9. We enjoyed ourselves very much in South America.
10. Which film is your favourite?

Unit 12

Section One

一、1. C 2. D 3. E 4. A 5. B

二、1. lucky 2. number 3. ticket 4. another 5. caught

三、1. B 2. B 3. B 4. C 5. D

四、1. Tom has not got any rulers.
2. Has she got any money?
3. They haven't got a ball of string or a kite.
4. What has Mary got?
5. have, learnt ; have learnt
6. has been; for
7. How many times has Mary been to Beijing?

五、1. Has Tom got a headache? He's got a headache, but he hasn't got a temperature.
2. Have they got any strawberries? They have got some strawberries, but they haven't got any cream.
3. Has Sue had flu yet? He's already had flu, but he hasn't had mumps.
4. Have they had a shave yet? They have already had a shave, but they haven't had a haircut.
5. I've got some. Have you got any?
6. I've got one. Have you got one?

六、1. F 2. G 3. A 4. C 5. B

Section Two

一、1. D 2. A 3. E 4. C 5. B

二、1. mind 2. getting 3. already 4. truant 5. lovely

三、1. D 2. A 3. B 4. C 5. B

四、1. I have been to the library. 2. Have you been to the park?
3. No, he hasn't. 4. She's just been to the doctor's.
5. How long have you been here? 6. have found; already
7. Did he do his lessons this morning?

五、1. No, they didn't. They haven't been to the library yet.
2. No, I didn't. I haven't been to the watchmaker's yet.
3. Yes, she has. She's already been to Asia. She was in Asia last year.
4. Yes, he has. He's already been to Russia. He was in Russia a fortnight ago.
5. Yes, they have. They have already been to the park. They were in the park last Sunday.

六、1. B 2. F 3. G 4. A 5. D

Section Three

一、1. E 2. D 3. C 4. B 5. A

二、1. market 2. unusual 3. suits 4. show 5. since

三、1. D 2. C 3. D 4. D 5. B

四、1. She has been here since 1982. 2. No, he hasn't.
3. What have you done? 4. How long have they lived here?
5. has she

五、1. C 2. B 3. A 4. D 5. A 6. B 7. C 8. A 9. B 10. D

六、1. E 2. A 3. F 4. C 5. D

Section Four

一、1. C 2. D 3. A 4. E 5. B

二、1. while 2. Chief 3. famous 4. scientist 5. robberies

三、1. count counted counted 2. turn turned turned 3. answer answered answered
4. carry carried carried 5. live lived lived 6. knock knocked knocked
7. visit visited visited 8. open opened opened 9. try tried tried
10. play played played 11. stop stopped stopped 12. stir stirred stirred

四、1. C 2. B 3. C 4. D 5. B

五、1. has been away since 2. When did Mr. Bean tell them a story?
3. hasn't; yet 4. Have, found, yet; haven't
5. has already got 6. What have you done?
7. have been; since
8. They didn't do their homework late last night.

六、1. B 2. B 3. D 4. A 5. C

Section Five

一、1. unusual 2. suit 3. robbery 4. slippery 5. accident
6. draw another number 7. quite a while 8. play truant 9. a famous scientist
10. a few moments ago

二、1. C 2. B 3. C 4. A 5. B

三、1. C 2. B 3. B 4. A 5. A

四、1. C 2. B 3. A 4. D 5. C 6. C

五、1. draw 2. prize 3. truant 4. unusual 5. suits

6. shut 7. robbery 8. tread 9. muddy 10. on

六、1. never 2. already; since 3. for 4. ever; never 5. yet; already

七、1. has seen 2. have written 3. has done 4. have; seen
5. has bought 6. has lived 7. has broken 8. haven't finished
9. Have; borrowed 10. have drunk 11. has left; called 12. have seen, love
13. Have you heard, have; told, did; did he tell

八、1. have you 2. Has, found; hasn't found
3. has taught 4. doesn't have; Does, have
5. How long have they lived here? 6. have been to; haven't you
7. What have you done?

九、1. Jim has finished his homework. He is free now.
2. He has received that letter.
3. My father has been to the Great Wall before.
4. She hasn't seen that new film yet.
5. She has been to Shanghai.
6. Where has he gone these days?

十、1. G 2. A 3. F 4. C 5. B

十一、1. B 2. D 3. C 4. B 5. A 6. B 7. C 8. D 9. B 10. A

十二、1. D 2. C 3. A 4. D 5. C

Unit 13

Section One

一、1. D 2. E 3. C 4. A 5. B

二、1. say said said 2. get got got 3. light lit lit 4. find found found
5. tell told told 6. hear heard heard 7. meet met met 8. set set set
9. spend spent spent 10. read read read 11. cut cut cut 12. shut shut shut
13. put put put 14. hit hit hit 15. have had had

三、1. accident 2. tread 3. slippery 4. polished 5. dangerous

四、1. bought 2. are repairing 3. have eaten 4. have flown 5. has taken

五、1. A 2. D 3. C 4. C 5. D

六、1. has been open
2. How many times have; cleaned
3. I spoke to your mother on the phone yesterday.
4. took; ago

七、1. Mother's just shut the window. She shut the window a few minutes ago.
2. Sue's just set the table. She set the table at six o'clock.
3. The children have woken up.
When did they wake up? They woke up at seven.
4. The girl has seen a movie.
When did she see a movie? She saw a movie this evening.

八、1. B 2. F 3. G 4. A 5. E

Section Two

一、1. E 2. A 3. D 4. C 5. B

二、1. give gave given　2. do did done　3. see saw seen　4. begin began begun
5. run ran run　6. come came come　7. go went gone
8. set set set　9. rise rose risen　10. wake woke woken
11. speak spoke spoken　12. break broke broken

三、1. newspaper　2. lit　3. needed　4. tricks　5. Blow

四、1. B　2. A　3. B　4. C　5. C　6. C

五、1. has had; for
2. Have you finished your homework yet?
3. What has your friend just bought?
4. He has got an old coat.
5. When did Mr. Bean tell them a story?
6. How many times have; cleaned

六、1. We've already thrown away the waste paper. We threw it after the lesson.
2. We've already ridden our bicycles. We rode them during the day.
3. They've just drawn pictures.
When did they draw pictures? They drew pictures at lunch time.
4. They've just taken off shoes.
When did they take off shoes? They took off shoes in the evening.

七、1. E　2. A　3. G　4. C　5. F

Section Three

一、1. E　2. C　3. A　4. D　5. B

二、1. cross　2. lovely　3. kicked　4. During　5. throw

三、1. ring rang rung　2. write wrote written　3. sing sang sung
4. feel felt felt　5. wear wore worn　6. stand stood stood
7. sleep slept slept　8. shine shone shone　9. sit sat sat
10. hold held held　11. think thought thought　12. fight fought fought

四、1. A　2. D　3. D　4. D　5. A

五、1. Whose report has Daddy read?
2. Has, left; has ; did, leave; left
3. has he
4. have been; for
5. What did the boy do just now?
6. How long has your father lived in Tianjin?

六、1. C　2. D　3. A　4. B　5. F

七、1. D　2. A　3. B　4. B　5. D　6. C　7. B　8. D　9. A　10. C

Section Four

一、1. E　2. A　3. B　4. C　5. D

二、1. take　2. while　3. parcel　4. moment　5. sheet

三、1. say said said　2. get got got　3. light lit lit
4. find found found　5. run ran run　6. come came come
7. go went gone　8. set set set　9. sit sat sat
10. hold held held　11. think thought thought　12. fight fought fought

四、1. A　2. D　3. B　4. C　5. C

五、1. Have, had; did, have; had　2. Have, written; have; wrote

3. Has; finished
4. Have; been
5. has; finished
6. finished
7. learned
8. haven't read
9. has; gone
10. Have; drunk

六、1. have been in
2. I haven't done my homework yet.
3. been; for two weeks
4. Why did he see the doctor?
5. Have, ever read; read

七、1. C 2. A 3. C 4. B 5. A

Section Five

一、1. waste 2. parcel 3. ground 4. lovely
5. match 6. play a trick on 7. throw away 8. blow up
9. light a fire 10. knock at the door

二、1. C 2. C 3. C 4. C 5. B

三、1. B 2. C 3. A 4. C 5. B

四、1. B 2. D 3. D 4. D 5. B

五、1. light 2. trick 3. sheet 4. parcel 5. waste
6. puppet 7. wore 8. During 9. cross 10. worn

六、1. in 2. before 3. around 4. at 5. with
6. between 7. After 8. During 9. to 10. for

七、1. has gone to 2. went to 3. has been in 4. have; been in
5. have been in 6. Have; been to; have been 7. have been in
8. has gone to 9. did, go; went 10. go to; have been

八、1. has lived 2. have been 3. came 4. has passed; left
5. has lost; Have, seen 6. Have; found 7. have; had
8. have; returned 9. Have; built 10. haven't finished
11. has read 12. bought

九、1. haven't seen; last Wednesday
2. How long has he learnt Japanese?
3. When did Mr Bean tell them a story?
4. has been to; twice
5. hasn't he

十、1. B 2. A 3. F 4. C 5. E

十一、1. C 2. B 3. A 4. D 5. D 6. B 7. C 8. A 9. B 10. C

十二、1. B 2. A 3. C 4. D 5. C

Unit 14

Section One

一、1. Where would you like to
2. somewhere relaxing
3. would like you to fetch a towel
4. Would you like to give me
5. Would you like to have a picnic with me?

二、1. to go 2. travel 3. exciting 4. about 5. relax 6. sounds

三、1. Would; like to have 2. Would; some 3. Where would; like 4. I'd like to

四、1. Canada sent the most tourists to the US.
2. Japanese visitors spent the most.
3. Canada. 4. France. 5. Open answer.

五、1. belonging 2. chicken 3. farm 4. Paris 5. glasses

六、1. What book did you read recently?
2. Have you got any plans for this evening?
3. I'm afraid that I can't come tonight.
4. We don't have to go far.
5. John's grandmother likes to go somewhere clean and quiet.

Section Two

一、1. B 2. D 3. A 4. D 5. C 6. A 7. C 8. C 9. B 10. C

二、1. The party is on Saturday, March 22nd. 2 p. m.
2. It is Megan's fifth birthday party.
3. People can contact Sara at 407-333-4444.
4. It is held at Bubble Gum Playland.

三、1. invite 2. reply 3. footballer 4. picnic 5. dream

四、1. B 2. big fork 3. big knife 4. The small knife and the fork 5. on the left
6. napkin 7. Glasses

五、1. Professor Smith 2. on Monday, June 28 3. at 6 : 30 in the evening 4. wedding anniversary party 5. contact Albert Shaw at 3445902334

Section Three

一、1. C 2. D 3. B 4. D 5. D 6. A 7. C 8. B 9. D 10. B

二、1. to have 2. cleaning 3. helps 4. doesn't rain 5. ask 6. to learn 7. going 8. were; doing 9. called 10. stop

三、1. don't think; right 2. fly to 3. would like 4. isn't young enough; so, that 5. on the right side

四、1. busy 2. Suddenly 3. quickly 4. answer 5. mother's 6. forgot 7. love 8. enough 9. remember 10. show

五、1. B 2. A 3. B 4. C 5. C 6. B 7. D 8. B 9. A 10. C 11. D 12. B 13. B 14. D 15. D

Section Four

一、1. B 2. B 3. B 4. D 5. B 6. B 7. B 8. C 9. A 10. C

二、3241675

三、A: cup B: rinse C: add; boil D: put; cook E: fork

四、1. C 2. D 3. A 4. C 5. A

Section Five

一、1. A 2. B 3. A 4. B 5. A

二、1. C 2. B 3. B 4. B 5. A

三、1. B 2. B 3. C 4. C 5. A 6. C 7. B 8. A 9. A 10. B

四、1. B 2. A 3. B 4. B 5. C

五、1. A 2. A 3. C 4. D 5. B 6. A 7. C 8. A 9. B 10. D

六、1. A 2. D 3. B 4. B 5. D 6. A 7. D 8. A 9. B 10. D 11. D 12. B 13. D 14. A 15. D

七、1. D 2. D 3. A 4. D 5. D 6. D 7. A 8. B 9. B 10. D

八、1. stand　2. nothing　3. recipe　4. lay　5. chopsticks
6. invitation　7. top　8. main　9. instructions　10. peeling

九、1. What would you like to do?
2. What about going for a walk in the park?
3. There isn't much orange juice in the jar or any water in the bottle.
4. Where is big hole?
5. What does he like doing?

Unit 15

Section One

一、1. C　2. D　3. D　4. C　5. A　6. B　7. B

二、1. a cinema; on the corner
2. get to the hospital; at the traffic lights
3. is the car park; in the square
4. van; at the roundabout
5. get to the petrol station; across the bridge
6. bus station is; at the crossroads

三、1. By school bus; It takes
2. Where is the library? How can I get there?
3. Is there a bank (near here)? Is it far from here?
4. How can I get to the bakery? Where is the subway station?

四、1. A museum is near here.　2. Could you tell me the way?
3. The traffic lights are far from here.　4. There isn't a sports centre down the road.
5. Can she show me the way?　6. How far is it?

Section Two

一、1. A　2. C　3. A　4. B　5. B　6. B　7. B

二、1. Yes, there is.　2. It's between the post office and the restaurant.
3. Yes, there is.　4. It's 300 yards away.
5. It's 200 metres away.　6. You may walk there.
7. No, there isn't.　8. It's at the roundabout.

三、post office　hospital　museum　inn　station　park　bank　school
theatre

四、1. Yes　2. way　3. course　4. for　5. take　6. Turn　7. on　8. walk　9. on　10. Either

Section Three

一、1. A　2. B　3. C　4. B　5. C　6. B　7. B

二、1. Don't turn left.　2. Turn right.　3. Don't spit.
4. Go across the road.　5. keep cell phone silent.　6. Don't litter.　7. Keep it dry.

三、1. B　2. D　3. D　4. B　5. C

四、1. Traffic　2. bridge　3. Running　4. collect　5. directions　6. writing

Section Four

一、1. B　2. C　3. C　4. A　5. C　6. C　7. B

二、1. how to get to the National Gallery
how we can get to the National Gallery
2. which bus to take
Which bus he can take
3. what presents to buy
What presents I shall buy
4. where to go
Where we will go

三、1. was; was sold 2. fell; hurt 3. think 4. make 5. travelling 6. bought 7. smoked 8. moving 9. clean/to clean 10. put

四、1. C 2. C 3. A 4. B 5. D 6. A 7. A 8. A 9. D 10. A

五、1. The sign says, "No spitting."
2. Jerry sent the letters for them yesterday.
3. I want a room that has a great view of the sea.
4. Would you like me to make a booking for you?
5. It's my job to help the seniors cross the roads.
6. He saw a boy knock into the lamppost.

Section Five

一、1. into; along 2. lights 3. information 4. crossroads 5. hall

二、1. A 2. B 3. A 4. C 5. B 6. B

三、1. B 2. C 3. C 4. D

四、1. D 2. C 3. D 4. A 5. far; straight; along; minutes; left ; beside; party

五、1. C 2. C 3. B 4. B 5. B 6. C

六、1. picked 2. see 3. saved 4. carried 5. wanted 6. put

七、1. A 2. D 3. A 4. B 5. C 6. C 7. B 8. D

八、1. Why wouldn't you join us?
2. He turned off the lights when he was out.
3. Shirley cut the watermelon into halves.
4. They turned right at the crossroads and then walked on.
5. How did he achieve this?

九、1. A 2. D 3. D 4. C 5. A 6. C 7. A 8. B 9. B 10. D 11. B 12. D 13. A 14. B 15. B

十、1. tell 2. answered 3. is doing 4. waiting 5. explained

Unit 16

Section One

一、1. picnic 2. spend 3. village 4. library 5. churches 6. cinema

二、1. will/shall leave; will/shall finish; leave 2. will; study; plan; hope; will; do; leave; will/shall return; get 3. am; will/shall go 4. will give 5. will snow

三、1. C 2. D 3. D 4. D 5. D 6. B 7. C

四、1. A 2. D 3. C 4. D

Section Two

一、
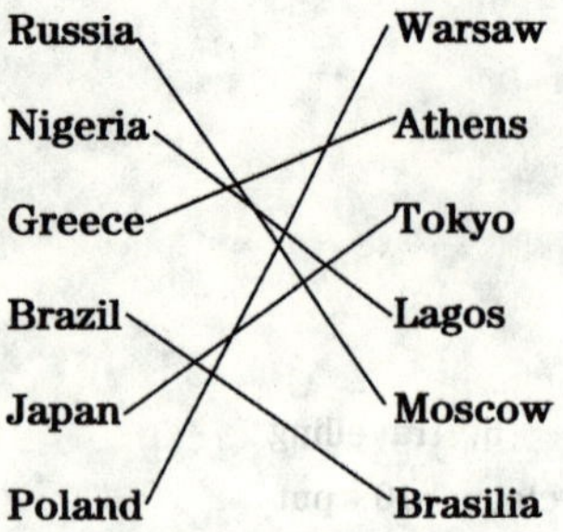

二、1. professors 2. robots 3. Setting 4. Because 5. front

三、1. Are they going to Tahiti to spend summer holiday?
2. I shall not arrive at Prague in 24 hours.
3. Where will Steven join us?
4. How long will the journey take us to finish?

四、1. D 2. B 3. B 4. C 5. C 6. B

五、1. D 2. A 3. D

Section Three

一、1. pass 2. make 3. sweep/clean 4. shut/close 5. turn

二、1. Will; be; will visit 2. Shall; get 3. will be 4. loves; has read
5. will lose 6. went; will fly 7. didn't believe; saw 8. will win

三、1. D 2. B 3. A 4. D 5. B

四、1. They will go to Mr. Wang's in three minutes.
2. Tom and Jerry will go to Mr. Yao's in a moment.
3. Sheila will go to Texas in a month.
4. We will go to Tahiti next week.
5. He will go to the fun fair in one hour.

五、1. A 2. C 3. C 4. B 5. A 6. B 7. A 8. B 9. D 10. B

Section Four

一、1. D 2. A 3. B 4. D 5. A

二、1. F 2. C 3. B 4. E 5. D

三、1. B 2. A 3. A 4. A 5. D

四、1. The CEO won't make a speech at the meeting next week.
2. Will there be any sea fish served at the buffet?
3. Where will Sylvia go on a business trip?
4. When will Samuel be back from Hong Kong?

五、1. T 2. F 3. T 4. T 5. T

Section Five

一、1. A 2. C 3. C 4. C 5. B

二、1. B 2. B 3. C 4. C 5. B 6. C 7. B 8. C 9. A 10. A

三、1. A 2. C 3. A 4. B 5. C

四、1. fifth 2. built 3. with 4. filled 5. heard

五、1. player 2. sunny 3. skating 4. careful 5. forgetful

六、1. C 2. B 3. B 4. C 5. B

七、1. The Obamas won't come home soon.

2. Have they lived here for ten years?

3. Who didn't finish homework until the day before yesterday?

4. What will you do at night?

5. Who is going to join the army next month?

八、1. C 2. D 3. A 4. C 5. B 6. C 7. A 8. A 9. B 10. B 11. A 12. C 13. A 14. B 15. A

九、1. B 2. A 3. B 4. A

Unit 17

Section One

一、1. are 2. work 3. likes 4. studies 5. playing 6. Finish

二、1. on 2. for 3. by 4. in 5. like 6. at 7. in 8. as

三、1. C 2. E 3. B 4. A 5. D

四、1. Excuse me, could you tell me how I can get to the train station please?

2. sells good 3. The price of; at least

4. In the past; as 5. It is said; been to

6. sooner or later

五、1. middle 2. friendly 3. with 4. born 5. rich

6. everything 7. afternoon 8. for 9. When 10. punish

Section Two

一、1. tell 2. does; come 3. wants; to look 4. give; Go

5. to be 6. swimming; teaches; to swim 7. is; going to

8. are 9. takes 10. are climbing

二、1. sleepy; asleep 2. its 3. everyday 4. service

5. the second 6. travel 7. lively 8. on

三、1. D 2. B 3. B 4. C 5. A

四、1. Where are you going 2. What happened to her

3. I'm sorry to hear that 4. I hope she will be all right

5. Can I go to see her with you

五、1. C 2. D 3. D 4. D

Section Three

一、1. dealing 2. repairing 3. held 4. mainly 5. decision 6. carefully

二、1. washes 2. drove 3. satisfied 4. realize 5. made 6. dead 7. leave

三、1. B 2. A 3. D 4. C 5. B

四、1. C 2. A 3. D 4. D 5. B

五、1. T 2. F 3. F 4. F 5. T

Section Four

一、1. are 2. gets; is 3. spend 4. shall; do 5. listen
6. doesn't; will take 7. will go 8. is 9. are going
二、1. D 2. C 3. C 4. A 5. C 6. A 7. C 8. C
三、1. F 2. B 3. A 4. C 5. D
四、1. according 2. should 3. discussing 4. themselves 5. not 6. beginning 7. or

Section Five

一、1. C 2. A 3. A 4. C 5. A
二、1. A 2. C 3. B 4. A 5. B 6. C 7. A 8. C 9. A 10. A
三、1. C 2. A 3. C 4. A 5. B
四、1. French 2. careless; careful 3. second 4. Eastern 5. the Clarks 6. quiet; quietly
五、1. called 2. shopping 3. after 4. newspapers 5. tell
6. started 7. celebrate 8. parents 9. together 10. why
六、1. D 2. A 3. C 4. A 5. A 6. C 7. B 8. C 9. B 10. D
七、1. has been interested in; since 2. have taken place; in the past years
3. always clever enough; come up with 4. be strict with; in daily life
5. provide us; to learn team spirits
八、1. D 2. C 3. B 4. B 5. A 6. C 7. A 8. A 9. D 10. D
九、1. 9,000. 2. Africa, South America and parts of Asia. 3. 75% .
4. People do not have enough food to eat and they live in poor housing; children get little or no time at school and people suffer from many kinds of diseases.

Unit 18

Section One

一、1. B 2. C 3. B 4. B 5. D 6. B 7. A
二、1. CBDAFE 2. CBDEA 3. CBADE
三、1. They're going to Peru. 2. They're coming to see her.
3. She's going to the dentist's. 4. She's heading for Prague.
5. He's taking the 6 p. m. train.
四、1. plan 2. offer 3. cinema 4. garage 5. reason 6. vacation
五、1. He is sitting under the tree.
2. Who offers to buy the tickets?
3. I'm afraid they can't go there tomorrow.
4. Let's not fix a time.
5. Is he working on the farm right now?
6. What are the Simons doing for the vacation?

Section Two

一、1. B 2. A 3. B 4. C 5. C 6. B 7. B 8. C
二、1. Can I help you 2. the tickets are sold out 3. What about 4. How much is it 5. Which would

you like

三、1. B 2. E 3. D 4. A 5. C

四、1. I'm writing to tell you about my new flat.
2. Lying on the grass, he finds it pleasant to relax a little bit.
3. Why don't you tell me the truth?
4. Lillie is visiting her grandparents this Spring Festival.
5. Where shall we go tomorrow morning?

五、1. making 2. help 3. have; Come 4. to go; am 5. wore 6. starting 7. do 8. is singing 9. are sleeping 10. break; have broken; be

六、1. I am taking the dance lessons next year.
2. My classmates are putting up the posters here.
3. Are we meeting Aeron at 11：00 tomorrow morning?

Section Three

一、1. A 2. A 3. D 4. C 5. C 6. C 7. C

二、1. E 2. C 3. B 4. A 5. D

三、1. Would you like 2. would like 3. why not 4. Why don't you 5. What about 6. Do you mind

四、1. A 2. B 3. B 4. A 5. C 6. B 7. A 8. D 9. A 10. A

五、1. cash 2. performance(s) 3. advertisements 4. exactly 5. earned 6. address

六、1. Why don't you have a second thought on this plan?
2. He will return home next Tuesday.
3. How about booking the room on the Internet at a lower price?

Section Four

一、1. B 2. B 3. B 4. D 5. C 6. C 7. A 8. C

二、1. I played basketball.
2. How much did it cost?
3. What will you do?
4. He goes to work by bike every day.

三、1. He is going to spend the holiday in Greece.
2. Who are planting trees over there?
3. Would they like to stop for a moment?
4. She had better not drop that stupid topic.
5. What is he going to do?
6. What would you like to do?

四、1. D 2. C 3. A 4. B 5. B

Section Five

一、1. B 2. C 3. B 4. A 5. A 6. A

二、1. A 2. B 3. A 4. A 5. A

三、1. C 2. B 3. C

四、3. Boil water.
1. Choose the tea leaves.
4. Put the tea and boiling water into a cup.
2. Get enough tea.

五、1. C 2. C 3. B 4. B 5. C 6. A 7. B 8. C

六、1. C 2. A 3. B 4. D

七、1. bed 2. glad 3. sleep 4. flowers 5. friend 6. where

八、1. A 2. B 3. D 4. C 5. B 6. A 7. A 8. B

九、

<table>
<tr><td>arrive</td><td>arrived</td><td>arriving</td><td>eat</td><td colspan="2">ate</td><td>eating</td></tr>
<tr><td>stop</td><td>stopped</td><td>stopping</td><td>lie</td><td>lied</td><td>lay</td><td>lying</td></tr>
<tr><td>write</td><td>wrote</td><td>writing</td><td>set</td><td colspan="2">set</td><td>setting</td></tr>
<tr><td>rise</td><td>rose</td><td>rising</td><td>take</td><td colspan="2">took</td><td>taking</td></tr>
</table>

十、1. B 2. A 3. C 4. B 5. C 6. C 7. C 8. C 9. B 10. B

十一、1. A 2. C 3. D 4. B 5. A

期末考试(一)

第一部分

1—5 ABACC 6—10 BCBAA 11—15 BBCBC 16—20 BCBAB 21—25 CCBCC
26—30 BABBC 31—35 ACDBA 36—40 DCDAB 41—45 ABCAC 46—50 DBBAC
51—55 CDCCD 56—60 BABBA 61—65 CAACC 66—70 BAACB 71—75 BADDC
76—80 DACDA

第二部分

一、1. calling 2. report 3. between 4. dropping 5. pick

二、1. B 2. C 3. E 4. A 5. D

三、1. to drink 2. teaching 3. doing 4. is 5. have ;had
6. responsible 7. invitation 8. to get 9. deliver 10. digging

四、1. Father wasn't able to fix the clock.
2. Lillian hasn't been to any foreign countries yet.
3. Did Sam cut his finger in the kitchen?
4. Did Tina leave her hometown when she was 16?
5. How much shampoo would you like?
6. What musical instrument could you play when you were young?
7. How far is it from the city park to your school?
8. When did James go to the theatre?
9. Jason always listened to the music on every Sunday afternoon last year.
10. Tom spent three hours finishing all his homework.

期末考试(二)

第一部分

1—5 ABACB 6—10 CCBBA 11—15 BCBBC 16—20 BBCBC 21—25 BBBCC
26—30 BABCB 31—35 BCCDC 36—40 CDBAD 41—45 ABDCC 46—50 CABAD
51—55 ACBBC 56—60 BBDAC 61—65 CDBAC 66—70 ABBDA

第二部分

一、1. hobbies 2. designs 3. interests 4. certain 5. value

二、1. D 2. E 3. A 4. C 5. B

三、1. silent 2. visiting 3. preparing 4. frightening 5. playing
6. attractive 7. have collected 8. exactly 9. planned 10. experienced

四、1. Bungee jumping didn't start on Pentecost Island.
2. Would she like to visit Greece one day?
3. How long has Tom been away from home?
4. I spent three hours cleaning the room.
5. How handsome the boy John is!

五、1. There was a big fire in town the other day.
2. If you don't take your rain coats, you'll be sorry.
3. You've only worn the shoes for a few hours, and they are already old.
4. He has a responsibility to children watching the programme.
5. In Britain, cars drive on the left-hand side of the road and drivers sit on the right-hand side of the car.